KV-371-723

OUT TO EAT

The Editor

Elizabeth Carter is a food journalist, author and experienced restaurant/hotel inspector. She ran her own restaurant in Kensington for five years and has also written a book entitled *Majorcan Food and Cookery* (Prospect Books, 1989) based on her experiences of living and working in Majorca.

OUT TO EAT

Edited by Elizabeth Carter

Published by Consumers' Association and Hodder & Stoughton

Which? Books are commissioned and researched by The Association
for Consumer Research and published by Consumers' Association,
2 Marylebone Road, London NW1 4DX and Hodder & Stoughton,
47 Bedford Square, London WC1B 3DP

Cover design by Splash Studio
Cover illustration by Paul Cox
Indexes compiled by Paul Nash

First edition April 1991

Copyright © 1991 Consumers' Association Ltd

British Library Cataloguing in Publication Data
Out to eat.
1. Great Britain. Catering establishments.
I. Carter, Elizabeth   II. Consumers' Association
647.9541

ISBN 0-340-53901-1

No part of this publication may be reproduced or transmitted in any
form or by any means, electronically or mechanically, including
photocopying, recording or any information storage or retrieval
system without prior permission in writing from the publisher. The
publication is not included under licences issued by the Copyright
Agency. No part of this publication may be used in any form of
advertising, sales promotion or publicity.

Designed and typeset by
Barbican Print & Marketing Limited, London

Printed and bound in England by
Richard Clay Limited, Bungay, Suffolk

Contents

INTRODUCTION

At the expensive end of the eating scale we in Britain fare reasonably well, with talented chefs and some outstanding native-grown produce making a smart but pricey combination. Yet Britain is not noted for its food culture. This country does not stop for lunch, as the inhabitants of France, Spain and Italy do, to go and eat freshly cooked food at home or in an inexpensive restaurant. In France you can eat very well at a Routier (no more than a transport café) for under £6, and the food will be a freshly prepared, balanced meal, not a greasy fry-up. In Britain rock-bottom prices and generous quantities, rather than the quality of the food and the skill of the kitchen staff, are often cited by customers as the reason for recommending an eating establishment. But there is a growing number of Britons who enjoy good food, are inspired by the healthy regard which their fellow Europeans have for it, envy their informal, inexpensive and professionally run cafés and restaurants and want the same on their own doorsteps. Similarly, if they are travelling and want to stop off for a satisfactory meal in an unfamiliar area, they want to be able to find somewhere serving good, reasonably priced food in decent surroundings. This book aims to satisfy the needs of that ever-increasing band of eaters-out.

Low prices, high standards – the search

In the current economic climate, in which money is counted carefully and even restaurant critics are beginning to remark on the size of their wining and dining bills, the need for a food guide devoted to the less expensive is stronger than ever. Here it is, the only current guide to inexpensive eating out in Britain. Our criterion was that two courses and a drink should cost no more than £10 a head (£15 in London). Pubs, cafés, ethnic and other low-price restaurants, wine bars, hotel lounges, tea-rooms, pizza parlours, fish and chip shops, even sandwich bars, came under close scrutiny. Our intention to bring to the fore those places providing good, honestly priced food was greatly aided by the tremendous effort made by *Good Food Guide* inspectors. In many cases they themselves searched out suitable candidates as well as inspecting those recommendations made by readers of *The Good Food Guide*. No establishment presented itself for inclusion; all were inde-pendently recommended and all inspections were anonymous.

We toured Britain and found that at the cheaper end of the eating scale low standards still persist: 'home-made' soup based on canned tomatoes, a stock cube and yesterday's left-over vegetables; cartons of UHT milk when the kitchen can perfectly easily supply fresh milk; sachets of sauces. One inspector braved a trifle topped by a custard so rubbery that his spoon could only indent it, and sporting a hazel-nut decoration 'retrieved from a Topic bar'. Another inspector had a bad experience in a vegetarian restaurant where she could not bring herself to eat the dish ordered – it had been prepared from very stale mushrooms which were oozing an acrid-tasting black liquid over the plate. She complained. The owner staunchly maintained, in spite of evidence to the contrary, that the mushrooms used were fresh, delivered that day. While loudly extolling the purity of the kitchen, mainly for the benefit of the other, staring, customers, a waitress was theatrically summoned to clear the offending plate. In her nervousness she accidentally tipped the contents down the inspector's leg.

We have also retreated from pubs, without eating, unable to cope with the foul smell of cooking oil or able to face the lengthy menu offering the contents of some food manufacturer's deep-frozen list. The worst offenders are the same manufacturers' 'specialist' dishes, which are seemingly designed to look as if prepared within the establishment serving them. They dominate many a menu and give a sameness of taste throughout the country in exactly the same way that every high street sporting the same shops now looks identical. Do we really want such a standardised Britain?

Making more of pubs
Highlighted in this guide are the establishments offering food and atmosphere that bear their unique signature. Some are close to motorways and these have been flagged in the guide with a special motorway symbol for easy recognition. There are also a number of pubs. Drink-driving laws are forcing more and more pubs, especially in rural areas, to provide food, and those that are good are popular, as the relevant entries point out. Pubs can be very pleasant places nowadays. No-smoking areas are becoming more common and children are being made more welcome with the setting-up of family-rooms. (London, however, is lagging behind in the provision of no-smoking areas, family-rooms and better food.) In fact the progressive Scots, whose licensing laws are several years ahead of those in England and Wales, have recently introduced a new law concerning children in pubs. If a pub or hotel obtains the relevant permission (known as a children's certificate) then children under the age of 14 years, if accompanied by an adult, can be legally in the bar in order to eat a meal during opening hours from 11am to 8pm.

Unfortunately, throughout Britain many town and city-centre pubs cling to the traditional image of a smoky, boozy atmosphere. And even in the more civilised places there are still some problems deterring many would-be pub-goers. We feel the obvious place for a snack or light meal in any town or village should be a pub, but, as the few hundred pub entries in this guide show (and there are over 40,000 pubs in Britain), there are not enough dedicated souls prepared to tackle what must be the most under-rated, under-used catering outlet in Britain.

At Easter 1991, nearly three years into the change in the English and Welsh licensing law allowing pubs which so desire to stay open all day, we still cannot get a snack at 4pm. Many pubs in areas popular with tourists do not even bother with all-day opening, or if they do it is for drinks only; meal times have not been expanded beyond the usual restricted hours for lunch and dinner. While researching a number of popular tourist areas we were frequently confronted with tiny tea-rooms packed to the gunnels at 3.30pm while the nearby pub, often an ancient, atmospheric place complete with garden, was firmly closed. What a waste of potential!

Pubs need to be viewed with more flexibility. Why are young chefs who struggle to survive in heavily mortgaged restaurants not encouraged into lucrative pub tenancies? While they sort out their reputations in the restaurant the drinks and bar snacks trade will keep them going, and if they have any sense they will follow the Continental custom of keeping the bar and light snacks on the go all day, and will serve espresso coffee and tisanes as well as alcohol.

This would set to rights some of the great areas of Britain where good food is hard to find. *Out to Eat*'s dearth of entries in Bedfordshire, Cleveland, Humberside, Lincolnshire, Northamptonshire, Shropshire, Staffordshire and Warwickshire is not in any way due to cursory inspecting, but to a surprising shortage of inexpensive eating establishments of any quality. We looked at each county individually, with a view to showing the best on offer regardless of how they compared with London establishments, where fierce competition leads to a finer tuning of operations. This still left a shortfall in the above counties. It also produced some surprises. Surrey could well claim to be the pizza county of Great Britain with no less than 16 pizza parlours listed, both chain and individual. But unfortunately there is little else there. Our inspectors found Surrey expensive; even good pub food is pricey and often fell outside our price bracket. But there is obviously a market for good, inexpensive food, which the pizza chains have noted.

Smoke gets in your eyes

One criticism we thought would have been levelled almost exclusively at pubs never materialised. Smoky atmospheres in those pubs that are noted for their food just do not seem to exist – possibly a combination of the welcome establishment of no-smoking rooms or areas and the fact that the sort of people who go to pubs to eat are not usually smokers. We would have trouble finding a pub where an inspector had been smoked out but could recall vividly all those wine bars and restaurants where it has happened.

The scenario is a common one. The restaurant is closely packed with tables, a mere matter of inches separating you from your neighbours. You are half-way through your meal when the next table is taken by a couple who immediately light up. What do you do? You cannot move, and the waiters seem oblivious to your plight; asking the smokers to desist could result in a row as smoking is not officially discouraged. You finish your meal hurriedly, leave without giving a tip and vow never to go back, despite the fact that the food was very good. To endure the smoke of others' cigarettes while eating a meal is a very unpleasant experience for diners, and one proprietors should be more aware of, especially when tables have to be close-packed to keep the prices down. While this has to be accepted as a fact of life in budget eating places, there is all the more need for positive no-smoking policies.

Turn it down

Music is another problem, and one the inspectors were quick to comment on if it was played too loudly. Inexpensive establishments tend to be informal and there is nothing wrong with background music so long as it is unobtrusive and allows diners to carry on a conversation. It is when the volume creeps up and customers have to shout at each other that one wonders for whose benefit the music is being played, the staff's or the client's? Indeed, it can make communication with waiting staff virtually impossible. One lunchtime, an inspector visited a wine bar with a friend where the din was ear-splitting. The friend ordered mushrooms and was brought, after a long wait, moules. She was allergic to shellfish and by then their time was up so she left unfed. Although customers can request some volume adjustment, loud music is a problem and proprietors should again be more aware of it, especially when leaving staff to their own devices.

Good ingredients

The most heartening sign to come out of our research has been the sheer number of caterers who care about where their food comes from, buy organic supplies where possible, and support local producers (even, as in the case of one restaurant, visiting a farm to check that the eggs really were free-range). Some places list their suppliers on the menu; one even has a list on the counter giving details of all the ingredients in each dish. This is all the more laudable in the context of the keen prices these places offer. They have not fallen into the trap of regarding food as a mere commodity, of buying cheap, whatever the quality, to sell cheap; instead they strive hard to buy the best they can, and it shows in the end result. Where we have been made aware that organic produce is used, a comment has been made in the entry. We did find ourselves wondering how long it would take for this policy to cease being a rarity, at which time there will be no further need to comment upon it.

Over to you

Out to Eat sets out to be the definitive guide to less expensive eating out in Britain, but to remain so it requires your support. Use it and write to us about your experiences, good or bad, so that we can keep our records up to date. Let us know about new places. It is a fallacy to think that by keeping some interesting discovery out of the guides the place will remain exactly the same and tables will always be available at short notice. This can sometimes happen, but the danger of the reverse – no spreading of the word, no written praise or printed accolade – is that the place may go out of business. Good eating out places need recognition and support to survive, especially in the economic climate of the early 1990s, and guides are one of the best ways to give them this. Your reports are important, and the report forms at the back of the book are there to be used. We look forward to hearing from you.

Elizabeth Carter

HOW TO USE THIS GUIDE

Regions
England has been divided up into counties for ease of reference. East and West Sussex have been combined under Sussex, and North, South and West Yorkshire appear under Yorkshire. Within each county, eating-places are listed alphabetically, according to city, town or village. London (the first section in the book) is listed alphabetically by name of eating-place. Scotland and Wales are not divided into counties or regions, but have their eating-places listed alphabetically according to city, town or village. (The relevant county or region is, however, given after each location.) At the back of the book are two indexes of eating-places: one according to location, the other according to the name of the establishment. There is also a listing of London eating-places according to cuisine-type (see page 337).

Prices
Specific prices quoted in the text are correct at the time of going to press. They are intended as general guidelines and may change in the course of a few weeks or months. Our cost criteria are that a two-course meal, plus a drink, should cost £10 or less a head (£15 or less in London).

Alcohol licence
Establishments are licensed unless otherwise indicated in the entry. We say when a 'bring your own' policy is adopted, and whether there is a corkage charge.

Children
Children accompanied by adults are generally welcomed, unless otherwise stated in the entry. There may be restrictions on the times and places within the eating-place where families with children can eat. As there are legal restrictions on children under 14 in licensed premises in England and Wales where alcohol is served, it is always worth asking the landlord or proprietor if he or she has any objections. In Scotland, a licensed premises can obtain a 'children's certificate', which allows children under 14 to be legally in a bar, if accompanied by an adult, in order to eat a meal during opening hours from 11am to 8pm.

Wheelchairs
'Wheelchair access' in the details indicates that, according to the proprietor, entrances are at least 33 inches wide, passages 4 feet wide, and that there is a maximum of two steps. We also mention if there is access to a WC .

Opening and closing times
The majority of opening times cover lunch and dinner, but they can also cover breakfast, morning coffee, afternoon tea and snacks. Food may be available at times other than those listed – we may omit a restaurant's evening opening hours if dinner is too expensive according to the cost criteria of this guide (see opposite), for example. The letters L and D are used to denote lunch and dinner where clarification is needed. Pub times relate only to when food is available – the licensing hours may be different.

Symbols
★ indicates an eating-place that is one of the best found by the Editor during research for this book (see page 14 for a list of the stars).

 indicates a pub.

ⓣ indicates that an eating-place is within 5 miles of the nearest motorway junction. We give the relevant motorway and junction in the details. Eating-places in cities and large towns, where traffic, parking and route-finding may cause delay, do not have this symbol.

Directions
Directions are given where an eating-place may be difficult to find.

Car-parking
If an eating-place has its own car-park, this is mentioned in the entry.

Smoking
Where there are restrictions on smoking, and where a no-smoking area is provided, this is mentioned in the entry. If you are in any doubt, it is best to check beforehand.

THE STARS

LONDON

Bedlington Café, W4
Bistrot 190, SW7
Casale Franco, N1
Museum Street Café, WC1
Patisserie Bliss, EC1
Place Below, EC2
Quality Chop House, EC1
Ragam, W1
Tea Time, SW4

ENGLAND

Angel, Hetton
  (N Yorkshire)
Baldry's, Grasmere
  (Cumbria)
Bell Inn, Alderminster
  (Warwickshire)
Bettys, Harrogate
  (N Yorkshire)
Bettys, Ilkley (W Yorkshire)
Bettys, Northallerton
  (N Yorkshire)
Bettys, York (N Yorkshire)
Black Chapati, Brighton
  (Sussex)
Food for Friends, Brighton
  (Sussex)
Gallery Coffee Shop,
  Hemel Hempstead
  (Hertfordshire)
Jules, Weobley (Hereford
  & Worcester)
Moon, Kendal (Cumbria)
Moorings, Wells-next-the-
  Sea (Norfolk)
Mulberry Room, Torquay
  (Devon)
Plough, Ivy Hatch (Kent)
Polly Tea Rooms,
  Marlborough (Wiltshire)
Primrose Cottage,
  Lustleigh (Devon)

Queen's Head, Newton
  (Cambridgeshire)
Ram, Firle (Sussex)
Roebuck, Brimfield
  (Hereford & Worcester)
Royal Oak, Yattendon
  (Berkshire)
Sharrow Bay, Ullswater
  (Cumbria)
Sheila's Cottage, Ambleside
  (Cumbria)
Sonny's, Nottingham
  (Nottinghamshire)
Stone Close, Dent
  (Cumbria)
Stones, Avebury
  (Wiltshire)
Village Bakery, Melmerby
  (Cumbria)
Wine Bar, Woodbridge
  (Suffolk)
Wykeham Arms, Winchester
  (Hampshire)

SCOTLAND

Crannog Seafood
  Restaurant, Fort William
  (Highland)
Kalpna, Edinburgh
  (Lothian)
Kilberry Inn, Kilberry
  (Strathclyde)
Loch Fyne Oyster Bar,
  Cairndow (Strathclyde)

WALES

Griffin Inn, Llyswen
  (Powys)
Hive on the Quay,
  Aberaeron (Dyfed)
Queen's Head, Glanwydden
  (Gwynedd)
Tu Hwnt I'r Bont, Llanrwst
  (Gwynedd)

LONDON

Accademia Italiana   map 13

24 Rutland Gate, SW7
☎ **071-225 3474**

Open Tue to Sat L 1–2.30
Closed Sun, Mon, Christmas and bank
hols

Cooking is often regarded as an art form, so it is fitting that at the Italian Academy for art and applied arts there is not only a bookshop and art gallery but also a lunchtime restaurant serving authentic, traditional Italian dishes. It offers robust food, simple in concept, strong on flavour, the sort Italians eat at home, including homely zuppas (earthy, peasant-style soups ladled over thick slices of bread) crisp salads of rocket, radicchio and wild mushroom, bufala mozzarella with tomatoes and basil, rich lasagne, and veal or chicken with potatoes. The menu changes daily, service is pleasantly informal, and the espresso superb.

Unlicensed, but bring your own: no
corkage

Adams Café   map 12

77 Askew Road, W12
☎ **081-743 0572**

Open Mon to Sat D 7.30–10.30
Closed Sun, Christmas and New
Year

By day, this modest café in the grey reaches of West London serves full English breakfasts, mixed grills and boiled bacon and cabbage. By night, candlelight and a few carefully draped cloths create a softer setting for the same kitchen's Mediterranean and

Turkish dishes. Brik of egg and tuna or vegetables, or chorba, a lamb soup of a rich, deep colour, make good starters. Couscous is a speciality, but gargoulette, a spicy Tunisian lamb casserole, slow-cooked to an intense, memorable flavour, is equally noteworthy. Finish with mint tea. The charming, relaxed service from both Frances and Abdel Boukraa includes the sprinkling of jasmine water on your hands as you leave.

Unlicensed, but bring your own: no
corkage

African Pot   map 12

236 High Street, NW10
☎ **081-453 0453**

Open all week noon–1am

Ghanian, Nigerian and Caribbean dishes appear on the menu and there is a ready explanation for the uninitiated. Very generous quantities mean that a main course of waatse (black-eyed beans with rice and fish) or an aubergine stew would constitute a meal in itself. Fried plantain or yams accompany. An easy, laid-back atmosphere prevails. There is also a branch at 9–10 Balham Continental Market, 31 Bedford Hill, SW12.

No-smoking area

You will find report forms (write a letter if you prefer) at the back of the book so that you can tell us about your experiences of going *Out to Eat*. We'll put the information to good use when we're compiling the next edition.

Ajimura
map 14

51–3 Shelton Street, WC2
☎ 071-240 0178

Open Mon to Sat noon–3 (exc Sat),
6–11
Closed Sun and bank hols

Ajimura's style is more informal than that of most Japanese restaurants – staff are young and relaxed, the menu fresh and inventive and prices are realistic. The £7.50 set lunch of tempura or chicken teriyaki with rice or sushi, all served with miso soup, Japanese pickles, salad and fresh fruit, is excellent value and there is a light, pre-theatre dinner for £11.50.

Access, Amex, Visa

Albion
map 13

10 Thornhill Road, N1
☎ 071-607 7450

Open Mon to Sat noon–2.30,
7.30–9.30, Sun noon–2
Closed Christmas Day

A popular pub in the heart of Georgian Islington, which has something for everyone – a traditional turn-of-the-century-style front bar with much heavy dark wood, a pastel, modern non-smoking sitting-room, and a large walled beer garden. Food includes hot salt-beef, steak and kidney pie, ham, egg and chips and sausage and mash.

No-smoking room • Garden •
Wheelchair access, also WC • Access,
Amex, Diners, Visa

Ali Baba
map 13

32 Ivor Place, NW1
☎ 071-723 5805

Open all week midday–midnight

A plain, spotless room, tucked away at the back of a gleaming take-away, serving good, carefully cooked, inexpensive Middle Eastern food. Melokhia and foul reflect the owner's Egyptian origins, while falafel, couscous, moussaka and shawarma cover a broader area. Bamia (lamb with okra) is excellent. For dessert, both Om Ali and mohalabieh are a must.

Almeida Theatre
Wine Bar
map 13

1A Almeida Street, N1
☎ 071-226 0931

Open Mon to Sat 12.30–2.30, 6–9.30
Closed Sun and Christmas

On performance evenings the pressure is on the food-counter, so time your arrival. Lunch is a more leisurely affair with a laid-back table service to suit the bare boards, rickety tables and short blackboard menu strong on vegetarian choices – honestly made minestrone, thick with fresh vegetables; vegetable fritters; and stuffed aubergine. Beef bourguignonne for meat-eaters.

No-smoking area • Wheelchair access,
also WC • Access, Diners, Visa

Anwar's   map 13

64 Grafton Way, W1
☎ 071-387 6664

Open all week 10am–10pm

Opened in 1962 and still one of the
cheapest Indian eating places in the
area. A board outside proclaims that
this is 'a budget curry house' and it
offers excellent value for money. The
décor may resemble a café, with
Formica-topped tables and queues by
the serving-counter, but the food is
genuine. Big pans of ready-prepared
dishes such as kofta curry and chicken
dhansak are supplemented with
vegetables, rice, tandooris and
savoury snacks including keema
samosa and potato chop, plus breads.
Also look for specials: karahi gosht,
chicken tikka masala, prawn patia.
The curries respond better to the
microwave re-heating than the breads
and deep-fried snacks.

Unlicensed • Wheelchair access

Athenaeum Hotel   map 13

116 Piccadilly, W1
☎ 071-499 3464

*Open Mon to Sat 11am–11pm, Sun
noon–3, 7–10.30*

Strikingly decorated in modern
country-house style – boldly striped
wing chairs and sofas, strong floral
drapes, games tables and huge lamps
– the Windsor Lounge presents a
peaceful front for all-day snacks or
afternoon tea (3–6pm). Salads, Welsh
rarebit, club or open sandwiches, and
croque-monsieur are well-made and
served with great style.

Access, Amex, Diners, Visa

All letters to this guide are acknowledged.

Aziz   map 12

116 King Street, W6
☎ 081-748 1826

*Open Mon to Sat noon–3, 6–midnight
(12.30am Fri and Sat)
Closed Sun*

Supporters rate this as one of the
most authentic North Indian
restaurants in London. It stands in a
shopping development not far from
the Lyric Theatre, and inside the
style is 'old-fashioned curry house'.
The menu follows suit with a well-
tried mix of distinctively flavoured
tandooris and curries with plenty of
punch. Shami kebab, lamb madras,
prawn patia and sag bhaji have all
been recommended; the speciality
chicken kyberi kebab is good, too.
Rice and other details are up-to-the-
mark. Drink Kingfisher beer or lassi.

*Wheelchair access • Access, Amex,
Diners, Visa*

Balls Brothers   map 13

**2–3 Old Change Court,
St Paul's Churchyard, EC4**
☎ 071-248 8697
6–8 Cheapside, EC2
☎ 071-248 2708
42 Threadneedle Street, EC2
☎ 071-628 3850
**Bucklersbury House,
Cannon Street, EC4**
☎ 071-248 7557
**Hays Galleria,
Tooley Street, SE1**
☎ 071-407 4301
**Hop Cellars,
24 Southwark Street, SE1**
☎ 071-403 6851
King's Arms Yard, EC2
☎ 071-796 3049
**Great Eastern Hotel,
Liverpool Street, EC2**
☎ 071-626 7919

Moor House,
London Wall, EC2
☎ 071-628 3944
St Mary at Hill, EC3
☎ 071-626 0321

Open Mon to Fri 11am–8pm

Lavishly filled sandwiches are a feature at this group of city wine bars, washed down by some excellent wines. Smoked turkey mayonnaise, roast beef with horseradish, avocado and cream cheese, pastrami and occasionally hot salt-beef are made to order. There is also a selection of cheeses including Stilton, ripe Brie and mature cheddar, moist fruit cake and fresh fruit. No sandwiches are served in the evening.

Bambaya   map 12

1 Park Road, N8
☎ 081-348 5609

Open Tue to Sun D 6.30–11 (10.30 Sun)
Closed Mon and bank hols

Afro-Caribbean dishes and specialities from the southern United States co-exist happily in Rosamund Grant's cool, calm restaurant. The mood is relaxed; most of the trade comes late in the evening. Spiciness and an all-pervading use of coconut are the hallmarks of the kitchen. Typically there might be torpedo-shaped salt-fish-cakes with warm chutney; delicately herbed fish chowder; Louisiana king prawn Creole and specials such as 'Run Down Fish' (meaty pomfret in coconut sauce). Imaginative salads and brown rice dishes; very creamy home-made ice-creams; interesting, non-alcoholic cocktails.

Unlicensed • Wheelchair access, also WC • Access, Visa

Bangkok   map 13

9 Bute Street, SW7
☎ 071-584 8529

Open Mon to Sat 12.15–2.15, 6.30–11
Closed Sun and bank hols

Probably London's oldest Thai restaurant, family-run and offering a limited-choice menu in an informal setting. Main courses (better than starters) are fresh and well-made. Try a generous portion of Thai rice noodles with crisp vegetables and a carefully spiced chicken curry. Finish with mango sorbet or coconut ice-cream.

Access, Amex, Visa

Basil Street Hotel   map 13

Basil Street, SW3
☎ 071-581 3311

Open all week 4–5.30pm

Afternoon tea in the second-floor lounge is quintessentially English, old-fashioned and comfortable, in a manner long lost by the grand hotels. The trolley trundles round laden with well-filled sandwiches, whole pots of jam to accompany scones, creamy cakes and fruit tarts. It is a relaxing refuge from Harrods close by, and there is no fuss or pretence, just tea.

Access, Amex, Diners, Visa

Bedlington Café ★   map 12

24 Fauconberg Road, W4
☎ 081-994 1965

Open Mon to Sat 8.30am–2, 6.30–10, Sun D 7–9

The décor is Formica and lino, the tables are crowded together and the atmosphere can be smoky, but to eat the fresh, aromatic Thai food here it is essential to book or queue in the street. Every time a dish goes by to another table you get a heady waft of basil, coriander, garlic and ginger. Red chicken curry, chilli beef and squid with garlic and peppers are particular strengths, but the chicken and coconut milk soup is considered to be outstanding. Bananas in coconut milk for dessert comes hot, sweet/salt, and is delectable. Service is friendly and relaxed. By day there are incongruous fry-ups of bacon, egg, tomatoes and mushrooms; the Thai food is available evenings only.

Unlicensed, but bring your own: corkage 50p • No-smoking area • Wheelchair access

Bibendum Oyster Bar map 13

**Michelin House,
81 Fulham Road, SW3
☎ 071-589 1480**

*Open all week noon–11
Closed 4 days Christmas and New Year's Day*

The thought of all those white tiles and marble-topped tables combined with cold food is a rather chilling one in inclement weather. The light, elegant food, however, makes a stylish snack. Six oysters and a glass of champagne (£12.25), a salad of crab (£9.95) or smoked duck (£7.95) are not cheap, but the quality is first-class and the food does not disappoint.

Wheelchair access, also WC • Access, Visa

The factual details under each eating-place are based on information supplied by the restaurateur.

Bistrot 190 ★ map 13

**190 Queen's Gate, SW7
☎ 071-581 5666**

Open all week 7am (11.30 Sun)–12.30am

On the ground floor of the Gore Hotel, but run by chef Anthony Worrall-Thompson as an inexpensive alternative to his Restaurant 190 next door. The inventive menu and the strong espresso speak of the Mediterranean; even breakfast (7am–11.30am) has a cosmopolitan feel raising it beyond the traditional English fry-up to minute steak with hash potatoes and eggs Benedict. The main menu is robust and earthy, offering hearty portions and excellent bread. Garlic terrine comes with hummus, tapenade and roast aubergines, chargrilled squid with outstanding pommes frites, the calf's liver with polenta mash and tortellini. Long hours are a great plus point.

Garden • Access, Amex, Diners, Visa

Bizzarro map 13

**18–22 Craven Road, W2
☎ 071-402 4695**

Open all week noon–3, 6–11.30

This long-standing Italian restaurant is just two minutes' walk from Paddington Station. Don't dine downstairs unless you want to dance – the ground floor is more peaceful, offering generous portions of veal with aubergines, tomatoes and mozzarella, or leg of lamb covered in wine, onions and pepper from a large choice of poultry, fish, meat and pasta.

Access, Amex, Diners, Visa

Blooms
map 12

90 Whitechapel High Street, E1
☎ **071-247 6001**
130 Golders Green Road, NW11
☎ **081-455 1338**

*Open Sun to Thur 11am–9.30, Fri
11am–2*
*Closed Sat, Christmas Day and Jewish
hols*

An old-established kosher restaurant
where the idiosyncratic waiters elicit
as much comment as the hearty but
variable quality food. Huge bowlfuls
of heimishe barley soup or bortsch,
hot salt-beef with good tzimmas
(little dumplings) and potato latkes,
and hot, spiced apple strudel will
bring in a bill well under £15, and a
desire to diet.

*Wheelchair access • Access, Amex,
Diners, Visa*

Blueprint Café
map 12

**Design Museum, Butlers Wharf,
SE1**
☎ **071-378 7031**

*Open all week noon–3, 7–11 (exc Sun
and Mon D)*

It is fitting that the Design Museum
should boast a carefully designed café
by Terence Conran, who should be
pleased that his love of gutsy
Mediterranean cooking is so well
interpreted by American chef Paul
Delfavero. Sweeping views of the
river at Tower Bridge and free
(daytime) entry into the museum
afterwards compensate, in a small
way, for the fact that the food can be
pricey. But it is worth it. Olive oil is
extra virgin and stars with tuna
carpaccio, fennel and red pepper
(£5.25), and farfalle, wild mushrooms,
basil and rosemary (£7). All pasta is
home-made and there is grill-

emblazoned red snapper, salmon and
calf's liver. There is a special brunch
at weekends from 11am.

*Wheelchair access, also WC • Access,
Visa*

Boardwalk
map 14

18 Greek Street, W1
☎ **071-287 2051**

*Open all week noon–11.30, exc Sat L
and Sun D*
Closed Christmas and bank hols

An attempt to fashion a New
Orleans-style theme restaurant in
Soho. Dominated by a fountain
(which tends to promote extra trips
to the loo), this is a big place where,
either upstairs or down, office parties
are likely to be in progress. Most of
the menu, including steaks, burgers
and salads, is familiar and not very
New Orleans in style. However,
deep-fried smoked chicken with a
mustard and honey sauce is good, as
are hot king prawns 'rolled in bacon
and served with a selection of dips'.
Specials include Louisiana 'gumbo'
(prawns, seafood and the like fried
and spiced) and 'Florida trifle' (a lot
like any other trifle). This is fun food
so behave accordingly.

Wheelchair access • Access, Visa

Bon Ton Roulet
map 12

127 Dulwich Road, SE24
☎ **071-733 8701**

*Open Mon to Sat D 7–10.30, Sun L
12.30–2.30*
*Closed 1 week end August and 1 week
Christmas*

A well-established neighbourhood
restaurant (midway between Brixton
and Dulwich Village) with a

commendable pricing structure: all starters are £2.50, all main courses £6.50. The menu shows many influences – to be seen in such dishes as samphire and prawn salad, tempura vegetables, southern fried chicken, lamb strudel and beef Catalan. Open for lunch all week in the two weeks before Christmas.

Wheelchair access

La Bouffe map 12

13 Battersea Rise, SW11
☎ **071-228 3384**

Open all week 12.30–2.30 (exc Sat), 7–11 (exc Sun)
Closed 1 week Christmas

A very French menu offers good-value food. For lunch there is a set three-course meal for £9.95 or just some simple snacks: croque-monsieur, of course, as well as an omelette, a blue cheese and bacon salad or a salad paysanne. In the evening, for £12.95, there is a small-choice three-course menu. Good bread, cheerful service and a limited wine list.

Wheelchair access • Access, Visa

Brahms map 13

147 Lupus Street, SW1
☎ **071-834 9075**

Open Mon to Sat noon–3, 7–midnight, Sun noon–11

One of Peter Ilic's lively group of informal restaurants. See entry for Lantern.

Wheelchair access, also WC • Access, Visa

Brewer Street Buttery map 14

56 Brewer Street, W1
☎ **071-437 7695**

Open Mon to Fri 8.30am–5.30
Closed Sat and Sun, Christmas Day, Boxing Day and Easter Mon

Making a refreshing change from the area's sandwich bars, the Brewer Street Buttery sets a gentle pace, serving simple home-cooked food in a tea-shop-style setting. There is an East European influence to the food: cucumber soup, savoury potato cakes, veal loaf, all freshly made and served in generous portions. Espresso is excellent.

Unlicensed • Wheelchair access

Bridge map 12

74–6 Battersea Bridge Road, SW11
☎ **071-738 0198**

Open Mon to Sat noon–3, 7–midnight, Sun noon–11
Closed Christmas Day and Boxing Day

One of Peter Ilic's lively group of informal restaurants. See entry for Lantern.

No-smoking area • Wheelchair access, also WC • Access, Visa

Brompton Brasserie map 12

222–4 Fulham Road, SW10
☎ **071-351 3956**

Open all week 10am–midnight (10.30 Sun)
Closed Christmas Day

Brasserie by name and brasserie by nature, with big mirrors on the walls, ceiling fans, wicker chairs and photographs of pop heroes all round the room. A standard menu of burgers, pizzas and pasta is boosted by more adventurous blackboard specials. Brompton Blini is an excellent muffin with smoked salmon, cream cheese and Danish caviare; and the fish pie is packed with good things. Fruit pies, crumbles and sorbets to finish. No bookings – which is an advantage on Saturday nights when other places are full.

Wheelchair access • Access, Visa

Burgh House Buttery

map 12

New End Square, NW3
☎ **071-431 2516**

Open Wed to Sun 11am–5.30 (7.30 Fri)
Closed Mon, Tue and 3 weeks Christmas

On fine days, visitors to this handsome Queen Anne mansion eat in the pretty rose garden. Otherwise, the basement buttery is always busy. The aim is to serve tourists and locals with honest home cooking. Salads are arrayed on a counter, and the blackboard menu lists a range of hot and cold buffet dishes from coq au vin and beef Stroganoff to fresh salmon, coronation chicken and broccoli quiche. Puddings are crumbles, pies and scones. The place does a roaring trade with Sunday lunches. Wine by the glass.

No-smoking area • Garden

Bu San

map 12

43 Holloway Road, N7
☎ **071-607 8264**

Open all week noon–2.30 (exc Sat and Sun), 6–11

This tiny, six-table dining-room has the cosy intimacy of a café and the quality of a good restaurant. Chef/proprietor Young Heung Lee cooks a menu dominated by specialities from his native Korea, plus a few personal versions of Japanese dishes like sashimi. Korean favourites include bulgogi (marinated strips of beef cooked at the table), meaty chunks of eel in batter, and pa jeon (Korean-style pizzas). Also kim chee and cold salads. Flavours are authentic and presentation is beautiful. Good-value set meals. Drink saké or tea.

Wheelchair access

Café Anjou

map 12

394 Green Lanes, N3
☎ **081-886 7267**

Open Tue to Sun noon–3, 7–11
Closed Mon and Christmas Day

A softly lit, cream-painted café in a parade of high-street shops. Soups, salades niçoise and anjou, grilled steak, lamb kebab with ginger, veal chops, salmon fish-cakes and stuffed aubergine can all be found on the menu. The cooking is honest and sound, and prices are reasonable, especially for the two-course set menus at £6.25 and £7.25.

Wheelchair access • Access, Amex, Visa

Café de Columbia   map 13

**Museum of Mankind,
6 Burlington Gardens, W1
☎ 071-287 8148**

*Open Mon to Sat 10am–4.30, Sun
2.30–5pm*

A small, comfortable and stylish café
with table service making the whole
affair civilised. Mornings and
afternoons bring a choice of cakes –
chocolate, ginger and cinnamon,
lemon crunch – or croissants, and
excellent Columbian coffee. For
lunch you can choose a vegetarian
soup, sandwiches made with ciabatta
bread, chicken with tarragon and
mayonnaise, or gravad lax – nothing
too complicated but all freshly
prepared. Justin de Blank oversees
the operation. The café name
suggests South American food, or at
least some ethnic bearing, but the
concept is light and fashionable
rather than innovative. A place to
remember, as it is inexpensive for
the area.

*No smoking • Wheelchair access, also
WC*

Café Delancey   map 13

**3 Delancey Street, NW1
☎ 071-387 1985
32 Proctor Street, WC1
☎ 071-242 6691**

Open all week 8am–midnight

A large café of the bare-floorboards-
and-blackboard variety where you
can get anything (including breakfast)
any time. A short menu offers a
selection of typical London brasserie
dishes: calf's liver with bacon, rack of
lamb, steak, sausages. Rösti come
with everything. Croque-monsieur,
salads and omelettes for quick snacks.

*Garden • Wheelchair access, also WC •
Access, Visa*

Café Kensington   map 12

**Lancer Square, W8
☎ 071-938 2211**

*Open Mon to Sat 8am–11.30pm, Sun
10am–10.30pm
Closed Christmas Eve to 27 Dec*

There are few cafés in London that
are open all day and can sustain the
standards of cooking achieved here.
From breakfast – bagels, perfect
waffles, scrambled egg – on to the all-
day menu of crab-cakes, chargrilled
chicken, pizza with leeks, red peppers
and goats'-milk cheese, to afternoon
tea, inventive and assured cooking is
the keynote. The versatility of the
menu combined with real attention
to small details – bread and pastries
are excellent, staff well-trained –
should make this a role model for all
future ventures. The daytime menu
gives a taste of what's available on the
more expensive evening carte.

*No cigars/pipes • Wheelchair access, also
WC • Access, Visa*

Café Pelican   map 14

**45 St Martin's Lane, WC2
☎ 071-379 0309**

*Open Mon to Sat 11am–5, 5.30–12.30,
Sun noon–3, 7–11
Closed Christmas Day*

A cheerful Gallic atmosphere
pervades this busily situated café, a
sister to Café Pelican du Sud (see
following entry). Weather
permitting, there are pavement
tables, otherwise you can sit in the
brasserie area and opt for the all-day
snack menu – served 11am–12.30am

– of onion soup, substantial salads, baguette sandwiches, croque-monsieur and a tempting selection of cakes.

Wheelchair access, also WC • Access, Amex, Visa

Café Pelican du Sud   map 13

Hays Galleria, Tooley Street, SE1
☎ **071-378 0096**

Open Mon to Fri 11am–9.30, Sat and Sun noon–5
Closed 1 week Christmas

At last a proper French café in a poorly served part of London – no frills, an authentic Gallic feel to the menu, food and service, with tables spilling out into the Galleria. The menu offers snacks and full meals, taking in splendidly made soups, croque-monsieur, assiette de charcuterie, Toulouse sausages and pommes frites, crisp, well-dressed salads, good-looking pastries and desserts.

Wheelchair access, also WC • Access, Amex, Diners, Visa

Café Rouge   map 12

19 Hampstead High Street, NW3
☎ **071-433 3404**

Open all week 10am–midnight (10.30pm Sun)
Closed Christmas Day and Boxing Day

One of four look-alike bistros – a slick, pseudo-French appearance belies careful, consistent-quality cooking at reasonable prices. Expect lamb casserole with vegetables (£5.95), hot smoked sausage with warm potato salad (£4.95), and grilled fillet of red bream with Pernod (£5.95). This is the kind of place

where chain-smokers like to hang out. The cappuccino is good, but the service is usually too fast. Other branches at 31 Kensington Park Road, W11 (071-221 4449), 200 Putney Bridge Road, SW15 (081-788 4257), and 7A Petersham Road, Richmond, Surrey (081-332 2423).

No-smoking area • Wheelchair access • Access, Visa

Café Sud Ouest   map 13

27–31 Basil Street, SW3
☎ **071-584 4484**

Open Mon to Sat 11am–11pm
Closed Sun

If overcome by fatigue in Harrods, make for this relaxed, informal café behind that emporium. Good, strong espresso, delicious prune or apricot tarts, a sandwich made from ciabatta or a croissant will put you back on your feet. Lunch, a crowded affair, can comprise a lamb chop and lentils or baked duck with petits pois, and great pommes frites. Evenings are quieter.

Calabash   map 14

38 King Street, WC2
☎ **071-836 1976**

Open Mon to Sat 12.30–3 (exc Sat), 6–10.30
Closed Sun, Christmas Day, Boxing Day and bank hols

A stern warning, 'No drugs (of any sort)', pinned up in the entrance should not be viewed as a barrier. The basic, laid-back, batik/cultural centre-style dining-room provides a generally spicy cuisine and is ideal for African lovers of vegetarian food. Prices aren't bad. Aloco, a starter made of fried plantain with hot sauce, is £2.70. The speciality here is 'peanut butter', a combination of sweetcorn, carrots, peas, green beans, pepper and potatoes, which can be heavy-going. If you are incredibly hungry, order a side dish of pounded yam.

Access, Amex, Diners, Visa

Camden Brasserie   map 13

216 Camden High Street, NW1
☎ **071-482 2114**

Open Mon to Sat noon–3, 6–11.30, Sun 12.30–3.30, 6–10.30
Closed Christmas Day, New Year's Eve and bank hols

Everything appears to be well-prepared at this popular brasserie, with simplicity and quality the keynotes. Chargrilling is a speciality, with lamb brochettes or leg steaks, salmon, halibut and various cuts of beef being fairly representative of the choice. These are all accompanied by large bowls of irresistible matchstick pommes frites. The fact that only good-quality ingredients are used enhances such dishes as fresh scallops and arugula or bufala mozzarella with plum tomatoes and fresh basil. The adjoining Underground Café (see entry) is under the same ownership but has a separate kitchen, simpler menu and lower prices.

Visa

Camden Tandoori   map 13

114 Camden Road, NW1
☎ **071-482 2717**

Open all week noon–2.30, 6–midnight
Closed Christmas Day and Boxing Day

Handily situated close to the Camden Road BR Station, this tandoori restaurant is modestly decorated, and has an agreeable ambience and food that is distinctively flavoured. First-rate ingredients and clear-tasting sauces are the hallmarks of the kitchen, which delivers spot-on tandoori trout, chicken korma and prawn sag. Rice is excellent, too. Good-value thalis from £7.50.

Wheelchair access • Access, Amex, Visa

Canal Brasserie   map 12

Canalot Studios,
222 Kensal Road, W10
☎ **081-960 2732**

Open all week 9.30am–10.30pm, exc Sat L and Sun D

A spacious, all-day brasserie in a converted warehouse – now Canalot Studios – on the south side of the Grand Union Canal. The walls are hung with large paintings, and the short menu is full of variety: sauerkraut with Toulouse sausage, lambs' kidneys provençale, tagliarini dolcelatte, vegetable tempura. Breakfast is served from 9.30am and there is afternoon tea.

Garden • Access, Visa

Caravan Serai   map 13

50 Paddington Street, W1
☎ **071-935 1208**
also Buzkash at 4 Chelverton Road, SW15
☎ **081-788 0599**

Open all week noon–3 (exc Sun), 6–11

Afghan food that borrows from its Iranian and Indian neighbours, combining inventive use of the tandoor and hot spices with the gentler, more fragrant Persian style.

Coriander is a dominant taste, yoghurt an important vehicle for sauces. Lamb or veal cooked in the tandoor are nicely marinated and well-flavoured; rice and nans elaborate. There is another branch, Buzkash, address above.

No-smoking area • Access, Amex, Diners, Visa

Carriages   map 13
43 Buckingham Palace Road, SW1
☎ 071-834 0119

Open Mon to Fri noon–2.30, 5.30–10.30
Closed Christmas Day and bank hols

Owned by the Ebury Wine Bar (see entry), Carriages is a stylish wine bar opposite the Royal Mews. A good selection of wines by the glass is matched by an inventive choice of snacks at the bar: well-flavoured soup with seed bread or an unusual lamb satay with a spicy yoghurt dip. The restaurant menu offers a more substantial grilled calf's liver or seafood pie.

Wheelchair access • Access, Amex, Diners, Visa

Casale Franco ★   map 13
134–7 Upper Street, N1
☎ 071-226 8994

At rear of 134–7 Upper Street

Open Fri to Sun L noon–2.30, Tue to Sun D 6.30–11
Closed Mon, Christmas Day L and New Year's Day

Casale Franco is hard to find, takes no bookings and queues form by

8pm. It is a seriously popular Italian restaurant that has got the price and product just right. You can start with great olive bread, then move on to enormous pizzas with thin, light crisp bases and toppings such as Parma ham, mozzarella, olives and tomatoes, excellent pasta – penne with four cheeses and pasta i fagioli – chargrilled aubergines in olive oil, and cuttlefish in wine or spicy sausages, both served with squares of freshly grilled polenta. Tables are closely packed, the décor is ultra-minimal and service is very attentive. Espresso is heartstoppingly strong.

Wheelchair access • Access, Diners, Visa

Le Casino   map 13
77 Lower Sloane Street, SW1
☎ 071-730 3313

Open Mon to Sat noon–3, 7–1am, Sun noon–11

One of Peter Ilic's lively group of informal restaurants. See entry for Lantern.

Access, Visa

Cherry Orchard   map 12
241 Globe Road, E2
☎ 081-980 6678

Open Tue to Sat noon–3, 6.30–10.30
Closed Sun, Mon and Christmas

One of London's longest-standing vegetarian restaurants; a gently run co-operative with simple, daily-changing menus and a popular following. In the evening, waitress service and candles accompany mushroom moussaka or stir-fried vegetables with peanut sauce. Salads are satisfying, and there is a good choice of desserts and a wide selection of herb teas.

Unlicensed, but bring your own: corkage £1 • No smoking inside • Garden • Wheelchair access • Access, Visa

---

Chiang Mai   map 14

48 Frith Street, W1
☎ 071-437 7444

Open all week noon–3, 6–11.30

A simply decorated restaurant specialising solely in Northern Thai cooking. Fresh ingredients are carefully and subtly spiced and can produce quite unique flavours. Starters, such as grated papaya in a hot-and-sour salad, and noodle dishes are considered the best, though some of the curries, especially the chicken with coconut cream, are worth exploring.

Access, Amex, Visa

Chimes   maps 13/12

26 Churton Street, SW1
☎ 071-821 7456
91 Wimbledon High Street, SW19
☎ 081-946 2471

Open Mon to Fri noon–3.30, 5.30–10.30, Sat and Sun noon–10.30
Closed 3 days Christmas and New Year's Day

Plain wood tables, dried flowers and bare boards are the setting for a pair of restaurants serving wholesome, traditional English food. Pies dominate from steak and mushroom to pheasant, orange and walnut. Cold cuts, quiches and salad are alternatives. Daily specials could be gammon with parsley sauce, rabbit

and mustard pie. Good, old-fashioned puddings.

Wheelchair access • Access, Amex, Visa

China China   map 14

3 Gerrard Street, W1
☎ 071-439 7511

Open all week noon–midnight (1am Fri and Sat)

A fast-moving, no-frills Cantonese café. There is a long menu, but the Chinese generally tuck into the very cheap one-plate dishes of rice or noodles which are China China's strength. There is a freshness and quality to the food which, for the price, is remarkable. Everything comes at once, bills are brought the instant you finish, and service is brisk rather than impolite.

Access, Amex, Diners, Visa

Chinatown   map 12

795 Commercial Road, E14
☎ 071-987 2330/987 6720

Open all week L noon–3, Sun to Tue D 6–10, Wed and Thur D 6–10.30, Fri and Sat D 6–11

Limehouse, at the turn of this century, was home to the first Chinese restaurants in London. The rough dockland area was approached with some trepidation – still necessary as this restaurant faces four lanes of fast-moving traffic. It is rather faded, though much liked by East Enders, and goes in for decent Cantonese dishes served in enormous portions by remarkably cheerful waiters. Booking essential.

Wheelchair access, also WC • Access, Amex, Diners, Visa

Cho Won   map 14

27 Romilly Street, W1
☎ **071-437 2262**

Open Mon to Sat noon–3, 6–11
Closed Sun and 3 days Christmas

A well-established Korean restaurant offering good value and authentic cooking. Starters include hot and spicy fish soup laced with fiery chilli oil, while main dishes feature several items cooked at the table. Chicken is sautéed with garlic, leeks and mushrooms; coarsely shredded beef comes with 'Korean Secret Sauce'. The menu also has the obligatory kim chee (pickled cabbage), salads and Korean-style pancakes. Good-value set lunches. Drink barley tea.

Wheelchair access, also WC • Access, Amex, Diners, Visa

Chuen Cheng Ku   map 14

17 Wardour Street, W1
☎ **071-437 1398**

Open all week 11am–midnight (11.30 Sun)

A large and impersonal Cantonese restaurant with lunchtime dim-sum its strongest point. Waitresses trundling around the huge trolleys are not always able to explain their wares, and it helps to know the system. Beef in black-bean sauce, char siu, spare ribs and yam fritters are very good. One-plate rice and noodle dishes, chosen from the menu, are excellent value.

Wheelchair access • Access, Amex, Diners, Visa

Please let us know if you think an eating-place should be included in this guide; report forms are at the back of the book.

Chutneys   map 13

124 Drummond Street, NW1
☎ **071-388 0604**

Open all week noon–2.45, 6–11.30
Closed Christmas Day

A cool, fashionable Indian vegetarian restaurant on the site of the legendary Shah. Inside, it is all black and white, with a few prints on the walls, hanging baskets and steel-framed chairs. Best value is the remarkable lunchtime buffet – an assortment of starters, vegetable curries, breads, rice, pickles and a sweet, all for £3.95 (children eat for half price). The full menu stays in familiar territory for thalis, dosas, bhel pooris and the like, produced with varying degrees of success. Drink lassi or lager.

Wheelchair access, also WC • Access, Amex, Diners, Visa

La Cloche   map 12

304 Kilburn High Road, NW6
☎ **071-328 0302**

Open Mon to Sat noon–3, 7–midnight, Sun noon–11

One of Peter Ilic's lively group of informal restaurants. See entry for Lantern.

Wheelchair access • Access, Visa

Coffee House, Inter-Continental Hotel   map 13

1 Hamilton Place, W1
☎ **071-409 3131**

Open all week 7am–3.30, 6–11.30

From Japanese breakfasts (English for the faint-hearted) through monumental club sandwiches to elegant salads guaranteed organically grown, the smart, ground-floor Coffee House offers sophisticated, carefully prepared food which, if chosen with care, is not too expensive. In calming surroundings with attentive service, a wholesome kidney bean and pepper 'cauldron' with garlic bread, followed by a risotto with lambs' kidneys, chipolatas and mushrooms, could be enjoyed for no more than £12. Or you could just indulge in a beefburger with French fries or a croque-monsieur and finish with a rich bitter chocolate fudge cake. Afternoon tea is served in the hotel lounge.

Unlicensed • No-smoking area • Car-park • Wheelchair access, also WC • Access, Amex, Diners, Visa

Como Lario   map 13

22 Holbein Place, SW1
☎ 071-730 2954

*Open Mon to Sat 12.30–2.30,
6.45–11.30
Closed Sun*

A huge mirror and a charming painting of Lake Como by one Winston S. Churchill catch the eye in this long-established trattoria with four separate rooms. Generous pasta dishes and daily specials such as breast of pheasant in tomato and mushroom sauce back up a menu of familiar Continental dishes including scallopine alla romana. The sweets trolley may feature an excellent summer tart filled with all kinds of seasonal fruit. First-class coffee and drinkable house wine by the glass. Remarkably good value for SW1.

Wheelchair access • Access, Visa

F. Cooke   map 12

41 Kingsland High Street, E8
☎ 071-254 2878

*Open Mon and Thur 10am–8, Tue and
Wed 10am–6, Fri and Sat 10am–10pm
Closed Sun and bank hols*

Still boasting the original Victorian interior, F. Cooke serves that East End speciality, eels, to eat in or take away – pie and mash, hot eels and mash, both served with parsley sauce (liquor), or jellied eels. There are facilities to store eight tons of live eels on the premises and guided tours are given to groups by arrangement.

*Unlicensed, but bring your own: corkage
£1.50 • Wheelchair access*

Cork and Bottle   map 14

44–6 Cranbourn Street, WC2
☎ 071-734 7807

Open all week 11–3, 5–11

The warm, friendly personality of Don Hewitson is faithfully reflected in his staff's manner and the Cork and Bottle's atmosphere, unusual for a wine bar in so populous an area as Leicester Square. Food does not come up to the standard of the excellent, all-encompassing wine list, but is adequate and competent, including raised ham and cheese pie, salads, meat loaf and Catalan chicken.

Access, Amex, Diners, Visa

All details are as accurate as possible at the time of going to press, but chefs and owners often change, and it is wise to check by telephone before making a special journey.

Costas Fish Restaurant   map 12

18 Hillgate Street, W8
☎ 071-727 4310

Open Tue to Sat noon–2.25, 5.30–10.25
Closed Sun, Mon, last week July and
first 2 weeks Aug

This Greek restaurant offers
generally well-executed food, and is
supported by a regular clientele
drawn by the value, quality and
unpretentiousness of the décor and
service. Kleftiko is succulent and falls
off the bone, kleftedes well-made, or
there is the familiar hummus,
moussaka or sheftalia and charcoal-
grilled fresh fish.

Country Life   map 13

1B Heddon Street, W1
☎ 071-434 2922

Open Mon to Fri L 11.30–3 (2 Fri)
Closed Sat, Sun and 2 weeks Christmas

An unremarkable basement serving a
remarkable vegan buffet. Everything
is prepared on the premises and
dishes change regularly. Soups (such
as pumpkin), marvellous breads,
spreads and an impressive salad bar
featuring up to 18 different
vegetables are backed up by jacket
potatoes and hot specials including,
perhaps, chickpea à la king or tofu
lasagne. Fresh fruit salads can be
topped with all manner of seeds,
dried fruits and grains. True to the
healthy philosophy of the enterprise
there's no smoking and no alcohol
allowed on the premises.

Unlicensed • No smoking • Garden

See the back of the guide for a breakdown
of London eating-places into type of
cuisine.

Cranks   maps 13/14

8 Marshall Street, W1
☎ 071-437 9431

Open Mon to Fri 8am–8pm, Sat 9am–8
Closed Sun

11 The Market,
Covent Garden, WC2
☎ 071-379 6508

Open Mon to Sat 10am–8, Sun 10am–6

9–11 Tottenham Street, W1
☎ 071-631 3912

Open Mon to Fri 8am–8pm, Sat 9am–6
Closed Sun

17–19 Great Newport Street,
WC2
☎ 071-836 5226

Open Mon to Fri 8am–7, Sat 10am–
7.30, Sun 10am–6

8 Adelaide Street, WC2
(take-away)
☎ 071-836 0660

Open Mon to Fri 8am–7, Sat 9am–6
Closed Sun

23 Barrett Street, W1
☎ 071-495 1340

Open Mon to Fri 8am–7, Sat 9am–7
Closed Sun

Unit 31, The Circle, Broadgate,
EC2
☎ 071-256 5044

Open Mon to Fri 7.30am–6
Closed Sat and Sun

13–15 Leadenhall Market, EC3
☎ 071-283 8527

Open Mon to Fri 7.30am–6
Closed Sat and Sun

5 Cowcross Street, EC1
☎ 071-490 4870

Open Mon to Fri 7.30am–4
Closed Sat and Sun

43 Leather Lane, EC1 (take-away)
☎ 071-430 2064

Open Mon to Fri 8am–4
Closed Sat and Sun

Thirty years ago the first Cranks opened, to great acclaim. It has now evolved into an established group of vegetarian cafés/take-aways with a familiar formula: soups, baked potatoes, pizza, quiches, nut roast, vegetable casseroles and healthy fibre-loaded cakes, all keenly priced. There is also a strong commitment to organic produce. But with expansion, some blandness has crept in, and the formula, much copied elsewhere, can appear tired. The best bets remain the various inventive salads, filled wholewheat rolls, the banana bread and the cheese scones.

No smoking

Curry Paradise   map 12

49 South End Road, NW3
☎ 071-794 6314

Open all week noon–3, 6–11.30
(midnight Fri, Sat and Sun)
Closed Christmas Day

Much smarter and more in keeping with Hampstead than it was in its early days as a flock-wallpapered curry house, Curry Paradise now has spotlights, shiny glass and stainless steel, which gives it the feel of a new-wave Indian restaurant. The long menu makes familiar reading but food is carefully prepared and meals are excellent value. Aloo chop and prawn puri are good starters; chicken jalfrezi is laced with devastatingly hot green chillies. There is also a good choice of vegetables: look for rich sag paneer with plenty of aromatic spinach, and rather unusual capsicum bhaji. Kingfisher beer on draught.

Wheelchair access • Access, Amex, Diners, Visa

Cutty Sark   map 12

Ballast Quay, Lassell Street, SE10
☎ 081-858 3146

Open all week noon–3, 6–9.30

Not near the actual ship but downstream where the Thames turns, the Cutty Sark offers great views of developments in Docklands. The bar food in this listed (1695) bow-fronted pub is surprisingly good. Chalked on a blackboard will be seafood pasta (creamy, with spinach tagliatelle and fresh prawns), steak and Guinness pie, whitebait with chips and salad, and a steak sandwich. Try the pumpkin pie around Hallowe'en. Friendly, charming and good value.

Wheelchair access, also WC • Access, Amex, Diners, Visa

Czech Club   map 12

Czechoslovak National House,
74 West End Lane, NW6
☎ 071-372 5251

Open Sat and Sun L noon–3, Tue to
Sun D 6–10.30
Closed Mon

It is best to be very hungry when entering the Czech Club. Don't be distracted by the patriotic, yet incongruous, wall of fame: portraits of the Queen, Winston Churchill and Vaclav Havel. They watch, you eat. The food here is authentic; the same fare that sustained generations of Bohemian peasants. To start, there will be potato or noodle soup or Debrecin sausage. Next, there is beef, more beef, pork or roast duck. The latter is crisp and non-fatty. The sauerkraut is particularly good and dumplings are served with everything. Try to make room for the cheesecake or the kolac, which is apricot cake.

Dalat   map 12

11 Willesden Lane, NW6
☎ 071-624 8521

Open all week D 6–10.45
Closed 3 weeks Aug

Mr and Mrs Lam offer authentic South Vietnamese cooking in their inexpensive café-restaurant. The décor is functional, the tables are closely packed, but the food is the real thing. A well-described menu of more than 40 dishes includes plenty of choice for vegetarians. Look for specialities such as spring rolls and rice pancakes (both served with fish sauce); chicken with lemon grass and chilli; spicy grilled pork on sticks; and barbecued king prawns with a do-it-yourself selection of rice-paper for wrapping and sauce for dipping. Set dinners for less than £8 per person. Drink tea, saké or Vietnamese beer.

Access, Visa

Daphne   map 13

83 Bayham Street, NW1
☎ 071-267 7322

Open Mon to Sat noon–2.30, 6–11.30
Closed Sun

A cut above the average Greek taverna and still exceptional value.

Inside it feels smartly rustic, with green colour schemes and old Greek photographs on the walls. Meze is a real bargain at £7.25 per person. The standard menu of tsatsiki, dolmades, kebabs and kleftiko is backed up by enterprising and unexpected blackboard dishes with strong fish and vegetarian leanings: artichoke hearts with tomato and onion sauce, black-eyed beans cooked with spinach and olive oil, broad beans in their pods and chargrilled, marinated monkfish are all good. Service is always friendly, although the quality of food can vary, especially on busy, noisy nights. House French wine by the glass.

Roof-top garden • Wheelchair access, also WC • Access, Visa

Daquise   map 13

20 Thurloe Street, SW7
☎ 071-589 6117

Open Mon to Sun noon–10.45, lower restaurant Mon to Fri noon–3, 5.30–midnight, Sat and Sun noon–midnight
Closed Christmas Day, Boxing Day and Easter Sun

A long-established, all-day restaurant of Polish origin. East European dishes, albeit rather watered-down versions, tend to be the best bet, especially the bortsch, potato pancakes with beef goulash and the stuffed cabbage. Cakes are disappointing. The set lunch is keenly priced at £4.30. Drink Polish Tatra lager or vodka.

No cigars/pipes • Wheelchair access in upper restaurant

All letters to this guide are acknowledged.

Diana's Dining Room

map 13

30 Saint Cross Street, EC1
☎ 071-831 7261

Open Mon to Fri 8am–3.30
Closed Sat, Sun and Christmas to New Year

A cheerfully smart, roomy deli/café serving some Jewish and Middle Eastern dishes among the usual deli menu of salads, cold cuts, cheeses and quiches. Cooked-to-order breakfasts – eggs any style, light omelettes and cappuccino – are a strength. Hot salt-beef with latkes, lamb or chicken kebabs, fresh fish poached or fried in matzo-meal are some of the lunch options to eat in or take away. The mainstays of the take-away business are the generously filled, imaginative sandwiches – pastrami on rye, avocado and bacon, prawn mayonnaise – backed up by a variety of crisp salads and kebabs in pitta bread.

Access and Visa applied for

Diwana Bhel Poori House

maps 13/12

121 Drummond Street, NW1
☎ 071-387 5556/380 0730

Open all week noon–11.30
Closed Christmas Day

50 Westbourne Grove, W2
☎ 071-221 0721/229 7689

Open Tue to Fri noon–3, 6–11, Sat and Sun noon–11
Closed Mon

Two simple Indian vegetarian cafés serving inexpensive snacks and meals, all day at the original Drummond Street branch. Newcomers to this style of cooking should try one of the keenly priced thalis – set meals.

Otherwise, there are dosas, various pooris and a selection of specially made kulfi for dessert. Drink lassi or Masala Indian tea.

Unlicensed, but bring your own: no corkage • Wheelchair access • Access, Diners, Visa

Don Pepe

map 13

99 Frampton Street, NW8
☎ 071-262 3834

Open Mon to Sat noon–3, 7–1am
Closed Sun

London's first and still most authentic tapas bar, with basic décor, a lively, informal atmosphere and a TV tuned to Spain and sport. A strong Spanish clientele ensures that the tapas here are just that bit more original than those found elsewhere. Hence you can try earthy, peasant-style lentils with ham and potatoes, whole roasted quail, a rough, hearty pork brawn, as well as the usual meatballs, tortilla, sardines and mussels. There are over 30 tapas to choose from, most of which are on display. Others, such as the excellent pulpo à la Galega can be ordered from the menu. There is a wide selection of Spanish wines, brandies and liqueurs and good, strong espresso.

Access, Amex, Diners, Visa

Dorchester, Promenade

map 13

Park Lane, W1
☎ 071-629 8888

Open Mon to Sat 3pm–6pm
Closed Sun

The long promenade sweeps the length of the hotel, washed by light, soft colours, ornate gilding and divided by statement-making arrangements of flowers. It is an elegant setting for afternoon tea (£11), which the superb service enhances completely. Delicate sandwiches, light fresh scones and tiny gâteaux and pastries are all excellent. Dress accordingly. No bookings taken.

Wheelchair access, also WC • Access, Amex, Diners, Visa

Dragon Inn   map 12

63 Westbourne Grove, W2
☎ **071-229 8806**

Open all week noon–11.45

A light, smart Cantonese restaurant serving excellent dim-sum (noon–5pm). For Western tastes the dim-sum menu is broken up into sections, ending with sweet choices, while the Chinese mix them all up: a sweet steamed bun filled with lotus-seed paste happily precedes chicken feet in black-bean sauce. Turnip mousse and lotus-wrapped glutinous rice are highly recommended. The parent Dragon Inn, 12 Gerrard Street, W1 is less successful.

Access, Amex, Visa

East West   map 13

188 Old Street, EC1
☎ **071-608 0300**

Open all week 11am–9.30 (3 Sat and Sun)
Closed 24 Dec to 2 Jan

A comfortably informal self-service restaurant run on strict macrobiotic lines. The food concept may be simple but the results can be inventive. There is an oriental

influence in baked tofu in peanut butter sauce, seaweed-wrapped sushi rolls and miso soup, while blanched greens, vegetable soup, cucumber and pulse salad have a fresh flavour. Good wholesome sweets.

No smoking • Access, Visa

Ebury Wine Bar   map 13

139 Ebury Street, SW1
☎ **071-730 5447**

Open Mon to Sat noon–2.45, 6–10.30, Sun noon–2.30, 6–10

A popular wine bar with a strong emphasis on food of consistent quality. Pink but toothsome saddle of lamb, breast of duck with ginger and lemon grass sauce, suprême of cod in herb crumbs and shrimp sauce, grilled steaks, lamb cutlets and wild salmon show an imaginative selection. Good puddings include a cinnamon and orange bread-and-butter pudding.

Access, Amex, Diners, Visa

Efes Kebab House   map 13

80 Great Titchfield Street, W1
☎ **071-636 1953**

Open Mon to Sat noon–11.30
Closed Sun

A large, Turkish restaurant generally loved for its bustle and liveliness, although close-packed tables, smokiness and unitemised bills can rightly irritate. Main courses of enormous size – kebabs, kofte, steaks and grilled chicken – are great value, with hummus and fried cheese pastries rated as the very best meze. Both baklava and Turkish coffee are excellent. There is another branch, Efes II, at 175-7 Great Portland Street, W1 (071-436 0600).

No-smoking area • Access, Amex, Visa

Emile's   map 12

144 Wandsworth Bridge Road, SW6
☎ **071-736 2418**
96 Felsham Road, SW15
☎ **081-789 3323**

Open Mon to Sat D 7.30–11
Closed Sun

A bistro with a touch of class. The ground floor has all the classic trappings with candles on the tables; downstairs is a quarry-tiled basement with painted brick walls. The set menu (£12 for three courses) is excellent value for, say, crab pâté with poppy-seed wafers, chargrilled marinated chicken, and chocolate crème brûlée. Main dishes range from breast of duck glazed with plum and fresh ginger to nut and herb roast with watercress sauce. House wines by the glass. Emile's second, more spacious branch in Felsham Road has drawn encouraging early reports.

Wheelchair access • Access, Visa

Enoteca   map 12

28 Putney High Street, SW15
☎ **081-785 4449**

Open all week 12.30–3 (exc Sat), 6–11.30
Closed Boxing Day and New Year's Day

Italian regional restaurants are obviously in style, and Enoteca has the added advantage of being very good value. Try the unusual pasta dishes, the lentil and bacon salad,

involtini of ham, aubergine, courgette and pepper, an excellent rolled breast of pork stuffed with sultanas, apple and herbs, and tender duck in lentil sauce.

Wheelchair access, also WC • Access, Visa

Escape Coffee House   map 12

141–3 Greenwich South Street, SE10
☎ **081-692 5826**

Open Mon to Fri 8.15am–10.30pm, Sat 10am–10.30pm, Sun noon–8.30
Closed 3 days Christmas

A plain, small vegetarian café in the stripped-wood-tables and candles-in-a-bottle mould. The cooking shows some flair despite microwave short cuts: a woodland casserole of mushrooms, chestnuts, potato, leek and string beans comes with a good, nutty sauce; butter-bean bake with an inventive date topping. Good cakes and friendly service.

Unlicensed, but bring your own: corkage 50p per person • No-smoking area • Wheelchair access • Access, Amex, Visa

Ethiopia in the Year 2002   map 12

341A Harrow Road, W9
☎ **071-286 5129**

Open all week D 6.30–11

A fun place to go in a crowd as the food is eaten with fingers from shared trays. The basis of Ethiopian cooking is a flat, sour-dough bread called injera on to which various spiced dishes are placed, including chicken, lamb, mushrooms, mixed vegetables and lentils. Starters and desserts are missable, which keeps the price down. Drink strong Jamaican beer and tea made with coffee leaves.

No cigars/pipes • Wheelchair access • Access, Visa

Falafel House   map 12

95 Haverstock Hill, NW3
☎ 071-722 6187

Open all week D 6–11.30
Closed Christmas, New Year's Day and bank hols

If you like falafel – spiced rissoles made from white, dried beans deep-fried in oil – then this could be your place. Décor is pine, and ceiling lamps contain red and green light-bulbs, to further ensure cheerfulness. There is a good range of soups and starters; lamb and beef kebabs are good quality and there is no skimping. Most of what you order is served without grease and with a smile.

Wheelchair access • Access, Visa

Faulkners   map 12

424–6 Kingsland Road, E8
☎ 071-249 5661

Open Mon to Sat noon–2, 5–10
Closed Sun

Fish and chips no longer constitutes a cheap meal with the high price of fish nowadays, but this informal, popular East End café certainly gives value for money with £15 buying a filling meal for two. The fish is fresh and portions are generous, especially the children's half-price ones. Chips could be better.

Licensed, but bring your own: corkage £2 • No-smoking area

First Floor   map 12

186 Portobello Road, W11
☎ 071-243 0072

Open all week 12.30 (Sat and Sun 8.30am)–3.30, 7.30–11.30

An obviously named and deeply trendy restaurant reached via a stone-strewn corridor. The light, airy room offers artfully draped net curtains, a few broken pillars, close-packed tables and uncomfortable chairs. The menu is diverse, the food imaginatively ambitious if not always successful. Black-bean, coriander and yoghurt soup came up with the right off-beat flavour that the dish suggested and squid salad with pesto was well-judged, but risotto with fennel and sun-dried tomatoes lacked interest. Grazing amongst the starters is all part of the style (and actively encouraged at certain times), otherwise the bill could be high.

Access, Visa

Fleet Tandoori   map 12

104 Fleet Road, NW3
☎ 071-485 6402

Open Mon to Sat noon–2.30, 6–11.30, Sun noon–11.30

An unpretentious tandoori house at the back of the Royal Free Hospital. Consistently sound cooking and pleasant service account for its popularity. Chicken tandoori, lamb pasanda and chicken bhuna have all been especially praised. The tandoori mixed dish is good value at £8.45 and there are well-priced vegetarian and non-vegetarian thalis. There is another branch at 346 Muswell Hill Broadway, N10 (081-883 8252).

Wheelchair access • Access, Amex, Diners, Visa

Food For Thought   map 14

31 Neal Street, WC2
☎ **071-836 0239**

Open Mon to Sat 8.30–11.30am,
noon–2.45, 3–7.45
Closed Sun and 2 weeks Christmas

A former banana warehouse is home to this imaginative vegetarian restaurant. Goats'-milk cheese and spinach filo, Thai curry, lasagne, gado-gado with a spiced peanut sauce and stir-fried vegetables feature on the daily changing menu. Home-made bread, carrot cake and almond flapjacks can be enjoyed at any time. Healthy breakfasts are available, with vegan scones.

Unlicensed, but bring your own: no corkage • No smoking

Formula Veneta   map 12

14 Hollywood Road, SW10
☎ **071-352 7612**

Open all week 12.30–3, 7–11.30 (exc Sun D)

Food from the Veneto region of Italy with regional specialities well-represented: pasta and bean soup, several risottos, polenta and the ubiquitous tiramisu. A heady, pungent pesto enlivens carpaccio, chargrilled vegetables are satisfyingly fresh and rib of beef is generous good value. Finish with good espresso.

Access, Amex, Diners, Visa

When you book a restaurant table, you're making a contract with the restaurant and you must be given a table, within reasonable time of your arrival. If not, the restaurant is in breach of contract and you can claim a reasonable sum to cover any expenses you had as a result, e.g. travelling expenses.

Four Seasons   map 12

84 Queensway, W2
☎ **071-229 4320**

Open all week noon–11
Closed Christmas Day and Boxing Day

Those of you mourning the demise of Hung Toa as the foremost venue for Cantonese one-dish meals can take heart. The duo that formed the backbone of that operation have set themselves up 50 yards away at the Four Seasons. These inexpensive one-dish meals of rice with up to a maximum of three combinations of either char siu, soya chicken, spare ribs or roast duck for £3.75 including tea are amazing value for money and available for lunch all week. Otherwise, the secret of the carte is to ask for the Chinese menu supplement and insist on a translation in order to try the real dishes: the humble village specialities.

Access, Amex, Diners, Visa

Fox and Anchor   map 13

115 Charterhouse Street, EC1
☎ **071-253 4838**

Open Mon to Fri 7am–10.30am,
noon–2.30
Closed Sat and Sun

A solid, old-fashioned Victorian pub, famous for providing a hearty, meaty, sustaining breakfast to Smithfield market workers and intrepid tourists. This must be one of the few pubs in the country where you can wash breakfast down with a beer (the licence starts at 6am). There are also prime grilled steak, pork or lamb and cold cuts at lunchtime.

Visa

Frascati   map 12

33 Heath Street, NW3
☎ 071-431 3274

Open Tue to Sun noon–2.30, 6–11.30
Closed Mon, Christmas Day and Easter
Sun

A wholly unpretentious, relaxed
trattoria of diminutive size close to
Hampstead tube station. It is cheap
and cheerful with the best bets being
the freshly made pasta which comes
in generous portions. Both tortellini
parmigiana and spaghetti pescatore
have proved to be richly sauced and
fresh-tasting.

No-smoking area • No very young
children

Gandhi's   map 13

35 Gray's Inn Road, WC1
☎ 071-831 6208

Open all week noon–2.30, 6–11.30

This well-reported Indian restaurant
seems closer to the new wave than
the old curry-house style. Excellent
vegetarian thalis are full of distinctive
flavours and textures; king prawn
masala comes in a richly spiced,
buttery sauce; Bengal-style chingri
jhol is good, too. Otherwise, the
menu ranges from shami kebab and
tandoori mixed grill to karahi murg
and rogan josh. Vegetables can be
ordered as accompaniments or main
dishes.

Wheelchair access, also WC • Access,
Amex, Diners, Visa

Please let us know if you think an eating-
place should be included in this guide;
report forms are at the back of the book.

Ganpath   map 13

372 Gray's Inn Road, WC1
☎ 071-278 1938

Open all week noon–3 (exc Sun),
6–midnight
Closed Christmas, New Year and bank
hols

Ganpath is close to King's Cross
Station, and it is best if you ignore
the surroundings and concentrate on
the food, notably the South Indian
starters and the vegetable dishes.
Lentil doughnuts, uthappam, onion
bhajias and masala dosai draw
unanimous praise, while in the
vegetable department Bombay aloo is
crisp, dry and flavourful and green
bananas different and tasty. Good
chicken tikka and sag josh.

Wheelchair access • Access, Visa

Gardners   map 12

156 Chiswick High Road, W4
☎ 081-995 1656

Open all week D 7.30–11, Sun L
12.30–2

An attractive restaurant done out in
understated tones of beige, with pink
carnations and candles on the tables.
Best value is to be found in the
basement bistro, although meals in
the main dining-room are quite
affordable. The style is Anglo-French
with a loyalty to free-range poultry
and naturally reared meat; vegetarian
dishes are always on offer. Roast duck
breast comes with morello cherries,
boeuf en daube is served with
béarnaise sauce, and the menu also
takes in first-rate moules marinière,
Lancashire hot-pot and nut and
cabbage mould with tomato and basil
sauce. Chocolate mousse laced with

Grand Marnier is a fine sweet. Useful, varied set meals.

Wheelchair access • Access, Amex, Diners, Visa

La Gaulette   map 13

53 Cleveland Street, W1
☎ 071-580 7608/323 4210

Open Mon to Sat noon–3 (exc Sat), 6.30–11
Closed Sun

One of the best-kept secrets of the area – a wine bar in the basement of a Mauritian fish restaurant which serves huge portions of imaginatively cooked fish at low prices. Moules Mauritian is a great bowl of plump, spicy molluscs, fish soup is thick and deeply flavoured, while exotic fish like vacqua come with ginger and spring onions in a well-judged sweet-and-sour sauce. Leave room for the rich tarte tatin.

Access, Amex, Diners, Visa

Geales   map 12

2 Farmer Street, W8
☎ 071-727 7969

Open Tue to Sat noon–3, 6–11
Closed Sun and Mon, 2 weeks Christmas, 1 week Easter and 2 weeks Aug

Famous for its fresh fish (still delivered daily) and old-fashioned style – nothing has changed here for years. The menu is chalked up on a blackboard and can include anything from cod and plaice to salmon and shark. Portions are daunting, the batter light, the chips hand-cut. The image of a superior fish and chip shop is enhanced by champagne on the wine list.

No cigars/pipes • Wheelchair access, also gents WC • Access, Visa

General Trading Company   map 13

144 Sloane Street, SW1
☎ 071-730 2607

Open Mon to Sat 9am–5.15, 6–10.15 (exc Sat D)
Closed Sun, 10 days Christmas and bank hols

Well-heeled but weary shoppers head for Justin de Blank's basement restaurant to be revived – the bright, glassed-in terrace and high-walled garden attract lunchtime queues. Fresh, well-prepared food includes spinach roulade, well-flavoured soups, good bread, roast beef, chicken salad and quiches. In the evening there is a more adventurous set menu (£11.95 for two courses) and a pre-theatre supper of soup and salad (£4.95).

No-smoking daytime area • Access, Visa (evenings only)

Gopal's of Soho   map 14

12 Bateman Street, W1
☎ 071-434 1621/0840

Open all week noon–3, 6–11.30 (11 Sun)
Closed Christmas Day and Boxing Day

Currently the pick of central London's new-wave Indian restaurants. Sequined prints and fashionable pinks and beiges set the tone in the classy dining-room, which is convivial and cramped at the front, spacious and formal at the back. The kitchen delivers excellent North Indian curries and tandooris backed up by a few regional specialities such as fiery Goan chicken with coconut.

Potato 'patties', kadai murgh, prawns cooked with spring onions, and vegetable dishes have all been recommended. Pilau rice is outstanding. Good-value thalis. Drink Kingfisher beer.

No-smoking area • Wheelchair access • Access, Amex, Diners, Visa

---

Govinda's   map 13

9 Soho Street, W1
☎ 071-437 3662

Open Mon to Sat noon–7
Closed Sun and New Year's Day

This vegetarian restaurant, run by Hare Krishna followers and only yards from Oxford Street, is a haven of peacefulness. Ultra-basic pine furniture and a few flowers pass for décor. Head for the self-service food counter after studying the blackboard menu which, while limited, changes daily. Expect two hot curry dishes, plain boiled rice, salads and a good selection of chutneys and pickles. For dessert there is fresh fruit. To drink there are kiwi fruit and melon juice and banana lassi. Soft smiles, soft voices and soft on your wallet.

Unlicensed • No smoking • Wheelchair access • Access, Diners

Grahame's Seafare   map 13

38 Poland Street, W1
☎ 071-437 0975/3788

Open Mon to Sat noon–2.45, 5.30–9
(8 Fri and Sat)
Closed Sun

Grahame's is a crowded, old-fashioned Jewish dining-room, not cheap, but offering value with good, fresh ingredients simply cooked. Fish is fried, steamed or boiled and served

with potatoes chipped (could be better), creamed or boiled. Jewish specialities of gefilte fish and bortsch are popular and there are also potato latkes, cheese blintzes and various salads.

Wheelchair access • Access, Amex, Visa

Grapes ⊚   map 12

76 Narrow Street, E14
☎ 071-987 4396

Open Mon to Fri L noon–3, Tue to Sat D 7–9
Closed Sun, 10 days Christmas and bank hols

Once used as a model by Dickens for his 'Six Jolly Fellowship Porters' in *Our Mutual Friend*, this small, narrow pub is nevertheless off the tourist track – customers are East End or City. Fillet of plaice, lightly battered with hand-cut chips and home-made tartare sauce, is the most popular choice in the bar. Otherwise, there is a simple selection of sandwiches or salads of home-cooked ham, fresh crab or beef. The tiny upstairs restaurant, known for fresh fish, has a fine river view and acknowledges its East End location with jellied eels.

No-smoking area • Children restricted • Access, Visa

Great Nepalese   map 13

48 Eversholt Street, NW1
☎ 071-388 6737

Open all week noon–2.45, 6–11.30
Closed Christmas Day and Boxing Day

If you brave this insalubrious street next to Euston Station and enter the Great Nepalese, you will be rewarded with a warm welcome and food of unusual spicing and flavours which are distinctly different from other Indian restaurants. Good, moist chicken tikka, tender Nepalese mutton curry, and well-flavoured chicken jhalphiraji have all been praised. Fresh coriander pickle is exemplary and service is everything it should be.

Wheelchair access • Access, Amex, Diners, Visa

Greenhouse   map 13

16 Chenies Street, WC1
☎ **071-637 8038**

Open Mon to Sat noon–9 (exc Mon D)
Closed Sun and bank hols

This 'greenhouse' is a dimly lit basement full of healthy plants, wooden tables and green chairs. A short, daily-changing menu always features a soup, hot dishes, pizzas and quiches. The style is 'multinational wholefood', ranging from walnut balls with tomato and basil sauce to French and kidney bean casserole to kebabs with hot-and-sour sauce. It gets very busy at lunchtime; limited choice 3pm–5pm. Take-aways are available.

Unlicensed, but bring your own • No smoking • Wheelchair access by prior arrangement, also WC

Gurkhas Tandoori   map 13

23 Warren Street, W1
☎ **071-388 1640**

Open all week noon–2.45, 6–11.45
Closed Christmas Day and Boxing Day

One of the first restaurants in central London to feature authentic Nepalese specialities. The small, box-like dining-room reinforces the geographical links, with gurkhas' medals, photographs and other memorabilia on the walls. The menu is a mixed bag, indiscriminately listing Nepalese dishes alongside curry house/tandoori stalwarts. Look for specialities such as thupa (noodle soup flavoured with herbs) and kukura masu (chicken on the bone with a sweetish mellow sauce). Vegetables and side dishes are a strong point: excellent ungreasy spinach, aloo bodi tama, thick raita and boiled Basmati rice are always good. Useful, cheap lunch menu. Drink lager.

Wheelchair access • Access, Amex, Diners, Visa

Häagen-Dazs   maps 14/12

14 Leicester Square, WC2
☎ **071-287 9577**

Open all week 10am–midnight (1am Fri and Sat)

75 Hampstead High Street, NW3
☎ **071-794 0646**

Open all week 10am–10pm (11pm Fri to Sun)
Closed Christmas Day and Boxing Day

A light, stylish American ice-cream parlour. One part is take-away, the other contains waitress-served tables for which there is generally a queue. Ice-cream is marvellous, made from pure ingredients and offering fresh flavours in generous portions. Some of the composite offerings on the menu are worth exploring. Chocoholic sundae is self-descriptive or try raisin muffin with vanilla ice-cream.

Unlicensed • No smoking

Haandi
map 13

161 Drummond Street, NW1
☎ 071-383 4557

*Open all week noon–2.30, 6–11.30
(midnight Fri and Sat)
Closed Christmas Day and bank hols*

This newest Indian arrival in
Drummond Street is a classy relative
of the nearby Ravi Shankar and
Chutneys (see entry). Unlike its
neighbours it is not exclusively
vegetarian, although dishes such as
dahi vada and potato bonda feature
on the menu, and vegetables are a
high point. Best value is the excellent
lunchtime buffet (£5.50), which has a
mix of vegetarian starters, meat and
vegetable curries, bread, rice and
sweets, backed up by a remarkable
array of eight chutneys and pickles.
The full menu takes in familiar
tandooris, bhunas, kormas and the
like. Drink lager.

*Wheelchair access • Access, Amex,
Diners, Visa*

Hodja Nasreddin
map 12

53 Newington Green Road,
N1
☎ 071-226 7757

*Open Mon to Thur noon–1.30am, Fri
and Sat noon–3am
Closed Christmas Eve and Christmas
Day*

Richly patterned fabric drapes the
room, and the ceiling is hung with
Moorish brass lamps. This is a
friendly Turkish restaurant where
long hours and value for money are
the main selling points. The menu
holds no surprises: dolmades,
hummus, taramasalata, excellent
börek, with variations on the kebab

theme dominating main courses.
Good Turkish coffee to finish. There
is also a take-away.

Wheelchair access • Access, Amex, Visa

Honeymoon
map 12

33–5 Park Road, N8
☎ 081-341 5113

*Open all week noon–2.30, 6–11.30
Closed 3 days Christmas and half-day
bank hols*

A highly agreeable Peking/Szechuan
restaurant where the owner may
serenade birthday parties by playing
his violin. The décor is quite elegant,
but understated, with rag-rolled walls
and some colourful Chinese screens
in the archways. The mixed plate of
appetisers is a good starter; crispy
aromatic duck is authentically
prepared; and other recommended
dishes have included sliced steak in
mandarin sauce, garlicky Szechuan
lamb and gwa-tar chicken. Good-
value set 'feasts' for two or more
people. Drink wine, saké or Tiger
beer.

*Wheelchair access, also WC • Access,
Amex, Visa*

Hubble & Co
map 13

55 Charterhouse Street, EC1
☎ 071-253 1612

*Open Mon to Fri noon–10.30
Closed Sat and Sun*

Opposite Smithfield, this ground-
floor wine bar carved out of a
Victorian warehouse offers some
relief from the surrounding greasy
spoons; hence the need to book at
lunchtime. Stick to the well-priced

snacks and main course dishes: Smithfield steak or Cromer crab sandwich, wild-boar sausages and salmon fish-cakes. There is a more expensive basement restaurant.

Wheelchair access, also WC • Access, Visa

Hungrys   map 13

37A Crawford Street, W1
☎ **071-258 0376**

*Open Mon to Fri 7am–5, Sat 8.30am–3
Closed Sun, 1 week Christmas, Easter
and bank hols*

Half sandwich bar, half café, with blue plastic table-covers and waitress service. An astonishing range of sandwiches, including double- and triple-deckers, is the mainstay, but there are also lunchtime specials such as pea soup, salt-beef with latkes and jacket potato with sausage and beans. First-class ingredients, and exceptional value for money.

Unlicensed • Access

ICA Café   map 13

The Mall, SW1
☎ **071-930 8535**

Open all week noon–9pm

Return to the 1980s and have a light, professionally cooked lunch or supper in the civilised, art-filled café/ bar of the ICA. The scene is black chrome, rubber floor covering and designer lighting. The paintings on show, generally, do not hinder digestion. This is a polite, counter-service canteen which has, for the past five years, been operated by Work in Progress caterers. Each day they prepare simple baguette

sandwiches, soup, imaginative salads, such as cauliflower and raisin, and vegetable-based, Italian-style hot dishes. Try the calamari con piselli – squid with peas in a pepper brine; or the ratatouille – served over a rich tomato sauce. For afters there are nut loaf, tiramisu, truffle cake and ricotta pie. You will have to pay £1.50 to get into the ICA.

No smoking in restaurant • Wheelchair access, also WC

Ikkyu   map 13

67A Tottenham Court Road, W1
☎ **071-636 9280/436 6160**

*Open Mon to Fri 12.30–2.30, 6–10.30,
Sun 6–10.30
Closed Sat*

A lively, down-to-earth Japanese restaurant, serving a good, robust style of cooking to an equally lively and varied clientele. Set meals of sushi, herring or deep-fried pork are excellent value and give the best introduction, for unless you are familiar with the food the menu can be confusing and the staff are not always up to explaining it. It is essential to book.

Access, Amex, Diners, Visa

Indian Veg Bhel-Poori House   map 13

92–3 Chapel Market, N1
☎ **071-837 4607**

*Open all week noon–3, 6–11
Closed Christmas Day and Boxing Day*

Tables are squeezed tightly together and service can be indifferent here, but for sheer value for money the £2.95 buffet (£3.95 evenings) would be hard to rival. The crisp, subtly seasoned samosas and stimulating (cold) bhel poori are particularly recommended as starters; alternatively, choose from various thalis, which may include salad (not too adventurous), dhal, puris, chapatis, assorted vegetable curries and masala dosai. The House Special Thali at £4.95 is the most expensive dish on the menu. For those who have not over-indulged at the buffet – easily done – kulfi (Indian ice-cream) is a good dessert. Bottled Dortmund beer is cheaper than in most pubs.

No-smoking area • Wheelchair access • Access, Amex, Visa

Italian Graffiti   map 14

163–5 Wardour Street, W1
☎ **071-439 4668**

Open Mon to Fri noon–3, 6–11.45, Sat noon–11.45
Closed Sun, Christmas and New Year

This is a small, independent pizzeria, rivalling the nearby branch of Pizza Express. Inside, it feels intimate, with dark marble-topped tables and upholstered banquettes, bare brick walls and a tiled floor. Pasta dishes such as fettucine with salmon back up a range of decent pizzas with some imaginative toppings. Real Italian ham, good-quality mozzarella and juicy anchovies show that the kitchen cares about ingredients. Interesting starters include slivers of grilled pepper with olive oil. House wine by the glass.

Wheelchair access • Access, Amex, Diners, Visa

Jade Garden   map 14

15 Wardour Street, W1
☎ **071-437 5065**

Open all week noon (11.30am Sat and Sun)–11.30 (10.30 Sun)
Closed Christmas Day and Boxing Day

Some of the best dim-sum in Chinatown are served here; join the queue at 11.30am on Sundays to ensure a seat. Fresh-tasting and piping-hot come ginger beef ball dumplings, stuffed bean curd roll, char siu buns, delicious glutinous rice wrapped in lotus leaves, and good chueng fun. The carte can be expensive and less exciting.

Wheelchair access • Access, Amex, Visa

Jason's   map 12

50 Battersea Park Road, SW11
☎ **071-622 6998**

Open Mon to Sat D 6.30–11.45

Nothing changes at this long-established, good-value taverna jointly run by an Englishman and a Cypriot. Dim lights, unobtrusive music and red-painted walls set the scene, while the menu centres on the classics. Meze (£7.50 per head) spans the full range of dishes; otherwise, look for garides (prawns split lengthways with onions, oil and lemon), chargrilled shashlik and slowly braised kleftiko. Reasonable sweets, unlimited coffee, full-bodied Cypriot red wine.

Wheelchair access

Jigsaw   map 12

74 Askew Road, W12
☎ 081-746 0397

*Open Mon to Sat noon–3, 7–midnight,
Sun noon–11*

One of Peter Ilic's lively group of
informal restaurants. See entry for
Lantern.

Access, Visa

Jin   map 14

16 Bateman Street, W1
☎ 071-734 0908

*Open all week noon–3 (exc Sun), 6–11
Closed Christmas Day and Boxing Day*

Korean and minimalist, with black
veneer tables and Rennie
Mackintosh-style chairs. The set-
price lunch might be soup, bulgogi
(cooked on a gas grill set into the
table), kim chee (pickled cabbage),
rice, 'silk noodles' and tea. Bulgogi
meat will be sizzled by your waiter,
and it should be a generous portion.
The service can be absent-minded.

*Wheelchair access • Access, Amex,
Diners, Visa*

Julie's   map 12

137 Portland Road, W11
☎ 071-727 7985

*Open Mon to Sat 11am–midnight, Sun
noon–10.30
Closed Easter, Christmas and bank hols*

A quietly successful wine bar
concealed amid a backwater of
antique shops near Holland Park.
Ignore the adjoining restaurant and
climb the stairs to discover a
comfortable bar-room and
conservatory stuffed with sofas and
the ransacked remnants of more than
one Victorian church: dark wood
pews, stained-glass and tapestries.
Potted palms, gothic arches and a few
British Raj artefacts are also scattered
around for good measure. Food
quality is average but acceptable. You
won't go wrong with leek and potato
soup or duck and chicken liver pâté,
or with Cumberland sausages and
mash or roast loin of pork with apple
sauce, red cabbage and new potatoes.
The wine list is exclusively French
but includes a few organic
experiments. The service is confident
and your coffee cup is replenished at
no extra cost.

Access, Visa

Just William Wine Bar   map 12

6 Battersea Rise, SW11
☎ 071-228 9980

*Open all week noon–3, 7.30–11
Closed 1 week Christmas and 1 week
Easter*

A neighbourhood wine bar with a
folksy welcome and better-than-
average food. The wine list isn't bad
either. There is only one picture of
'William' and there are only a few
tables. Almost everything has a
home-made touch including lentil
and vegetable soup, lamb steak au
poivre and pheasant and chicken
casserole. Also, there are excellent
desserts. Generous portions and a
relaxed atmosphere.

Wheelchair access • Access, Visa

See the front of the guide for a list of each
eating-place given a star for being one of
the best found by the Editor during
research for this book.

Kenny's

map 12

70 Heath Street, NW3
☎ 071-435 6972

Open all week 11.45am–midnight

Not unlike your average pizza/pasta joint from without, Kenny's is, in fact, different: a well-run Cajun/Creole restaurant using properly trained and motivated staff. The food is fresh, the cooking style generous and very assured. There is alligator sausage, succulent grilled shrimp wrapped in bacon, catfish lafayette and spicy po'man's jambalaya. Superb desserts.

No cigars/pipes • Wheelchair access • Access, Amex, Visa

Kettners

map 14

29 Romilly Street, W1
☎ 071-734 6112

Open all week 11am–midnight

Kettners is primarily known for its pizzas and on these the current feeling is that they are not as good as they used to be. But it is still a great place to go, especially in a group, for the reasonable prices and because the grand, historic Soho building has such stylish décor and a lively atmosphere. Steak, burgers, chilli, BLT and egg and bacon for non-pizza lovers.

Wheelchair access • Access, Amex, Diners, Visa

You will find report forms (write a letter if you prefer) at the back of the book so that you can tell us about your experiences of going *Out to Eat*. We'll put the information to good use when we're compiling the next edition.

Lantern

map 12

23 Malvern Road, NW6
☎ 071-624 1796

Open Mon to Sat noon–3, 7–midnight, Sun noon–11

Peter Ilic's lively group of informal restaurants is run to the same formula – prices are fixed so that main courses, for instance, are all £4.85. Some dishes are standard throughout the group: moules marinière, duck en croûte and lamb steak, although each restaurant offers some variation plus daily specials. Tables are always close-packed, candles often the only form of lighting, the staff bright and cheerful.

Access, Visa

Latymers ⊛

map 12

157 Hammersmith Road, W6
☎ 081-741 2507

*Open Mon to Sat noon–2.30, 6–10
Closed Sun, Christmas Day, New Year's Day and bank hols*

Lurking behind an incredibly glitzy, chrome-laden pub saloon bar is the Thai café part of Latymers. This is a pleasant mini-restaurant decorated in an eclectic style. Non-Thai food as well as a few vegetarian dishes are posted on a blackboard. The menu offers an excellent and variable choice of noodle, stir-fry, curry and rice dishes. Almost everything can be ordered to include either beef, chicken, pork or prawns. The tom yam goong fragrant lemon grass soup is authentic, while the spring rolls are eminently non-greasy and delicately parcelled. Just about everything is pretty hot and spicy.

Wheelchair access • Access, Diners, Visa

Lauderdale House   map 12

Waterlow Park, Highgate Hill, N19
☎ 081-348 8716

Open Tue to Sun Apr to Oct 9am–5.30, Nov to Mar 9.30am–5
Closed Mon and 3 weeks Christmas

Once the home of the poet Andrew Marvell, this gracious building in the grounds of a beautiful park is now used for exhibitions, concerts and craft fairs. The café is in a small downstairs room leading in from the rose garden, and snacks can be eaten outside when the weather allows. A menu based on grills, salads, pizzas and quiches ranges from liver and bacon to specials such as fresh salmon pancakes. Cheddar cheese and apple salad is piled high with healthy ingredients. Warm, home-made apple tart or Loseley ice-creams to finish. Pots of tea, coffee, or wine by the glass.

Garden • Wheelchair access, also WC • Access, Visa

Laurent   map 12

428 Finchley Road, NW2
☎ 071-794 3603

Open Mon to Sat noon–2.30, 6.30–11
Closed Sun and first 3 weeks Aug

Laurent Farrugia does one thing and he does it well – couscous, undoubtedly the best in London. It is all he offers in his spic and span little restaurant, in just three versions: vegetarian, complet and royale. Brique à l'oeuf is the sole starter and there are a few simple desserts. Drink North African wines and mint tea.

Wheelchair access • Access, Visa

Ley-On's   map 14

56–8 Wardour Street, W1
☎ 071-437 6465

Open all week 11.30am–11.15pm
Closed Christmas Day and Boxing Day

One of the oldest Cantonese restaurants in Soho, cavernous and faded with an encyclopaedic menu of nearly 200 dishes. The food is pricier than in nearby Chinatown, but the atmosphere is calmer, especially in the evenings. During the day the menu is better value, with well-prepared, inexpensive one-plate meals and some 30 choices of dim-sum (11.30am–4.30pm).

Wheelchair access • Access, Amex, Diners, Visa

Lorenzo   map 12

73 Westow Hill, SE19
☎ 081-761 7485

Open all week noon–2.30 (exc Sat), 6–11

A pizzeria/restaurant with a wood and glass frontage and green gingham tablecloths. It can get busy and noisy. The menu is dominated by 18 pizzas, including calzone and a dessert version topped with grated apple and served with ice-cream. They are thin and crisp in the Italian style with good, plentiful toppings; thick American pizzas can be produced for a small extra charge. Otherwise, there are familiar starters, plenty of pasta dishes and blackboard specials. House wine by the glass. Booking essential. There is also a branch at 122 Streatham High Road, SW16 (081-664 6033).

Wheelchair access • Acess, Amex, Diners, Visa

Los Remos
map 13

38A Southwick Street, W2
☎ 071-723 5056

Open Mon to Sat noon–11
Closed Sun, Christmas Day, Boxing Day
and New Year's Day

A basement tapas bar with its own
entrance to distinguish it from the
restaurant above. It is handy for
Paddington Station as the efficient
all-Spanish staff understand the basic
concept of tapas as fast food. This is a
cheerful place with lively Spanish
music on tape, and a fresh, tempting
display of over 20 tapas dishes. The
food is excellent and of a consistent
standard: roasted pimentos are fleshy
and garlicky, patatas bravas spicy, and
chicken in white wine is tender.
Portions are generous and
complemented by Spanish wines and
strong espresso coffee.

Access, Amex, Diners, Visa

Lou Pescadou
map 13

241 Old Brompton Road, SW5
☎ 071-370 1057

Open all week noon–3, 7–midnight
Closed 2 weeks Christmas

A lively seafood restaurant with an
authentic French atmosphere. Best
value is fish soup with its proffered
second helping; then choose moules
marinière, omelette or the generously
topped pizzas. Avoid being parked in
the bar (no bookings) and watch out
for the cover and service charges, all
bill bumpers.

Wheelchair access • Access, Amex,
Diners, Visa

Louis
map 12

**12 Harben Parade, Finchley Road,
NW3**
☎ 071-722 8100

Open all week 8.30am–7

Formerly owned by Louis Patisserie
of Hampstead, this patisserie has
changed little under the new
ownership and Louis still supplies the
cakes. There is a light snack menu
which takes in sandwiches, salads,
sausage rolls and a Hungarian
goulash soup, but it is the cakes that
excel – rich creamy confections
accompanied by excellent espresso.

Unlicensed • No-smoking area •
Wheelchair access

Louis
map 12

32 Heath Lane, NW3
☎ 071-435 9908

Open all week 9.30am–6
Closed Christmas Day and Boxing Day

A mouth-watering display of cakes in
the window draws you inside this
decidedly old-fashioned patisserie of
long standing. There is not much
choice, just good coffee and tea (no
specialities), sausage rolls, croissants
and a choice of delicious cakes, with
maybe a rich chocolate cake of light
sponge, liqueur and cream, or a
cream-based strawberry tart.

Unlicensed • No-smoking area

A restaurant manager can't insist on
people not smoking, unless it's specifically
a no-smoking restaurant or a no-smoking
area. If it is, smokers could be asked to
leave if they don't stop. If in doubt, check
beforehand what the smoking
arrangements are.

Maison Bertaux   map 14

28 Greek Street, W1
☎ 071-437 6007

*Open Mon to Sat 9am–7.30, Sun
9am–1, 3–7
Closed Christmas Day and Boxing
Day*

Despite a change of hands, this tiny
Soho patisserie continues to produce
some high-quality baking. Individual
quiches are outstanding, while the
range of cakes is huge, taking in
mille-feuilles, colourful fruit tarts,
plump eclairs and varied gâteaux.
There are a few tables in the shop
itself and a tiny tea-room for some
excellent light snacks.

No-smoking area • Wheelchair access

Maison Sagne   map 13

105 Marylebone High Street, W1
☎ 071-935 6240

*Open Mon to Fri 9am–4.45
Closed Sat and Sun*

Established in 1921, Maison Sagne is
a decidedly old-fashioned tea-room
with faded trompe-l'oeil walls and a
sparkling cleanliness reminiscent of
French patisseries. The baking does
not always come up to scratch
though: strawberry tarts have had
inedible, hard pastry cases. For lunch
there are omelettes and salads.
Popular, and for a pit-stop the best
the area can offer.

*Unlicensed, but bring your own: no
corkage • Wheelchair access*

Makan   map 12

270 Portobello Road, W11
☎ 081-960 5169

*Open Mon to Sat 11am–8
Closed Sun, Christmas and New
Year*

This is one of the best places in
Notting Hill for cheap, nourishing
and tasty food. Authentic, popular
Malaysian dishes are available to take
away or to eat in. For breakfast, try
either gado-gado (£2.20), laksa
(£2.80) or nasi lemak (£2.50). Almost
everything is cooked with chicken or
prawns although there is a good
choice for vegetarians.

*Unlicensed • No smoking • Wheelchair
access*

Malabar   map 12

27 Uxbridge Street, W8
☎ 071-727 8800

*Open all week noon–2.45, 6–11.15
Closed last week Aug, 4 days Christmas
and bank hols*

The interior of Malabar is cool and
white. It is advisable to book as this
North Indian restaurant offers both
high quality and low prices. Kerahi of
chicken, beef and lamb, dhansaks,
kormas, tandooris and tikkas form the
short menu. Dishes are carefully
cooked and there is good nan and
pilau rice. Close tables and smoking
neighbours can be annoying.

Wheelchair access • Access, Visa

Mandalay map 12

100 Greenwich South Street, SE10
☎ 081-691 0443

Open Tue to Sat D 7–10.30, Sun L
12.30–3
Closed Mon

The only Burmese restaurant in
England. The menu has descriptions
of the dishes but explanations help
and are readily given. Starters of
marrow in batter, and minced pork
deep-fried in wun-tun leaf, with a
main course of beef and potato
tamarind fry, all come highly
recommended. Stir-fried cabbage is a
good accompaniment. Order soup
with the main course.

Children by arrangement only

Mandeer map 13

21 Hanway Place, W1
☎ 071-323 0660/580 3470

Open Mon to Sat noon–3, 6–10
Closed Sun, Christmas and bank hols

Since 1960 Ramesh and Usha Patel
have been serving vegetarian food
from their native Indian province of
Gujerat. For all these years they have
eschewed artificial colouring,
preservatives and additives and use
just the minimum of fats and oils.
Fashion has now caught up with
them. Unspiced dishes are available,
prepared in special pans to preserve
their more gentle flavours, while
spiced dishes are subtle with well-
balanced flavours. The food is very
good value, with the familiar starters
of bhel poori, dosas, samosas and
bhajias giving way to more unusual
vegetable curries. Good Indian
desserts.

Access, Amex, Diners, Visa

Manna map 12

4 Erskine Road, NW3
☎ 071-722 8028

Open all week D 6.30–11
Closed Christmas Day and Boxing Day

Opened in 1968, Manna is a firmly
established, well-loved and informal
vegetarian restaurant. A recent, much
needed refurbishment has replaced
some of the large, shared tables with
smaller ones for two. Hearty portions
of robust food are accompanied by
hunks of home-made wholemeal
bread, inventive salads and washed
down by mugs of hot, spicy apple
juice.

No-smoking area • Wheelchair access

Maple Leaf ⊚ map 14

41 Maiden Lane, WC2
☎ 071-240 2843

Open Mon to Sat 11am–11pm (Sun
sandwiches only)
Closed Christmas Day and New Year's
Day

The food bar at the back of this pub
serves substantial, moderately priced
grub. Sometimes it is grub prepared
from a Canadian recipe book. The
Montreal smoked meat is no longer
served but you may be able to try an
'imported from Canada' hot-dog,
which is far superior to the British
imitation. Meatloaf, a Canadian
staple since the 1950s, is also popular,
as is beef pie cooked with Molson
beer. This is Covent Garden's
homage to the Mounties, the Yukon,
ice hockey, *et al*. Excellent lager and
raucous conviviality.

No children in evenings • Access, Amex,
Diners, Visa

Marine Ices   map 12

8 Haverstock Hill, NW3
☎ 071-485 3132

Open Mon to Sat noon–2.45, 6–10.15
Closed Sun and 3 weeks Aug

Ice-cream is the main reason
everyone goes to Marine Ices. The
Mansis have been making it since the
turn of the century and have
developed a range of exquisite
flavours which come in every
conceivable combination. The ice-
cream menu is backed up by excellent
pasta and pizzas, and dishes of
chicken, veal and calf's liver. It is all
well-made and great value for money.

Wheelchair access, also WC

Masters Super Fish   map 13

191 Waterloo Road, SE1
☎ 071-928 6924

Open Tue to Sat 11.30am–10.30
(11 Fri)
Closed Sun, Mon, 23 to 27 Dec, New
Year's Day and bank hols

A useful place to know for take-aways
as well as for a keenly priced sit-down
supper. The style is holiday villa
blended with extra polystyrene. The
fish, from Billingsgate, is fresh and
fried in groundnut oil. Supply varies,
so forget the menu and ask what is
available on the night. There should
be excellent calamari fritters,
ungreasy and succulent. The grilled
halibut steak is also recommended.
Decent house wine.

'Wheelchair access' indicates that,
according to the proprietor, entrances are
at least 33 inches wide, passages 4 feet
wide, and that there are a maximum of
two steps. If there is access to a WC, we
mention it.

Melati   map 14

21 Great Windmill Street, W1
☎ 071-437 2745
30-1 Peter Street, W1
☎ 071-437 2011

Open Mon to Sat noon–3, 6–11.30
Closed Sun, 3 days Christmas and
bank hols

Despite a face-lift and lots of new
pine woodwork, the downstairs
dining-room still feels like a café,
with closely packed tables, lots of
atmosphere and a fast turnover. Two
upstairs rooms fill up quickly as the
crowds arrive. A long menu of
Malaysian and Indonesian dishes
makes few compromises to Western
tastes, and flavours pack a hefty
punch. Best value is found with the
one-dish meals of rice and noodles,
huge bowls of laksa soup, potent
curries of chicken, mutton and fish,
plus vegetarian specialities such as
gado-gado (cold, raw vegetables
topped with dollops of peanut sauce).
Sweets verge on the bizarre: green
pancakes floating in coconut milk;
puréed jackfruit with crushed ice,
served in a tall glass with a straw.
Tiger beer is the essential
accompaniment.

Wheelchair access, also WC • Access,
Visa

Men's Bar Hamine   map 14

84 Brewer Street, W1
☎ 071-439 0785/287 1318

Open Mon to Sat noon–3, 6–10.30
Closed Sun, 3 days Christmas and
bank hols

There is nothing untoward
happening, unless it's the time-
honoured oriental habit of noisily
slurping noodle soup – 'men' means
noodle in Japanese. As well as the

three different kinds of noodle soup there are grilled dumplings and Japanese curry rice. Small menu, filling portions, low prices (pay at the bar before being seated) and cheerful, friendly service.

Le Mercury   map 13

140 Upper Street, N1
☎ 071-354 4088

*Open Mon to Sat noon–3, 7–midnight,
Sun noon–11*

One of Peter Ilic's lively group of informal restaurants. See entry for Lantern.

*No-smoking area • Wheelchair access •
Access, Visa*

Meson Don Felipe   map 13

53 The Cut, SE1
☎ 071-928 3237

*Open Mon to Sat noon–3 (exc Sat),
5.30–11
Closed Sun*

Handy for the Old Vic, Young Vic and the South Bank complex, this is one of the more atmospheric Spanish tapas bars. It is popular and lively, with a hard-working, friendly Spanish staff. The tapas list is standard – patatas bravas, tortillas, meatballs, prawns in garlic, stuffed peppers – all perfectly acceptable. The comprehensive Iberian wine list is keenly priced.

*Wheelchair access, also WC • Access,
Visa*

All letters to this guide are acknowledged.

Microkalamaras   map 12

76–8 Inverness Mews, W2
☎ 071-727 9122

*Open Mon to Sat D 7–11
Closed Sun, Christmas and bank hols*

A simpler, homespun version of the adjacent (macro) Kalamaras. Bring your own wine (not beer) and relax in a casual, intimate atmosphere. Intimate may verge on cramped but the reasonable prices preclude grumbling. The food is Greek as opposed to Greek-Cypriot. Adept staff patiently explain items on a menu which varies according to what was available at the market that morning. Try melitzands scordalia (aubergines cooked with garlic) or arnaki-spanaji (baby lamb with spinach and onions). Precise cooking and generous portions.

*Unlicensed, but bring your own: no
corkage • Access, Amex, Diners, Visa*

Mildred's   map 14

58 Greek Street, W1
☎ 071-494 1634

*Open Mon to Sat noon–10
Closed Sun*

A minimalist modern café whose walls sport regularly changing painting or photographic exhibitions. The assured, inventive, mainly vegetarian cooking draws on world-wide inspiration: hot-and-sour vegetable soup, penne with mushrooms and peppers, Waldorf salad, vegetable Stroganoff, Ukrainian poppy-seed cake. Organic produce is used if available.

No smoking • Wheelchair access

Mr Kong   map 14

21 Lisle Street, WC2
☎ 071-437 7341

Open all week noon–1.45am
Closed 4 days Christmas

A fairly smart Cantonese one-up,
one-down in a decidedly seedy street.
It is best to eat downstairs where
there is marginally more comfort.
The wun-tun soup contains
dumplings of superior quality; the
deep-fried crab claws are,
unfortunately, smothered by inferior
batter. Braised venison in ginger wine
sauce is a treat and the squid is above
standard. There is little sparkle in the
service and the air-conditioning can
be fierce.

Access, Amex, Diners, Visa

Mongolian Barbecue   map 12

187 South Ealing Road, W5
☎ 081-569 7171

Open all week noon–2.30 (exc Sat),
6.30–11.30

The owners describe this informal,
fun place as a 'participation
restaurant', with the emphasis on
'Mongolian'-style stir-fries cooked on
a large, round iron hot-plate. Select
your choice of meat, poultry or fish,
plus raw vegetables from a chill
cabinet; add sauces, herbs and spices;
collect your ceramic bowl and
chopsticks and wait for the chef to
prepare your own unique creation.
You can also go back for refills – all
for a set price of £7.95 (children
£4.95). To start there is Mongolian
chicken broth or cashew-nut pâté; to
finish look for 'Total Eclipse' – a
kind of alcoholic ice-cream soda
sucked through a straw. Chinese or
Russian beers, saké and wine to drink.
There are also branches at 65

Richmond Road, Twickenham (081-
744 2782) and 162 The Broadway,
Wimbledon, SW19 (081-545 0021).

Wheelchair access • Access, Amex, Visa

Moti Mahal   map 13

3 Glendower Place, SW7
☎ 071-584 8428

Open Mon to Fri noon–3, 6–11.15, Sat
and Sun noon–11.15

An above-average tandoori restaurant
made special by extremely pleasant
service, with plain décor dominated
by plants. Prawn puri, samosas and
thali (two onion bhajias) to start;
chicken jalfrezi (chargrilled), kari
gosht (lamb with onions) and
vegetable curry (cauliflower and
potato) to follow. Good dhal. Decent
prices in an indecently priced
neighbourhood.

No children under 5 • Access, Amex,
Visa

Museum Street Café ★   map 13

47 Museum Street, WC1
☎ 071-405 3211

Open Mon to Fri 12.30–2.30, 7.30–9
Closed Sat, Sun, last 2 weeks Aug,
Christmas and Easter

It looks like a converted old
bookshop, but it is actually a café to
beat all cafés. Flair and imagination
are apparent in the use of prime
ingredients, and lunch is a bargain.
The place is packed, so it is best to
book, and even then you may have to
share a table. A fish chowder, chunky
with salmon, white fish, potato,
cabbage and bacon, or penne with
beef, tomato and pancetta sauce

could be followed by chargrilled chicken with pesto, a burger or salmon and tuna skewer with sun-dried tomato mayonnaise. Bread is excellent, and tarte Tatin and the chocolate cake are both superb. The cheeses are from Neal's Yard Dairy. Good coffee and a range of herbal teas. Evenings are more expensive.

Unlicensed, but bring your own: no corkage • No-smoking area at lunchtime • Wheelchair access

Mustoe Bistro　　　map 13

73 Regent's Park Road, NW1
☎ 071-586 0901

Open all week D 6.30–11.30, Sun L 1–3

'Rather cheap' is the owner's understatement for the excellent-value, good-quality food served in her Primrose Hill bistro. Inside, it feels like someone's house, with a cosy atmosphere, wooden floors and half-pine walls. Dark and neat sums it up. The menu is classic bistro home-cooking, with dishes such as beef casserole topped with pungent horseradish, pork with tomato and chilli, and succulent breast of chicken with fennel and Pernod. Good soups and salads to start, sorbets and mousses to finish. House wine by the glass.

Unlicensed, but bring your own: corkage £1.50

All details are as accurate as possible at the time of going to press, but chefs and owners often change, and it is wise to check by telephone before making a special journey.

National Gallery　　　map 14

Trafalgar Square, WC2
☎ 071-839 3321

Open all week 10am–5
Closed Christmas Day and New Year's Day

A spacious, well-maintained basement restaurant, designed to complement the gallery, offering an array of food with daily specials chalked up on a blackboard. Soup, vegetarian pasta, rabbit pie, cod in batter, quiches, roulades and pâtés are backed up by hunks of bread, cheeses, creamy desserts and a selection of herbal teas.

No-smoking area • Wheelchair access, also WC

Navigator　　　map 12

Polish Air Force Club, 14 Collingham Gardens, SW5
☎ 071-370 1229

Open Tue to Sun noon–3, 6–11
Closed Christmas Day, Boxing Day and New Year's Day

A windowless basement where the quality of the Polish food overcomes any drabness in the décor. For the price it is remarkable: generous portions, first-rate ingredients and sound cooking. That the majority of the clientele are Polish adds to the obvious authenticity of the place. Intensely flavoured bortsch, a light apple blini, pierogi of potato and cheese, excellent potato latke, outstanding zrazy, goulash and duck with apple are all served with simple courtesy. Make room for pancakes with cheese and sultanas or poppy-seed and honey cake. Drink Polish lager, East European wines or vodka.

Neal's Yard Bakery Co-operative   map 14

6 Neal's Yard, WC2
☎ 071-836 5199

Open Mon to Sat 10.30am–6.30
Closed Sun

With prices for a main dish of the day at no more than £2.20, it is no wonder that things can get hectic, rather as they did when this was a fruit and vegetable market. Self-service vegetarian wholefood includes vegetable pasties, pizza, quiche, stuffed pitta bread, sugar-free cakes and excellent bread. The take-away eases the strain on the tea-room.

Unlicensed • No smoking • Wheelchair access to take-away section

New Restaurant   map 13

Victoria & Albert Museum,
Cromwell Road, SW7
☎ 071-581 2159

Open all week 10am–5

To avoid an unplanned tour, enter via the Henry Cole Wing. The restaurant is all light and space – high ceilings, pale brick, bright pine and well-segregated smokers – the food plain and copious with an honest worthiness to some dishes rather than cooking talent. But sound ingredients can produce good cauliflower and broccoli soup, ratatouille, salads and cakes.

No-smoking area • Wheelchair access, also WC • Access, Amex, Visa

New Serpentine   map 13

Hyde Park, W2
☎ 071-402 1142

Open summer all week 8am–10.30pm,
winter 10.30am–4.30pm
Closed Christmas Day

The New Serpentine occupies a splendid position in Hyde Park on the edge of the Serpentine. Under the aegis of Prue Leith, simple freshly prepared modern food is prettily presented. Skip miserly portioned starters for mains of chargrilled Scotch salmon, sausage and mash and finish with steamed sponge pudding. Open for morning coffee, afternoon tea, and for dinner in summer.

Wheelchair access, also WC • Access, Amex, Visa

New Shu Shan   map 14

36 Cranbourn Street, WC2
☎ 071-836 7501

Open all week noon–11.30

If you want a change from Chinatown, then head for this delightful family-run restaurant on its borders – New Shu Shan is a world apart. The cooking covers Szechuan and Cantonese dishes, the former picked out on the menu in red. Ingredients are first-class, and the flavours fresh. Staff take time to explain and recommend. Booking is advisable at popular times.

Access, Amex, Diners, Visa

New World   map 14

1 Gerrard Place, W1
☎ 071-434 2508

Open all week 11am–11.45pm

For many, this is the place to go in
Chinatown for dim-sum (11am–
6pm), with the depth and range of
flavours on offer complemented by
generally cheaper prices. Noodle
soup with barbecued pork is
consistently good as are char siu
buns. For the adventurous, tangy
chickens' feet are worth trying.
Occasionally indifferent service can
irritate.

Wheelchair access, also WC • Access,
Amex, Diners, Visa

Ninjin   map 13

244 Great Portland Street, W1
071-388 4657

Open Mon to Sat noon–2, 6–10 (exc
Sat D)
Closed Sun

A basement Japanese restaurant
serving inexpensive lunches, the price
depending on the main course
chosen. A tonkatsu lunch starts with
an appetiser, miso soup, then the
tonkatsu of pork cutlet with rice and
pickles and half an orange for dessert.
There are sashimi and sushi lunches
for raw-fish addicts as well as the
wafu steak lunch – a beef steak with
teriyaki sauce.

No children under 10 • Access, Amex,
Diners, Visa

Nontas   map 13

16 Camden High Street, NW1
☎ 071-387 4579

Open Mon to Sat 8.30am–11.30pm
Closed Sun, Christmas Day, Easter and
bank hols

Nontas is still cosy, but more
comfortable since expansion into the
building next door. Most dishes taste
fresh, and the kalamaria are usually
above-average. Psari (fish kebab) is
consistently excellent. The 'Nontas
special' is smoked sausage and pork,
marinated in red wine and served
with pourgouri (described as 'ground
wheat'). No Greek coffee, but there is
a choice between Turkish and
French.

Garden • Wheelchair access • Access,
Amex, Diners, Visa

Odette's   map 13

130 Regent's Park Road, NW1
☎ 071-586 5486

Open Mon to Sat 12.30–2.30,
7.15–10.30
Closed Sun, 1 week Christmas and 2
weeks Aug

A small cellar wine bar, an offspring
of the imaginative parent restaurant.
It is a decent spot for light snacks.
Salmon trout with potato salad,
vegetable and cheese pie and sardines
with tomato coulis are standard
offerings complemented by an all-
encompassing wine list.

Access, Amex, Diners, Visa

Ognisko Polskie   map 13

55 Exhibition Road, SW7
☎ 071-589 4635

Open all week 12.30–3, 6.30–11

A grand, if faded, ground-floor
restaurant and bar in the premises of
the Polish Hearth Club. The cooking
is gutsy, East European, strong on
flavour and the portions are
generous. Beetroot soup with a meat
roll, blinis, zrazy, bigos and pierogi
all feature, as do game, boiled beef
and knuckle of pork. Pancakes stuffed
with sweet cheese to finish.

Garden • Access, Amex, Diners, Visa

Oliver's   map 12

10 Russell Gardens, W14
☎ 071-603 7645

Open all week noon–11.30
Closed Christmas Day and Boxing Day

The beat of the latest sounds throbs
relentlessly, incongruous against the
bare brick, scrubbed floor and plain
tables of a neighbourhood bistro
serving simple, old-fashioned food.
You can enjoy some keenly priced
and satisfying dishes: steak and
kidney pudding, duck with orange
sauce, lasagne.

Unlicensed, but bring your own: corkage
£1.50 • Wheelchair access • Access,
Diners, Visa

Ooblies   map 12

78 Chester Road, N19
☎ 071-263 3899

Open Mon to Sat D 6.30–11.30
Closed Sun and Christmas Day

Handy for visitors to Highgate
cemetery, Ooblies offers crêpes

tempting enough to raise the dead.
Only prime ingredients are used –
free-range eggs and chicken, organic
vegetables and beef – and to good
effect. Of the many exotic
combinations, simpler fillings such as
ratatouille or beef bourguignonne
work best. The pancake theme
extends to desserts – better than the
ice-creams. Friendly service.

Unlicensed, but bring your own: no
corkage • Wheelchair access, also WC

Osteria Antica Bologna   map 12

23 Northcote Road, SW11
☎ 071-978 4771

Open Mon to Sat 11am–11pm, Sun
12.30–4pm
Closed Christmas Day, Boxing Day and
New Year's Day

Aurelio Spagnuolo was born in Sicily
and raised in Bologna, so his cooking
strongly reflects both regions. The
long and absorbing menu
(accompanied by a thoughtful Italian
wine list) tends, in execution, to be
varied in quality: there is an excellent
bread, cabbage and bean soup,
properly made grainy soft polenta,
but pasta dishes can be disappointing.

Wheelchair access • Access, Visa

Papadams   map 13

125 Great Titchfield Street, W1
☎ 071-323 2875/2879

Open Mon to Sat noon–3 (exc Sat),
6–11.30
Closed Sun

The particular strength of this Indian
restaurant is the good-value lunch
and dinner buffet for £6.50. A

satisfying three-course meal can be had by starting with nan, tikka and onion bhajia and some of the chef-made chutneys, then pilau rice with spinach and potato curry and lamb pasanda. Finish with Indian rice pudding or gulab juman.

No-smoking area • Wheelchair access • Access, Amex, Diners, Visa

---

Patisserie Bliss ★   map 13
428 St John Street, EC1
☎ 071-837 3720

Open Mon to Fri 8.30am–6, Sat 9am–6, Sun 10am–6
Closed Christmas Eve to New Year's Day and bank hols

The baking in this tiny, simple café with minimal décor and crowded tables is of a very high standard. The credit goes to Robert Didier, formerly pastry chef at the famous Maison Blanc bakery in Oxford. Unbleached, additive-free flour and organic produce, where possible, go into the eight or so varieties of bread, sausage rolls, quiches and sandwiches, and also into the delectable cakes: pain au chocolat, superb almond croissant, chocolate layer cake and apple slice. Counter sales are as brisk as the café. Excellent espresso.

Unlicensed, but bring your own: no corkage • No smoking

Patisserie Valerie   map 14
44 Old Compton Street, W1
☎ 071-437 3466

Open Mon to Sat 8am–8pm, Sun 10am–5.30

There is obviously a market for more patisseries of this quality in Soho, for Patisserie Valerie is always full. In the

morning there are buttery croissants, cinnamon toast, brioche and pain au chocolat. All day there are salads, toasted sandwiches, quiche and the sheer delight of the cakes, perhaps cream-filled mille-feuilles or eclairs, accompanied by good espresso coffee.

Unlicensed • No-smoking area • Wheelchair access

Le Petit Prince   map 12
5 Holmes Road, NW5
☎ 071-267 0752

Open Tue to Fri L 12.30–2.30, all week D 7–11.30
Closed bank hols

A simple, informal restaurant where couscous dominates the menu. The vegetable broth is now cooked without mutton for the benefit of vegetarians but then a choice of meat – lamb cutlets and kebabs, meatballs, chicken or merguez sausages – is added and served with a hot chilli sauce. Portions are daunting but the chocolate mousse is worth sampling, as is the peppermint tea.

Wheelchair access

Pigeon   map 12
606 Fulham Road, SW6
☎ 071-736 4618

Open Mon to Sat noon–3, 7–1am, Sun noon–11

One of Peter Ilic's lively group of informal restaurants. See entry for Lantern.

Access, Visa

The factual details under each eating-place are based on information supplied by the restaurateur.

Pizza Express   maps 12/13/14

29 Wardour Street, W1
☎ 071-734 0355
30 Coptic Street, WC1
☎ 071-636 3232
363 Fulham Road, SW10
☎ 071-352 5300
137 Notting Hill Gate, W11
☎ 071-229 6000
10 Dean Street, W1
☎ 071-437 9595
15 Gloucester Road, SW7
☎ 071-584 9078
84 High Street, SW19
☎ 081-946 6027
14 High Parade, High Road, SW16
☎ 081-677 3646
26 Porchester Road, The
Colonnades, W2
☎ 071-229 7784
11 Knightsbridge, SW1
☎ 071-235 5273
305 Upper Richmond Road West,
SW14
☎ 081-878 6833
154 Victoria Street, SW1
☎ 071-828 1477
35 Earls Court Road, W8
☎ 071-937 0761
252 Chiswick High Road, W4
☎ 081-747 0193
227 Finchley Road, NW3
☎ 071-794 5100
456 High Road, Wembley,
Middlesex
☎ 081-902 4918
2 College Road, Harrow,
Middlesex
☎ 081-427 9195
335 Upper Street, N1
☎ 071-226 9542
230 Lavender Hill, SW11
☎ 071-223 5677
64 Tranquil Vale, SE3
☎ 081-318 2595
94 Golders Green Road, NW11
☎ 081-455 9556
144 Upper Richmond Road, SW15
☎ 081-789 1948

895 Fulham Road, SW6
☎ 071-731 3117
23 Bond Street, W5
☎ 081-567 7690
820 High Road, N12
☎ 081-445 7714
70 Westow Hill, SE19
☎ 081-670 1786
46 Battersea Bridge Road, SW11
☎ 071-924 2774
The Chapter House, Montague
Close, SE1
☎ 071-378 6446

Open all week 11.30am–midnight

Using first-rate ingredients combined
with a great formula for putting it all
together makes the Express chain the
pick of the pizza bunch. Bases are
thin, crisp and light, toppings, from a
straight margherita to a spicy
American hot, are generous and
fresh. The restaurants themselves are
styled on clean, functional lines.
Service is fast and efficient.

*No-smoking area • Access, Amex,
Diners, Visa*

Pizza Piazza   map 12

St John's Parish Hall, 374 North
End Road, SW6
☎ 071-386 7225

Open all week 11am–11.30pm

Pizza Piazza is one of the best of the
large pizza chains in the country.
Expertly made dough bases, plain or
wholemeal, are topped with some
striking combinations – spinach,
cottage cheese and garlic; pepperoni
and hot sweet peppers. A fresh, clean
spacious look is common to all
branches. Cheerful, willing service.

Access, Visa

Pizza Place   map 13

5 Lanark Place, W9
☎ 071-289 4353

Open all week 11.30am–11pm
Closed Christmas Day and Boxing Day

A decent pizza place, very much on the tiny side with just 24 places. Deep-pan pizzas come with standard toppings: pepperoni with pepper and onion, mozzarella and cheddar cheese, seafood and vegetarian. Lasagne and a salad bar selection are alternative choices. Hot rum baked banana is a must. Good espresso.

Wheelchair access • Access, Visa

Pizzeria Castello   map 13

20 Walworth Road, SE1
☎ 071-703 2556

Open Mon to Fri noon–11, Sat 5–11
Closed Sun

The pilgrimage to Newington Butts roundabout, the unlikely location for London's most written-about pizzeria, is not for the faint-hearted. The emphasis is strongly on pizza (pasta is not praised): thick-based, doughy, crisp on the outside, chewy inside, and liberally topped. Service can be erratic.

Wheelchair access, also WC • Access, Visa

A restaurant manager can't insist on people not smoking, unless it's specifically a no-smoking restaurant or a no-smoking area. If it is, smokers could be asked to leave if they don't stop. If in doubt, check beforehand what the smoking arrangements are.

Pizzeria Condotti   map 13

4 Mill Street, W1
☎ 071-499 1308

Open Mon to Sat 11.30am–midnight
Closed Sun

The flagship of the Pizza Express chain. Stylish, the walls crowded by a covetable modern art collection, yet priced affordably, the Condotti is almost impossible to get into for lunch, and there is always a queue. Evenings are more relaxed. Pizzas come with light, crisp bases and generous toppings, backed up by salads and some good desserts. Fast, efficient service.

Wheelchair access • Access, Amex, Diners, Visa

Place Below ★   map 13

St Mary-le-Bow Church, Cheapside, EC2
☎ 071-329 0789

Open Mon to Fri 7.30am–3, Thur D 6–9.30
Closed Sat, Sun, Christmas and New Year

To be precise, Place Below is in the church crypt. It is a stylish, vegetarian self-service restaurant open for breakfast and lunch and attracts a new species of City bohemian. Medieval stone – with ancient mortar still visible – glows under subdued lighting; square tables are decorated with candles, and chairs have flat cushions. Freshly squeezed orange juice, croissants and good scrambled eggs feature at breakfast time. For lunch, you can have roast pepper and aubergine salad, and carrot and coriander gâteau, served with roast potatoes, red cabbage and mange-tout, or walnut and mushroom rice-cakes with redcurrant sauce and fennel. The exquisite quiches are memorable, and imaginative, fresh salads are served with well-prepared dressings. Also open Thursday evenings.

Unlicensed, but bring your own (D only): corkage £1 • No smoking

The Place to Eat   map 13

John Lewis, Oxford Street, W1
☎ **071-629 7711**

Open Mon to Sat 9.30am–5, exc Thur 9.45am–7.30
Closed Sun, Christmas Day and Boxing Day

Department store self-service food (a problem if laden with packages though), that is fresh-looking, of good quality and outstanding value. Different counter sections specialise in different dishes; the best are crêpes, sweet or savoury, seafood, perhaps a grilled-to-order plaice or the cold table offering sole and salmon terrine, roast beef, salmon and salads. Breakfast is served all day.

No smoking • Wheelchair access, also WC

Poons   map 14

4 Leicester Street, WC2
☎ **071-437 1528**

Open all week noon–11.30

Brave the basic décor, for good-standard Cantonese cooking at reasonable prices is what you are here for. Wind-dried meats are a speciality, and the duck in particular is richly flavoured. The various hot-pots of spiced beef, fried chicken, braised eel or spare rib are filling

meals in themselves, so are the one-plate rice dishes.

Poons   map 14

27 Lisle Street, WC2
☎ **071-437 4549**

Open all week noon–11.30
Closed Christmas

Poons offers the simplest of surroundings, yet the Cantonese cooking here is among the most authentic available in Chinatown. It is famous for wind-dried dishes, especially the duck, which make marvellous and inexpensive one-plate meals with rice. The barbecued pork is outstanding. Oil-soaked squid indicates a far more adventurous menu than is normal and is well worth trying.

Unlicensed, but bring your own: no corkage

Poons at Whiteleys   map 12

Queensway, W2
☎ **071-792 2884**

Open all week noon–midnight
Closed Christmas Day and Boxing Day

A fresh branch of Poons with décor in keeping with the setting – the second-floor food boulevard of Britain's classiest new-age shopping emporium. Good, varied Cantonese dishes spiced with some Szechuan choices produce excellent meals, based on quality raw materials cooked without fuss. Set menus are great value: lunch £7, dinner £12 and dim-sum (noon-5pm) £5.65.

Access, Amex, Diners, Visa

Portobello Gold map 12

95 Portobello Road, W11
☎ 071-727 7898

Open all week 12.30–2, 7.30–10.45 (exc Sun D)

A mini Caribbean resort hiding behind the saloon bar of an agreeable Portobello Road pub. Greenhouse-effect palms and hanging plants combine with fan-backed wicker chairs to create an oddly convincing tropical trompe-l'oeil. Casual service has also been in character. A big menu is supplemented by blackboard specials. The signature dish here is 'Jamaican bacon', a starter comprising bananas and back bacon topped with grilled cheese and chilli: excellent and satisfying. Baby squid come fresh and accompanied by chilli and peanut dips. An eclectic selection of main courses allows Asian, Italian, stir-fry and ordinary bistro favourites. The bar boasts nine tequilas, American beer, Chilean wine and Gosset champagne.

Access, Amex, Visa

Le Poulbot map 13

45 Cheapside, EC2
☎ 071-236 4379

*Open Mon to Fri 7.30am–10am (brasserie only), noon–3
Closed Sat and Sun*

The pub/brasserie fronting the Roux Brothers' pricier basement restaurant is looking dated these days but it still offers good value. Breakfast is served from 7.30am, while lunch ranges from a simple snack, perhaps a steak sandwich or an omelette, to a more sustaining daily special like cassoulet with a green salad.

Quality Chop House ★ map 13

94 Farringdon Road, EC1
☎ 071-837 5093

*Open Mon to Fri 7am–9.30am, noon–3, Mon to Sat D 6.30–11.30, Sun noon–3
Closed Christmas and New Year*

A place that buys well and cooks simply with a café style of shared tables and a complete lack of pretension. Breakfast is served Monday to Friday from 7am to 9.30am, otherwise there is a modern café menu of scrambled eggs with smoked salmon, eggs Benedict, salads from Caesar or spinach and Roquefort to fresh anchovies or endive and bacon. The menu also includes the British café staples of egg and chips, sausage (veal or Toulouse) and mash or salmon fish-cakes. Grills – lamb chops, calf's liver and bacon, Dover sole – come emblazoned with grill marks and represent the best quality produce. Chips come with everything. Great atmosphere, good food, excellent value.

Ragam ★ map 13

57 Cleveland Street, W1
☎ 071-636 9098

Open all week noon–3, 6–11.30

A small, clean-looking restaurant with a plain, neutral décor, closely packed tables and charming, courteous service. It specialises in the cooking of Kerala in South West India. Much of the menu is familiar, with dosai, uthappam (the pizza-style pancake), dhal dishes, puri, chapati and filled paratha covering the vegetarian side, while various meat birianis, vindaloos, kormas and dopiazas are equally well-known. More unusual dishes are avial, a

Kerala dish of vegetables cooked with coconut, yoghurt, curry leaves and spices, and sambar, a curry cooked with lentils, vegetables and tamarind juice.

Wheelchair access, also WC • Access, Amex, Diners, Visa

Raj Bhel Poori House   map 13

19 Camden High Street, NW1
☎ **071-388 6663**

Open all week noon-11.30
Closed Christmas Day

Locals appreciate the virtues of this good-value Indian vegetarian restaurant on Camden High Street. The décor is deliberately 'anti-flock', with pine tables and wallpaper created from skeletal pressed leaves. Aloo chana chaat is an excellent starter, otherwise the menu covers familiar ground with bhel pooris, dosas, fresh-tasting samosas, raita and pistachio kulfi. Vegetable curries may be disappointingly greasy.

Unlicensed, but bring your own: no corkage • Wheelchair access • Access, Amex, Diners, Visa

Rajput   map 12

144 Goldhawk Road, W12
☎ **081-740 9036**

Open all week noon-2.30, 6-midnight
Closed Christmas Day and Boxing Day

Raja and Aziz Meah have been running this reliable neighbourhood curry house since 1984 and it continues to offer quality and good value. There are few surprises on the menu, which covers the usual tandooris and North Indian curries such as chicken dhansak, king prawn

masala and navratan pilau with mixed vegetables. One unexpected dish is podina gosht – mutton cooked with mint. Good-value thalis for vegetarians and meat-eaters. On Sundays there is a help-yourself buffet (£6.50). Drink Dortmunder lager.

Access, Amex, Visa

Rani   map 12

3 Long Lane, N3
☎ **081-349 4386/2636**

Open Wed to Fri and Sun L 12.30–2.30, all week D 6–10.30
Closed Christmas Eve, Christmas Day and New Year's Day

Rani is spacious, immensely popular and designed along clean, bright lines. It is without doubt one of the best Indian vegetarian restaurants in London, with a large following of Indian customers. Close attention to detail means that even chutneys are made on the premises, and the fresh flavours of these encapsulate the fine balance and style of the kitchen. Set menus are a good introduction, offering a simple two-course meal for £11.80 or a blow-out for £17. There are various thalis, and curries of imaginative combination – aubergine and Lima bean, for example – with the special daily curries well worth exploring. On Monday night only there is just a fixed-price menu for £10.

No-smoking area • Wheelchair access • Access, Visa

See the back of the guide for a breakdown of London eating-places into type of cuisine.

Rasa Sayang
maps 12/14

10 Frith Street, W1
☎ 071-734 8720

*Open Mon to Thur noon–2.45,
6–11.30, Fri and Sat noon–2am,
Sun noon–10
Closed Christmas Day and Boxing Day*

3 Leicester Place, WC2
☎ 071-437 4556

*Open as above
Closed as above*

**5–6 Kingswell Shopping Centre,
Heath Street, NW3**
☎ 071-435 6508

*Open all week D 6–11
Closed Christmas Day*

**146 The Broadway, West Ealing,
W13**
☎ 081-840 4450

*Open Tue to Sun noon–2 (exc Sat),
6–11
Closed Mon, Christmas Day and Boxing
Day*

38 Queensway, W2
☎ 071-229 8417

*Open Mon to Fri noon–2.45, 6–10.45,
Sat noon–10.45, Sun noon–10.15
Closed Christmas Day and Boxing Day*

Each link in this pioneering chain of
Malaysian/Singaporean restaurants
manages to retain its own
individuality despite the similarities
in menu and prices. The latest
branch, in Queensway, is a lesson in
bright, neon-lit modernity with a
cosmopolitan clientele to match,
while Leicester Place has a shabby,
used look in keeping with its
environment, attracts many South
East Asians and is considered to offer
the best food. Standards tend to be
high in all branches, with an
emphasis on freshness in both
ingredients and flavour. Portions are
generous, which means that noodle
dishes such as mee goreng can be
happily shared by two, with a sambal
and kari of meat or fish, a portion of
rice, and some vegetables providing a
filling meal for under £10 a head.

Access, Amex, Diners, Visa

Raw Deal
map 13

65 York Street, W1
☎ 071-262 4841

*Open Mon to Sat 10am–10pm (10.30
Sat)
Closed Sun and bank hols*

Raw Deal as a name does not do this
place, occupying a corner site close to
Baker Street, justice. It is a small,
slightly cramped vegetarian self-
service café/take-away offering sound
food. This includes some 10 different
salads, a couple of hot dishes – one
always vegan – pastas, an array of
cakes and an unusual brown bread-
and-butter pudding.

*Unlicensed, but bring your own: no
corkage • No-smoking area*

Redfords
map 12

126 Golders Green Road, NW11
☎ 081-455 2789
**313 Hale Lane, Edgware,
Middlesex**
☎ 081-958 2229

*Open all week noon–2.30 (3 Sun),
5–10.30*

A couple of up-market fish and chip
restaurants that use fresh fish only.
Frying is in groundnut oil and the
batter a light egg and matzo meal
mixture. There is a Jewish flavour to
the menu with bortsch, smetana,

chopped herring and gefilte fish backing up the plaice, haddock and lemon sole. Grilled fish is available and jacket potatoes are an alternative to chips.

No-smoking area • Wheelchair access, also WC • Access, Visa

Reuben's   map 13

20A Baker Street, W1
☎ 071-486 7079 (snack bar)/
935 5945 (restaurant)

Snack bar open Mon to Fri 11am–10 (early closing Fri), restaurant open Mon to Fri noon–3, 5–10 (exc Fri D), Sun noon–10
Closed Sat and Jewish hols

On the ground floor is a busy, kosher take-away bar serving big portions of salt-beef, gefilte fish and latkes to a high-turnover passing trade. Upstairs is a dining-room with panelled walls, done out in shades of blue. Good, filling soups such as lentil or onion can be followed by grilled haddock, chicken schnitzels or barbecued spare ribs; there is always a choice for vegetarians. Choose carefully to keep the bill under £15 a head. The restaurant is licensed; the take-away bar is not.

Wheelchair access to snack bar • Access, Visa

Ritz Hotel, Palm Court   map 13

Piccadilly, W1
☎ 071-493 8181

Open all week 8am–11.30am, tea served 3 and 4.30

Afternoon tea at the Palm Court is firmly on the tourist circuit – book well in advance for both sittings (3pm and 4.30pm). In such opulent surroundings, and at £12 a head, the mêlée that can occur at the steps before being allocated a table is unfortunate, but the polished service, the finger sandwiches, scones and delicate little cakes smooth any ruffled nerves. Continental breakfast (8am–11.30am) makes a more decorous alternative.

Wheelchair access, also WC • Access, Amex, Diners, Visa

Rive Gauche   map 13

Warren Street, NW1
☎ 071-387 8232

Open Mon to Fri 9am–3.30
Closed Sat and Sun, 3 days Christmas, New Year's Day and bank hols

A highly popular French-style café with an excellent take-away. The tables are closely packed and the café fills up early. Light snacks are the main attraction at lunchtime, and most people opt for crêpes, salads, steak and frites, omelettes and stuffed brioches – all served with a salad garnish. Otherwise, there might be excellent watercress soup and more substantial French provincial dishes such as cassoulet and choucroute. Pastries and breads are out of the top drawer. Full English breakfasts start the day, otherwise have a croissant. Wine by the glass, superb coffee.

No cigars/pipes • Wheelchair access

When you book a restaurant table, you're making a contract with the restaurant and you must be given a table, within reasonable time of your arrival. If not, the restaurant is in breach of contract and you can claim a reasonable sum to cover any expenses you had as a result, e.g. travelling expenses.

Rouxl Brittania Café   map 13

Triton Court, 14 Finsbury Square, EC2
☎ 071-256 6997/8

Open Mon to Fri 7.30am–9.30am, noon–3
Closed Sat and Sun

A bustling, inexpensive part of the Roux Brothers' empire, offering the option of choosing just one dish. Good-quality, brasserie-style dishes include a crisp chef's salad of salmon and excellent mayonnaise (£4.95), and Toulouse sausages with onion confit (£7.90). However, tables are very close together, smokers are not segregated and wines are expensive.

Sabras   map 12

263 Willesden High Road, NW10
☎ 081-459 0340

Open Tue to Fri 12.30–3, 6–10, Sat and Sun 1–10
Closed Mon and Christmas Day

Imaginative Indian vegetarian food, all made on the premises, draws the crowds to this restaurant; to accommodate them tables are far too close together. To start there are hot Gujerati savouries, samosas and onion bhajias being the most familiar, or puris and dosas, to be followed by spicy vegetable curries and home-made Indian sweets. Finish the meal with gingery Gujerati tea.

No-smoking area • Wheelchair access • Access, Visa

Out to Eat has been compiled in the same way as *The Good Food Guide* and is based on reports from consumers and backed up by anonymous inspections.

Saheli Brasserie   map 13

35 Great Queen Street, WC2
☎ 071-405 2238

Open Mon to Sat noon–3, 5.30–11.30
Closed Sun and Christmas Day

The most recent branch of the Fleet Tandoori mini-chain (see entry) dresses up for its central London address and plays to its audience with set lunches for office workers and early evening menus for theatre-goers. Otherwise, the menu is recognisably North Indian with tandooris and curries ranging from tandoori lamb chops and Kashmiri lamb tikka to murgh makhani, rogan josh and niramish mixed vegetables. Karahi kebab khyberi, sag paneer and mushroom bhajia are recommended. Drink Kingfisher beer or a jazzy cocktail.

No-smoking area • Wheelchair access, also WC • Access, Amex, Diners, Visa

---

St John's Café   map 13

120 St John's Wood High Street, NW8
☎ 071-586 1162/722 8366

Open Mon to Sat 9.30am–10.45pm
Closed Sun, Christmas Day, Boxing Day and New Year's Day

An ornate public house converted into a large café/bistro. Close-packed tables and obvious popularity make for a lively, noisy atmosphere. Light meals offered from noon to 4pm include first-class pasta, smoked salmon bagels, omelettes and salads. Coffee and pastries are served pre- and post-lunch and there is a more elaborate dinner menu. Desserts can be dull.

No young children • Wheelchair access • Access, Amex, Visa

Sala Thai   map 12

182 South Ealing Road, W5
☎ **081-560 7407**

Open Mon to Sat noon–2.30 (exc Sat),
6–11.30
Closed Sun

In what was once the sitting-room of an Ealing family there is now an authentic, unpretentious Thai restaurant. The setting is still comparatively domestic, with a small upright piano nestling against one wall. Tables are wonky and chairs don't match but the menu lists 111 dishes. 'We offer more choice than any Thai restaurant in the UK,' says chef P. Klinchui. Most dishes can be altered to customers' specific requirements. To start, try hoih josh: fried bean curd skin stuffed with crab meat and minced pork served with plum sauce. Then, move on to kang kheaw wharn, which is green curry in coconut milk: hot and spicy but with clean flavours coming through loud and clear.

Access, Diners, Visa

Samsun   map 12

34 Stoke Newington Road, N16
☎ **071-249 0400**

Open all week 11am–10

A very basic, spotless Turkish café dominated by the take-away side of the business. There are a few, neat tables to eat at. Totally Turkish – some of the staff speak no English – the food is genuine, plain and simple. Slow-cooked stews like lamb and mushroom are a speciality but there are also good kebabs and mixed grills. Excellent bread and unusual home-made desserts.

No children • Wheelchair access

Savoy Hotel, Thames Foyer   map 14

Strand, WC2
☎ **071-836 4343**

Open all week 3–5pm

Relax into the elegant and sophisticated world of discreet surroundings and impeccable service created by the Savoy. Afternoon tea (£11) is a memorable way of sampling the style. It is a leisurely experience of finger sandwiches, scones with clotted cream and delicate cakes. No bookings are taken so there may be a wait.

Unlicensed • No-smoking area • Wheelchair access, also WC • Access, Amex, Diners, Visa

Seafresh Fish Restaurant   map 13

80–1 Wilton Road, SW1
☎ **071-828 0747**

Open Mon to Sat noon–10.45
Closed Sun and 10 days Christmas

Long-established and of some renown, this is a superior chippie. No-nonsense décor helps focus attention on a very wide choice of fish and seafood. The owners claim to have their own agents at ports in Scotland to ensure quality and variety. The latter is demonstrated by red mullet, halibut cutlets and squid. The Dover sole is a triumph. Massive portions and relaxed service.

Wheelchair access • Access, Visa

'Wheelchair access' indicates that, according to the proprietor, entrances are at least 33 inches wide, passages 4 feet wide, and that there are a maximum of two steps. If there is access to a WC, we mention it.

Seashell   map 13

49–51 Lisson Grove, NW1
☎ 071-723 8703

*Open Mon to Fri noon–2.15,
5.15–10.30, Sat noon–10.30
Closed Sun, Christmas Day, Boxing Day
and New Year's Day*

There are still queues for tables
despite complaints that Seashell is
not quite the fish and chip shop it
used to be. Certain things do niggle:
over-sweet tomato ketchup, acidic
tartare sauce and only one lager,
Stella Artois, is available. But the fish
is still fresh, the batter light, the
whole decidedly non-greasy. A no-
frills family restaurant with half-
portions for children.

*No-smoking area • Wheelchair access •
Access, Amex, Diners, Visa*

Seasons   map 13

22 Harcourt Street, W1
☎ 071-402 5925

*Open noon–10pm
Closed Christmas*

Slightly off the beaten track in a quiet
street near Paddington is this good-
value, prettily decorated vegetarian
restaurant. Lunch is self-service;
dinner is slightly more formal, with
waitresses and a reasonably varied
menu. Stuffed vine leaves are a good
starter, before mushroom crêpes, stir-
fried tofu or a special such as
tagliatelle with leeks in cream sauce.
Salads are copious, puddings are
home-made. Basic wines and soft
drinks.

*No-smoking area • Wheelchair access •
Amex, Diners, Visa*

7 Pond Street   map 12

7 Pond Street, NW3
☎ 071-435 1541

Open all week 11–10.30

The restaurant menu and a lighter
blackboard choice are available in the
upstairs wine bar, but it is best to go
there for the light, quick snacks to
which the blackboard is geared:
croque-monsieur, soup, sandwiches.
For serious dining you might as well
eat in comfort downstairs, where
lamb with flageolets and a mushroom
tart have pleased on a variable menu.

Access, Visa

Shampers   map 13

4 Kingly Street, W1
☎ 071-437 1692

*Open Mon to Sat 11–3, 5–10.45 (exc
Sat D)
Closed Sun*

A lively wine bar with Don
Hewitson's absorbing, all-
encompassing wine list and a varied
menu to match. Sweetbread and veal
terrine, apricot-glazed ham,
tagliatelle, raised ham and cheese pie
and grilled Toulouse sausages all
appear on the regularly changing
menu. See entry for Cork and Bottle.

*Wheelchair access • Access, Amex,
Diners, Visa*

Simpsons of Cornhill   map 13

38 Cornhill, EC3
☎ 071-626 9985

*Open Mon to Fri 11.30am–3
Closed Sat and Sun*

Tucked away down an alleyway off
Cornhill, Simpsons is one of the last

surviving bastions of the old England still imagined to exist by tourists. It is a city institution unashamedly Dickensian in décor and with a menu where oxtail soup, bubble and squeak, pease pudding, steak and kidney pie and, of course, roast beef reign supreme. Generous quantities are served in a good-hearted manner and the atmosphere is lively. Best to book for lunch.

Access, Amex, Diners, Visa

Singapore   map 12

95 Chiswick High Road, W4
☎ 081-995 7991

Open all week noon–2.30, 6–11.30

A handy neighbourhood restaurant serving a mix of Chinese and Singaporean dishes. Wun-tun soup and kway-pietie (little pastry baskets filled with prawns, chicken and vegetables) are good starters. Otherwise, the menu takes in satays, fried meehoon noodles, beef in coconut sauce and fried sambal squid. Prawn crackers with red-hot dips arrive before the meal. Drink lager or house wine by the glass.

Wheelchair access • Access, Amex, Visa

Singapore Garden Restaurant   map 12

83–83A Fairfax Road, NW6
☎ 071-328 5314

Open all week noon–2.45, 6–10.45
(11.15 Fri and Sat)
Closed 4 days Christmas

Chinese and Malaysian/Singaporean dishes share the bill in this spacious, plant-filled restaurant with dark green curtains at the windows. Barbecued spare ribs, vegetarian

spring rolls and mixed satay are typical starters. Main dishes range from prawns with spring onion and ginger to Szechuan crispy beef. Among the list of Singaporean specialities look for ho jien (oyster omelette), kway tiow rice stick noodles, and prawn sambal. Drink wine by the glass, saké or Tiger beer.

Wheelchair access • Access, Amex, Diners, Visa

Smokey Joe's Diner   map 12

131 Wandsworth High Street, SW18
☎ 081-871 1785

Open Mon to Sat noon–3, 6–11, Sun 3.30–11

A diner, not a restaurant, right on the High Street – not a place to park or dawdle. The sunshine yellow paintwork, with emerald green counterpoint, is as cheerful as the calypso, jazz or blues tapes (bring your own) coming from the deck by the counter. Joe is a good cook, so is his Brazilian wife, as well as a friendly patron. Jerk chicken or pork, good plantains, roties (Jamaican patties) and giant ribs are always available; special dishes vary each day, sometimes it is lobster, oxtail on Thursdays, or red-bean stew on Tuesdays. Basic food prepared with honesty and sometimes great style.

Unlicensed, but bring your own: no corkage • Wheelchair access

You will find report forms (write a letter if you prefer) at the back of the book so that you can tell us about your experiences of going *Out to Eat*. We'll put the information to good use when we're compiling the next edition.

Sonny's

map 12

94 Church Road, SW13
☎ 081-748 0393

Open all week 12.30–2.30 (exc Sat),
7.30–11

A very modern neighbourhood bistro, spacious, bare-floored and noisy. The charcoal grill features prominently on an inventive, eclectic menu – salmon with herb aïoli, breast of pigeon with pancetta and cabbage. The menu changes regularly, reflecting seasonal produce and there is always an excellent-value set menu at £10.50. Sticky toffee pudding remains the favourite dessert.

Wheelchair access • Access, Visa

Spago

map 13

6 Glendower Place, SW7
☎ 071-225 2407

Open all week noon–2.45, 6–11.45
Closed Christmas Day and Boxing Day

Spago's strength lies in honest Italian food of generally sound quality at keen prices. Unusually varied pasta dishes, pizzas and robust Italian sausage and beans are supplemented by enterprising daily specials. Cramped (possibly smoky) shared tables when busy.

Wheelchair access

Spices

map 12

28–30 Stoke Newington Church
Street, N16
☎ 071-254 0528

Open all week noon–2.30, 6–midnight

A spacious Indian vegetarian restaurant, with tasteful décor, worth noting for reasonable prices. The standard of cooking is par for the course for this type of restaurant, with some surprises: kulfi served with a pot of evaporated milk was outstanding, and papri chaat and potato puri were faultless.

Wheelchair access, also WC • Access,
Amex, Diners, Visa

Sporting Page

map 12

6 Camera Place, SW10
☎ 071-376 3694

Open all week noon–2.30, 7–10
Closed 2 days Christmas

A light, airy pub with pale wood, paddle fans and sporting motifs, in a quiet backstreet of Chelsea's World's End. A blackboard menu offers (for London) a decent selection: spinach-enriched Popeye salad, salmon fish-cakes, smoked salmon and scrambled eggs, garlic mushrooms and bacon, good bread. A cheerful place with attentive service.

Wheelchair access

Sree Krishna

map 12

192–4 Tooting High Street, SW17
☎ 081-672 4250/6903

Open all week noon–3, 6–11 (midnight
Fri and Sat)

South Indian vegetarian dishes get top billing in this highly popular restaurant lined with religious pictures. Masala dosai, idli and dahi vadai sit alongside specialities from the Kerala coast, including uthappam (a pizza-style spicy pancake made from rice and lentil flour) and avial – mixed vegetables cooked with coconut milk and curry leaves. Also look for the green banana bhajia,

vegetable malabar and lemon rice.
The menu has a full complement of
meat, chicken and seafood curries for
those with carnivorous tendencies.
Drink lassi or Kingfisher beer.

*Wheelchair access, also WC • Access,
Amex, Diners, Visa*

Sri Siam   map 14

14 Old Compton Street, W1
☎ 071-434 3544

*Open all week noon–3 (exc Sun),
6–11.15*

Very good, well-presented Thai food
is the order of the day here. A green
curry of chicken and coconut milk or
steamed trout with chilli and
tamarind and palm-sugar sauces show
prime ingredients complemented by
fresh herbs and judicious spicing.
The sense of fine food and elegant
surroundings can, however, be
dispelled by cramped tables and
smoking neighbours.

Access, Amex, Diners, Visa

Star Café   map 13

22 Great Chapel Street, W1
☎ 071-437 8778

*Open Mon to Fri 7am–10pm
Closed Sat, Sun and bank hols*

Probably the best value for hearty
home cooking on the fringes of Soho.
The corner building with its stripped
pine and check tablecloths does a
frantic trade with breakfast fry-ups
and English roast lunches, as well as
serving fish and pasta dishes. The
place now stays open for dinner. As a
starter, vegetable dip is a serious
understatement: it is actually a huge
plate of deep-fried vegetables with a
bowl of Stilton and herb dip. Pies

dominate the main courses, and there
are more pies among the sweets.
Drink wine, tea or coffee.

No-smoking area • Access, Diners, Visa

Supan   map 12

4 Fernhead Road, W9
☎ 081-969 9387

*Open Mon to Sat noon–3 (exc Sat),
6.30–11.30
Closed Sun and 1 week Aug*

Flock wallpaper, stark lighting and a
small front room full of close tables
give no hint of the subtly spiced,
delicate cooking this marvellous little
Thai restaurant produces, seemingly
without effort. The menu, short and
to the point, offers a gentle balance of
flavours and textures, skilful spicing
that allows main ingredients to retain
individual identity: deep-fried fish-
cakes, gently curried with a proper
sweet-and-sour sauce, a fresh-tasting
chicken soup with coconut milk and
spices, thick red curries with creamed
coconut, delicious stir-fried dishes
with fresh herbs. Service is solicitous
and charming.

Access, Visa

Surinder's   map 12

109 Westbourne Park Road, W2
☎ 071-229 8968

*Open Fri L noon–2.30, Tue to Sat D
7–11
Closed Sun and Mon*

This is the neighbourhood restaurant
many would wish for. A pleasant
room, a short, daily-changing menu,
charming service and chef-patron
cooking that displays old-fashioned,
honest principles. The accent is
French – crêpes de poisson, foie de

veau, selle d'agneau – handled with simplicity and enjoyable for that. The price is good – £12.95 for three courses.

Wheelchair access • Access, Amex, Visa

Suruchi   map 13

18 Theberton Street, N1
☎ 071-359 8033

Open all week noon–2.30, 6–11

The bhel poori and aloo papri might not be as crisp and crunchy and coriander-laden as in former years but Suruchi still remains one of North London's better Indian vegetarian options. The short menu of pooris, dosas and thalis offers great value for money. It is essential to book evenings. There is also a branch at 82 Mildmay Park, Newington Green, N1 which is licensed and meat-biased.

Unlicensed, but bring your own: no corkage • Amex, Visa

Surya   map 12

59–61 Fortune Green Road, NW6
☎ 071-435 7486

Open all week D 6–10.30, Sun L noon–2.30
Closed Christmas Day, Boxing Day and New Year's Day

Tastefully decorated by Indian restaurant standards, Surya has a relaxed atmosphere and particularly helpful staff. This is a fully fledged Indian vegetarian restaurant. To start, aloo papri chaat (flat, crispy puri topped with chickpeas, potatoes and yoghurt sauce with fresh mint chutney) is both spicy and refreshing. Masala dosai (a pancake made from rice flour and accompanied by a

tamarind sambar and coconut chutney) is good. For each day of the week there is a special dish: stuffed green chillies on Wednesday, spicy lentil fritters on Thursday, and so on. Choose between Omar Khayam Indian sparkling wine and Becks beer.

No-smoking area • No children under 6 after 7pm • Wheelchair access • Access, Amex, Diners, Visa

Taj Oriental   map 12

102 Queensway, W2
☎ 071-727 0830

Open all week 11am–1am (2am Fri and Sat)

A Pakistani restaurant offering excellent-quality snacks and take-aways, even more valuable for being in an area of London which is increasingly expensive. This is the place to try a shawarma. What looks like a doner kebab at a distance is, on closer inspection, succulent, fresh, lean lamb – spiced with lemon, vinegar and black and white pepper and roasted on a spit. Carved shawarma meat is deposited into freshly tandoor baked bread. Next comes tahini (paste made from crushed sesame seeds), chilli sauce and some shredded red and white cabbage and onions. For afters, there are wondrously syrupy baklavas.

Wheelchair access • Access, Amex, Diners, Visa

You will find report forms (write a letter if you prefer) at the back of the book so that you can tell us about your experiences of going *Out to Eat*. We'll put the information to good use when we're compiling the next edition.

Tea Time ★   map 12

21 The Pavement, Clapham Common, SW4
☎ 071-622 4944

Open Tue to Sun 10am–6
Closed Mon and 2 weeks Christmas

At face value just a simple tea-room fronted by a small cake shop, but a closer look reveals as much care in the purchasing of ingredients as in the cooking; eggs are free-range, preserves free of additives, and all cakes home-baked by local ladies. Open for breakfast, which could be smoked salmon and scrambled eggs or pancakes, or just a buttery croissant, lunch, when some simple savouries are served, and for various set afternoon teas. Cakes are available all day, from cream-filled eclairs to a fine-textured carrot cake, as are an imaginative choice of sandwiches either plain or toasted. Good cafetière coffee or properly served leaf tea to drink.

Unlicensed • No-smoking area • Wheelchair access

Terrace Café Restaurant, Museum of London   map 13

150 London Wall, EC2
☎ 071-726 4446

Open Tue to Sat 10am–5
Closed Sun and Mon

A concrete-scape, not particularly edifying in terms of view or atmosphere, but the simple self-service café provides plainly cooked, inexpensive food. The quality can vary and tiredness can be seen in dishes kept on offer for too long. But good, crisp salads, chicken and mushroom rice, apple crumble and huge scones for tea are worth trying.

No-smoking area • Garden • Wheelchair access, also WC

Thai Garden   map 12

249 Globe Road, E2
☎ 081-981 5748

Open Mon to Sat noon–3 (exc Sat), 6–11
Closed Sun

The black-and-white minimalist décor was inherited from the previous incarnation, a wine bar. It is now a Thai restaurant specialising in vegetarian food (with some fish dishes). There is hot-and-sour seafood soup, aubergine in a green curry with coconut cream, water-chestnuts with dry chilli and beans, and fried noodles, Thai-style, with seafood.

Access, Diners, Visa

Le Tire Bouchon   map 13

6 Upper James Street, W1
☎ 071-437 5348

Open Mon to Fri 8am–9.30pm
Closed Sat and Sun, Christmas and New Year

A dark, appealing French café full of atmosphere and Gallic charm. Start the day with breakfast of croissant, scrambled eggs and good coffee. From 11am there is a choice of hot dishes, a fish soup, lamb with flageolets, poached salmon and a set lunch menu for £11.85 plus service. Try the superb chocolate mousse for dessert or some excellent French cheeses.

Access, Amex, Visa

Titchfield Café   map 13

71 Great Titchfield Street, W1
☎ 071-636 1780

Open Mon to Sat 8am–10pm (3pm Sat)
Closed Sun

A fast-moving café on a busy corner, specialising in Continental dishes with some Greek overtones. Bottles of beer and house white stand ready and waiting on ice by the door. The menu deals in pasta, omelettes, veal milanese and fish, backed up by such dishes as spinach and cheese roll in filo pastry. There are tables outside for fair-weather eating. Excellent value and a useful venue away from the Oxford Street crush.

Topkapi   map 13

25 Marylebone High Street, W1
☎ 071-486 1872

Open all week noon–11.30

A long-standing fixture among London's crop of Turkish restaurants, although recent reports suggest that the generally excellent quality of the food could be dropping. Meze, both hot and cold, are still the best bets, along with starters such as stuffed aubergines, triangular cheese-filled pastries and peppers in olive oil. Close-packed tables.

Wheelchair access, also WC • Access, Amex, Diners, Visa

See the front of the guide for a list of each eating-place given a star for being one of the best found by the Editor during research for this book.

Topsy Tasty   map 12

5 Station Parade, Burlington Lane, Chiswick, W4
☎ 081-995 3407

Open Mon to Sat D 6.30–11
Closed Sun and bank hols

Much more of a restaurant than its sister the Bedlington Café (see entry). It is not the place for an intimate tête-à-tête, yet the noise of laughter and chatter is part of the fun. The menu is predominantly Thai, although some Japanese, Vietnamese and Laotian choices are featured. Dishes descend to the table in garlic- or basil-scented clouds, and even those destined for other tables look and smell wonderful as they float past. Tender squid salad, Siamese fried pork, stir-fried king prawns with baby sweetcorn and bananas in coconut milk to finish were the constituents of one memorable meal. It is essential to book.

Unlicensed, but bring your own: corkage 70p per person

Tui   map 13

19 Exhibition Road, SW7
☎ 071-584 8359

Open all week noon–2.30, 6.30–10.45
Closed Christmas Day and bank hols

Watch out for those bill bumpers the cover charge and the $12\frac{1}{2}$ per cent service charge at this stylish, courteous Thai restaurant. The food is authentic, carefully judged, judiciously spiced and worth exploring. Seafood items and the tom yum soup are pricey.

Access, Amex, Visa

Tuk Tuk

map 13

330 Upper Street, N1
☎ 071-226 0837

Open Mon to Sat noon–3 (exc Sat),
6–11.30
Closed Sun

An informal Thai café specialising in
one-course meals. Starters are
missable. Fried beef with chilli and
black-bean sauce is more delicate
than its Chinese counterpart, while
chicken curry with rice, and fried
noodles with mixed seafood, show a
characteristic Thai sweetness. Ideal
for a quick snack (especially if visiting
the Screen on the Green cinema
opposite).

Wheelchair access • Access, Amex, Visa

Underground Café

map 13

214 Camden High Street, NW1
☎ 071-482 0010

Open Mon to Sat noon–3, 6–11 (11.30
Fri and Sat), Sun noon–10.30

Owned by and umbilically linked to
Camden Brasserie (see entry), but
with a separate kitchen. As the name
suggests, this is a basement café and it
specialises in keenly priced modern
Italian cooking. Bruschetta, grilled
vegetables with pesto on polenta,
zampone on lentils and pine nuts are
featured, as well as freshly made
pasta.

No cigars/pipes • Visa

Upper Street Fish Shop

map 13

324 Upper Street, N1
☎ 071-359 1401

Open Tue to Sat L noon–2, Mon to Fri
D 5.30–10
Closed Sun

Smart for a fish and chip shop, with
bistro-style décor and the ebullient
Olga Conway pacing around to make
sure you enjoy everything. Fish is
either traditionally battered and
served with chips, or else poached or
steamed and served with salad. In
season, there are Irish rock oysters
and the fish soup wins praise both for
price and quality. Stodgy puddings.

Unlicensed, but bring your own: no
corkage • Wheelchair access

Valentino's

map 12

147 Green Lane, N13
☎ 081-889 1847

Open Mon to Sat 12.30–2.30, 6–11.30
Closed Sun and Christmas Day

Paintings, wine bottles and dim red
lights set the scene in this warm and
cosy trattoria. Twenty-eight starters
head the vast menu. Pasta dishes offer
the best value, but there are other
options such as chicken in wine and
cream sauce and peppered steak with
brandy. Portions are generous, prices
are affordable, and service comes
with a friendly smile. Average wines.

Access, Visa

Villa Estense   map 12

642 King's Road, SW6
☎ 071-731 4247

Open all week 12.30–2.30 (3 Sat and Sun), 7–11.30 (midnight Fri and Sat) Closed Christmas Day, Boxing Day and bank hols

Friendly, prompt service marks out this cheerful, spacious Italian restaurant. Home-made pastas and pizzas feature strongly on the printed menu and the daily blackboard also offers some reasonably priced dishes such as bacon and lentil soup, gnocchi with dolcelatte among the pricier fish and meat. Fine touches include freshly grated Parmesan and strong espresso.

Wheelchair access • Access, Amex, Visa

Village Bistro   map 12

38 Highgate High Street, N6
☎ 081-340 5165

Open all week noon–2.30, 6–11.30 (11 Sun)

A pretty bistro with a widely influenced décor: close-packed carved and painted tables and benches, chintz curtains, Dutch plates, tiles and Russian dolls. The menu plays it safe with filled avocado pears, marinated king prawns with rice and garlic butter, and aubergines stuffed with vegetables, all greatly enhanced by sound ingredients and careful cooking.

Access, Amex, Diners, Visa

All letters to this guide are acknowledged.

Vrisaki   map 12

73 Myddleton Road, N22
☎ 081-889 8760

Open Tue to Sat noon–2.30, 6–11.30 Closed Sun, Mon, 2 weeks Christmas and bank hols

Easily mistaken for a down-at-heel kebab house, this is a professionally operated Greek-Cypriot restaurant of some size and with a considerable local (Greek-Cypriot) following. The highlight here is meze: a minimum of two diners could have 11 cold starters, including freshly made tahini, tsatsiki, octopus and mussels, boiled beetroot and tuna, followed by grilled halloumi (Cyprus cheese) served on a slice of grilled lountza (smoked pork loin), and then have the giant king prawns, the lamb or sheftalia – minced meat with onions, parsley and spices wrapped in sheep's gut and cooked on charcoal. Service is generally efficient and well-timed.

Wheelchair access

Waterside Café   map 13

Barbican Centre, EC1
☎ 071-638 4141 ext 664

Open all week noon–4, 5–8 Closed 3 days Christmas

A large seating area spills out on to a fair-weather terrace, where the view is dominated by the grey concrete of the Barbican. The food, by Justin de Blank, is more cheerful: attractively laid-out salads, fresh-looking haddock and broccoli roulade, mushroom and ricotta strudel and various flans. Casseroles can look fatigued, vegetables are sometimes badly cooked, but an appealing display of cakes makes up for this.

No-smoking area • Wheelchair access, also WC • Access, Visa

White Horse on Parsons Green   map 12

1–3 Parsons Green, SW6
☎ **071-736 2115**

Open Mon to Fri noon–2.30, 5–10, Sat 11–2.30, 7–10, Sun 12.30–2.30, 7–9.30
Closed Christmas Day and Boxing Day

It is good to see such a well-patronised London pub, known for its extensive wine list, attempting to provide decent food. A cold-display cabinet offers ham off the bone, English cheeses, quiches and Spanish tortilla, while dishes of the day could be seafood pasta or a bolognese.

No-smoking area • No children in evening • Wheelchair access, also WC

Wilkins   map 13

61 Marsham Street, SW1
☎ **071-222 4038**

Open Mon to Fri 11.30am–3
Closed Sat and Sun

This family-run vegetarian restaurant has been going strong for 15 years, serving wholesome food to eat in or take away. Soups, home-made pizzas, wholemeal quiches and dishes such as mixed vegetables and beans in cheese sauce are backed up by an impressive array of sweets and cakes. Organic vegetables are used when available; eggs are always free-range.

Unlicensed • No smoking • Wheelchair access

Wine Gallery   map 12

49 Hollywood Road, SW10
☎ **071-352 7572**

Open all week noon–3, 6–11.45

A regularly changing exhibition of paintings, a good wine list and some competent, straightforward cooking using sound ingredients draws a smart crowd. Lunch is less busy than dinner. Bangers and mash, fish-cakes with good chips and the occasional cordon bleu standby of coronation chicken compete with pasta, beef Stroganoff and ratatouille. Cheerful, efficient service.

Wheelchair access • Access, Visa

Woodlands   maps 12/13/14

37 Panton Street, SW1
☎ **071-930 8255**
402 High Road, Wembley, Middlesex
☎ **081-902 9869**
77 Marylebone Lane, W1
☎ **071-486 3862**

Open all week noon–2.30, 6–10.30
Closed Christmas Day and Boxing Day

The London branches of a large chain in India specialising in South Indian vegetarian cooking. This style of food is often associated with informality and simple surroundings, but this is not the case at the Woodlands with their smart décor and courteous service. The set meals (thalis) are a good and inexpensive introduction, and dosas, uthappam and idli are well-executed.

Access, Amex, Diners, Visa

Out to Eat is totally independent, accepts no free hospitality and makes no charge for inclusion.

Yerakina   map 12

10 Kentish Town Road, NW1
☎ 071-485 5743

Open all week noon–3 (exc Sat),
6–midnight

A dependable local taverna
specialising in larger-than-average
portions, mostly fresh ingredients
and a sense of humour. Yerakina's
business card promises 'an
unforgettable evening'; on belly
dancing nights the boast is more than
justified. The schmaltzy music may
be piped but the kalamaria are non-
greasy and the fish is likely to be
moist. Try the galatoboureko, an
extra-sweet, gooey dessert.

Access, Amex, Diners, Visa

Zamoyski   map 12

85 Fleet Road, NW3
☎ 071-794 4792

Open Mon to Sat noon–2 (exc Sat),
5.30–11
Closed Sun

A mid-European wine bar-cum-
restaurant with a folksy atmosphere,
especially on Friday and Saturday
evenings, when there is live music.
Mainly Polish dishes dominate the
menu with cold stuffed carp, apple
blini (topped, for a price, with
caviare), pierogi, bigos and zrazy
being particular strengths. Desserts
are missable.

No-smoking area • Wheelchair access,
also WC • Access, Visa

Yoshino   map 14

Japan Centre, 66–8 Brewer
Street, W1
☎ 071-287 6622

Open Mon to Sat 11am–7 (6 Sat)
Closed Sun, Christmas Day, Boxing Day
and 1 to 4 Jan

Well worth seeking out is the
esoteric Yoshino in the basement of
the Japan Centre. The cramped
counter-seating necessitates queuing
after first ordering and paying. The
seven-piece nigiri shushi is a
beautifully presented bargain at
£3.80, while pork or chicken cutlets
with rice and/or curry are filling
alternatives. Cheerful fast food,
popular with the Japanese.

Unlicensed • No smoking

Zazou Brasserie   map 13

74 Charlotte Street, W1
☎ 071-637 1285

Open Mon to Fri noon–3, 7–10.30
Closed Sat and Sun, Christmas to New
Year (exc New Year's Eve) and bank hols

A clean and thorough remodelling
gives a pleasantly retro-brasserie air
to this ground-floor off-shoot of the
dearer fish restaurant in the
basement. Pop music gives aural
wallpaper. Vegetable or onion soups;
a stir-fry of squid, prawns and
mussels; spaghetti with mussels; or
'cannelloni' of aubergine are done in
a robust bistro fashion and are none
the worse for that. Service is amiable
and French.

Access, Amex, Diners, Visa

We consume some 13 million sandwiches a week in Britain and sandwich bars are sprouting up everywhere. As fast food they can be far healthier and much more satisfying than a hamburger or fish and chips and have the added attraction of an ability to evolve to reflect current food styles. But to be successful they need imaginative, inventive handling.

Birley's

12–13 Royal Exchange, EC3 • 17 Cullum Street, EC3 • 5 Bow Lane, EC4 • Unit 2, Cannon Street Station, EC4 • 14 Moorfields, EC2

Style is the keynote at Birley's, with chandeliers an incongruous touch for a take-away sandwich bar. Open for breakfast with egg and bacon muffin, sausage in Italian bread (ciabatta), then on to prawn avocado, curried turkey, good ham with cheddar or Jarlsberg; pricey but generously filled.

Brick Lane Beigel Bake

159 Brick Lane, E1

Piles of bagels (or 'beigels') filled with smoked salmon, egg or cheese sell fast, and you can see the bagels being made in the background. There is also a little stand-up counter space to eat in.

Diana's Dining Room

30 St Cross Street, EC1

Generously filled sandwiches at this smart deli/café are imaginative: pastrami on rye, avocado and bacon, prawn or egg mayonnaise, hot salt beef, kebabs in pitta bread. (See main entry.)

John Charlick Foods

142 Gray's Inn Road, WC2

A take-away sandwich bar of some renown. Plump, well-filled sandwiches are made to order from a list that takes in egg mayonnaise, Brie with sugar roast ham and mozzarella, tomato and black olive paste on ciabatta. Black rye and whole-meal bread are also available, plus superb

quiches, ham, roast beef, pâté and mayonnaise, all home made.

Onion

1 Sicilian Avenue, WC1

A tiny but charming take-away sandwich bar (there is a small eating area) with a good-looking display of ingredients – excellent rare roast beef, freshly sliced ham, good cheeses, eight different kinds of bread, including rye to make a meaty pastrami, and bagels for filling cream cheese and smoked salmon.

Phood

29–31 Fouberts Place, W1

Primarily a deli which cooks and bakes on the premises and provides a varied selection of sandwiches, savouries and salads to take away. Good ham, roast beef, egg mayonnaise, smoked salmon, various cheese combinations such as mozzarella, tomato and black olive paste, are all made to order in generous portions.

Ridley Hot Bagel Bakery

13–15 Ridley Road, Dalston, E8

This has become something of an institution. The 24-hour bakery is full of people at any time of the day or night, attracted by the excellent filled bagels of smoked salmon and cream cheese, egg, cheese or chopped liver. There is a deli counter, and there are hot tea and cakes. Branches at 116 Upper Clapton Road, E5; 14 Ashfield Parade, Southgate, N14; 105 High Road, East Finchley, N2.

LONDON'S CHINATOWN

London's Chinatown takes in an area of Soho bounded by Wardour Street, Shaftesbury Avenue, Charing Cross Road and Lisle Street. It provides a colourful insight into the Chinese food culture – not just restaurants, but also herbalists, greengrocers, supermarkets, fishmongers, butchers and bakeries. It is, of course, a major tourist attraction, but this constant source of one-off custom has led to some bad habits and low standards. We are all getting tired of being snapped at by Chinatown waiters, especially when some of the food served defies eating and you know that none of the Chinese staff would touch it. Yet there is outstanding, authentic food – Poons in Lisle Street is a consistent good example – and in our edited map of Chinatown we have done our best to highlight the better restaurants and cafés. But it is advisable in any case to approach Chinatown with a spirit of adventure, eschewing the obvious concessions to western tastes by choosing specialities such as eel or belly pork and the general items that these mainly Cantonese restaurants do so well, namely dim-sum (usually served all day up to 5–6pm) and one-plate rice and noodle dishes. We have also listed the best of the Chinese food shops and herbalists.

1 **Joy King Lau**
3 Leicester Street
(restaurant)

2 **Poons**
4 Leicester Street
(restaurant – see entry)

3 **Jade Garden**
15 Wardour Street
(restaurant – see entry)

4 **Chuen Cheng Ku**
17 Wardour Street
(restaurant – see entry)

5 **Kai Kee**
19 Wardour Street
(café)

6 **Super Cake Shop**
21 Wardour Street
(bakery)

7 **Yungs**
23 Wardour Street
(restaurant)

8 **Welcome Supermarket**
32 Wardour Street
(shop)

9 **Dragon's Nest**
58–60 Shaftesbury Avenue
(restaurant)

10 **Mayflower**
68 Shaftesbury Avenue
(restaurant)

11 **Kowloon**
21 Gerrard Street
(restaurant and bakery)

12 **Tai Ko Lok**
18 Gerrard Street
(restaurant)

13 **Lee Ho Fook**
15 Gerrard Street
(restaurant)

14 **Lee Ho Fook**
4 Macclesfield Street
(restaurant)

15 **Golden Gate Bakery**
13 Macclesfield Street
(bakery)

16 **Far East**
13 Gerrard Street
(bakery)

17 **Dragon Inn**
12 Gerrard Street
(restaurant)

18 **Super**
11 Gerrard Street
(bakery)

19 Fook Lam Moon
10 Gerrard Street
(restaurant)

20 Loon Moon Supermarket
9 Gerrard Street
(shop)

21 Dragon Gate
7 Gerrard Street
(restaurant)

22 China China
3 Gerrard Street
(restaurant – see entry)

23 New World
1 Gerrard Street
(restaurant – see entry)

24 Friendly Inn
47 Gerrard Street
(restaurant)

25 Loon Fung Supermarket
31 Gerrard Street
(shop)

26 Phoenix
39 Gerrard Street
(take-away)

27 London Chinatown
27 Gerrard Street
(restaurant)

28 Golden Gate Supermarket
14 Lisle Street
(shop)

29 Fung Shing
15 Lisle Street
(restaurant)

30 See Woo Supermarket
18 Lisle Street
(shop)

31 Mr Kong
22 Lisle Street
(restaurant – see entry)

32 Po Sau Tang
24 Lisle Street
(herbalist)

33 Chan Mai May
25 Lisle Street
(restaurant)

34 Man Lee Hong
26 Lisle Street
(restaurant)

35 Poons
27 Lisle Street
(restaurant – see entry)

36 Good World
8 Little Newport Street
(restaurant)

37 Shing Wo Hong Greengrocer
12 Little Newport Street
(shop)

38 Sun Luen Snack Bar
14 Little Newport Street
(café)

39 Hong Ning Co
15 Little Newport Street
(medicinal herbalist)

40 Chinatown Tourist Information Centre
27 Newport Court

41 Sunki Supermarket
Newport Court
(shop)

42 Hop Hing Hong Supermarket
33 Newport Court
(shop)

43 Garden
37 Newport Court
(bakery and snack bar)

44 Man Poh
59 Charing Cross Road
(restaurant)

45 Golden Gate Supermarket
16 Newport Place
(shop)

46 Chinatown Fish and Meat Market
14 Newport Place

London's Chinatown

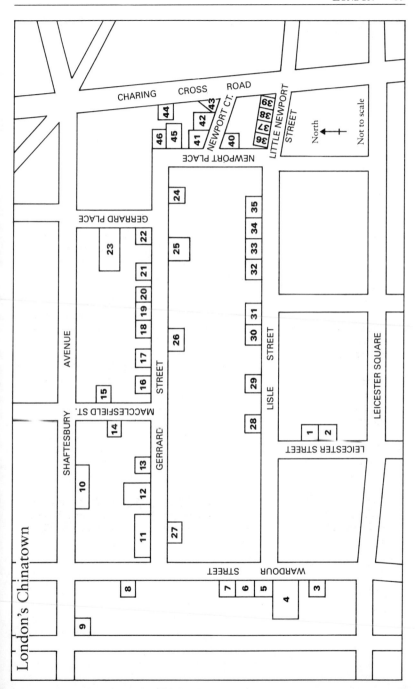

LONDON – DRUMMOND STREET

Drummond Street is a slightly shabby street running west from Euston Station. It is hardly more than 200 yards long, yet for the last 30 years it has earned a reputation as one of the most vivid centres of Indian food and culture in north London. In the 1950s, many immigrant families moved into the area to set up little shops, restaurants and other businesses. Some of these places, like the legendary Shah Restaurant, have since disappeared; others such as the Ambala Sweet Centre and Viniron Traders (originally opened by one of the Patak family) are still going strong. Alongside the grocers and restaurants are halal butchers, video shops, even an Islamic book centre. We list the best of the food shops as well as eating-places.

Since the late '70s, Drummond Street has been famed for its vegetarian restaurants. The Diwana Bhel Poori House set the tone, and still draws crowds of tourists, celebrities and enthusiasts looking for good-value Gujerati food and snacks from the Indian west coast. Others – notably Ravi Shankar and Chutneys – have followed in its wake, but the most promising new arrival in the street is Haandi. This brings together the meat-eating traditions of the tandoori, regional dishes and a small showing of vegetarian specialities.

Ravi Shankar, Chutneys and Haandi share the same ownership, and it is not unusual to see waiters bustling from one venue to another with containers of prepared food. If Drummond Street's restaurants have a weak point, it is the lack of really interesting vegetable dishes. Grocers such as the Anglo Asian Food Supermarket and Viniron have an impressive array of ingredients – mustard leaf, karela, tinda, Kashmiri beans and much more besides – yet restaurant kitchens seem content to deliver potatoes, cauliflower, spinach and little else. Exotic vegetables are used as a matter of course in other Indian centres, such as the Sparkhill district of Birmingham. It would be good to see Drummond Street restaurants taking up the challenge.

1 **Anglo-Asian Food Supermarket**
115–17 Drummond Street
(supermarket and greengrocers)

2 **Viniron Traders**
119 Drummond Street
(grocers and greengrocers)

3 **Diwana Bhel Poori**
121 Drummond Street
(restaurant – see entry)

4 **Raavi Kebab**
125 Drummond Street
(restaurant)

5 **Savera Bakery**
129 Drummond Street
(bakery)

6 **Ravi Shankar**
133–5 Drummond Street
(restaurant)

7 **Eva Tandoori**
159 Drummond Street
(restaurant)

8 **Haandi**
161 Drummond Street
(restaurant – see entry)

9 **Ali & Son**
134 Drummond
Street
(grocer and
butcher)

10 **Chutneys**
124 Drummond
Street
(restaurant – see
entry)

11 **Universal Halal**
122 Drummond
Street
(butchers and
grocers)

12 **Ambala Sweet
Centre**
110 Drummond
Street
(sweet centre and
take-away)

13 **Gupta
Confectioners**
100 Drummond
Street
(sweet centre and
take-away)

14 **Nature's Delight**
96 Drummond
Street
(juice and paan
centre)

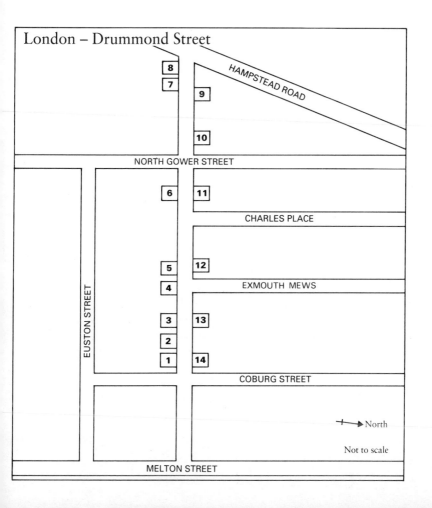

London – Drummond Street

HAMPSTEAD ROAD

NORTH GOWER STREET

CHARLES PLACE

EXMOUTH MEWS

EUSTON STREET

COBURG STREET

North

Not to scale

MELTON STREET

ENGLAND

AVON

Aust

map 2

Boars Head

Main Road
☎ PILNING (045 45) 2278

½ mile from M4 junction 21, off A403

Open Mon to Sat noon–2, 7.30–9.45
Closed Sun

A very friendly village pub, the open fires reflecting the warm welcome. A cold buffet dominates the range of bar snacks with its spread of salads and cold cuts. But there is hot food too: cauliflower cheese and bacon, seafood lasagne, Yorkshire pudding with a choice of fillings and jacket potatoes. The adjoining restaurant is more expensive.

Garden and family-room • Car-park •
Wheelchair access, also WC (ladies) •
Access, Amex, Visa

Bath

map 2

Cedars

2 Margarets Building
☎ BATH (0225) 310064

Open Mon to Sat 12.30–2.30, 7–10.30
Closed Sun, Christmas Day and Boxing
Day

The name refers to Cedars of Lebanon – the geographical basecamp for this restaurant with two little dining-rooms. Spend £10 or less by staying with the selection of meze, which can be served as starters or main courses. Puréed, grilled aubergine with tahini is best eaten as a dip with pitta bread; vine leaves are stuffed with rice, raisins and spices. Good main dishes are barbecued baby chicken with cold garlic vinaigrette and kofte mafroumi – chunks of minced lamb in a buttery tomato sauce, served with a curious mix of rice and minute bits of vermicelli. Wines by the glass.

Wheelchair access • Access, Amex,
Diners, Visa

Pasta Galore

31 Barton Street
☎ BATH (0225) 463861

Open Mon to Sat noon–2.30,
6–10.30 (11 Sat)
Closed Sun

A few doors from the Theatre Royal, this restaurant is popular for pre- and post-theatre suppers. Bright and clean inside with a log-effect gas fire in the corner and Italian colours on the ceiling. You will find more than pasta: begin with bresaola (dried salt-beef with a slice of Parmesan, olive oil and black pepper), fagioli all' arrabbiata (borlotti beans in a chilli, tomato and garlic sauce) or peperoni col tonno (baked red peppers sliced and rolled round a garlic tuna mayonnaise). Lots of tagliatelle and spaghetti combinations, and a short, reasonably priced list of Italian wines. Service, courtesy of a young staff, is friendly and helpful.

No-smoking area • Garden •
Wheelchair access • Access, Amex,
Visa

Pizza Express

1 Barton Street
☎ BATH (0225) 420119

Open all week 11.30am-midnight

Part of the popular chain which is the pick of the pizza bunch. See London entry.

No-smoking area • Access, Amex, Diners, Visa

Pump Room

Stall Street
☎ BATH (0225) 444488

Open all week 10am–5.30 (6.30 July and Aug, 4.30 Nov to Feb)
Closed Christmas Day and Boxing Day

Droves of tourists flock to see the spectacular Georgian architecture of the Pump Room, with its Corinthian columns, great chandelier and statues. A trio plays on the galleried podium and visitors relax under the immensely high ceiling. It is a perfect, civilised setting for morning coffee or afternoon tea, which includes classic Bath buns and Sally Lunns, scones with clotted cream, and toast with gentlemen's relish. At lunchtime there are also hot dishes, salads, freshly-made club sandwiches and ploughman's. Fruit flans, ice-creams and English cheeses complete the picture. Seven wines by the glass.

No-smoking area • Wheelchair access, also WC

Out to Eat is totally independent, accepts no free hospitality and makes no charge for inclusion.

Sally Lunn's House

4 North Parade Passage
☎ BATH (0225) 461634

Open all week 10am–6
Closed Christmas Day, Boxing Day and New Year's Day

The oldest house in Bath, a medieval bakehouse, was in 1680 the home of a French refugee, Sally Lunn. Here she made the eponymous brioche that became famous all over the city. Today, Sally Lunn buns are still baked on the premises and come topped with tuna, prawns or goats'-milk cheese, toasted with scrambled egg or as part of a cream tea with strawberry jam and clotted cream.

No smoking • Access, Visa

Tarts

8 Pierrepont Place
☎ BATH (0225) 330280

Open Mon to Sat noon–2.30, 6.45–10.45 (11 Fri and Sat)
Closed Sun, Christmas Day, Boxing Day and New Year's Day

The high level of praise for this intimate cellar restaurant has put us in a quandary; although the flexible, cheaper lunch menu allows light choices, it can get a bit pricey with a simple cream of nettle soup £2.90, fillet of John Dory with home-made seaweed pasta £6.80, and vegetables a naughty £1.50 extra. For the quality, however, the value is hard to beat.

No cigars/pipes in dining-room • Access, Visa

Bristol   map 2

Arnolfini

Narrow Quay, Prince Street
☎ BRISTOL (0272) 279330

Open all week noon–10
Closed 1 week Christmas and Easter Sun

The Arnolfini is a dockside
warehouse converted into a stylish
arts complex which includes an all-
day café. Free-range and organic
produce is used where possible and
used inventively. Mozzarella and
spinach pancakes, gnocchi with salsa
verde and chicken tarragon cider pie
are backed up by lighter snacks of
salads and a range of cakes and
sandwiches.

Wheelchair access, also WC

Café de Daphne

12 York Road, Montpelier
☎ BRISTOL (0272) 426799

Open all week 8am–4 (2 Sat to Mon)
Closed 1 week Christmas

Breakfast on a Jamaican brunch –
fried banana, eggs, beans and
Jamaican bread – lunch on a Middle
Eastern platter of spicy bulgar wheat
or an Italian risotto. The menu is
eclectic, the cooking inventive and
assured. Good food is more
important than the décor at this plain
café, anything from a Tuscany bean
soup, bagel with curd cheese, meat
pasty or pork in sour cream.

No-smoking area • Wheelchair access

The factual details under each eating-
place are based on information supplied
by the restaurateur.

Le Château

32 Park Street
☎ BRISTOL (0272) 268654

Open all week L noon–2.30, Mon to
Thur D 5.30–8
Closed Christmas Day and Boxing Day

Near the university and subject to
fierce competition, this is a dark but
ungloomy wine bar festooned with
William Morris-style wallpaper and
lace curtains. Recent refurbishment
has revealed gleaming, highly
polished panelling. For more light
there is a conservatory downstairs.
The simpler dishes are more
successful, and the best choice may be
a plate of rare, cold roast beef and a
glass of wine from an adequate list.
Snack on cockles, fruits de mer, fresh
sardines or tuck into whole lemon
sole, rack of lamb or Stroganoff.
Despite the bustle, service is
generally prompt.

Accompanied children over 14 only •
Wheelchair access • Access, Visa

Cherries

122 St Michael's Hill
☎ BRISTOL (0272) 293675

Open Mon to Sat D 7–10.30
Closed Sun and first half Sept

Staff and students from the nearby
university and hospitals frequent this
lively evening bistro. On busy nights
you may need to wait for a table in
the pub across the road. A varied
menu of vegetarian and vegan dishes
is chalked on a blackboard; flavours
are forthright, and garlic is used
freely. Arame seaweed with cucumber
and radish sticks, or smoked tofu and
vegetable kebabs, line up with home-
made hummus and meatless lasagne.
Nut roast comes with apple sauce;

rich spinach and cream cheese frittata is served with fresh tomato sauce. Cherry and almond pie is a good sweet. Acceptable wines and imported beers to drink.

No-smoking area • Wheelchair access, also WC • Access, Visa

Ganges

368 Gloucester Road, Horfield
☎ BRISTOL (0272) 245234/428505

Open all week noon–2.30, 6–11.30
Closed Christmas Day and Boxing Day

The menu claims that the food represents the three main regions through which the Ganges flows – but the influence is heavily northern Indian. Bhuna gosht and chicken dansak are highly recommended, while mutter panir is outstanding, enhanced by lime and fresh coriander. Spicing is consistently imaginative and sauces are individual and harmonious to each dish. Kingfisher beer is the best accompaniment.

Wheelchair access • Access, Amex, Diners, Visa

Pizza Express

31 Berkeley Square
☎ BRISTOL (0272) 260300

Open all week 11.30am–midnight

Part of the popular chain which is the pick of the pizza bunch. See London entry.

No-smoking area • Access, Amex, Diners, Visa

Pizza Piazza

8–10 Baldwin Street
☎ BRISTOL (0272) 293278

Open all week 11am–11.30pm

A branch of one of the best pizza chains in the UK. See London entry.

Access, Visa

Rocinante's

Whiteladies Road
☎ BRISTOL (0272) 734482

Open all week noon–11
Closed Christmas Day and Easter

Not far from the BBC West of England headquarters, this large, clean and uncluttered wine and tapas bar is one of the best spots in an area well supplied with restaurants. The menu, of course, goes far beyond tapas with paella (for two people), bouillabaisse and daily specials such as fried red mullet and fillet of beef. Tapas include calamares, and chickpea and spinach tortillas – denoting a Mexican enthusiasm as well as purely Spanish. Prices for the tapas are affordable; much of the food supplied is organically reared or grown and it makes a change to sit in a place that is not too cluttered by futile ornament nor too dark for diners to see the food on offer.

Car-park • Wheelchair access, also WC • Access, Visa

See the front of the guide for a list of each eating-place given a star for being one of the best found by the Editor during research for this book.

Nailsea

map 2

Courtyard

120 High Street
☎ NAILSEA **(0275) 810137**

On B3130 E of M5 junction 20

Open all week noon–2.30, 6.30–9.30
Closed New Year's Day

Tucked deep into a modern courtyard development along the high street in Nailsea are two storeys (connected only by steel stairways and balconies) of a French colony – La Cour restaurant above, the Courtyard wine bar below – benevolently ruled by André Pierre Baqué. The wine bar is significantly cheaper and, while making concessions to English taste such as bottled mayonnaise, manages fair soups and notable bargains like roast pheasant on braised cabbage for under £5.

Wheelchair access, also WC • Access, Visa

Oldbury-on-Severn

map 2

Anchor Inn

☎ THORNBURY **(0454) 413331**

Off B4061 2m NW of Thornbury

Open all week noon–2, 6.30 (6 Sat and Sun)–9.30
Closed Christmas Day evening

This riverside country pub serves imaginative and fresh food. The dining-room, entered from the bar, is pretty and floral. Once seated at the pine tables the choice may be between 'pork Normandy', poached wild salmon or charcoal-grilled sirloin steak. All will very likely be cooked with professionalism and may be accompanied by courgettes or cauliflower florets. Sweet-tooths should not leave without sampling the 'Oldbury Mud Pie'. Attentive service.

Garden • Car-park • Wheelchair access, also WC • Access, Visa

BEDFORDSHIRE

Bedford   map 5

Park 🏵

98 Kimbolton Road
☎ BEDFORD (0234) 54093

*Open Tue to Sun 12.30–2.30 (exc Sat),
7–9 (exc Sun)*
Closed Mon

A solid mock-Tudor pub with an airy
conservatory and spacious beer
garden. The big draw here is the 18-
strong English cheese selection.
Choose any three of them to
accompany your ploughman's,
preceded perhaps by home-made
soup, or eschew cheese altogether in
favour of roast beef, steak and kidney
pie or lasagne.

*Garden • Car-park • Wheelchair access
• Access, Amex, Diners, Visa*

Pizza Express

22 St Peter's Street
☎ BEDFORD (0234) 53486

Open all week 11.30am–midnight

Part of the popular chain which is the
pick of the pizza bunch. See London
entry.

*No-smoking area • Access, Amex,
Diners, Visa*

'Wheelchair access' indicates that,
according to the proprietor, entrances are
at least 33 inches wide, passages 4 feet
wide, and that there are a maximum of
two steps. If there is access to a WC, we
mention it.

Leighton Buzzard   map 4

Swan Hotel

High Street
☎ LEIGHTON BUZZARD (0525)
372148

Open Mon to Sat noon–2
Closed Sun

A Georgian coaching-inn, now a
comfortably appointed hotel, offering
good-value bar food: soup, home-
made pasta, beef and venison pie,
sandwiches and salads. In the
restaurant the Busy Body's Lunch of
one course and coffee for £5.95 could
include a choice of smoked salmon
omelette, pork cutlet or lambs'
kidneys Turbigo.

*No-smoking area • Car-park •
Wheelchair access, also WC • Access,
Amex, Diners, Visa*

Milton Ernest   map 5

The Strawberry Tree

Radwell Road
☎ OAKLEY (023 02) 3633

Open Wed to Sun 11.30am–5.30
Closed Mon, Tues and Jan

The archetypal cottage tea-room –
thatched, painted white with an
impeccably kept interior. John and
Wendy Bona do just a few things but
they do them well: light lunches of
sandwiches, fish pie and a salad of
home-baked ham; set teas, including
a boiled-egg tea; and cakes baked on
the premises – light scones served

with home-made preserves, and rich, cream-filled gâteaux.

No-smoking area • Car-park • Wheelchair access, also WC

Turvey   map 4

Ye Three Fyshes

Bridge Street
☎ TURVEY (023 064) 264

On A428 Bedford–Northampton road

Open all week noon–2, 7–9

The River Ouse runs close to this seventeenth-century village pub.

Inside, it still feels like a local watering-hole. 'Dynamic rolls', filled with steak, onions, fried egg and melted cheese, are a standard fixture of the bar menu. Otherwise, a blackboard advertises specials which may include excellent local venison steak with mushrooms, and pork with green peppercorn sauce, as well as pub stalwarts such as scampi. Reid ales and fine cider drawn from a cask behind the bar.

Garden • Car-park • Wheelchair access • Access, Visa

★ after an eating-place indicates that it is one of the best found by the Editor during research for this book (see page 14 for a list).

⊛ after an eating-place indicates that it is a pub. The opening and closing times we give only relate to when food is available – the licensing hours may be different.

⊞ after an eating-place indicates that it is within five miles of the nearest motor-way junction. We give the relevant motorway and junction in the details. Eating-places in cities and large towns, where traffic, parking and route-finding may cause delay, do not have this symbol.

BERKSHIRE

Cookham Dean map 2

Jolly Farmer

☎ MAIDENHEAD (0628) 482905

Off A404 S of M40 junction 4

*Open all week 12.30–2, 7.30–10
(exc Sun D)
Closed Christmas Day evening*

The Jolly Farmer offers some of the
best bar meals in Berkshire. It is
small, neat and tidy and the food
portions are generous. At lunch you
might choose haddock and leek
crumble or lasagne, at dinner, home-
made pâté, rainbow trout with
almonds or steak and kidney pie.
Good value for Sunday lunch.

*No children in bar • Garden • Car-park
• Wheelchair access*

Eton map 2

Eton Wine Bar

82–3 High Street
☎ ETON (0753) 855182

*Open all week noon–3.15, 6–10.45
Closed 5 days Christmas*

A friendly wine bar offering decent, if
pricey, food. The day's menu is
chalked up on a blackboard: perhaps
a trio of starters, and half a dozen
main dishes – sound tomato, haricot
and herb soup, pancake stuffed with
smoked salmon, fish and broccoli,
lamb and cumin pie with coriander.

*No cigars • Wheelchair access, also WC
• Access, Visa*

Inkpen map 2

Swan Inn

Lower Inkpen
☎ INKPEN (048 84) 326

On W side of Inkpen on Hungerford road

*Open Wed to Sun L noon–1.45, Tue to
Sat D 7–9.30
Closed Mon, 1 week Jan and 1 week
Sept*

Part of the charm of this old village
pub is its incongruity; in the evening
one sits beneath old beams, in a
traditional setting eating Singaporean
and Chinese food. Szechuan chicken
is for the adventurous, but the milder
satay, drunken prawns, beef rendang
and nasi goreng are all carefully
prepared. Standard bar food, such as
steak and kidney pie, or cottage pie, is
available at lunchtimes.

Garden • Car-park • Access, Visa

Kintbury map 2

Dundas Arms

☎ KINTBURY (0488) 58263

1m off A4 between Newbury and
Hungerford

*Open Mon to Sat 12.30–1.30,
7.30–9.30 (exc Mon D)
Closed Sun and Christmas to New Year*

With the Kennet and Avon Canal
flowing on both sides, this small
Victorian pub enjoys a waterside
setting. The bar has a restrained,
traditional feel. Lunchtime bar snacks

include sandwiches, ploughman's and soup, with boned quail filled with pâté backed up by jugged hare, steak and kidney pie and fresh pasta with pesto sauce. Bread-and-butter pudding for dessert.

Garden • Car-park • Wheelchair access, also WC • Access, Amex, Visa

Pangbourne   map 2

Copper Inn
Church Road
☎ READING (0734) 842244

N of M4 junction 12

Open all week 12.30–2 (exc Sat), 7.30–9.30

An unprepossessing mock-Tudor pub with a homely bar. Bar food, chosen from the standard printed menu, is the usual fare of sandwiches and some very well cooked dishes such as steak and kidney pie. It is the blackboard specials that provide the more imaginative choices: watercress and potato soup, a selection of game with herbs or pork chop and apple.

Access, Amex, Diners, Visa

Reading   map 2

Pizza Express
56 St Mary's Butts
☎ READING (0734) 391920

Open all week 11.30am–midnight

Part of the popular chain which is the pick of the pizza bunch. See London entry.

No-smoking area • Access, Amex, Diners, Visa

Stanford Dingley   map 2

Old Boot Inn
☎ READING (0734) 744292

5m SW of Pangbourne W of M4 junction 12

Open all week noon–2, 6–10 Closed Christmas Day evening

Over the years, this village local has seen its share of changes. Currently, it is all exposed beams, with a recently revealed inglenook and scaled-down public bar. Customers now drive from miles around for a meal here. The menu runs to several pages, taking in thick fish soup, garlic mushrooms, grilled swordfish steaks and pork Chinese-style. Some main courses, such as steak au poivre and roast duck, may bump up the bill. Courage beers.

Garden • Car-park • Wheelchair access • Access, Visa

West Ilsley   map 2

Harrow
☎ EAST ILSLEY (063 528) 260

Off A34 10m N of Newbury

Open all week noon–2.15, 6–9.15

A village pub overlooking a cricket pitch, with a varied choice of hot and cold dishes. The speciality is rabbit pie, made with local wild rabbit. Vegetarians and vegans are supplied with a tremendous series of daily specials – hazelnut and courgette bake, spinach and mushroom roulade and stuffed cabbage rolls baked in coconut sauce. Good coffee.

No-smoking area at lunch • Garden • Car-park • Wheelchair access, also WC • Access, Visa

---

Yattendon   map 2

Royal Oak ★

The Square
☎ HERMITAGE **(0635) 201324**

5m W of Pangbourne E of M4 junction 13

Open all week 12.30–2.30, 7.30–10

The charms of this ivy-clad sixteenth-century village inn, with a comfortable, dark-panelled interior and log fires, are considerable; the sort of pub that makes an ideal local, especially when the bar food is so good. Although the prices reflect the high quality of the food, it is possible to eat simply: a ploughman's with a selection of superb farmhouse cheeses (£8.95), maybe moules marinière (£4.75) or fish soup (£4.25) followed by lemon tart or an almond parfait with coffee sauce. Well-chosen wines and good coffee. It is essential to book for lunch.

Garden • Car-park • Wheelchair access, also WC • Access, Amex, Diners, Visa

---

If there are restrictions on children, these are mentioned in the details at the end of each entry.

Amersham   map 4

Eton Wine Bar

1 Market Square, Old Amersham
☎ HIGH WYCOMBE (0494) 727242

Open all week noon–3.15, 7–11
Closed 5 days Christmas

This wine bar is housed in a seventeenth-century building in the middle of the old high street. It is spacious, with a glass-covered conservatory, lots of period feel, and is very popular. Decent but pricey food includes prawn-and-sweet-pepper-filled pasta shells, lamb, artichoke and mange-tout pancake, old English turkey and parsley pie.

No cigars • Garden • Access, Visa

Beaconsfield   map 2

China Diner

7 The Highway, Station Road
☎ BEACONSFIELD (0494) 673345

N of M40 junction 2

Open all week noon–2.30, 6–11.30

Specialising in Peking and Szechuan cooking, this restaurant has stark, modern décor of Venetian blinds, tiled floor and ceiling fans. It gets noisy on busy evenings. Skip indifferent hors d'oeuvres and bland soups and concentrate on main courses; crispy aromatic duck is highly praised. Good for eating in a crowd with prices reasonable enough to order widely.

Wheelchair access, also WC • Access, Amex, Diners, Visa

Royal Standard of England

Forty Green
☎ BEACONSFIELD (0494) 673382

NE of M40 junction 3

Open all week noon–2.30, 6–10.30
Closed Christmas Day evening

History looms large in this ancient rambling pub. Some of the beams date back 900 years, and the place is crammed with stained-glass, pewter tankards and other treasures. There is finely carved antique panelling and Charles II is supposed to have hidden in the rafters above what is now the food bar. Today's visitors can choose from an impressive selection of cheeses, home-made pies such as venison or pigeon, flans and hot dishes including fritto misto. Well-kept real ales including Owd Rodger, which was originally brewed here, before the recipe was passed on to Marstons.

No-smoking area • Garden and family-room • Car-park • Wheelchair access, also WC

Chesham
map 4

Swan

Ley Hill
☎ CHESHAM **(049 478) 3075**

2m E of Chesham

Open all week noon–2, 7–9

Ancient oak beams, big open fireplaces and a feeling of congenial snugness are the hallmarks of this busy, old-fashioned pub. Food is served in the bar and restaurant, with the emphasis on grills, salads and traditional English pies such as game and port. Also, there are daily specials along the lines of beef and vegetable soup, lamb steak in spinach sauce and apple strudel. Ind Coope beers on draught, decent coffee and drinkable house wine.

No-smoking area • No children in bar • Garden • Car-park • Access, Visa

Dinton
map 4

Bottle and Glass

Gibraltar
☎ AYLESBURY **(0296) 748488**

Off A418, 4m SW of Aylesbury

Open all week 12–2, 7–10 (exc Sun D)
Closed Christmas Day and Boxing Day

This fifteenth-century thatched pub's big attraction is the food. Simple snacks, salads and sandwiches can be eaten in the bar at lunchtime; more imaginative evening meals are served in the restaurant (booking essential). Menus change every month, but cream of celery soup or gravlax might be followed by baked brill in chervil sauce, chicken with leeks and almonds, or vegetables in filo pastry with yoghurt, banana and coriander sauce. Real ales.

No children in pub • Garden • Car-park • Wheelchair access • Access, Amex, Diners, Visa

CAMBRIDGESHIRE

Barrington

map 5

Royal Oak

West Green
☎ CAMBRIDGE (0223) 870791

Off A10 SW of M11 junction 11

Open all week noon–2, 6.30–10.30

Vegetarians get a better-than-average deal in this timber-framed pub within striking distance of Cambridge. The kitchen scores because it offers fresh, cooked-to-order dishes, not the commercial, ready-prepared items found in so many pubs looking for vegetarian trade. Nuts are the trademark: the Cambridgeshire cutlet is embellished with walnuts and cashews; bean and cheese loaf gets a peanut sauce, while 'challis cottage crumble' includes almonds, along with leeks, mushrooms and tomatoes. For carnivores, there are steaks, curries and liver and bacon. Well-kept beers from Adnams and Greene King.

No-smoking area • Garden and family-room • Car-park • Wheelchair access, also WC • Access, Visa

Cambridge

map 5

Browns

23 Trumpington Street
☎ CAMBRIDGE (0223) 461655

Open all week 11am–11.30pm
Closed Christmas Eve to Boxing Day

Browns is one of a family of three informal, lively, American-style restaurants (see entries for Brighton and Oxford) with continuous service from breakfast to 11.30pm. The menu offers pasta, salads and hot sandwiches with game, chicken and fisherman's pies, roast ribs, vegetarian dishes and fresh fish. Desserts are gooey and satisfying.

No-smoking area • Wheelchair access, also WC • Access, Amex, Visa

Catering Training Restaurant

Cambridge Regional College, Newmarket Road
☎ CAMBRIDGE (0223) 324455

Open L Mon to Fri noon–1.15, D Tue and Thur 7–7.45 (1 sitting)
Closed college hols

This restaurant is different every time you visit, as its function changes daily to meet the syllabus needs of the students (check the menu when booking). What is on offer is some of the best-value food in Cambridge. The students cook and serve under supervision, providing a set lunch for £3.50 and, on two evenings a week, a four-course dinner for £8.

No smoking • Wheelchair access, also WC • Access, Visa

All details are as accurate as possible at the time of going to press, but chefs and owners often change, and it is wise to check by telephone before making a special journey.

Free Press

Prospect Row
☎ CAMBRIDGE (0223) 68337

Open all week noon–2, 6.30–8.30

Tucked away and not easy to find is this small, unspoilt and very atmospheric pub. Rowing memorabilia deck the bars, and there is a splendid mix of town and gown. Locally made raised pies – chicken and ham, game and duck with walnut and orange – are especially popular. Soup, inventive salads, a couple of hot dishes and treacle tart are always available.

No-smoking area • Garden • Wheelchair access, also WC

Greenhouse

Eaden Lilley dept store, 12 Market Street
☎ CAMBRIDGE (0223) 358822

Open Mon to Sat 9.30am–5 (7.15 Wed)
Closed Sun

A rarity these days, an old established department store that still maintains an air of breeding. On its second floor is a pleasant self-service restaurant much patronised by the lady shoppers of Cambridge. Everything is made on the premises: poached salmon with home-made mayonnaise, chicken and ham pie, delicious puddings – and there is some sound baking.

No-smoking area • Wheelchair access, also WC

Hobbs Pavilion

Park Terrace
☎ CAMBRIDGE (0223) 67480

Open Tue to Sat noon–2.30, 7 (8.30 Thur)–9.45 (exc Sat D)
Closed Sun, Mon and 1 month from mid-Aug

A cheery crêperie with vegetarian emphasis housed in a former cricket pavilion on the edge of Parker's Piece. The menu concentrates almost exclusively on pancakes savoury – sausage and black pudding, spicy ratatouille, Dijon mushroom – and pancakes sweet with nursery fillings of Smarties or Maltesers and cream. Sheep's-milk ice-cream for the grown-ups.

No-smoking area

Little Tea-room at Perfect Setting

1 All Saints Passage
☎ CAMBRIDGE (0223) 63207

Open Mon to Sat 9.30am–5.30
Closed Sun, Christmas Day and Boxing Day

Entrance to this delightful cottage-style tea-room is via Perfect Setting, a shop devoted to exquisite bed linen. Open for a breakfast of fruit juice, croissant and coffee through lunch of baked potato or sandwiches made from freshly cut home-made bread, to afternoon tea of scones and cakes. Try the lemon special – hot lemon cake with lemon curd and cream.

Unlicensed • No smoking • Access, Visa

Martins Coffee House

4 Trumpington Street
☎ CAMBRIDGE (0223) 61757

Open Mon to Fri 8.30am–5.30,
Sat 8.30am–5, Sun 9.30am–5
Closed 1 week Christmas and Good Fri

A converted coffee bar off the tourist
track, away from the crowds and the
students. Mrs Fawkes serves the best
coffee in Cambridge and also
produces an array of home-baked
scones, eclairs, lemon meringue pies
and cakes. Full cooked breakfasts are
served 8.30–11am; lunches include
soup, filled jacket potatoes and
substantial hot dishes such as beef
and vegetable casserole.

Unlicensed • No-smoking area •
Wheelchair access

Nettles

6 St Edward's Passage
☎ CAMBRIDGE (0223) 872419

Open Mon to Sat 9am–8
Closed Sun, Christmas Day and
bank hols

A diminutive vegetarian take-away
squeezed down a little side passage; at
a pinch it could seat 10 people.
Thick, nourishing soups, well-
flavoured vegetable chilli, filling pasta
and vegetable dishes, quiches and
pizza – the menu varies but it is all
cooked with flair and imagination.
Puddings include a superb apple
crumble.

Unlicensed, but bring your own: no
corkage • No smoking

See the back of the guide for an index of
eating-places and an index of locations.

Pizza Express

7 Jesus Lane
28 St Andrews Street
☎ CAMBRIDGE (0223) 324033/
61320

Open all week 11.30am–midnight

Part of the popular chain which is the
pick of the pizza bunch. See London
entry.

No-smoking area • Access, Amex,
Diners, Visa

Tai Cheun

12 St John's
☎ CAMBRIDGE (0223) 358281

Open all week noon–2, 6–11
Closed Christmas

A small, intimate Chinese restaurant
opposite St John's College,
specialising in Beijing and Szechuan
dishes. Crab and sweetcorn soup,
pork ribs and stir-fried beef in black-
bean and green pepper sauce are well
done and there is decently prepared
chicken in garlic with stir-fried
vegetables. Service can be brusque.

Wheelchair access, also WC • Access,
Amex, Visa

Ely   map 5

Dominique's

8 St Mary's Street
☎ ELY (0353) 665011

Open Tue to Sun 10am–6
Closed Mon and 2 weeks Christmas

A huge picture window allows
passers-by a glimpse of the tempting

array of cakes and pastries; the best advert Dominique's could have, not that they just do tea and cakes. Salade tiède, ratatouille, filled jacket potatoes (properly cooked, not microwaved), sandwiches and baguettes represent the light side of the menu with jugged hare, rabbit, barley and mushroom casserole or chicken escalope in a cream sauce adding the substance. The cooking is sound and thoroughly enjoyable, even more so when one contemplates the keen prices and generous portions.

No smoking • Wheelchair access

Peking Duck

26 Fore Hill
☎ ELY (0353) 662063

Open Tue to Sun D 6–11
Closed Mon and Christmas Day

A classic version of the eponymous centrepiece dish is served in this Chinese restaurant. Other high points on the menu have included the assorted hors d'oeuvre (a cold plate of sliced meats surrounding a mound of pickled cabbage, onions and carrots, topped with bits of braised fish); hot-and-sour soup; almond chicken and battered sweet-and-sour prawns. Excellent Chinese-style toffee apples to finish.

Wheelchair access • Amex

You will find report forms (write a letter if you prefer) at the back of the book so that you can tell us about your experiences of going *Out to Eat*. We'll put the information to good use when we're compiling the next edition.

Fowlmere   map 5

Chequers Inn

☎ ROYSTON (0763) 82369

Between Royston and Cambridge on B1368 W of M11 junction 10

Open all week noon–2, 7–10
Closed Christmas Day

Log fires, a pleasant garden and the knowledge that Samuel Pepys spent the night here in 1660 are part of the charm of this restored sixteenth-century coaching inn. Bar food in the form of garlic mushrooms, lasagne, breadcrumbed pork chop, crab au gratin and ploughman's are comple-mented by a good selection of wines by the glass and espresso coffee.

Garden • Car-park • Wheelchair access, also WC • Access, Amex, Diners, Visa

---

Huntingdon   map 5

Old Bridge Hotel

1 High Street
☎ HUNTINGDON (0480) 52681

Open all week noon–2.30, 6–10.30

An ivy-clad Georgian hotel which is busy and very popular, with gardens running down to the River Ouse. The Terrace offers a lunchtime buffet with an unusually comprehensive selection of wines by the glass. Hot dishes include lasagne, stir-fried chicken and vegetarian kebab. Afternoon tea is served in the lounge or the garden in fine weather.

Garden • Car-park • Wheelchair access, also WC • Access, Amex, Diners, Visa

Keyston

map 5

Pheasant Inn

☎ BYTHORN (080 14) 241

Open all week noon–2, 6 (7 Sun)–10
Closed Christmas Day evening and
Boxing Day

Service is exemplary for a pub, with small touches such as crudités, dips and spiced sausages provided on the bar. Sofas and an open fire create a comfortable environment. Good bar food includes roast pork with apple sauce and onion gravy, crab Mornay and lamb casserole, with bread-and-butter pudding and praline bavarois to finish.

Car-park • Access, Amex, Diners, Visa

Madingley

map 5

Three Horseshoes

1 High Street
☎ MADINGLEY (0954) 210221

W of M11 junction 14

Open all week noon–2.30, 7–10.30
Closed Christmas Day evening and
Boxing Day

A smart, thatched pub, two miles out of Cambridge, right by the gates of Madingley Hall. Go for the good-value meals in the comfortable bar, such as kipper mousse, kedgeree, ham hocks in mushroom sauce, and bread-and-butter pudding. To drink, there are local beers and some decent wines by the glass. More expensive meals are available in the pink dining-room.

Garden • Car-park • Wheelchair access,
also WC • Access, Amex, Diners, Visa

Newton

map 5

Queen's Head ★

☎ CAMBRIDGE (0223) 870436

On B1368 S of M11 junction 11

Open all week noon–2.15, 6.30–10
Closed Christmas Day

It is hard to describe the Shaws' delightfully traditional country pub. Beer is served direct from the cask behind the bar, the only noise to disturb conversation is that of a loudly ticking clock and the food is outstanding because it is so simple. For 28 years the approach has been the same – soup, baked potato and sandwiches at lunchtimes, soup and cold cuts in the evening – but only the very best ingredients are used. Thick soup, based on good stock, comes in a mug with a hunk of locally baked granary bread and all sandwiches are cut to order. Beef is Scottish topside cooked rare, ham is succulent and thickly sliced. If only more pubs were like this.

No children in bar • Car-park •
Wheelchair access

Wansford

map 5

Haycock

☎ STAMFORD **(0780) 782223**

On A1, nr A1/A47 intersection

Open all week 7.30am–11pm

Easy access from the A1 has encouraged the addition of a business centre and ballroom to this former coaching-inn. The Orchard Room, a series of characterful rooms leading on to a terrace and formal garden, provides first-rate food. A lunchtime buffet offers excellent ham, rare roast beef, poached salmon, dressed lobster, but at a price, and it is easy to go over budget. On the other hand, portions are generous, quality high and you can help yourself to as much salad as you want. Otherwise, choose from the printed menu of reasonably priced favourites: steak and kidney pie, lasagne or curried beef. Open also for breakfast and afternoon tea. Service is very good.

No-smoking area • Garden • Car-park • Wheelchair access, also WC • Access, Amex, Diners, Visa

---

★ after an eating-place indicates that it is one of the best found by the Editor during research for this book (see page 14 for a list).

🍺 after an eating-place indicates that it is a pub. The opening and closing times we give only relate to when food is available – the licensing hours may be different.

🛉 after an eating-place indicates that it is within five miles of the nearest motor-way junction. We give the relevant motorway and junction in the details. Eating-places in cities and large towns, where traffic, parking and route-finding may cause delay, do not have this symbol.

Alderley Edge   map 7

Alderley Rose

34 London Road
☎ **ALDERLEY EDGE (0625) 585557**

*Open Mon to Fri noon–1.45, 5.30–
11.15 and Sat to Sun noon–11.15*

An unattractive modern building with
brushed-concrete walls, incongruous
in this well-heeled village. But the
Alderley Rose fills a gap in an
expensive part of Cheshire with some
good-value, generously portioned
Cantonese cooking. Chow-mein and
fried rice one-plate dishes, together
with dim-sum, are good value.

Wheelchair access • Access, Visa

Bickley Moss   map 7

Cholmondeley Arms

☎ **CHOLMONDELEY (0829) 720300**

On A49 nr Malpas

*Open all week noon–2.15, 7–10
Closed Christmas Day*

A Victorian schoolhouse
imaginatively converted into a pub.
Pastel-shaded, rag-rolled 18-foot-
high walls, a clutter of kitchen tables
and open fires create an eye-catching,
stylish effect. Well-presented food
includes stuffed pancakes, various
home-made pies – steak and kidney,

chicken and leek – omelettes, goujons
of plaice, salads and sandwiches.
Friendly, cheerful service.

*Garden • Car-park • Wheelchair access,
also WC • Access, Visa*

Chester   map 7

Abbey Green

**2 Abbey Green, off Northgate
Street**
☎ **CHESTER (0244) 313251**

*Open Mon to Sat noon–2.30, 6.30–10
Closed Sun*

Very pleasant, popular vegetarian
restaurant. With its cheerful sitting-
room and open fire and two intimate
dining-rooms it's rather like eating in
a private house. The lunch menu
offers a fairly inventive choice, but
with rather small portions. Salads
accompanying the main course can
be dull and unimaginative, and carrot
and orange soup was found to be thin
and too orangey. But spiced carrot
kofte with lentil and orange sauce and
spinach roulade with chestnut,
mushroom and leek filling have both
pleased; and desserts, especially the
vegan tart, are enjoyable. More
expensive evening meals.

*No-smoking area • No children in
evening • Garden • Wheelchair access •
Access, Visa*

La Brasserie

**Chester Grosvenor Hotel,
Eastgate Street**
☎ CHESTER **(0244) 324024**

Open all week 6.30am–11pm
Closed Christmas Day and Boxing Day

A spacious, light, stylish place which
for breakfast (6.30am–11am) offers
calf's liver, lamb kidneys and
kedgeree as well as traditional
choices. A lounge menu runs until
6pm with a simple choice of club or
'bookmaker' sandwiches, scrambled
eggs, salads, omelettes, terrines, cakes
and afternoon tea (3pm–5.30pm).
Service can be erratic. More
expensive evening meals.

*No-smoking area • Wheelchair access,
also WC • Access, Amex, Diners, Visa*

Francs

14 Cuppin Street
☎ CHESTER **(0244) 317952**

*Open Mon to Sat noon–11, Sun noon–3,
6.30–10*

A self-consciously French café with a
modest frontage and pleasantly
spacious interior. Quite the 'in' place
for young fogeys and middle-aged
professionals. There's an interesting
selection of crêpes, also of French
charcuterie, cassoulet, splendidly
herby boudin blanc, rillettes, moules,
boeuf bourguignonne. Lively
atmosphere, must book.

*Wheelchair access, also WC • Access,
Amex, Visa*

Mamma Mia

St Werburgh Street
☎ CHESTER **(0244) 314663**

Open Mon to Sat noon–2.30, 6–11
*Closed Sun, Christmas Day and
Boxing Day*

A fun place, full of the sort of bustle
Italian waiters create so well. Avoid
the main dishes, which are not such a
success anyway. Go for the real
Italian stuff – the pizzas, the pastas
and the ice-cream (the coppa tiramisu
is imported from Italy) – with a glass
of the Italian house wine. Good value
for money.

Access, Amex, Diners, Visa

Philpotts

**2 Cross Street, off Watergate
Street**
☎ CHESTER **(0244) 345123**

Open Mon to Sat 8am-2.30

Made to order, take-away sandwiches
are all Philpotts do, but they do them
well. The permutations are inventive:
black pudding, bacon and tomato;
bacon and avocado; crispy bacon;
smoked trout in dill sauce; pastrami
and mustard with dill pickle; and
coronation chicken. There are five
kinds of cheese, a daily breakfast and
lunchtime special, soups and
espresso.

Unlicensed • No smoking

All letters to this guide are acknowledged.

Congleton   map 7

Odd Fellows

20 Rood Hill
☎ CONGLETON (0260) 270243

Open Mon to Sat noon–2, 6.30–10.30
Closed Sun, 23 Dec to 1 Jan and bank
hol Mons

The Kirkham family's busy wine bar
(on the ground floor) and bistro
(upstairs) attract a loyal following.
The dark Victorian décor creates an
intimate atmosphere in which to
enjoy steak and kidney pie, drunken
bullock, garlic lamb kebabs or black-
eye bean and mushroom curry from a
strong vegetarian choice. Desserts,
especially the crème brûlée, are
excellent.

No-smoking area • Garden • Access,
Amex, Visa

Henbury   map 7

Flora Tea Room

The Garden Centre
☎ MACCLESFIELD (0625) 422418

Open Tue to Sun 10am–5
Closed Mon

Floral décor sets the tone in this tea-
room attached to a 'flower, gift and
garden centre'. Cooking facilities are
limited, but the food is fresh and
home-made. Colourful salads, filled
jacket potatoes and plain or toasted
sandwiches are bolstered by daily
specials such as cottage pie and chilli.
Slices of hot beef and chicken are
served in soft baguettes. Fruit
crumbles, pies and ice-creams to
finish.

Unlicensed • No-smoking area • Garden
• Car-park • Wheelchair access, also
WC • Access, Visa

Lower Peover   map 7

Bells of Peover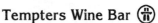

The Cobbles, nr Knutsford
☎ KNUTSFORD (0565) 722269

Open all week L noon–2, Mon to Fri D
6.30–8.30

You will find this ancient inn,
overgrown with creeper and wistaria,
opposite the thirteenth-century
church at the end of a narrow
cobbled lane off the B5081. A
sympathetic extension has enlarged
the seating area for bar food. This is
standard but well prepared fare: well-
flavoured soups, deep-fried
mushrooms, halibut in parsley sauce,
beef in red wine. There is also a
restaurant, open from Tuesday to
Sunday, except for Saturday lunch
and Sunday dinner.

No children in pub • Car-park •
Wheelchair access • Access, Visa

Middlewich   map 7

Tempters Wine Bar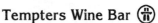

11 Wheelock Street
☎ MIDDLEWICH (060 684) 5175

On A54 E of M6 junction 18

Open Tue to Sun noon–1.45, 5.30–9.45
(exc Sun D)
Closed Mon

A split-level wine bar furnished with
plain, natural wood tables. A printed

menu, supplemented by blackboard specials, offers a varied choice: savoury pancake, garlic mushrooms, mariner's crumble, beef in red wine. A lunchtime snack menu includes filled jacket potatoes, chilli and pitta bread stuffed with tuna and salad.

No children under 14 • Garden • Wheelchair access • Access, Visa

Prestbury   map 7

Steak and Kabab Restaurant

New Road
☎ MACCLESFIELD **(0625) 829640**

Open Mon to Fri noon–4, 6–11.30, Sat 5.30–11.30pm, Sun noon–11 Closed Boxing Day and New Year's Day

A misleading name for a restaurant whose menu encompasses trout and plaice roulade, mushroom and nut terrine, poacher's pot and chicken tikka. There are, of course, steaks, even salmon steaks. The cooking is enjoyable, although desserts can be carelessly prepared,

and for the area – picture postcard Prestbury is very smart – offers excellent value.

Wheelchair access, also WC • Access, Visa

Sutton   map 7

Sutton Hall ⓦ

Bullocks Lane
☎ SUTTON **(026 05) 3211**

Open all week noon–2, 7-10

Sutton Hall has seen quite a slice of life in its 490-year-old existence; once it was a baronial residence, later it became a convent, now it is an inn of obvious atmospheric charm. Dishes on the bar menu are fairly standard – vegetable soup, eggs florentine, ploughman's, lasagne, steak and kidney pie – but honestly prepared from good ingredients.

No children exc weekends • Garden • Car-park • Wheelchair access • Access, Amex, Visa

Easington   map 10

Grinkle Park Hotel

☎ GUISBOROUGH (0287) 640515

Open all week 12.15–2, 7.15–9 (9.30 weekends)

A spacious, comfortable hotel beside a small duck-strewn lake at the end of a half-mile drive. Conferences and weddings can disturb the peace. Otherwise, the lunchtime buffet of cold cuts and salads is very good value and this is backed up by soup, cod and chips and steak and kidney pie and vegetables. There are old-fashioned homely puds like lemon snow and fruit tart.

Garden • Car-park • Wheelchair access, also WC • Access, Amex, Diners, Visa

Middlesbrough   map 10

Rooney's

23 Newport Road
☎ MIDDLESBROUGH (0642) 223923

*Open Mon to Sat 9am–10.30pm
Closed Sun*

A comfortable and popular fish and chip restaurant above a large bar. Cod, haddock, plaice and skate come fresh each day from Whitby and are served up in enormous portions – desserts are non-existent for no one ever asks for one. There is a £2.95 shoppers' special of cod or haddock and chips with mushy peas, bread and butter and a pot of tea. English breakfasts are served 9am–11am.

No-smoking area • Wheelchair access • Access, Visa

Stockton-on-Tees map 10

Waiting Room

9 Station Road
☎ EAGLESCLIFFE (0642) 780465

*Open Mon to Sat 11.30–4.30,
6.30–9.45
Closed Sun and Christmas to New Year*

An Edwardian three-storey terrace house with the ground floor opened up into a vegetarian restaurant and wholefood shop. It is run by the effervescent Jenny Harding and her team of lively women helpers who put the accent strongly on green issues. The menu encompasses soups, salads, quiches, casseroles, crêpes, great garlic bread, organic wines and excellent baking.

Wheelchair access, also WC

Bodmin
map 1

Pots Coffee Shop

55 Fore Street
☎ BODMIN **(0208) 74601**

Open Mon to Sat 9am–5.30, Fri and
Sat D 7.30–late
Closed Sun

Judging by the logo, 'pots' refers to
potatoes. The menu in this informal
coffee-shop/restaurant on two floors
is dominated by 'suggested
combinations' for jacket potatoes,
and there are scores of possibilities.
Otherwise, the daytime choice
includes steaming hot-pots, salads
and ploughman's, as well as assorted
sandwiches. Clotted cream
embellishes most of the sweets. On
Friday and Saturday evenings, the
basement functions as a good-value
bistro. Teas, milk shakes and wine by
the glass.

Wheelchair access • Access, Visa

Waffles

Market House Arcade, Fore Street
☎ BODMIN **(0208) 75500**

Open Mon to Sat 8.30am–5.30
Closed Sun

Waffles is highly recommended for
lunch. The menu varies considerably,
and the influence-of-the-day may be
Italian, French, Indian or Greek.
There is always at least one hot
vegetarian dish, such as lentil and
mushroom bake with herb dumplings

or vegetable lasagne, and no shortage
of good salads, cakes and pastries.

No-smoking area • Wheelchair access

Chapel Amble
map 1

Maltsters Arms

☎ WADEBRIDGE **(0208) 812473**

2m N of Wadebridge

Open all week noon–2.30 (3 summer),
7–9.30 (6.30–10.30 summer)
Closed Christmas Day evening

Since the closure of the unsuccessful
upstairs restaurant, the downstairs
bar has served good food. Blackboard
specials like grilled goat's cheese and
moules marinière are now favourites.
As a main course, you may be offered
moussaka or a plump, meaty fillet of
red mullet. Serious bread-and-butter
pudding and treacly tart.

No children if not eating • Garden •
Car-park • Access, Visa

Falmouth
map 1

De Wynne's Coffee House

55 Church Street
☎ FALMOUTH **(0326) 319259**

Open Mon to Sat 10am–5
Closed Sun

A waterfront coffee-house with gas
lights and bow windows. Home-made
cakes are the big attraction – chocolate

cake, scones, meringues with local cream, a Fiji slice of chocolate, coconut and whisky, various fruit pies – freshly made each day from sound ingredients. Light lunches include lasagne, cheese and onion pie and jacket potatoes.

No-smoking area • Wheelchair access

Gweek
map 1

Mellanoweth

☎ HELSTON (0326) 22271

Just N of B3291 Helston/Falmouth road at Gweek

Open summer all week noon–2

During the summer months, this flower-covered cottage serves good-value lunches centring on crêpes with fillings such as spiced beef or garlic mushrooms. There are wholesome soups to start, fresh crisp salads as accompaniments, and spectacular ice-creams to finish. At other times, the place becomes a full restaurant providing more expensive meals. The Gweek Seal Sanctuary is nearby.

Garden • Wheelchair access • Access, Visa

Helford
map 1

Shipwrights Arms

☎ MANACCAN (032 623) 235

Open all week (exc Sun and Mon winter) noon–2, 7–9
Closed Sun and Mon winter

A charming thatched pub with tables by the riverbank and better-than-average food based on fresh

ingredients. Local fish, such as mussels and goujons of monkfish, back up home-made dishes including tomato soup, garlic mushrooms and steak and kidney pie. Hot apple cake is served with clotted cream. Devenish beers or wines by the glass.

Manaccan
map 1

New Inn

☎ MANACCAN (032 623) 323

Open all week noon–2, 7–9

Deep in the yachting country of the Helford River, this sleepy coastal village gets rudely awakened at weekends and in the summer months. Its charming sixteenth-century thatched pub is best viewed at quiet times. Good, plain bar food includes walnut and mushroom pâté, chicken soup, hunks of granary bread, bangers and mash, and meat and potato pie. Local fish when available.

Garden • Wheelchair access, also WC

Marazion
map 1

Sail Loft

St Michael's Mount
☎ PENZANCE (0736) 710748

Open all week 12.15-5
Closed 1 Nov to 31 Mar

Walk across the cobbled causeway or take the ferry at high tide to this National Trust restaurant in a converted carpenter's shop and boat store. A ferryman's lunch of two English cheeses and home-made bread or a hot seafood casserole awaits. Afternoon tea is enhanced by home-made cakes and biscuits. A traditional roast Sunday lunch is great value at £4.95.

No smoking • Wheelchair access • Access, Amex, Visa

Marhamchurch   map 1

Bullers Arms

☎ BUDE (0288) 361277

2m SE of Bude off A39

Open all week noon–2, 6.30–9.30 (9 winter)

This friendly local is the focal point of village life and, consequently, the repository of many 'private', well-used tankards. The locals also take advantage of the generous set-price lunch for around £9, which might offer lobster bisque or sautéed king prawns to start, with steak or grilled trout, or a roast on Sundays, to follow. Good bar snacks include French onion soup and fish pie. Real ales from the St Austell brewery.

Garden and family-room • Car-park • Wheelchair access, also WC • Access, Visa

---

Mevagissey   map 1

Mr Bistro

East Quay, The Harbour
☎ MEVAGISSEY (0726) 842432

Open all week noon–3, 7–10
Closed Nov to Feb

A converted pilchard store by the quay serving fresh fish bought from the local fishermen. Cod or lemon

sole and chips, with perhaps moules marinière or leek, potato and onion soup to start, would make a satisfying lunch. The evening menu is pricier and would take the bill over £10.

Wheelchair access • Access, Amex, Diners, Visa

Mylor Bridge   map 1

Pandora Inn

Restronguet Creek
☎ FALMOUTH (0326) 72678

4 miles N of Falmouth off A39, follow signs to Mylor Bridge, then through village to Restronguet Creek

Open all week noon–2 (2.15 summer), 6.30–9.30 (10 summer)

A medieval thatched pub, in a beautiful position overlooking a tidal creek. It is especially popular during the summer months when the patio and pontoon on the water come into their own. Bar food is simple, with the local seafood being the best choice: crab salad or thermidor, mussels in white wine or the Restronguet fish pie. Jam roly-poly, spotted dick or treacle tart to finish.

No-smoking area • Car-park • Access, Visa

When you book a restaurant table, you're making a contract with the restaurant and you must be given a table, within reasonable time of your arrival. If not, the restaurant is in breach of contract and you can claim a reasonable sum to cover any expenses you had as a result, e.g. travelling expenses.

Penzance map 1

Parrot of Penzance

Abbey Slip
☎ PENZANCE (0736) 50515

*Open Easter to Sept all week noon–3
(exc Sun), 7.30–10, Sept to Easter Thur
to Sat D 7.30–10
Closed Christmas Eve and Sun to Wed
Sept to Easter*

A small, elegant restaurant with good
views of Penzance harbour and
Mounts Bay. Inside, there are
paintings on the plain walls and the
ceiling is cedar-clad. Both lunch and
dinner are affordable, and there is
plenty of choice for vegetarians.
Good dishes include ratatouille with
garlic bread, richly flavoured steak
and mushroom pie, and coffee-
flavoured 'mocha log'. Otherwise, the
menu might take in chicken with
orange and mint sauce; coquilles St
Jacques; and sweet-and-sour tofu.
Wines by the glass or carafe.

*Garden • Wheelchair access, also WC •
Access, Amex, Visa*

Philleigh map 1

Roseland Inn

☎ PORTSCATHO (087 258) 254

*Open all week noon–1.45,
D summer 7–9
Closed Christmas Day*

One of Cornwall's prettiest pubs –
the paved courtyard and the bars
bloom with flowers, setting off
sturdy, old-fashioned furniture,
flagstoned floors and low beams.
Simple bar food includes sandwiches,

a hot-pot broth, rabbit terrine, fresh
local crab and home-made apple pie
or treacle tart with lashings of cream
to finish.

Car-park

Polperro map 1

Sun Lounge

Little Green
☎ POLPERRO (0503) 72459

*Open Mon (Wed winter) to Sat
10–2.30, 6.30–10
Closed Sun, Mon and Tue winter, and
2nd week Jan to Easter*

A real find in such a tourist trap, the
Sun Lounge is not particularly smart
but the food is good. This takes in an
English breakfast fry-up, light snacks
of jacket potatoes, sandwiches, crab
salad and soups of rich French onion,
dark olive-green pea and lettuce and
the more substantial spaghetti
bolognese and fresh but pricey fish.

Wheelchair access • Access, Visa

St Breward map 1

Old Inn

☎ BODMIN (0208) 850711

4m S of Camelford off B3266

*Open Mon to Sat noon–2.30, 6–10 and
Sun noon–2, 7–9.30
Closed Christmas Day*

The dining-room, at the back, is only
open in the evening. At lunchtime
there is an ample bar snacks menu.
Night or day, it is best to decide what
to eat while enjoying a drink in the

'snug' bar. And if it is chilly outside there will be a roaring fire. The food here is fresh and wholesome, somewhat plain but reasonably priced. The garlic mushrooms are huge, juicy and very garlicky. Trout with almonds is pink, succulent and local. Don't count on the wine list: have another beer.

No children under 14 in bar • Car-park • Wheelchair access

St Dominick   map 1

Cotehele Barn

Cotehele Estate
☎ **LISKEARD (0579) 50652**

Open all week noon–5.30 (exc Fri)
Closed Fri, open spasmodically 31 Oct to Good Fri or 1 Apr

An unaltered medieval manor house with lovely gardens, now run by the National Trust, affording a fascinating glimpse into the past. The Barn restaurant has a reputation for serving tasty lunches of home-made soup, savoury vegetable flan, spicy beef hot-pot and steamed sponge pudding. An excellent three-course Sunday lunch can be had for £9.25. Otherwise, there are snacks and Cornish cream teas.

No smoking • Wheelchair access, also WC • Access, Amex, Visa

You will find report forms (write a letter if you prefer) at the back of the book so that you can tell us about your experiences of going *Out to Eat*. We'll put the information to good use when we're compiling the next edition.

Tintagel   map 1

House on the Strand

Trebarwith Strand, nr Tintagel
☎ **CAMELFORD (0840) 770326**

Off B3263 Tintagel–Camelford road

Open Easter to Oct all week 10am–10pm, Nov to Easter Thur to Sat 6pm–10pm and Sun 10am–6pm Closed Jan to mid–Feb

You can almost hear the waves crashing on the Strand from this wonderfully atmospheric '70s-style bistro. The inventive menu is available 12 hours a day, served by efficiently casual and friendly staff. Choose from spicy lentil fritters, stuffed squid, black-bean chilli, Thai pork, king prawns with coconut rice, and finish with brown sugar meringues and clotted cream.

Garden • Wheelchair access (nearby toilets for disabled) • Access, Visa

Truro   map 1

Bustopher Jones

62 Lemon Street
☎ **TRURO (0872) 79029**

Open all week noon–2 (exc Sun), 6–10

A lively bistro popular with both locals and tourists. Dark panelling and stained-glass from a Nonconformist chapel add to, rather than detract from, the atmosphere. Lasagne, chilli and ratatouille feature regularly, while steak and kidney pudding, Chilean beef, stuffed cabbage and parsnips Molly Parkin are frequent specialities.

No-smoking area • No children in bar • Access, Visa

Wadebridge

map 1

Janner's

34 Molesworth Street
☎ WADEBRIDGE **(0208) 812833**

Open all week noon–2, 6–9.30
Closed New Year's Day

Janner's and the adjacent restaurant (renamed The Bistro) have separate entrances. The former is better value, with most main courses priced below £4. Narrow, and filled with plants and art deco-type posters, this is a stylish wine bar, with food betraying Mediterranean influences. Sample a simple, effective version of garlic prawns or try the smoked mackerel pâté. Most lasagne and fettucine creations are worthy. The wine list has bottles from Australia, New Zealand and California and there are tables and chairs for drinking the same on a patio outside, under hanging baskets of flowers.

Access, Visa

★ after an eating-place indicates that it is one of the best found by the Editor during research for this book (see page 14 for a list).

🔘 after an eating-place indicates that it is a pub. The opening and closing times we give only relate to when food is available – the licensing hours may be different.

🛆 after an eating-place indicates that it is within five miles of the nearest motorway junction. We give the relevant motorway and junction in the details. Eating-places in cities and large towns, where traffic, parking and route-finding may cause delay, do not have this symbol.

Barnard Castle   map 10

Market Place Teashop

29 Market Place
☎ TEESDALE (0833) 690110

*Open all week 10am (3pm Sun)–5.30
Closed 24 Dec to 5 Jan and Sun Jan to
early Mar*

Tea served in splendid repro-antique
silver pots matches the style of the
eighteenth-century building with its
antique furniture and flagstoned
floor. Honest home-cooked food of
hearty portions and low prices,
chosen from a long list, is
consistently good. The emphasis is
on simplicity: steak pies, chicken
casserole, meatballs, roast brisket and
Yorkshire pudding. Food is available
all day. Vegetarians are well catered
for with vegetable patties, samosas
and various vegetable bakes. Save
room for the cakes, especially the pies
bursting with fruit and cream, all very
temptingly on display. Despite being
constantly busy, service remains
attentive.

Wheelchair access

Priors

7 The Bank
☎ TEESDALE (0833) 38141

*Open all week 10am (noon Sun)–5
(5.30 Sat and Sun)*

A pleasant, plant-filled vegetarian
café-cum-art and craft gallery run by
various members of the Prior family
– some cook, some serve. Food is
attractively displayed at the counter
with dishes ranging from simple
sandwiches and ploughman's to a
wide range of inventive salads,
quiches, vegetable croustade, nut and
wine lasagne. There are some
excellent home-baked cakes.

*No-smoking area • Wheelchair access •
Access, Amex, Diners, Visa*

Burnopfield   map 10

Fairways ⦿

Hobson Golf Centre
☎ BURNOPFIELD (0207) 70941

*Open all week noon–2.30, 7–8.30
(exc Sun D)*

Described as a pub and restaurant,
Fairways is an independent enterprise
on a municipal golf course. It
occupies the upper floor of a
modernistic building and has chrome
and glass tables. The menu offers just
three combinations of table d'hôte
(one vegetarian) with the main course
setting the price, and starters,
puddings and salad bar common to
all three. Most main courses, steak
and kidney pie, a carvery selection
and steaks, are also available as bar
meals. The imaginative vegetarian
menu (£7.95) offers mushroom and
onion bordelaise, young corn and
Stilton casserole, cucumber in pink
peppercorn sauce. Superb value for
money.

Car-park • Wheelchair access

Durham
map 10

Almshouses

Palace Green
☎ 091-386 1054

Open all week 9am–5 (8pm June to Sept)

In the shadow of Durham Cathedral, the ancient almshouses have been turned into an atmospheric cafeteria. It is very popular with students and tourists alike, all attracted no doubt by the low prices and wholesome food. There are generally a couple of soups, filled rolls, a variety of salads, beef bourguignonne, vegetarian dishes and a range of cakes.

No smoking • Wheelchair access, also WC

And Albert

17 Hallgarth Street
☎ 091-384 1919

Open Mon to Sat noon–2.30, 6.30–9.30 Closed Sun

A small, cheerful restaurant opposite a Victorian pub and at the back of the prison. There are two rooms on the ground floor: one for smoking, the other no-smoking. Vegetarians are provided for, but simple, light dishes such as chicken cacciatore and Cumberland sausages predominate. A reasonably imaginative wine list. Big on puddings.

No-smoking room • Wheelchair access • Access, Visa

Ristorante de Medici

21 Elvet Bridge
☎ 091-386 1310

Open Mon to Sat 11.30–2.30, 6.30–11 Closed Sun, Christmas Day and Boxing Day

A scruffy entrance wedged between two shop doors and an even scruffier ascent of the stairs to the first-floor restaurant can be off-putting. The atmosphere, however, is warm and the food decent and inexpensive. There is a strong line of pizzas and pastas at very reasonable prices, fresh minestrone, garlic bread and frothy, boozy zabaglione.

Access, Visa

Greta Bridge
map 10

Morritt Arms Hotel

☎ TEESDALE (0833) 27232

Open all week noon–2

The Morritt Arms is one of those unspoilt, creeper-clad Georgian coaching-inns in a lovely, peaceful setting that instantly gives a sense of life lived at a slower pace. The faded but handsome bars – one sports a life-size Pickwickian mural – serve lunchtime dishes of soup, fresh salmon salad, grilled gammon, ploughman's, sausage and chips and sandwiches.

No children under 6 after 7pm • Garden • Car-park • Wheelchair access • Access, Amex, Diners, Visa

Summerhouse   map 10

Raby Hunt Inn 🏠

☎ DARLINGTON (0325) 374604

Open Mon to Sat noon–2
Closed Sun

Barbara Alison's plain country cooking requires a hearty lunchtime appetite to do it justice. A selection of four fresh vegetables plus potatoes accompany main courses of game pie, Cumberland sausage, steak pie and the perennial favourite – roast beef and Yorkshire pudding. A simple, friendly pub offering a warm welcome and honest good food.

Garden • Car-park • Wheelchair access

★ after an eating-place indicates that it is one of the best found by the Editor during research for this book (see page 14 for a list).

🏠 after an eating-place indicates that it is a pub. The opening and closing times we give only relate to when food is available – the licensing hours may be different.

🏠 after an eating-place indicates that it is within five miles of the nearest motor-way junction. We give the relevant motorway and junction in the details. Eating-places in cities and large towns, where traffic, parking and route-finding may cause delay, do not have this symbol.

Ambleside map 10

Drunken Duck Inn

Barngates
☎ HAWKSHEAD (096 66) 347

Turn off B5286 Ambleside–Hawkshead
road by Outgate Inn

Open all week noon–2, 6.30–9

A remote but extremely popular 400-
year-old pub in a lovely location with
distant views of Lake Windermere.
Plain, down-to-earth bar food,
offered on a blackboard, brings
plenty of game in season (game
terrine, home-made game pie), well-
filled sandwiches, ploughman's, spicy
red-bean crumble and Mediterranean
spiced lamb.

*No children in bar • Family-room •
Car-park • Wheelchair access, also WC*

Rothay Manor

Rothay Bridge
☎ AMBLESIDE (053 94) 33605

Open all week 10am-5.30
Closed early Jan to early Feb

Smart but not stuffy, Rothay Manor
is an informal, friendly hotel whose
style can be sampled inexpensively at
lunch. The simple menu offers soup,
cold cuts or cheese with salad and a
choice of desserts, with unlimited
coffee and wine by the glass.
Afternoon tea (£5.75) is a grand
buffet of superb cakes and excellent
savouries, plus a good selection
of teas.

*No smoking in dining-room • Garden •
Car-park • Wheelchair access, also WC
• Access, Amex, Diners, Visa*

Sheila's Cottage ★

The Slack
☎ AMBLESIDE (053 94) 33079

*Open Mon to Sat noon–3.30, 7–9.30
(exc Mon), Sun L noon–3
Closed Christmas and 1 week Jan*

Changes have taken place at the Lake
District's most popular tea-room.
The general consensus on the new
barn extension, and on opening for
dinner, is one of warm approval,
although the loss of morning opening
is regretted. Light lunches of
Cumbrian sugar-baked ham, open
sandwiches, well-flavoured soups,
rösti and perhaps seafood ragoût are
rounded off by great desserts; sticky
toffee pudding elicits ecstatic praise.
The afternoon tea menu is highly
imaginative, offering as good a
selection of well-made savouries as
sweet. Try the Solway shrimps
followed by Lakeland lemon bread
and be left with little room for
dinner, which is more expensive.
There is also a £10 three-course
Sunday lunch available in the
restaurant.

*No smoking • Wheelchair access •
Access, Visa*

Wilf's Café

3–4 Cheapside
☎ AMBLESIDE **(053 94) 34749**

Open all week 9am–4.30

Entered via the Rock and Run shop, purveyors of climbing and running gear, Wilf's is a no-smoking haven for climbers, hill walkers and cyclists. The food reflects the simplicity of the place: filled baked potatoes, sausage sandwich, egg on toast and a full breakfast for £2.50. Hearty daily specials include brown lentil chilli with brown rice and potato and broccoli bake.

No smoking • Access, Visa

Zeffirelli's

Compston Road
☎ AMBLESIDE **(053 94) 33845**

Open Sat and Sun L noon–2, all week D 5–9.45
Closed Jan Tue and Wed

Part of a complex which includes a cinema, arcade of shops, lounge bar and café. Zeffirelli's is a vegetarian pizzeria whose unusual pizza bases are wheatmeal rolled in sesame seeds. Various pastas or organic rice with a choice of sauces along the lines of Mexican red-bean and vegetable chilli bulk out the menu. The red and black Japanese décor is a bit of a surprise.

No smoking • Access, Visa

All letters to this guide are acknowledged.

Appleby   map 10

Royal Oak

Bongate
☎ KIRKBY **(0930) 51463**

Open all week noon–2, 6.30–9
Closed Christmas Day and
New Year's Day

A highly rated stone-built pub on the main road through Appleby. Food is served in the oak-furnished bar and the dining-room. Local specialities such as potted shrimps and Cumberland sausages share the bill with international dishes from Greece, Yugoslavia and Mexico. The lasagne is renowned in the neighbourhood. Also look for marinated herrings, leek and tomato croustade and chicken in cheddar cheese sauce. Langoustines come direct from creel fishermen around Loch Fyne; bread is baked on the premises. Excellent sweets might include chocolate roulade with chestnut and brandy cream. Real ales, including guest beers.

Car-park • Wheelchair access • Access, Amex, Diners, Visa

Bassenthwaite   map 9

Pheasant

Bassenthwaite Lake
☎ KESWICK **(076 87) 76234**

Open all week noon–2

A comfortable, peaceful and well-maintained inn in a beautiful setting.

Bar lunches, taken in the intimate, old-fashioned bar or in the bright, spacious lounge (bar only on Sundays), offer delicious soup with home-made rolls and a range of cold, light dishes such as salmon mousse, smoked chicken with salad and potted Silloth shrimps.

No smoking in restaurant • No children under 14 in bar • Garden • Car-park • Wheelchair access, also WC

Bowland Bridge   map 10

Masons Arms

Strawberry Bank, Cartmel Fell
☎ CROSTHWAITE **(044 88) 486**

Open all week noon–2, 6–8.45
Closed Christmas Day and Boxing Day

Not easy to find, but well worth the effort, this remote pub occupies an unrivalled setting in lovely countryside, has comfortable, relaxing bars and offers some 150 different beers as well as excellent, imaginative bar food based on sound, fresh ingredients. Large bowls of soup, possibly carrot and coriander or sweet potato and parsnip, come with warm crusty rolls, and there are lentil, mushroom and hazelnut pâté, a coachman's casserole of beef in red wine or aubergine and courgette korma. Service is excellent, even when the place is busy.

Garden and family-room • Car-park • Wheelchair access

Out to Eat has been compiled in the same way as *The Good Food Guide* and is based on reports from consumers and backed up by anonymous inspections.

Bowness-on-Windermere   map 10

Rastelli Pizzeria

Lake Road
☎ WINDERMERE **(096 62) 4227**

Open all week D 6–10.45 (exc Wed)
Closed Wed and end Dec to end Feb

A cheerful, polite and efficient pizza and pasta place. Seating is cramped but the hustle and bustle are usually endearing. There is a larger than average choice of reasonably priced classics as well as steaks, pork chops, trout and other Bowness favourites. Good cappuccino and espresso.

Wheelchair access • Access, Visa

Brampton   map 10

String of Horses

Faugh
☎ CARLISLE **(0228) 70297/70509**

4m S of Brampton and follow signs to Castle Carrock and Heads Nook

Open all week noon–2.15, 7.30–10
Closed Christmas Day evening

Hidden away in a peaceful village is this extremely popular seventeenth-century inn. Beams, panelling and roaring fires add greatly to the atmosphere. Bar food offers fisherman's pie, chicken curry and lasagne, together with some odd mixtures such as Yorkshire pudding topped with chilli. Leave room for the bread-and-butter pudding.

No-smoking area • Garden • Car-park • Wheelchair access, also WC • Access, Amex, Diners, Visa

Carlisle   map 10

Grapevine

22 Fisher Street
☎ CARLISLE (0228) 46617

Open Mon to Sat 11.30am–4
Closed Sun

A large coffee-shop tucked behind the covered market. Helpful counter service offers interesting salads, local roast ham, steak and kidney pie and fresh salmon. Vegetarians are especially well catered for. Borrowdale tea-bread and date and walnut cake are popular choices for morning coffee or afternoon tea.

Unlicensed, but bring your own: corkage £1 • No-smoking area • Wheelchair access, also WC

Casterton   map 7

Pheasant

☎ KIRKBY LONSDALE (052 42) 71230

Open all week noon–1.45, 6.30–9.15
Closed some Mons Jan and Feb

A neat, pebble-dashed village inn with fine views of the Lune Valley. Substantially portioned bar food includes a number of local and regional specialities – black pudding, Woodalls Cumberland sausage, naturally cured Cumberland gammon – as well as the more standard pub fare of steak and kidney pie, chicken curry and grilled plaice. Good puddings.

No children after 8pm • Garden and family-room • Car-park • Wheelchair access, also WC • Access, Visa

Cockermouth   map 9

Quince & Medlar

13 Castlegate
☎ COCKERMOUTH (0900) 823579

Open Tue to Sun from 7pm
Closed Mon, 1 week Oct and 3 weeks Feb

A vegetarian restaurant where the clientele is strong on non-vegetarians enjoying Colin le Voi's imaginative, assured food. Carrot and apricot pâté with oatcakes, honey-glazed radish and spring onion tartlet make highly unusual starters. Middle Eastern casserole, green lentil and potato galette topped with aubergine, courgette and peppers, and the baked curried vegetables and chickpea show the many influences at work. Desserts include a light and dark chocolate pie. Booking is essential as the restaurant is small.

No smoking • No children under 5 • Wheelchair access (notice must be given) • Access, Visa

Dent   map 10

Dent Crafts Centre

Helmside
☎ DENT (058 75) 400

Open all week 9.30am–5.30
Closed Mon to Fri from 6 Jan to end Feb

Well worth a visit for the scenic drive alone. There is also an imaginative selection of craftwork on sale, and the pleasant, flagstone-floored café offers excellent, carefully prepared food. Open all day for thick, satisfying soups with locally baked bread, sandwiches and home-baked cakes as well as offering a three-course lunch for £5.95.

No smoking in restaurant • Garden • Car-park • Access, Visa

Stone Close ★

Main Street
☎ DENT (058 75) 231

*Open all week 10.30am–3.15, D 7.30 (one sitting)
Closed Jan, 2 weeks Feb and mid-week Feb, Nov and Dec*

A converted seventeenth-century cottage tea-room in a lovely cobbled village offering simple, well-cooked food. Available all day are local cheeses with wholemeal bread served in a Dalesman's platter, cheese and onion pie, home-roasted ham salad and good soups. Sound baking is apparent in treacly parkin, light pastry in the Yorkshire curd tart, and moist fruit cake. A blackboard menu lists daily specials. Prices are admirably low. A three-course evening meal, restricted to one choice for the main course only, is remarkable value at £8.50 given the quality of the ingredients. Quiet, unobtrusive service.

No smoking in evening • Wheelchair access

Embleton   map 9

Wythop Mill

☎ KESWICK (076 87) 76394

*Open Sun to Thur 11am–5
Closed Fri, Sat and end Oct to Easter*

The mill's water wheel is still driven each day by the fast-flowing river

beside which it stands. Here, you will find a museum of woodworking tools and a pretty flower-filled restaurant serving commendable food. Everything is home-made, even the ice-cream. Celery and apple soup comes with a herb scone, smoked haddock and mushroom quiche in sesame pastry. Salads and desserts are excellent.

No smoking • Car-park

Grange-over-Sands   map 7

At Home

Danum House, Main Street
☎ GRANGE-OVER-SANDS (053 95) 34400

*Open Mon to Sat 10am–7 (5 winter)
Closed Sun*

This is indeed home from home for many local residents who enjoy the informal but civilised atmosphere of this simple restaurant open for morning coffee, light lunches (served until 5.30pm) and afternoon teas. There is a strong following for the home-made soups and carefully cooked omelettes and quiches, with beef and vegetable pie satisfying heartier appetites.

Wheelchair access, also WC • Access, Visa

A restaurant manager can't insist on people not smoking, unless it's specifically a no-smoking restaurant or a no-smoking area. If it is, smokers could be asked to leave if they don't stop. If in doubt, check beforehand what the smoking arrangements are.

Grasmere
map 10

Baldry's ★

Red Lion Square
☎ GRASMERE (096 65) 301

Open all week 11–3.30, 6–8

There is nothing fancy about Baldry's. It is a plain, functional café, popular with walkers, but with outstanding food. Quality is all-important and Paul and Blaine Nelson use only organic flour for baking, organic vegetables when available, bake their own ham, and make their own bread and ice-creams. Light broccoli quiche, full-bodied minestrone soup, mushrooms on toast, rarebits and Westmorland tatties epitomise the basic menu, daily specials enhance it, and the superb baking crowns it. Scones, Cumberland rum nicky, walnut cake, hot sticky gingerbread and almond tart are all utterly tempting.

No smoking • Garden • Wheelchair access, also WC

Rowan Tree

Langdale Road
☎ GRASMERE (096 65) 528

*Open all week (exc Tue) noon–9
Closed Tue and Jan*

Simple vegetarian snacks and main meals with sound home baking are the order of the day at this homely little café. Lunch includes filled jacket potatoes, home-made soups, sandwiches and quiches backed up by more substantial blackboard specials like the popular potato, apple and onion bake.

No smoking • Wheelchair access, also WC

Hawkshead
map 10

Grandy Nook Tea Room

Vicarage Lane
☎ HAWKSHEAD (096 66) 404

*Open Tue to Sun 10.30am–5
Closed Mon, Christmas Day and Boxing Day*

This tiny, rustic cottage is one of the best-loved tea-rooms in the Lake District. The excellent range of home-baked cakes and pastries is the highlight, with impressively-risen scones, gingerbread, lemon meringue pie and much more besides. Decent lunches of soup, cottage pie, quiches and salads.

Unlicensed, but bring your own: no corkage • No smoking • Wheelchair access

Kendal
map 10

Moon ★

129 Highgate
☎ KENDAL (0539) 729254

Open all week D 6–10 (10.30 weekends)

Well worth the detour off the M6, this is Lake District food at its best in an unpretentious setting. Val Macconnell takes great care in her buying with loyalty to local produce and quality her prime criteria. The carefully prepared, imaginative food elicits as much praise for vegetarian as for meat dishes. Carrot, parsnip and tomato soup and creamy, spiced curried mushrooms are both delicately flavoured, chicken in tarragon cream lauded for the use of fresh tarragon. Sticky toffee pudding and raspberry and elderflower cheesecake vie with the home-made ice-creams. Cheerful service and excellent value for money.

Unlicensed • No smoking • Wheelchair access, also WC • Access, Visa

Pizza Margherita

181 Highgate
☎ KENDAL (0539) 731303

Open all week 11am–11pm
Closed Christmas Day, New Year's Day and Good Fri

Although a chain, of four pizza houses (see entries for Blackburn, Bradford, and Lancaster), none of the Margherita restaurants is impersonal. Bright colours, tiled floors and marble-topped tables create a pleasant look, backed up by courteous service. Plain or wholemeal pizzas come generously topped in 16 popular combinations including quattro formaggi, quattro stagioni and Americana.

No-smoking area • Car-park • Wheelchair access • Access, Visa

Keswick   map 10

Wild Strawberry

54 Main Street
☎ KESWICK (076 87) 74399

Open all week (exc Wed) 10am (11 Sun)–5
Closed Wed and Feb

Some people come only to ogle the porcelain, which has a particularly pretty strawberry motif. Others come for the sticky toffee pudding, a super-sweet Cumbrian delicacy. Either way, they appear satisfied after their pilgrimage. Don't come expecting

meals: this self-service salon provides superior snacks, and good tea and coffee by the cafetière. The owners claim their scones are 'said to be the best in Cumbria'.

Unlicensed • No smoking • Wheelchair access • Access, Visa

Melmerby   map 10

Shepherds Inn

nr Penrith
☎ LANGWATHBY (076 881) 217

M6 exit 40, 10m A686 signpost Alston

Open all week 11 (noon Sun)–2, 6 (7 Sun)–9.45

A converted, beamed barn with an open fireplace forms the main eating area in this Lakeland village pub. Martin and Christine Baucutt's menu has some local specialities such as Cumberland sausage hot-pot with black pudding alongside more exotic dishes ranging from rogan josh to spicy Cajun burgers. Vegetarians might be offered mushroom and chestnut pie; fish-eaters could try grilled swordfish steaks. Sunday lunch is a major event, and the pub is renowned for its cheeseboard. Sweets are gargantuan. Real ales from Marstons.

Car-park • Wheelchair access • Access, Amex, Visa

'Wheelchair access' indicates that, according to the proprietor, entrances are at least 33 inches wide, passages 4 feet wide, and that there are a maximum of two steps. If there is access to a WC, we mention it.

Village Bakery ★

☎ LANGWATHBY (076 881) 515

*Open all week 8.30am (9.30 Sun)–5
(2.30 Mon), Jan and Feb Mon to Sat
8.30am–2.30
Closed Sun Christmas to end Feb*

Only high-quality ingredients are
used in the bakery and adjoining
restaurant including organic flour
from the local watermill and home-
grown organic produce. Bread, pies,
scones, croissants, biscuits and cakes
are all baked traditionally in a
specially built wood-burning oven.
The building itself is a fine barn
conversion with a bright conservatory
and old pine furniture. The day starts
with a superb breakfast of either
Inverawe kippers, cinnamon pancake
or a traditional English fry-up. Lunch
includes creamy vegetable pie,
Cumberland sausage with apple sauce
or Lakeland char – a local fish
speciality. A set afternoon tea,
quiches, pasties, rich fruit cake and
gingerbread take care of the gaps.

*No smoking • Wheelchair access •
Access, Visa*

Penrith   map 10

In Clover

Poets Walk
☎ PENRITH (0768) 67474

*Open Mon to Sat 9am–5 (2 Wed)
Closed Sun*

A self-service wholefood café in a
paved shopping walkway off Penrith's
main thoroughfare. The modern
surroundings are stark and functional
but there is a decent selection of
freshly cooked dishes: tomato-based
soups with good wholemeal rolls,

vegetable and red wine moussaka,
Stilton and watercress quiche, and
coffee fudge pudding give an idea of
the daily changing menu.

No smoking • Wheelchair access

Ravenstonedale   map 10

Black Swan

☎ NEWBIGGIN-ON-LUNE (058 73)
204

Open all week 11–2, 6–9

A riverside Victorian village inn set
among the south Cumbrian fells.
Gleaming copper-topped tables, a
comfortable lounge bar and open
fires create a warm atmosphere. Food
and drinks are offered briskly but not
hurriedly and include soup,
sandwiches and ploughman's as well
as steak and kidney pie and gammon
and egg. Treacle tart to finish.

*No smoking in dining-room • No
children under 14 in bar • Garden •
Car-park • Wheelchair access, also WC
• Amex, Visa*

Seatoller   map 9

Yew Tree

☎ BORROWDALE (076 87) 77634

On B5289 at foot of Honister Pass

*Open Tue to Sun noon–2.30 (3 Sat and
Sun), 6–9.30 (exc Fri L)
Closed Mon*

Set in a spectacular, remote location,
the Yew Tree, two converted
seventeenth-century cottages, makes
a marvellous detour. The snack lunch

menu is good value, with well-made soup, home-boiled Cumberland ham in a salad or in an omelette, game pie and filled baguettes. Hot gingerbread or Cumberland rum nicky feature among irresistible desserts. There are more expensive dinners.

Garden • Wheelchair access, also WC • Access, Visa

Skelwith Bridge   map 10

Chesters

Kirkstone Galleries
☎ AMBLESIDE (053 94) 32553

Open all week 10am–6 (5 winter)
Closed 3 days Christmas and 1 week Jan

On either side of Chesters are galleries displaying everything imaginable for sale in Kirkstone slate, and the self-service café echoes the theme with slate-topped tables, floors and terraces. Throughout the day there is a mouth-watering display of home-baked cakes and, at lunchtime, good soups, filled rolls, ploughman's, vegetarian lasagne and crisp salads.

Car-park • Wheelchair access

Skinburness   map 9

Skinburness Hotel
☎ SILLOTH (069 73) 32332

Open all week noon–2, 7–9.30

Splendid views across the Solway Firth to the Scottish hills inspire lunchtime appetites. Bar meals come in large helpings – safe standard dishes such as gammon steak with fried egg, chicken, ham and leek pie,

and steak and kidney pie. Chips are praised and there are sandwiches or cold meats and salad for a lighter meal.

Garden • Car-park • Wheelchair access, also WC • Access, Amex, Diners, Visa

Troutbeck   map 10

Mortal Man ⓦ
☎ AMBLESIDE (053 94) 33193

Open all week noon–1.45, 6.30–8.45 (exc Mon D)
Closed mid-Nov to mid-Feb

A low-beamed ceiling, large coal fire, relaxing atmosphere and fine valley views make this well-run inn a pleasure to visit. The plain, satisfying and very popular food fits in with the rustic image. Venison pie, steak and kidney pudding, Cumberland sausage and apple sauce, and mussels cooked with vegetables set the standard.

Garden • Car-park • Wheelchair access

Ullswater   map 10

Sharrow Bay ★

Lake Ullswater
☎ POOLEY BRIDGE (076 84) 86301

2m from Pooley Bridge on E side of lake, signposted Howtown and Martindale

Open all week 4–4.30pm (booking essential)
Closed end Nov to early Mar

Afternoon tea at Sharrow Bay is a memorable way of spending £8.50. It is, after all, fitting that Britain's first country-house hotel, the natural heir to the Edwardian country house, should serve such a magnificent, old-fashioned spread. Bread and butter, toast, wholemeal and fruit scones with home-made preserves and, of course, thick cream, finger sandwiches, freshly baked biscuits and cakes arrive elegantly piled on several trays and overflow from the low tables in the deeply comfortable lounge. Your choice of loose-leaf tea is replenished without request. Service is discreet without being stuffy, for Sharrow has never been pretentious, just charming.

No smoking in restaurant • No children under 13 • Garden • Car-park • Wheelchair access, also WC

Ulverston   map 7

Bay Horse Inn

Canal Foot
☎ ULVERSTON (022 95) 3972

Open Tue to Sun noon–2, Jan and Feb only 7–9
Closed Mon

The marvellous view across Morecambe Bay is boosted by the Bay Horse's excellent lunchtime bar food. Soup could be thick, satisfying mushroom and apple, or there is Cumbrian air-dried ham with melon and a damson tartlet. Cumberland sausage comes with onion and red pepper marmalade and there is a meat and potato pie. Filled home-made baps make a light snack.

Garden • Car-park • Wheelchair access, also WC • Access, Visa

Windermere   map 10

Miller Howe

Rayrigg Road
☎ WINDERMERE (096 62) 2536

Open all week 3–5pm
Closed Dec to Mar

Afternoon tea at Miller Howe is served against a breathtaking view of Lake Windermere from the terrace, conservatory or very comfortable lounge. The tea will probably take your breath away too – a laden tray of little sandwiches, tea-breads, light scones, jam and cream, and lovely cakes. Service is so discreet that it hardly feels like a hotel.

No children under 12 • Car-park • Access, Amex, Diners, Visa

Miller Howe Kaff

Lakeland Plastics Shop, Alexandra Buildings
☎ WINDERMERE (096 62) 6732

Open Mon to Sat 10.30am–4
Closed Sun

A bright and airy café, an offshoot of the celebrated Miller Howe Hotel. The menu gives a good indication of John Tovey's distinctive style, but at budget prices. Chicken and venison terrine, carrot and lentil soup, cod coated in savoury breadcrumbs, sticky toffee pudding show the range. When busy, the otherwise friendly service tends to be overwhelmed.

No smoking • Car-park • Wheelchair access, also WC

Ashbourne map 7

Gingerbread Shop

26 St John Street
☎ ASHBOURNE **(0335) 43227**

Open Mon to Sat (Sun summer)
8.30am–5
Closed Sun winter, Christmas Day and
Boxing Day

A bakery founded in 1805 and home to small, rectangular, crisp and legendary gingerbread. It also produces superb cakes, tarts and gâteaux, and is an excellent place for a good-value breakfast of bacon, eggs, tomatoes and *three* sausages. For lunch expect gammon and pineapple, burgers, jacket potatoes, salads and sandwiches. It is good to find somewhere that is not afraid to serve gammon and pineapple.

Unlicensed • Wheelchair access

Market Fish and Chips

7 Market Place
☎ ASHBOURNE **(0335) 44780**

Open all week noon–1.45 (exc Sun), 5–8

A tiny fish and chip shop in a 600-year-old building in Ashbourne's market place. Ten customers would be a crush but service is quick. Most eat in their car if the dining-room is closed. The fish is fresh, the batter crisp and the chips excellent. Proper mushy peas too, sage green and stodgy, not at all the bright green bullets normally served elsewhere.

Unlicensed No smoking

Bakewell map 7

Aitch's Wine Bar

4 Buxton Road
☎ BAKEWELL **(0629) 813895**

Open Mon to Sat noon–2, 7–10 (10.30
Fri and Sat)
Closed Sun, Christmas Day, Boxing Day
and New Year's Day

Plants on the windowsills, beamed ceilings and a spiral staircase set the scene in this warm, spacious wine bar. The menu globetrots through meze with pitta bread, boeuf bourguignonne, spare ribs and enchiladas, backed up by equally enticing specials. Spicy tandoori lamb is served with a cooling fruit raita; chicken lasagne has a sauce thickened with ground almonds. Most dishes come with appetising fresh salads. Sweets are not a strong point. Drinkable wines by the glass.

No children after 8.30pm • Wheelchair
access, also WC • Access, Visa

Green Apple

Diamond Court, Water Street
☎ BAKEWELL **(0629) 814404**

Open all week noon–2 (exc Sun winter),
Wed to Sat D 7–9.30
Closed 3rd week Jan to 2nd week Feb

An attractive, flower-decked restaurant, made up of several cottages knocked together, with a positive no-smoking policy and a laudable use of organic vegetables where possible. The good-value lunch is simple, offering well-prepared, well-flavoured lamb casserole, hazelnut and vegetable loaf, a quiche or various salads and good puddings. Expensive evening meals.

Licensed, but you may bring your own: corkage £2 • No smoking • Garden • Wheelchair access • Access, Diners, Visa

Birchover   map 7

Druid Inn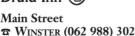

Main Street
☎ WINSTER (062 988) 302

Open all week noon–2, 7–9
Closed Christmas Day

Despite its remote setting, well off the beaten track in the White Peak area near Stanton Moor, this creeper-covered pub is remarkably busy. Food is the main attraction, and a vast menu chalked up on blackboards spans the globe. Moussaka and spaghetti bolognese line up alongside Turkish lamb with apricots, jambalaya, Chinese vegetables in sweet-and-sour sauce, and pork chop with apple and French mustard. Mussels are served with chilli and tomato sauce or put into a pie with steak; local Haddon trout gets a lemon and almond stuffing, and a massive saddle of lamb is glazed with honey sauce. Portions are geared to healthy appetites. The atmosphere bustles and there is no standing on ceremony. Marstons Pedigree on hand pump; basic pub wines.

No children after 8pm • Car-park • Wheelchair access • Access, Amex, Visa

The factual details under each eating-place are based on information supplied by the restaurateur.

Buxton   map 7

Dandelion Days

5 Bridge Street
☎ BUXTON (0298) 22843

Open Apr to Oct all week 10.30am–8, Fri and Sat D 7.30–10, Nov to Mar Tue to Sun 10.30am (noon Sun)–6 Closed Christmas Day, Boxing Day and New Year's Day

A 'wholefood' café/restaurant and shop combined, with daytime counter service and evening waiter service. Among the five main course options there is a curry, which is often the most tasty item – sometimes it is aubergine, usually served with basmati rice. Otherwise there are lots of baked vegetables (mushrooms, fennel and potatoes) and a few veggie pies and pizzas. Desserts are good.

No smoking

Castleton   map 7

Rose Cottage Café

☎ HOPE VALLEY (0433) 20472

Open all week 10am–5.30 Closed Christmas Eve, Christmas Day and all Jan

An attractive and popular cottage café, rustic in style and generous with the honestly cooked food. Home-made minced beef pie, toasted sandwiches, jacket potatoes and assorted home-baked cakes ranging from plain scones to a gooey chocolate cake provide something for all tastes. Good-quality ingredients are used. There is a pretty back garden for summer use.

Unlicensed • Garden • Wheelchair access

Chisworth map 7

Woodheys Farm

nr Hyde
☎ GLOSSOP (0457) 852704

On A626 between Marple and Glossop

Open Tue to Sun noon–2, 7–9.30 (exc Sun D)
Closed Mon

The view from this restaurant perched high above the Etherow Valley is spectacular, and is worth a visit. Lunch is good value with a fixed weekday two-course menu for £7.50. This takes in a roast, steak and dumplings or cold meats and salad. There is a three-course lunch on Saturday (£8.25) and Sunday (£9.50).

Garden • Car-park • Wheelchair access, also WC • Access, Diners, Visa

Derby map 7

Bennetts Coffee Shop

8 Irongate
☎ DERBY (0332) 44261

Open Mon to Sat 8.30am–4.30
Closed Sun

A coffee-shop offering solace and reasonably good food to shoppers in a traditional department store. Tables are arranged on balconies around an elegant staircase, and main courses are under £3. Apart from soup and sandwiches you could try good lasagne, seafood gratin, chicken curry and beef, kidney and onion pie. There is an admirable cake selection.

Unlicensed • No-smoking area • Wheelchair access • Access, Amex, Visa

Hathersage map 7

Longland's Eating House

Main Road
☎ HOPE VALLEY (0433) 51978

Open Tue to Sun 11am (9am Sat and Sun)–5 (5.30 Fri and Sat, 6 Sun), Fri and Sat D 6.45–9.15
Closed Mon

Walkers and climbers can check the weather forecast from a blackboard outside this enterprising restaurant. On the ground floor is an outdoor equipment shop; upstairs a modest dining-room with a balcony. During the day, Longland's is a café serving anything from sustaining chip butties and bowls of home-made soup to classic Bakewell tarts. In the evening it becomes a restaurant with an international menu: vegetable bhajias come with a blue cheese dip; steak teriyaki can be eaten with jacket potato, and vegetarians might opt for spicy aubergine bake. Sweets and cakes are a high point. Drink real fresh orange juice, herb tea or a glass of wine.

No smoking • Car-park • Access, Visa

Hope map 7

Hopechest

8 Castleton Road
☎ HOPE VALLEY (0433) 20072

Open Tue to Sat 9.15am–5
Closed Mon and Sun

An apt name for a village store – a treasure chest packed with high-quality goods in art, craft, gifts and foods. The back coffee-room is an attractive gem. The menu is small and all dishes home-made: fresh vegetable soup, a choice of five quiches, baked ham and pâté. A coffee gâteau and a brandy cake represent some sound home-baking.

No smoking • Garden • Wheelchair access • Access, Visa

Litton   map 7

Red Lion Inn

☎ TIDESWELL (0298) 871458

Off B6049 nr Tideswell

Open Sat and Sun L noon–1, Tue to Sat D 7–8.45
Closed Mon

A friendly, eighteenth-century hostelry serving unpretentious, down-to-earth food in a workmanlike way. There are no frills in presentation or table setting – tables are very close-packed – but the food is hearty, despite quantity defeating quality at times. Well-flavoured soup with great hunks of bread, venison pie, roast beef, Barnsley chop and heaped vegetables set the tone.

Wheelchair access, also WC • Access, Amex, Diners, Visa

Over Haddon   map 7

Lathkil Hotel

☎ BAKEWELL (0629) 812501

2m SW of Bakewell on B5055

Open all week noon–2, 7–8.45 (exc Sun D)

If you follow the footpath to the east of this robust country pub you can see the River Lathkill far below, flowing over a series of weirs. Returning to the pub, there is a place in the lobby to leave muddy boots. Further on, to the right, is a room with a fireplace (and a fire) and comfortable chairs; to the left, a spacious dining-room. At lunchtime, the bar serves admirable home-made soup, steak and kidney pie and lamb curry. In the evening, the restaurant comes into its own with predominantly local goodies: Lathkill trout and pheasant and chicken 'Hartington' (stuffed with leeks and served with Stilton sauce).

No-smoking area • No children under 14 • Family-room at lunchtime • Car-park • Access, Diners, Visa

DEVON

Barnstaple
map 1

Heavens Above

4 Bear Street
☎ BARNSTAPLE (0271) 77960

Open Mon to Sat 10am–6
Closed Sun, 10 days Christmas and
bank hols

Straightforward home-cooked
vegetarian food is served in this
upstairs café decorated with flowers
and paintings. At lunchtime the
familiar array of nut rissoles, vege-
burgers, jacket potatoes and salads is
augmented by a daily special such as
lentil and spinach lasagne or chestnut
casserole with 'cheesy nuggets'.
Sweets range from apple crumble to
ice-creams. Tea and cakes are the
mainstays in the morning and
afternoon. Organic ingredients are
used when possible.

No-smoking area

Lynwood House

Bishop Tawton Road
☎ BARNSTAPLE (0271) 43695

Open all week noon–2 (exc Sun), 7–10

The lighter menu offered by the
Roberts at their pleasant restaurant-
with-rooms gives an inexpensive
insight into the kitchen's style. Fish
soup or cheese beignets could be
followed by home-made sausages
with a piquant sauce or a pasta with
prawns and mussels in a langoustine
sauce – or maybe just a dish of
mussels. Those with smaller appetites
might enjoy a light, fluffy omelette.

No-smoking area • Car-park •
Wheelchair access, also WC • Access,
Visa

Bideford
map 1

Sloops

Bridge Street
☎ BIDEFORD (0237) 471796

Open Tue to Sat 10.30–2, 6.30–9
Closed Sun and Mon

Imaginative cooking and friendly
service are the hallmarks here. What
may be missing in consistency is
redeemed by inspiration: try pears
and Stilton grilled on toast or
bananas wrapped in bacon. The
lunch menu is conventional, featuring
lamb burgers and a fisherman's pie
made with cockles. In the evening
you can try lamb cutlets grilled with
goats'-milk cheese – well-executed
and popular – and pork with fennel
and coriander. The desserts are less
impressive, but fresh local produce is
a bonus. Be sure to arrive before last
orders at 9pm.

No smoking in dining area • No children
under 14 Fri or Sat pm • Wheelchair
access • Access, Visa

Bolham
map 1

Knightshayes

Knightshayes Court
☎ TIVERTON (0884) 259416

Open all week noon–5.30
Closed seasonally

The National Trust bills itself as a charity preserving the past for the future and certainly the restaurants on its premises in Devon, by strict adherence to local produce and traditional recipes, are doing just that. Knightshayes Court is no exception: traditional farmhouse cheese from Hawkridge Farmhouse Produce, Crediton, real ice-cream from Salcombe Dairy, local draught cider, English wine from Tiverton and locally made Devon pâté feature strongly on a simple, but well-executed menu. Home-baking produces bread as well as scones and cakes for the set afternoon teas. Good soups and a choice of hot dishes for lunch.

No smoking • Garden • Car-park • Wheelchair access, also WC • Access, Amex, Visa

Branscombe
map 1

Masons Arms ⊚

☎ BRANSCOMBE (029 780) 300

Open all week noon–2, 7–9

This creeper-clad fourteenth-century inn stands in the heart of one of Devon's most beautiful unspoilt villages. Inside are flagstoned floors, beams and a huge open fire (over which the spit roast is cooked on some weekdays in winter). Standards, which have flagged in the past few years, are being revived by a new regime and bar food featuring traditional English dishes is worth noting.

No children in bar • Car-park • Wheelchair access, also WC • Access, Visa

Broad Clyst
map 1

Killerton

Killerton House
☎ EXETER (0392) 881345

Open all week exc Tue 11am–5.30 (4 winter)
Closed Tue and 1 week Christmas

Famous for its beautiful hillside garden and the Pauline de Bush costume collection, Killerton House has a great deal to offer. This includes a splendid café which, like Knightshayes Court, Bolham (see entry), makes use of some of the best Devon produce, the suppliers of which are listed on the back of the menu. English wine comes from the Killerton estate and cakes and bread are baked on the premises. Steak and kidney pie followed by Dolbury pudding (steamed fruit pudding with fruit sauce) is a favourite lunch choice although lighter alternatives – smoked mackerel quiche or chicken and ham salad – are available. Devon clotted cream teas are very popular.

No smoking • Garden • Wheelchair access, also WC • Access, Amex, Visa

Dartington   map 1

Cranks

Dartington Cider Press Centre
☎ TOTNES (0803) 862388

Open Mon to Sat 10am–5

Thirty years ago, Cranks may have been cranky, but nowadays its vegetarian wholefood menu is a sane part of British mainstream eating-out. The restaurant services The Cider Press, a shopping centre that presents the commercial face of Dartington Hall. Crowds in the summer and at Christmas are thick, and queues at the assisted self-service counter can be lengthy – though never bad tempered. The quality of the materials is assured even if the cooking may be on the heavy side. A full range of cakes, yoghurts, snacks, drinks and good coffee is on offer as well as daily extras chalked up on a board. Soups are always restoring, bread is still inimitably Cranks.

No smoking • Garden • Car-park • Wheelchair access, also WC

Dartmouth   map 1

Cherub

11 Higher Street
☎ DARTMOUTH (0803) 832571

Open all week noon–2, 7–10

A fine timber-framed pub dating from 1380 and probably the oldest building in Dartmouth. The Hills are new owners, but they are maintaining the Cherub's wide reputation for sound, inexpensive bar food. Seafood pasta, a fisherman's lunch of hot smoked mackerel fillet, and avocado pear with local crab all come with

hunks of granary bread. Finish with treacle tart.

No children in bar • Access, Visa

Doddiscombsleigh   map 1

Nobody Inn

☎ CHRISTOW (0647) 52394

Off B3193 3m from Devon and Exeter Racecourse at Haldon Hill

Open all week L noon–2, Tue to Sat D 7.30–9.15

It is worth the effort to seek out this splendid old inn which dates, in parts, from the fifteenth century. The two decent-sized bars come complete with beams and walls stained a golden brown with age. Bar food includes a hearty Nobody soup, a range of six perfectly kept Devon cheeses served with locally baked bread and a home-made spiced bread pudding with local clotted cream.

No children under 14 • Garden • Car-park • Wheelchair access • Access, Visa

East Budleigh   map 1

Grasshoppers

16 High Street
☎ BUDLEIGH SALTERTON (039 54) 2774

Open all week 10am (2.30pm Sun)–5.30
Closed Christmas Day and Boxing Day, 1st week May and 2 weeks Nov

The gregarious Peggy Cooke dispenses tea, cakes, savouries and stories to visitors to her tiny gift- and tea-shop in the heart of this pretty Devon village. Everything is home-made, including the jam to go with the scones and thick clotted cream for tea. Soup, sandwiches, jacket potatoes, salads and ploughman's are available all day. Try the Devonshire apple cake.

Unlicensed • No smoking

Eggesford   map 1

Gardens Restaurant

Eggesford Garden Centre
☎ CHULMLEIGH **(0769) 80250**

Just off A377 Exeter–Barnstaple road at Eggesford

Open all week 10am–6 (5 winter)

A family-run restaurant serving good food in a garden centre. At lunchtime, help yourself to salads and choose from pies such as sausage, egg and onion, steak and kidney or cheese, onion and tomato, as well as pizzas, quiches and jacket potatoes. Wines, lager and cider can be ordered with lunch. Scones and home-baked cakes are served with tea or coffee.

No smoking • Garden • Car-park • Wheelchair access, also WC • Access, Visa

'Wheelchair access' indicates that, according to the proprietor, entrances are at least 33 inches wide, passages 4 feet wide, and that there are a maximum of two steps. If there is access to a WC, we mention it.

Exeter   map 1

Pizza Piazza

44–5 Queen's Street
☎ EXETER **(0392) 77269**

Open all week 11am–11.30pm

A branch of one of the best pizza chains in the UK. See London entry.

Access, Visa

Kingsteignton   map 1

Old Rydon Inn

Rydon Road
☎ NEWTON ABBOT **(0626) 54626**

From A380 take Kingsteignton/ Teignmouth turnoff, then 1st right into Longford Lane, then Rydon Road at bottom of hill

Open all week noon–2, 7–10
Closed Christmas Day

The Hrubys' grade 2 listed former farmhouse dates from the seventeenth century and the charming thatched pub is housed in the former stables and the old cider loft above. A lovely walled garden is a big summer attraction for eating out and it is for food that the Old Rydon is known. Bar food is adventurously eclectic with Indonesian nasi goreng, Chinese-style prawns and tandoori chicken comfortably sharing the menu with butter-bean and vegetable gratiné, farmhouse ham and rabbit and pigeon hot-pot, all carefully cooked. Desserts are served with rich clotted cream.

No-smoking area • Garden • Car-park • Access, Amex, Diners, Visa

Lifton
map 1

Arundell Arms

☎ LIFTON (056 684) 666

Open all week noon–2.30
Closed 4–5 days Christmas

A creeper-clad inn whose extensions
and modernisations have not
diminished its charm or its popularity
with anglers. Light lunches served in
the hotel bar are imaginative and well
presented. There is toasted Stilton
cheese on walnut bread, a
ploughman's with a trio of local
farmhouse cheeses, a casserole of
Teignmouth mussels or a down-to-
earth mixed grill.

Garden and family-room • Car-park •
Wheelchair access, also WC • Access,
Amex, Diners, Visa

Lustleigh
map 1

Primrose Cottage ★

☎ LUSTLEIGH (064 77) 365

Open all week 10am–5.30
Closed 3 weeks Christmas and Mon to
Fri Dec to Feb

This yellow thatched cottage, set in
an idyllic Dartmoor village, is the
stuff of picture postcards, the food is
the stuff of dreams. The antique-
crammed tea-room offers the best in
home baking, displayed on a lace-
hung table. Eclairs, meringues, fruit
cake, buttery shortbread, the lightest
of scones and the richest of chocolate
cake make a mouthwatering choice.
Dragging yourself away from the
cakes, the lunch menu offers
substantial, inventive dishes from
bacon, tomato and red pepper flan to

ham, asparagus and cream cheese
bake with caraway sauce, all served
with new potatoes and salads. Cheese
on toast and sandwiches are lighter,
more traditional tea-room offerings.

No smoking • Garden • Wheelchair
access

Modbury
map 1

Modbury Pippin

35 Church Street
☎ MODBURY (0548) 830765

Open Mon to Sat noon–2, 7–9.30 (exc
Mon winter)
Closed Sun, Jan and Mon winter

A small, family-run restaurant serving
the local community well. Fresh local
produce, including fish, is cooked in a
careful, homely manner and offered
at reasonable prices. Lunch includes
satisfying home-made soup, fluffy
omelettes, a richly flavoured lamb
casserole, and excellent chips. The set
dinner at £10.90 is good value.

No children under 5 • Wheelchair access
• Access, Amex, Diners, Visa

Moretonhampstead map 1

White Hart

The Square
☎ MORETONHAMPSTEAD (0647)
40406

Open all week 11.30–2.30, 6–8.30

A solid, well-run hotel on the edge of
Dartmoor offering good-value bar
meals. Home-made pasty and
country fried potatoes, plus locally
made ice-cream, costs just under £5.

Steak and kidney pie and treacle tart with Devon clotted cream are popular specialities while lesser appetites would be satisfied with a salad of home-cooked ham. Restaurant meals are more expensive.

No children in bar • Family-room • Car-park • Wheelchair access • Access, Amex, Diners, Visa

Peter Tavy   map 1

Peter Tavy Inn
☎ MARY TAVY (0822) 810 348

Open all week noon–2.15, 7–9.45

An ancient building, home to stonemasons and blacksmiths before it evolved into the village inn. The imaginative bar menu has a healthy, wholefood emphasis which, combined with sound cooking, draws the crowds. Homity pie, butter-bean, leek, sweetcorn and mushroom pie, wholemeal quiche, cauliflower croustade, meat and potato pasty show the range.

No children in bar • Garden and family-room • Car-park • Wheelchair access • Access, Visa

Plymouth   map 1

Clouds

102 Tavistock Place
☎ PLYMOUTH (0752) 262567

Open Mon to Fri L noon–2, Wed to Sat D 7–10
Closed Sun, bank hols and 1 week Christmas

A simple 36-seater basement restaurant serving soundly prepared

food. Lunch is good value, with starters of home-made pâté, tomato salad with Stilton vinaigrette and main courses of fisherman's pie, chicken à la king and beef bourguignonne. Dinner is more expensive.

Access, Amex, Diners, Visa

Training Restaurant

Plymouth College of Further Education, Kings Road, Devonport
☎ PLYMOUTH (0752) 385186

Open Fri breakfast 7.45–2, Mon to Fri L 12.15 (one sitting), Tue to Thur D 7.15 (one sitting)
Closed Sat, Sun and college hols

Catering for a variety of tastes is all part of the training for the students who run this forward-looking restaurant, under strict supervision. If it's Friday, it's the Great English Breakfast, served 7.45am–2pm. If it's Monday lunch or Thursday evening then the menu is vegetarian (four courses £6.50), offering the likes of savoury nut parcels with salad and ratatouille with parsley potatoes as a main course. Otherwise, £8.50 buys a four-course meal (plus coffee) which might include a starter of cheese fritters, a main course of roast Devon chicken with walnut stuffing and honey ice-cream to finish. A coffee-shop operates Monday to Thursday 9.30am–2pm.

No-smoking area • Garden • Car-park • Wheelchair access, also WC • Access, Visa

See the front of the guide for a list of each eating-place given a star for being one of the best found by the Editor during research for this book.

Yang Cheng

30A Western Approach
☎ PLYMOUTH (0752) 660170

Open Tue to Sun noon–2.30 (3 Sun),
6–11
Closed Mon, Christmas Day and
Boxing Day

One of only a handful of Chinese
restaurants away from the main
centres serving authentic old-style
Cantonese dishes. You can build a
decent lunch from a few dim-sum,
such as beef sui mai dumplings,
steamed spare ribs and spring rolls.
Otherwise, choose a one-plate meal
along the lines of roast pork on rice,
dry-fried rice stick with king prawns,
or roast duck and noodles in soup.
Drink tea or Chinese wine.

Access, Visa

South Molton   map 1

Stumbles

East Street
☎ SOUTH MOLTON (076 95) 3683

Open Mon to Sat 12.30–2.15,
7.30–9.30
Closed Sun

A town-centre wine bar which offers
an informal atmosphere and sound
cooking. Provençale-style fish soup,
wild field mushrooms with tomato
and Gruyère sauce, roast rack of lamb
and beef Stroganoff typify the wide-
ranging menu. Stumbles' own
commercial pasta machine makes
fresh pasta daily. There are
newspapers to hand and the service is
friendly and prompt.

Car-park • Wheelchair access • Access,
Visa

Torcross   map 1

Start Bay Inn

☎ KINGSBRIDGE (0548) 580553

Open all week 11.30–2, 6–10 (9.30 Sun
winter)

This inn is the winner of an award for
serving the freshest fish in Britain, so
it is no wonder that people queue up
outside before opening time to get
the pick of the catch. Portions are
generous and prices low, with cod,
haddock and plaice offered in various
sizes, grilled or fried. Popularity
causes delays but simple distractions
are offered by the beach setting.

Family-room • Car-park

Torquay   map 1

Mulberry Room ★

1 Scarborough Road
☎ TORQUAY (0803) 213639

Open Wed to Sun L 12.15–2.30, Sat D
7.30–9.30
Closed Mon and Tue

Everything seems just right at Lesley
Cooper's little café, from the
delightful furnishings to the aroma of
good cooking and the sight of a table
of home-made cakes. A blackboard
features regularly changing dishes of
admirable inventiveness: duck and
orange pancakes, filo chicken and
curd cheese pie. A simpler approach
is seen in fillets of fresh local sole,
pan-fried in butter and olive oil,
while desserts remain truly traditional
– steamed suet pudding, Bramley
apple pie, fruit fools, sticky toffee
pudding. A set-price lunch of three
courses and coffee is a remarkable

£7.50. Open, too, for morning coffee and afternoon teas.

Wheelchair access, also WC

Torrington   map 1

Rebecca's

8 Potacre Street
☎ TORRINGTON (0805) 22113

Open Mon to Sat noon–2 (exc Mon), 7–10
Closed Sun

The simple shop front disguises this light and pretty restaurant once considered a leading light in the area. The current owners are working hard to restore that reputation and the lunch menu is an inexpensive way of sampling their style. Whether it is just soup and sandwiches or fish pie, beef goulash or macaroni cheese you will find the cooking sound. Dinners are more expensive.

No-smoking area • Wheelchair access, also WC • Access, Visa

Totnes   map 1

Willow Wholefood Vegetarian

87 High Street
☎ TOTNES (0803) 862605

Open Mon to Sat noon–2.30, 6.30–9.30 (exc Mon D)
Closed Sun and 2 weeks Christmas

'An ethically run business with an ethnic atmosphere' is how the owners describe this easy-going wholefood/ vegetarian restaurant. Re-cycling and 'green' ideology set the tone of the place. The menu spells out exactly which ingredients are organic, from the wholemeal flour used for the bread and the milk in the ice-cream, to the celery in the celery and cashew nut soup and the mushrooms in the garlicky mushroom crumble. The kitchen seeks influence from around the world for dishes such as savoury tofu flan, Algerian couscous and Mexican frijoles con salsa. Wednesday night is vegetarian curry night. Organic wines and beers.

No smoking • Garden • Wheelchair access

Weare Giffard   map 1

Cyder Presse

☎ BIDEFORD (0237) 475640

Open Tue to Sun 12.30–1.45, 7–9.45
Closed Mon

A small, simple, whitewashed country pub with well-priced bar food drawing the crowds. The menu is overlong and slow-cooked dishes such as olde English pork with apricots tend to have the edge over deep-fried items. Other praiseworthy dishes include a vivid carrot soup, which is thick and well flavoured, Cumberland ham and good, fresh vegetables.

No children under 8 • Garden • Car-park • Wheelchair access • Access, Visa

Ansty map 2

Fox

nr Dorchester
☎ MILTON ABBAS (0258) 880328

Open all week noon–2, 7–10

A simple, friendly family pub which has a noted carvery. The choice could be between roast beef with Yorkshire pudding and roast pork with apple sauce; both are above average. The cold carvery can also be tempting. Start with either home-made soup or pâté and finish with fruit or pineapple crumble. Salads have been a let-down. Drink local Ansty ale.

No-smoking area • Garden and family-room • Car-park • Access, Amex, Visa

Askerwell map 2

Spyway Inn

☎ Powerstock (030 885) 250

Open all week noon–2, 6.45–9.15

A homely, relaxed and comfortable village pub, very popular with locals, anglers (who line their waders up outside) and tourists. Get there early for food, which is as unpretentious as the pub – no frills, just a good range of ploughman's, hot sausages and tomato pickle, home-cooked ham and sweet pickle, roast chicken and good chips or a three-egg omelette.

No children in bar • Garden • Wheelchair access • Access, Visa

Bournemouth map 2

Chez Fred

10 Seamoor Road, Westbourne
☎ BOURNEMOUTH (0202) 761023

Open Mon to Sat 11.30–1.45, 5–9.30
Closed Sun

A fish and chip shop using top-quality fresh fish fried in a dry, crisp batter and served on warm plates; cod, haddock and plaice are supplemented by a catch of the day. A microwave is much in evidence for heating pies and puddings, so have the apple pie made by Fred's aunt cold, and stick to the genuinely fried food cooked to order. There is also a children's menu.

No smoking • Wheelchair access

Coriander

14 Richmond Hill
☎ BOURNEMOUTH (0202) 552202

Open Mon to Sat L noon–2.30, all week D 6–10.30 (11 Fri and Sat)
Closed Christmas Day and Boxing Day

Well-meaning, fairly popular and as Mexican as you can get in Bournemouth. It is easy to forgive the home-spun décor: bright, efficient service means less time to examine the sombreros in detail. Under 'Gringo food' there is breaded plaice and steak, but experiment with the enchiladas selection. (Enchiladas are explained as flour tortillas rolled around a variety of fillings, baked with a tomato-based sauce and topped with cheese.) 'Peel and eat prawns' are exceptionally good value. By listing Mexican Riesling they sell even more Mexican beer.

No-smoking area • Wheelchair access • Access, Visa

Henry's Wholefood

6 Lansdowne Road
☎ BOURNEMOUTH (0202) 297887

Open Mon to Sat 11.30–2, 6–10 (exc Mon D)
Closed Sun

A friendly, informal atmosphere pervades this lively vegetarian/vegan restaurant and organic cellar wine bar. Quality ingredients make up the regularly changing dishes – comforting soups such as creamy parsnip, cheesy aubergine and red-bean bake, walnut and vegetable lasagne. They make their own bread and can offer gluten- and sugar-free dishes.

No-smoking area • Family-room in wine-bar • Wheelchair access

Pizza Piazza

1 Yelverton Road
☎ BOURNEMOUTH (0202) 552412

Open all week 11am–11.30pm

A branch of one of the best pizza chains in the UK. See London entry.

Access, Visa

All details are as accurate as possible at the time of going to press, but chefs and owners often change, and it is wise to check by telephone before making a special journey.

Bridport   map 2

George Hotel

4 South Street
☎ BRIDPORT (0308) 23187

Open all week noon–2.30 (exc Sun), 7–9.30

There is nothing old-fashioned about the George, apart from its classical Georgian façade and cask-conditioned beers on handpump. The atmosphere is lively, and John Mander and his staff are relaxed but attentive. Sound, well-cooked bar food includes fresh local fish such as whole grilled plaice, duck and bacon pie, Welsh rarebit, bubble and squeak and a good selection of cheeses.

No children under 14 in main bar • Family-room • Wheelchair access

Riverside

West Bay
☎ BRIDPORT (0308) 22011

Open all week July and Aug 10.30–3, 6–8, Tue to Sun Mar to June and Sept to Oct 10.30–3, 6–8 (exc Sun D)
Closed Mon Mar to June and Sept to Oct, and all week Nov to early Mar exc some weekends and school Christmas hols

An unpretentious seaside restaurant where the food, locally caught fresh fish, comes first. According to the season, the likes of grilled red mullet, John Dory or sole are offered side by side with simple fish and chips, and skate in black butter or hake provençale. Grills and meat dishes are available too. Ideal for children.

No cigars/pipes • Garden • Wheelchair access, also WC • Acces, Visa

Chedington   map 2

Winyard's Gap

☎ CORSCOMBE (093 589) 244

On A356 Crewkerne–Dorchester road

Open all week noon–1.45, 7–9.30

Thomas Hardy was so inspired by the spectacular view here that he wrote the poem 'At Winyard's Gap' to describe it. Today's visitors to this ancient inn can still appreciate the unspoilt setting. Bar food includes some splendid deep-filled pies of beef and game or steak, oysters and Guinness, home-made soups, Bridport smoked trout and local ham.

Garden and family-room • Car-park

Corscombe   map 2

Fox

☎ CORSCOMBE (093 589) 330

Open all week noon–2, 7–9

'Country cooking, no chips, no microwaves' states the sign outside. Indeed, cooking is done on the Aga and the food offered fits the style of this tiny, rural pub full of fox hunting memorabilia. There is excellent leek and potato soup with home-made bread, home cooked ham, gammon steak, beef stew, cauliflower cheese and very good puddings.

No children under 14 • Garden • Car-park

See the back of the guide for an index of eating-places and an index of locations.

Dorchester   map 2

Potter In

19 Durngate Street
☎ DORCHESTER (0305) 68649

Open Mon to Sat 10am–5
Closed Sun, Christmas Day and bank hols

Rosalind Armstrong does the baking in this pine-furnished wholefood café. Through the day there are scones and cakes to have with tea or coffee. Lunch brings more substantial dishes ranging from lamb hot-pot with broccoli to mushroom pancakes. Quiches, pizzas, jacket potatoes and excellent fresh salads complete the picture. Pleasant service by local women.

No smoking • Garden • Wheelchair access • Access, Visa

Plush   map 2

Brace of Pheasants

☎ PIDDLETRENTHIDE (030 04) 357

Open all week noon–2, 7–9.30

A country pub with a low-beamed bar, well patronised by locals. Very good bar food from an extensive menu includes a home-made leek and root ginger soup, local pork pie, liver and bacon and steak and kidney pie. Salads and ploughman's are available and there is a superb bread-and-butter pudding for dessert.

No smoking in restaurant • Garden and family-room • Car-park • Access, Visa

Powerstock   map 2

Three Horseshoes

☎ POWERSTOCK (030 885) 328

Open all week noon–2, 7–10

A secluded stone and thatch pub with highly polished old tables and paintings for sale on the walls. Fish is something of a speciality but can be quite expensive. Moules marinière, grilled sardines and fish pie are reasonably priced as is rabbit casserole and carbonnade of beef. Sticky toffee pudding and treacle tart for dessert.

No-smoking area • Garden • Car-park • Wheelchair access • Access, Amex, Diners, Visa

Tarrant Monkton   map 2

Langton Arms

☎ TARRANT HINTON (025 889) 225

Open Mon to Sat 11.30–2.10, 6–10.30, Sun noon–2.30, 7–10
Closed Christmas Day

A delightful thatched village pub in Hardy country. Standard bar food includes ploughman's, salmon mousse, steak and kidney pudding, shepherd's pie and lasagne backed up by blackboard specials. Speciality theme nights include Chinese on Thursdays and pizzas every Tuesday and Friday.

Garden • Car-park • Wheelchair access, also WC • Access, Amex, Diners, Visa

West Bexington   map 2

Manor Hotel

Beach Road
☎ BURTON BRADSTOCK (0308) 897616

Open all week noon–2, 6.30–10

An old manor house with some fine Jacobean carved panelling in the hall and a relaxing cellar bar where a log fire and horsey artefacts create a cosy atmosphere. Bar food includes good home-made soup, sandwiches, ploughman's, plenty of fresh fish, and steak and kidney pie. Puddings, such as poached whole pears and lemon mousse, are well made. There is a leafy no-smoking conservatory. Credit cards can only be used for bills over £15.

No-smoking area • Car-park • Garden • Access, Amex, Diners, Visa (all only over £15)

West Lulworth   map 2

Castle

Main Road
☎ WEST LULWORTH (092 941) 311

Open all week noon–2.30, 7.30–9.30

A trim, thatched pub with low-beamed ceilings and flagstone floors. The good food on offer includes filled rolls, salads and jacket potatoes, but the dishes to go for are the casseroles: rabbit in mustard sauce, hare in madeira sauce, venison or pigeon and bacon. There are good, plump mussels and home-made soup as well. A more expensive restaurant is available.

No-smoking area • Garden • Car-park • Wheelchair access, also WC • Access, Amex, Diners, Visa

---

Weymouth   map 2

Sea Cow

7 Custom House Quay
☎ WEYMOUTH (0305) 783524

Open all week noon–2, 7.15–10.15 (exc Sun D Oct to May)

A well-established harbourside bistro offering good-value lunches. Grilled sardines with garlic mayonnaise and jacket potatoes make simple snacks while fish and chips, local skate with capers and lemon butter, lamb in onion gravy are more substantial main courses. Finish with bread-and-butter pudding. More expensive evening meals are available.

No-smoking area • Wheelchair access, also WC • Access, Visa

You will find report forms (write a letter if you prefer) at the back of the book so that you can tell us about your experiences of going *Out to Eat.* We'll put the information to good use when we're compiling the next edition.

★ after an eating-place indicates that it is one of the best found by the Editor during research for this book (see page 14 for a list).

⊛ after an eating-place indicates that it is a pub. The opening and closing times we give only relate to when food is available – the licensing hours may be different.

ⓗ after an eating-place indicates that it is within five miles of the nearest motor-way junction. We give the relevant motorway and junction in the details. Eating-places in cities and large towns, where traffic, parking and route-finding may cause delay, do not have this symbol.

ESSEX

Brentwood   map 5

Pizza Express

4 High Street
☎ BRENTWOOD (0277) 233569

Open all week 11.30am–midnight

Part of the popular chain which is the pick of the pizza bunch. See London entry.

No-smoking area • Access, Amex, Diners, Visa

Burnham-on-Crouch   map 5

Polash

169 Station Road
☎ MALDON (0621) 782233/784930

Open all week noon–2.30, 6–11.30

A popular high-street tandoori restaurant, praised as much for its polite, pleasant, helpful waiters as for its food. Lamb badam pasanda, korai chicken and tandooris, all chosen from the carte, are consistently good. Set meals are around £12 a head for three courses. There is also a branch at 86 West Road, Shoeburyness, Essex.

No-smoking area • Wheelchair access • Access, Amex, Diners, Visa

Chelmsford   map 5

Kings Arms

Main Road, Broomfield
☎ CHELMSFORD (0245) 440258

Open all week noon–2, 6.30 (7 Sun)–9.30 (10 Sat)
Closed Christmas Day and Boxing Day

Robin Moore, formerly of the Eight Bells, Saffron Walden, is making a name for this traditional sixteenth-century pub by providing first-class bar food. Mushrooms baked in double cream and garlic au gratin, tagliatelle with mussels and prawns, duckling with black cherry sauce, al dente vegetables and treacle pudding elicit nothing but praise.

Car-park • Wheelchair access, also WC • Access, Visa

Pizza Express

219 Moulsham Street
☎ CHELMSFORD (0245) 491466

Open all week 11.30am–midnight

Part of the popular chain which is the pick of the pizza bunch. See London entry.

No-smoking area • Access, Amex, Diners, Visa

Clavering
map 5

Cricketers

☎ SAFFRON WALDEN (0799) 550442

Open all week noon–2.30, 7–10.30
Closed Christmas Day and Boxing Day

Crowds flock to this well-loved, old beamed pub with a modern extension. The main attraction is the food, and menus change every month. Full-flavoured crab bisque, crisp-skinned duck with orange sauce and tandoori chicken served with real chips and salad have been recommended. Tiered stands are loaded with home-made cakes and sweets: try the fruity summer pudding. You can eat in the bar or book a table in the restaurant. Traditional beers and reasonably priced wines.

No-smoking area • Family-room • Car-park • Wheelchair access • Access, Visa

Colchester
map 5

Tilly's

33 Crouch Street
☎ COLCHESTER (0206) 572780

Open Mon to Sat 9.30am–8.15 (10.45 Fri and Sat)
Closed Sun, Christmas Day and bank hols

A chintzy café serving a snack-style menu. Breakfasts run 9.30am–11.30am with a choice of croissants and scrambled or poached eggs. For the rest of the day the range of dishes encompasses soup, several varieties of quiche, chilli, moussaka or chicken curry, sandwiches and jacket potatoes.

No-smoking area • Wheelchair access, also WC • Access, Visa

Warehouse Brasserie

Chapel Street
☎ COLCHESTER (0206) 765656

Open Mon to Sat noon–2, 7–10.30
Closed Sun, Christmas Day and bank hols

Go at lunchtime for the best value in this highly popular brasserie, not far from the ABC cinema. The menu comprises a regularly changing and cosmopolitan choice of dishes: lamb tikka kebabs, herring fillets in oatmeal with gooseberry sauce, chargrilled sea trout, savoury stuffed marrow. Sweets are in a similar vein, taking in peach brûlée and iced hazelnut vacherin as well as steamed sponges and cheesecakes. Light main courses such as warm pigeon breast salad will keep the evening bill within limits. House wines by the glass.

Wheelchair access • Access, Visa

Dedham
map 5

Marlborough Head Hotel

Mill Lane
☎ COLCHESTER (0206) 323124

Open all week noon–2, 7–9.30
Closed Christmas Day and Boxing Day

Hearty food for big appetites is the order of the day in this 500-year-old beamed hostelry. Packed sandwiches and nourishing soups are backed up by dishes such as braised lamb and ratatouille, and wild rabbit with mustard sauce. There is always something for vegetarians, such as chestnut and mushroom bake.

Home-made treacle tart elicits particular praise. Wines by the glass. Well-behaved children are welcome in the large family-room.

Garden and family-room • Car-park • Wheelchair access, also WC

Gestingthorpe   map 5

Pheasant

Audley End, nr Halstead
☎ HALSTEAD (0787) 61196

Open Mon to Sat 11.30–2.15, 6.30–9.45, Sun noon–2.15, 7–9.15

One of the few unspoilt pubs in the area, with a country feel to the simple furnishings and a warm welcome. Satisfying bar food includes prawn, apple and celery salad, barbecued spare ribs, home-made soups, fisherman's pie and devilled chicken accompanied by excellent vegetables. Spotted dick with custard makes an old-fashioned finish.

Garden • Wheelchair access, also WC

Gosfield   map 5

Green Man

☎ HALSTEAD (0787) 472746

On A1017 4m NE of Braintree

Open all week 11.30–2, 7.30–9.30 (exc Sun D)

The exterior and interior are a little faded, but everyone is here for the keenly priced bar food. The lunchtime buffet offers home-cooked ham, rib of beef, salmon, tongue, pork and lots of salads. In the

evening, choose carefully from the menu's strengths: soups, casseroles such as beef with dumplings or partridge, and the home-made puddings.

Garden • Car-park • Wheelchair access • Access, Visa

Grays   map 3

R. Mumford & Son

6–8 Cromwell Road
☎ GRAYS THURROCK (0375) 374153

Open Mon to Sat 11.45–1.45, 5.30–10.30
Closed Sun and 10 days Christmas

A long-established fish and chip restaurant-cum-take-away still run by the Mumfords. Fish is delivered fresh each day from Billingsgate. Skate, cod, plaice and rock eel offer the cheapest choices, with the pricier lemon and Dover sole still representing good value at £7.25 and £8.25 respectively.

Wheelchair access, also WC

Great Dunmow   map 5

Chapslee

27A High Street
☎ GREAT DUNMOW (0371) 873299/ 875891

Open all week noon–2.30, 6–11.30

A local favourite with a small menu, which allows the kitchen to concentrate on tandoori items (the mixed grill is excellent) as well as authentically flavoured vegetable dishes like sag bhaji (spinach) and sag paneer (cottage cheese with spinach). The Sunday buffet lunch is particularly good value.

No-smoking area • Wheelchair access • Access, Amex, Visa

Harwich   map 5

Ha'penny Pier

The Quay
☎ HARWICH (0255) 241212

Open all week noon–2, 6–9.30

An offshoot of the more expensive fish restaurant upstairs (The Pier at Harwich), the Ha'penny Pier is a family restaurant specialising in fish and chips. A bright, nautical theme and busy harbourside views create a lively atmosphere. Locally caught fish provide the basis for the menu but there are also poached Scottish salmon, lasagne and steak.

Car-park • Wheelchair access, also WC • Access, Visa

Leigh-on-Sea   map 3

Osborne Bros

Billet Wharf, High Street
☎ SOUTHEND-ON-SEA (0702) 77233

Open Easter to Oct all week 8.30am–10pm, Oct to Easter Mon to Fri 10am–4pm, Sat and Sun 8.30am–5pm

Leigh High Street is not in the middle of town, but runs along the seafront on the other side of the railway tracks. Shellfish stalls are everywhere, and Osborne Bros is rated as the pick of the bunch. It is the only hut with Formica tables

inside as well as seats outside. The menu is a choice of 'teas' – mainly fresh cockles or shrimps with a roll and butter, plus a mug of strong tea to drink. Prawns, jellied eels and whelks can also be purchased to take away.

Unlicensed • Wheelchair access

Maldon   map 5

Wheelers

13 High Street
☎ MALDON (0621) 853647

*Open Tue to Sat 11.30–1.45, 6–9.30
Closed Sun, Mon and 2–3 days Christmas*

The Wheeler family continue to serve excellent fish and chips in their long-established business with its beamed dining-room and take-away. Portions are big and the choice can range from cod and plaice to skate and Dover sole. If you want a full meal, start with thick fish soup and finish with a sweet from the trolley.

Wheelchair access, also WC

Paglesham   map 3

Plough and Sail

☎ SOUTHEND-ON-SEA (0702) 258242

*Open all week noon–2, 7–9
Closed Christmas Day and Boxing Day*

An old timber-built inn located in an attractive spot near the marshes. The area is famous for its oysters, which, along with local river mussels and fresh fish, are the highlights of the menu. Other dishes, such as steak and kidney pie, are honestly and plainly cooked and come with piles of fresh vegetables.

No children under 14 • Garden • Car-park • Wheelchair access, also WC • Access, Visa

Saffron Walden   map 5

Eight Bells

18 Bridge Street
☎ SAFFRON WALDEN (0799) 22790

SE of M11 junction 9

Open all week noon–2.30, 6 (7 Sun)–9.30
Closed Christmas Day

A comfortable, roomy pub cheered in bad weather by a real log fire. The bar menu changes every two days and regularly features fish and local smoked foods. Smoked mushrooms with a spicy tomato sauce makes an unusual starter, followed perhaps by calf's liver with sage and bacon or good, old-fashioned steak and kidney pie. Chips are missable.

Garden and family-room • Car-park • Wheelchair access • Access, Amex, Visa

Old Hoops

15 King Street
☎ SAFFRON WALDEN (0799) 22813

Open Tue to Sat noon–2, 7–10
Closed Sun and Mon, 1 week Christmas and 2 weeks Aug

There is a noticeable sense of comfort combined with a genuine willingness to please in this first-floor dining-room. Lunch is particularly good value with well-made

'musselcress' soup (watercress and potato plus fresh mussels), a light tomato and herb omelette or a more substantial lamb's liver with onion sauce, all rounded off by perfectly made floating islands. Evenings are more expensive.

Access, Amex, Diners, Visa

Southend-on-Sea   map 3

Pipe of Port Wine Bar

84 High Street
☎ SOUTHEND-ON-SEA (0702) 614606

Open Mon to Sat 11.30–2.30, 6–10.30
Closed Sun

With your cheap-day return ticket secreted in your pocket and after a brisk promenade on the pier, repair to the thoroughly British Pipe of Port. If not pipes, there are bottles of port and sherry and a well-chosen assortment of wines supplied by Lay & Wheeler. The rooms in this subterranean wine bar have stone floors which are covered in sawdust. Popular starters are the fingers of toast with anchovy, Stilton and sardine and the over-generous chicken in curried mayonnaise and yoghurt. Pies are a speciality: they arrive in large earthenware pots. Try the 'celebrated' chicken and chestnut version or the quality steak, kidney and mushroom. Very busy at lunch, so book ahead.

No children under 14 • Access, Diners, Visa

Out to Eat is totally independent, accepts no free hospitality and makes no charge for inclusion.

Westcliff-on-Sea   map 3

Oldham's

13 West Road
☎ SOUTHEND-ON-SEA (0702) 346736

Open Mon to Sat 11.30am–9.30 (10 Fri and Sat), Sun noon–9
Closed Christmas Day and Boxing Day

One of a dying breed of classic, old-fashioned fish and chip restaurants. The dining-room with its Formica-topped tables is reached through a pair of glass-panelled doors from the take-away. Go for the fresh fish and chips – cod, skate, bass and haddock – and look for specials such as whole plaice on the bone, salmon cutlets with salad or fillet of lemon sole. Big portions, excellent value for money.

Wheelchair access

Witham   map 5

Crofters

25 Maldon Road
☎ WITHAM (0376) 511068

Open Mon to Sat noon–2, 7–10
Closed Sun

Oak beams, exposed brickwork, open fireplaces, treadle sewing-machine tables and blackboard menus feature in this good-value wine bar-cum-restaurant. Starters of mushrooms in Stilton, chicken liver pâté and orange, and pork terrine lead into well-made leek and ham pie and vegetable risotto.

Garden • Car-park • Access, Visa

See the front of the guide for a list of each eating-place given a star for being one of the best found by the Editor during research for this book.

GLOUCESTERSHIRE

Alderton
map 4

Gardeners Arms

Beckford Road
☎ CHELTENHAM (0242) 620257

*Open Tue to Sun noon–2, 7–9 (exc
Sun D)*
Closed Mon

One of those archetypal village pubs
we would all like to have as a local – a
thatched Tudor building with black-
and-white half timbering. The
lunchtime bar menu is very simple:
home-made soups, grilled king
prawns, grilled sardines, salads,
ploughman's and sandwiches. The
popular evening restaurant specialises
in more expensive game and fish
dishes.

*Garden • Car-park • Wheelchair access
• Access, Visa*

Bledington
map 4

Kings Head Inn

The Green
☎ KINGHAM (0608) 658365

Open all week noon–2, 7–9.30

A fine fifteenth-century inn in an
idyllic setting, next to the village
green with its stream and ducks. A
non-smoking area is as much a plus as
the beams, inglenook and flagstoned
floor. Bar food includes hot roast
beef sandwiches, steak and wine pie,
rabbit in cider and good basil and
mozzarella pancakes. There is always
a vegetarian dish.

*No-smoking area • Garden and family-
room • Car-park • Wheelchair access*

Blockley
map 4

Crown Hotel

High Street
☎ BLOCKLEY (0386) 700245

Open all week noon–2, 7–10

A mellow, honey-coloured inn,
Elizabethan in origin, upmarket in
style. Sandwiches only are available in
the bar, generously filled and of the
best quality; the former skittle alley
houses the restaurant. The inventive
fish dishes tend to be expensive –
smoked haddock and poached egg,
steak and kidney pie or spaghetti
bolognese are cheaper.

*No children in bar • Car-park •
Wheelchair access • Access, Amex, Visa*

Broad Campden
map 4

Bakers Arms

nr Chipping Campden
☎ EVESHAM (0386) 840515

On Chipping Campden–Blockley road

*Open Mon to Sat noon–2.30, 5.30–
9.45, Sun noon–2, 7–8.45*
Closed Christmas Day and Boxing Day

Broad Campden is one of the jewels
of the North Cotswolds and this
stone-built roadside pub fits the
scene. Inside, there are beamed
ceilings, open fireplaces – including

one huge inglenook – and bare tables for eating. The dining area is dominated by a large, colourful rug depicting the pub. There are signs of decent home-cooking on the menu – good tomato soup flavoured with herbs, vegetarian chilli packed with beans, vegetables and mushrooms, and well-made moussaka. There are also seafood and vegetarian versions of lasagne, as well as cottage pie and plaice Kiev. Wine by the glass.

No children in bar • Garden • Car-park • Wheelchair access, also WC

Cheltenham   map 4

Pizza Piazza

6–7 Montpellier Street
☎ CHELTENHAM (0242) 221845

Open all week 11am–11.30pm

A branch of one of the best pizza chains in the UK. See London entry.

Access, Visa

Chipping Campden   map 4

Greenstocks

Cotswold House Hotel, The Square
☎ EVESHAM (0386) 840330

Open all week 9.30am–9pm (10 Fri and Sat)
Closed Christmas Day and Boxing Day

A stylish, relaxed, well-run all-day restaurant where the ingredients are of sound quality, matched by competent cooking. Breakfasts are carefully prepared, the cafetière coffee is strong, and croissants are light and buttery. For lunch there is soup with an almost obligatory second helping, chicken cakes with herb mayonnaise, and vegetable Stroganoff, all priced keenly. The supper menu is more expensive, though it is possible to pick two courses for £10. In between, there are home-made scones, cakes and the highly recommended all-butter shortbread; plus an afternoon gap-filler – a toasted bap filled with grilled bacon and fried egg.

No-smoking area • Wheelchair access • Access, Amex, Diners, Visa

Cirencester   map 4

Number One

1 Brewery Court
☎ CIRENCESTER (0285) 659290

Open Mon to Sat 10am–5
Closed Sun

A laudable coffee-house whose principles are based on sound quality and wholesome simplicity. They prepare their own ham, make their own pasta, roast their coffee and bake their own bread. Needless to say, all cakes are home-made. Beef cobbler and mushroom and courgette roulade could feature as the daily hot lunch dishes.

No smoking at lunchtime • No-smoking area • Wheelchair access, also WC

See the back of the guide for an index of eating-places and an index of locations.

Tatyan's

27 Castle Street
☎ CIRENCESTER (0285) 653529

*Open Mon to Sat noon–2 (exc Sat),
6–10.30
Closed Sun, Christmas Day and Boxing
Day*

The floral patterns and pastel colour
schemes are closer to Laura Ashley
than Suzie Wong, but this light, airy
restaurant offers Chinese food well
above the provincial average. Peking
and Szechuan dishes dominate, but
the menu also has a few ideas from
Canton and Hunan. Sizzling scallops,
crispy shredded beef and chicken
with lemon sauce show the style.
Ingredients are fresh, cooking is fast
and flavours are vivid. Well-chosen
wines, otherwise drink tea or saké.

*Wheelchair access • Access, Amex,
Diners, Visa*

Corse Lawn   map 4

Corse Lawn House Hotel

☎ TIRLEY (045 278) 479

*Open all week noon–2, 7–10
Closed Christmas Day*

A fine Queen Ann house with some
carefully-prepared light food
available in the smartly re-styled bar.
Home-made sausages, hot crab
pancake, mushroom omelette and hot
shrimps en croustade come with
home-made bread rolls and salad.
Mousse of three chocolates or a
champagne sorbet are stylish desserts.
Service at times can be too casual for
the setting and prices.

*Garden • Car-park • Wheelchair access,
also WC • Access, Amex, Diners, Visa*

Cowley   map 4

Green Dragon Inn

Cockleford
☎ COBERLEY (024 287) 271

On Elkstone road between A417 and
A435

*Open all week 11.15 (noon Sun)–2,
6.15 (7.15 Sun)–10*

Rurally situated in the hamlet of
Cockleford, the popular Green
Dragon started life in the seventeenth
century as a cider house. Farm cider
is still available, nowadays
complemented by a range of real ales
served from the barrel. The bar menu
offers stalwarts such as Shrewsbury
lamb or beef and Guinness casserole
enlivened by such exotic dishes as
West African groundnut stew.

*No children in bar • Car-park •
Wheelchair access, also WC*

Ewen   map 4

Wild Duck Inn

Drakes Island
☎ CIRENCESTER (0285) 770310

Open all week noon–2, 7–10

Brian and Tina Mussell have taken
over this mellow sixteenth-century
village inn and put it on the food
map. The blackboard menu ranges
from home-made soup, pâté, a dish of
smoked salmon and crabmeat to giant
plaice, steaks and duck. Piles of
accompanying vegetables make it
hard to leave room for bread-and-
butter pudding.

*Garden • Car-park • Wheelchair access
• Access, Visa*

Gloucester

map 4

College Green

7-11 College Street
☎ GLOUCESTER (0452) 20739

Open Mon to Sat L noon–2, Wed to Sat
D 6.30–9.30
Closed Sun and bank hols

Gloucester's premier bistro is in a
fifteenth-century timbered building
by the cathedral. Lunchtime is best
value, when David Spencer offers a
set menu which might include spicy
tomato and garlic soup, sautéed
tenderloin of pork with creamy apple
and cider sauce and French lemon
tart. Evening meals will take the bill
beyond the £10 limit. The kitchen's
loyalty to fresh ingredients and
consistent standards are notable.
Decent wines by the glass.

Access, Amex, Visa

Pizza Piazza

1 Merchant's Quay, The Docks
☎ GLOUCESTER (0452) 311951

Open all week 11am–11.30pm

A branch of one of the best pizza
chains in the UK. See London entry.

Access, Visa

Guiting Power

map 4

Ye Olde Inne

Winchombe Road
☎ COTSWOLD (0451) 850392

Open all week noon–2, 7–9.30

A comfortable, tiny pub on the edge
of the village. Food reflects the

simplicity of the place with well-
made, down-to-earth dishes such as
minced pork rissoles, steak and
kidney pie and butter-bean bake.
Bread pudding just has the edge over
the coffee fudge pudding.

Garden • Car-park • Wheelchair access

Kingscote

map 4

Hunters Hall Inn

☎ DURSLEY (0453) 860393

Open all week 7.30am (8.30 Sun)–
9.30am, noon–2, 7–9.45

A spacious former coaching inn with
low beamed ceilings and roaring log
fires in winter. There is a large and
varied selection of bar food, buffet-
style at lunchtime: rare beef, thick
slices of ham, turkey, chicken, gala
pie and a range of salads. Hot dishes
include baked fish creole, steak and
kidney pie and seafood crumble.

Garden and family-room • Car-park •
Access, Amex, Diners, Visa

Little Washbourne

map 4

Hobnails

☎ CHELTENHAM (0242) 620237

On A438 6 miles E of Tewkesbury

Open all week noon–2, 7–9.30

An unassuming, plain pub, strong on
atmosphere and comfortably
informal. Food is a major feature and
there are tables everywhere,
including in the skittle alley (still in
operation). Copiously filled baps
ranging from egg and bacon to liver
and onion are justly popular, while

the home-made meringues and gâteaux are piled high. There is a good vegetarian selection.

No children in bar • Garden and family-room • Car-park • Wheelchair access, also WC • Access, Visa

Painswick   map 4

St Michael's

Victoria Square
☎ **PAINSWICK (0452) 812998**

Open Tue to Sun noon–2, 7.30–9 (exc Sun D)
Closed Mon, 10 days June and 2 weeks Nov

A small and charming tea-room-cum-restaurant (part of a well-run guest house) noted for friendliness and simple, good-value home cooking. Lunch might include home-made soup, lasagne, curry or carbonara of beef, while Sunday lunch (£8.75) always offers the choice of two roasts with a fresh and varied selection of vegetables. Cream teas are available. Dinner is more expensive.

Garden • Car-park • Wheelchair access

South Woodchester   map 4

Ram Inn

☎ **AMBERLEY (0453) 873329**

Off A46 between Stroud and Nailsworth

Open all week noon-2, 6.30-9.30

A lovely place in summer with a magnificent view down the valley from the flower-decked terrace. In winter, no fewer than three open fires cheer the beamed bar. Bar food is carefully prepared and consistent: beef and oyster pie, lamb and apple curry, spinach and cream cheese roulade, with the intriguingly-named 'open border pie' for dessert.

Garden • Car-park • Wheelchair access

Altrincham

map 7

French

25 The Downs
☎ **061-941 3355**

Open Mon to Sat noon–2.30 (exc Sat),
7–10.30 (11.30 Fri and Sat), Sun
noon–10.30
Closed Christmas evening and New
Year's Day

The good-value brasserie/café-bar is
directly across the road from the
well-established French Restaurant.
Like its neighbours it is a solid
Victorian brick building. Downstairs
is the bar with marble-topped
counter, large mirrors and frosted-
glass lights. On the ground floor is
the long, narrow dining-room. Food
is classic French brasserie-style: thick
fish soup, Roquefort salad, navarin of
lamb, chicken cooked in white wine
sauce with prawns and peppers,
stuffed aubergines and crème brûlée.
Fresh ingredients, generous portions,
and attractive surroundings. Decent
house wine by the glass.

No-smoking area • Access, Visa

Nutcracker Vegetarian

43 Oxford Road
☎ **061-928 4399**

Open Mon to Sat 10am–4.45 (2 Wed)
Closed Sun and bank hols

Altrincham is the UK Vegetarian
Society's home town, and this pine-
furnished restaurant is true to the
cause. Inside, there is a lot of space
amid simple décor. The menu is
chalked on a blackboard and dishes
are remarkably good value.
Specialities include Dutch zyldyke
casserole (mixed vegetables in a
curried cheese and spinach sauce with
a crisp breadcrumb topping) and
vegetable curry with brown rice,
backed up by monster jacket
potatoes, wonderful-looking salads
and home-made soup. Ice-creams
and sorbets are produced locally; fruit
pies and cakes are home-made. Fruit
juices and organic wines by the glass.

No-smoking area • Wheelchair access

Ashton-under-Lyne

map 7

Adam's Tandoori

215 Old Street
☎ **061-330 7183**

Open all week 5pm–1am

Ashton-under-Lyne is a former
cotton town on the edge of the
Pennines with a sizeable Asian
community and a good Indian
restaurant. Adam's décor is old-
fashioned – flock wallpaper, serried
ranks of close tables – with the long
menu representing a culinary tour of
Northern India. Bengali dishes are a
speciality and there is praise for the
tandooris and tikkas and for the
excellent nan.

Please let us know if you think an eating-
place should be included in this guide;
report forms are at the back of the book.

Bolton   map 7

Tiggis

63 Bradshawgate
☎ BOLTON **(0204) 397320**

Open Tue to Sun noon–2, 6–11.30 (exc Sun D)
Closed Mon, Christmas Day, Boxing Day and New Year's Day

One of a highly popular mini-chain of lively pizza/pasta restaurants dotted around North-West England. (For full details see Lytham St Anne's in Lancashire.)

Car-park (evening only) • Access, Visa

Manchester   map 7

Aladdin

529 Wilmslow Road
☎ **061-434 8588**

Open Tue to Sun 3pm–11pm
Closed Mon, Christmas Day and Boxing Day

Originally a take-away, Aladdin's now has a tiny dining-room at the back, with occasional overflow into the owners' living-room upstairs. It is run by two Syrians who deliver authentic Arabian and Middle Eastern dishes to equal anything in Cairo or Beirut. Some specialities are rarely found outside the Middle East. A range of classic starters, including excellent falafels, tabouleh and memorable potato kibbeh can be turned into a full meal; otherwise, there are fresh and perfectly executed main courses such as chicken kebabs, aromatic with lemon and garlic; shawarma flavoured with cinnamon and timbale of stewed lamb layered with rice, aubergines

and pine nuts. Delectable pastries and sweetmeats. Take-aways are available.

Unlicensed, but bring your own: no corkage

Café Istanbul

79 Bridge Street
☎ **061-833 9942**

Open Mon to Sat noon–3, 6–11.30
Closed Sun

Established for more than a decade, and a favourite haunt of expatriate Turks, Café Istanbul 'Wine and Meat' (to give it its full title) still scores heavily for its excellent-value set lunches: £4.50 pays for, say, spinach soup, lamb casserole or stuffed green peppers, a sweet and good Turkish coffee. Otherwise, the menu is dominated by classic meze such as tarama, stuffed vine leaves, cacik and cheese-filled pastries, followed by hefty well-timed grills and stews, with sticky Turkish pastries to finish. House wine by the glass.

Wheelchair access, also WC for ladies • Access, Visa

Gallery Bistro

Whitworth Art Gallery, Oxford Road
☎ **061-273 1249**

Open Mon to Sat noon–2.30
Closed Sun

A diminutive bistro housed within the Whitworth Art Gallery, popular for lunchtime snacks. Unfortunately, the lack of space and the congestion can be off-putting and it is best to arrive before 12.30pm to eat in comfort. Tomato and red pepper soup, beef goulash and sticky toffee pudding make a satisfying meal. Home-made cakes for morning coffee and afternoon tea.

No smoking • Garden • Car-park • Wheelchair access, also WC

Great Kathmandu

140 Burton Road, West Didsbury
☎ **061-434 6413**

Open all week noon–2.30, 6–midnight

Gopal Dangol was involved with the Kathmandu Tandoori in Sackville Street for six years before opening his own restaurant in Didsbury. Despite the strong Nepalese connections, the cooking is mostly North Indian, with only a few genuine specialities such as aloo tama from Gopal's home country. Spicing is subtle and herbs are fresh. Rani chicken and fish tikka are good starters, otherwise the menu takes in lamb biriani, chicken jalfrezi and kidneys masala, as well as madras and dhansaks. Vegetables are a strong point and there is a good-value vegetarian set meal for £6.95. Family lunches £3.75.

Wheelchair access • Access, Visa

Greenhouse

331 Great Western Street, Rusholme
☎ **061-224 0730**

*Open Mon to Sat noon–3 (exc Sat),
5.30–10.20, Sun noon–10.20
Closed 23 Dec to 2 Jan*

A relaxed and informal vegetarian restaurant with the added bonus of a real fire. The food is cosmopolitan. Indonesian peanut sauce accompanies satay mushroom pie, and there are curries, a goulash and lasagne. The popular Greenhouse strudel filled with mushrooms, spinach, cheese, wine and cream is never off the menu. The wine list includes organic wines.

No-smoking area • Wheelchair access

Hopewell City

45–7 Faulkner Street
☎ **061-236 0091**

Open all week noon–midnight

A canter through the fulsome Cantonese repertoire contained in a long menu reveals some authentic dishes; more than enough to satisfy average Chinese gastronomic curiosity. If you forget temptations like sea bass, scallops and lobster, there is good value to be had. Most dim-sum offerings merit some praise. An unusual main course – brisket casserole – is satisfying on a cold winter's night. Sautéed strips of duck in a sauce of onions, green peppers and black beans are salty but good. Decoration and warmth are minimal in these vast basement premises. Service can, on occasion, be frosty.

Wheelchair access • Access, Amex, Diners, Visa

Kathmandu Tandoori

42–4 Sackville Street
☎ **061-236 4684/2436**

*Open all week noon–2.30, 6–midnight
Closed bank hols*

A basement restaurant that is more North Indian than Nepalese. It offers excellent value for money, although occasional slips such as serving stale curried vegetables with the £4.95 set lunch have happened. Good chicken tandoori and chicken masala; lamb Kashmiri and pepper chicken kadai are some even spicier options.

No-smoking area • Wheelchair access • Access, Amex, Diners, Visa

Lime Tree

9–11 Wilmslow Road, Rusholme
☎ **061-225 7108**

Open Tue to Sat D 6–10.30
Closed Sun and Mon

This cheaper offshoot of the well-known Didsbury original is a corner building close to the Whitworth Art Gallery, with pine tables and lace curtains, ceramics on the walls and jazz coming through the speakers. Best value is the pre-theatre menu (£7.95 for two courses plus coffee) which can take in black pudding with apple and herb sauce, pan-fried salmon with fennel, and vegetable ragoût with celeriac. The full menu has a similar modern repertoire, ranging from asparagus with citrus butter to duck with orange and ginger. Decent bread, good espresso coffee and drinkable house wine.

Wheelchair access • Access, Visa

Little Yang Sing

17 George Street
☎ **061-228 7722**

Open all week noon–10.45

The close-packed basement of this restaurant is not for a romantic assignation and some may be irritated by the smaller portions and generally

higher prices than the rest of Chinatown. The food, however, is hard to fault. Dim-sum is a strength, as is vermicelli Singapore style from the one-plate dishes.

Access, Amex, Visa

On The Eighth Day

109 Oxford Road, All Saints
☎ **061-273 1850**

Open Mon to Sat 10am–7 (4.30 Sat)
Closed Sun

A vegetarian wholefood café – run as a workers' co-operative – of such long standing that it has become an institution, sustaining grant-impoverished students. Noon to 2pm should be avoided as it is the busiest time (hot food is available all day from 11am). On offer could be corn chowder soup, butter-bean and vegetable bake, chilli and Boston baked beans, and healthy cakes.

No smoking • Wheelchair access, also WC

Pearl City

33 George Street
☎ **061-228 7683**

Open Mon to Thur noon–2am, Fri and Sat noon–4am, Sun noon–midnight

Despite stiff local competition, regulars rate this as the pick of the old-style Cantonese restaurants in Manchester Chinatown. Fried crabmeat balls, sui mai, spring rolls and beef dumplings with ginger and spring onion are skilfully done, while steamed pork ribs and ducks' webs show the Chinese fondness for bony meats. Plates of three seafoods with rice; pork chop in special sauce; and brisket chow mein are excellent. The roast belly pork is outstanding.

No-smoking area • Access, Amex, Diners, Visa

Peppers

63 Bridge Street
☎ 061-832 9393

Open Mon to Sat noon–2 (exc Sat), 6–11
Closed Sun and bank hols

An array of gleaming metal chafing-dishes is visible from the windows of this Indian eating place just off Deansgate. Inside, it looks quite plush, with dim lighting, pots of greenery suspended from the dark-painted ceiling and attractive Indian pictures on the walls. Food is served from a buffet, and meals are excellent value. The choice of starters, main dishes and sweets is drawn from an extensive list and items vary: lamb masala might be transformed into rogan josh with a little mixing and blending. Onion bhajias, chicken bhuna, aloo palak, dhal and pilau rice have all been good. The kitchen also produces its own versions of chilli con carne and – appropriately – stuffed peppers.

No very young children • Wheelchair access • Access, Diners, Visa

Philpotts

19 Brazenose Street
☎ 061-832 1419

Open Mon to Fri 8.30am–2.30
Closed Sat, Sun, Christmas Day, Boxing Day and Aug bank hol

Made to order, take-away sandwiches are all Philpotts do, but they do them

well. The permutations are inventive: blackpudding, bacon and tomato, bacon and avocado, crispy bacon, smoked trout in dill sauce, pastrami and mustard and dill pickle, coronation chicken. There are five kinds of cheese, a daily breakfast and lunchtime special, soup and espresso.

Unlicensed • No smoking

Pizza Express

Old Colony House, South King Street
☎ 061-834 0145

Open all week 11.30am–midnight

Part of the popular chain which is the pick of the pizza bunch. See London entry.

No-smoking area • Access, Amex, Diners, Visa

Royal Oak Hotel

729 Wilmslow Road, Didsbury
☎ 061-445 3152

Open Mon to Fri noon–2

Arthur Gosling has a passion for cheese and he indulges it totally at this splendidly old-fashioned pub in a smart suburb of Manchester. At lunchtime the bar is piled high with a great selection of French and English cheeses, but only one type can be selected. This is, however, a huge chunk, served with a pile of wholemeal bread, pickles, onion and beetroot.

No children • Wheelchair access

If there are restrictions on children, these are mentioned in the details at the end of each entry.

Sanam

145–51 Wilmslow Road
☎ **061-224 1008**

Open all week noon–midnight (1am Fri and Sat)

The largest of the Sanam restaurants in the centre of Manchester's 'Curry Alley' has been extensively refurbished, providing even more seating and eye-catching décor. Reports suggest that this place has the edge over its local competitors, thanks largely to the freshness and vividness of the food. Tandoori fish, karahi lamb, matar paneer and mushroom bhajia have all been outstanding. To finish, check out the contents of the take-away counter with its bewildering array of sweetmeats. A jug of lassi is the perfect accompaniment. Take-aways are available.

Unlicensed • No-smoking area • Car-park • Wheelchair access, also WC • Access, Visa

Siam Orchid

54 Portland Street
☎ **061-236 1388**

Open Mon to Sat 11.30–2.30 (exc Sat), 6.30 (6 Fri and Sat)–11.30, Sun 5–11

A refreshing change from the massed Chinese restaurants round the corner in Chinatown, this Thai restaurant scores with fresh flavours and well-balanced spicing. The set business lunch is real value at £4.80 (for two courses and a drink). Dinner is more expensive.

Access, Visa

Sinclairs Oyster Bar

Shambles Square
☎ **061-834 0430**

Open Mon to Sat noon–2.30 (3 Sat)
Closed Sun and Christmas Day

Architectural students should be compelled to visit Sinclairs, an uprooted fourteenth-century timbered building plonked in the middle of a concrete shopping centre where it looks highly incongruous, in order to learn how not to mix the old and the new. Once inside everything is reassuringly traditional – oysters of course, beef and oyster pie and steak pie are the best bets.

No-smoking area • No children • Wheelchair access • Access, Visa

Wong Chu

63/63a Faulkner Street
☎ **061-236 2346**

Open all week noon–midnight
Closed Christmas Day

'Born in Hong Kong, brought up in Manchester' is the slogan of this restaurant in the heart of Chinatown. The place is well-known for its soup and noodle dishes, as well as plates of roast meats on rice. Otherwise, the extensive menu deals in a mix of esoteric and familiar dishes, from steamed minced pork with salt fish and braised brisket with spices to lemon chicken and duck stuffed with prawn meat. Set meals for under £10 a head. Drink tea.

Wheelchair access • Access, Visa

Woo Sang

19–21 George Street
☎ 061-236 3697

Open all week noon–midnight
Closed Christmas Day and Boxing Day

The food overcomes the rather bleak, unwelcoming surroundings in this long-established Cantonese restaurant above a Chinese supermarket. Best bets from the long menu are the dim-sum, such as steamed prawn dumplings, crisp, ungreasy spring rolls and beef dumplings with ginger and spring onion. Otherwise, there are more substantial items ranging from fillet of chicken in bird's nest to delicate steamed cod with chilli and black-bean sauce. One-plate rice and noodle dishes are also good value. Drink tea or wine.

Access, Amex, Diners, Visa

Yang Sing

34 Princess Street
061-236 2200

Open all week noon–11

The best-known of Manchester's Chinatown establishments and frequently lauded as one of the best in the country. The pressures that this fame puts on staff and kitchen can sometimes cause cracks to appear in the service and cooking, which could leave a newcomer wondering what all the fuss was about. Dim-sum are still great value with glutinous rice in lotus leaves, char siu bau and steamed beef balls eliciting consistent praise. One-plate meals of roast duck or spiced assorted meat with rice or a soup noodle dish will also provide a simple, filling, inexpensive meal.

Wheelchair access, also WC • Access,
Amex, Visa

Marple   map 7

Little Mill Inn

Rowarth, Marple Bridge
☎ NEW MILLS (0663) 43178

1m NE of Marple

Open all week 12–2.30, 6.45–10.30

As the name suggests, this is a pub in a converted mill. Snacks and simple dishes are available in the bar, while full meals are served in the upstairs carvery. The centrepieces are excellent roasts with all the trimmings, steaks and casseroles such as chicken in sherry cream sauce. Try home-made soup or black pudding to start, and mousses or gâteaux to finish. A useful venue for families.

No-smoking area • Garden and family-room • Car-park • Wheelchair access, also WC • Access, Amex, Diners, Visa

---

Mellor   map 7

Devonshire Arms

Longhurst Lane
☎ 061-427 2568

Open Mon to Sat noon–2
Closed Sun and Christmas Day

A solid stone pub at the top end of a long straggling village, surrounded by high pastureland. Brian Harrison is very enthusiastic about food, and offers a daily-changing lunchtime menu of enterprising dishes. Excellent soups such as carrot and mint or lentil and ham share the bill with home-cured gravlax, potted shrimps and oysters. Smoked German sausage is served with ratatouille, beef stew comes with a jacket potato, and curries are vividly spiced. Perfect crêpes to finish. Reasonably priced wines.

No-smoking area • Garden and family-room • Car-park • Wheelchair access

Rochdale   map 7

Tony's

417 Oldham Road
☎ ROCHDALE **(0706) 42975**

Open Mon to Sat 11.30am–2, 8.30–midnight
Closed Sun and bank hols

Cars queue outside, waiting for this immensely popular local chippie to open. When it does, regulars tuck into freshly cooked fish and non-greasy chips. There isn't much else but no one cares. Low prices, massive portions.

Unlicensed

Sale   map 7

Yerevan

1B Ashton Lane
☎ **061-973 2577**

Open Tue to Sat D 6.30–midnight
Closed Sun, Mon and Christmas Day

Named after the capital of Armenia and tucked away in a quiet street by the law courts, this ethnic restaurant is slowly establishing a reputation beyond its neighbourhood. There are Armenian posters on the walls, and the menu has a range of authentic

specialities. Starters such as sarma (vine leaves stuffed with rice and walnuts), kibeh and spicy sausages can be followed by bamya (fillet of lamb cooked with okra and peppers) or ourfa kebab (rissoles served on a bed of fried aubergines). There are plenty of options for vegetarians. Armenian coffee or Greek wine (Demestica) to drink. Live music Friday and Saturday evenings.

Wheelchair access, also WC • Access, Visa

Salford   map 7

Mark Addy ⓦ

Stanley Street
☎ **061-832 4080**

Open Mon to Sat 11.30am–11, Sun noon–3, 7–10.30

A stylishly converted wharfside pub overlooking the River Irwell. Its popularity lies in the fact that the food is almost exclusively cheese, an extraordinary range of British, French and European, also some pâtés, and hunks of granary bread and pickled onions. Doggy-bags help cope with the enormous portions. There are chocolate fudge cake and espresso to finish.

A restaurant manager can't insist on people not smoking, unless it's specifically a no-smoking restaurant or a no-smoking area. If it is, smokers could be asked to leave if they don't stop. If in doubt, check beforehand what the smoking arrangements are.

Training Restaurant

**Salford College of Technology
Frederick Road
☎ 061-736 6541**

*Open Mon and Wed to Fri L 12.15 (one
sitting), Tue to Thur D 6.30 (one
sitting)
Closed Sat, Sun and college hols*

This is run by catering students
under strict supervision, so it is hard
to put a finger on the restaurant's
character. But one thing is certain, it
serves some of the best-value food in
the area. Lunch is a bargain at £8
(booking essential). Leeks wrapped in
ham and cheese, strips of lamb in
rosemary sauce, tipsy trifle typify the
menu. Dinner is £12.

*No smoking in restaurant • Car-park •
Wheelchair access, also WC*

Stockport   map 7

Peppermill

**37 St Petersgate
☎ 061-480 7013**

*Open Mon to Sat 10am–4
Closed Sun and bank hols*

The new incarnation of Coconut
Willie's. Pictures, prints and
upholstered chairs have replaced the
toy parrots and luxuriant greenery,
and the menu is no longer exclusively
vegetarian. Salads, baked potatoes,
pizzas and quiches are backed up by
specials such as lamb hot-pot and
cheesy vegetable pasta. Substantial
cakes and sponges to finish. There
are Cawston Vale whole-fruit drinks
as well as best bitter and wine by the
glass.

*No-smoking area • Wheelchair access,
also WC*

★ after an eating-place indicates that it is one of the best found by the Editor
during research for this book (see page 14 for a list).

Ⓒ after an eating-place indicates that it is a pub. The opening and closing times
we give only relate to when food is available – the licensing hours may be different.

Ⓜ after an eating-place indicates that it is within five miles of the nearest motorway junction. We give the relevant motorway and junction in the details. Eating-
places in cities and large towns, where traffic, parking and route-finding may cause
delay, do not have this symbol.

MANCHESTER'S CHINATOWN

Chinatown is a solid square of nineteenth-century cotton merchants' buildings, bounded by Charlotte Street to the north, Princess Street to the south and Moseley and Portland Street to east and west. It houses a vibrant Chinese community of hairdressers, acupuncturists, herbalists, bankers and lawyers and craft centres, as well as the usual restaurants and supermarkets. More spacious and more dignified than London's Chinatown, it contains some of the best Chinese restaurants in Britain. All are Cantonese except for Mr Kuk's (set somewhat apart, on the edge of Chinatown) which serves Pekingese dishes. Sunday, when Chinese families come en masse to eat lunch, is the liveliest time to visit. Prices and quality can vary, but dim-sum snacks, served during the day, and one-plate meals offer the best and most inexpensive choices.

1A **Wang Yip Supermarket**
45A Faulkner Street
(shop)

1B **Hopewell City**
45–7 Faulkner Street
(restaurant – see entry)

1C **New Hong Kong**
47 Faulkner Street
(restaurant)

1D **Wing Fat Chinese Supermarket**
49 Faulkner Street
(shop)

2 **Modern Chinese Cultural Services**
18 Nicholas Street

3 **Kai's**
16 Nicholas Street
(restaurant)

3A **Faulkner Chinese Supermarket**
Faulkner Street
(shop)

4A **Dragon Gate**
57 Faulkner Street
(restaurant)

4B **Happy Seasons**
59 Faulkner Street
(restaurant)

5A **New Jade Garden**
Faulkner Street
(restaurant)

5B **Hang Won Hong Supermarket**
56 Faulkner Street
(shop)

6 **Wong Chu**
63 Faulkner Street
(restaurant – see entry)

7 **Yang Sing**
34 Princess Street
(restaurant – see entry)

8 **Kwok Man**
28 Princess Street
(restaurant)

9 **Ho's Bakery**
85 Princess Street
(bakery)

10 **Wai Hong Supermarket**
83 Princess Street
(shop)

11 **Little Yang Sing**
17 George Street
(restaurant – see entry)

12A **Woo Sang Chinese Provisions**
Ground floor, 19–21 George Street
(shop)

12B **Woo Sang**
First floor, 19–21 George Street
(restaurant – see entry)

13 Pearl City
33 George Street
(restaurant – see
entry)

14 Leen Hong
35 George Street
(restaurant)

15 Charlie Chan's
41 George Street
(restaurant)

16 Connaught
56–60 George
Street
(restaurant)

17 Mr Kuk's
55A Moseley Street
(restaurant)

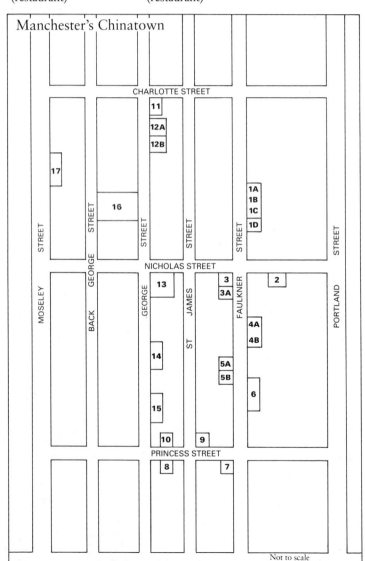

Manchester's Chinatown

Not to scale

MANCHESTER'S 'CURRY ALLEY'

Sandwiched between the university and medical faculties to the north and the prosperous Mancunian suburbs of Withington and Didsbury to the south, the inner-city area of Rusholme presents a down-to-earth but colourful face. For here, on a half-mile stretch of the Wilmslow Road are curry houses, sweet centres, supermarkets, and shops selling bright saris and exotic-looking household goods. The area is known locally as 'curry alley' and the air is pungent with the smell of spices. The restaurants offer popular North Indian, Punjabi and Bangladeshi dishes and prices are so keen, and competition so fierce, that it is generally the décor only that varies. Stop to peruse a menu in a window on a quiet evening and waiters will rush to the door offering a free drink or free starters as an inducement to eat there. The lack of variety in the food is balanced by the friendliness and sheer liveliness of the area. It is not unusual to see a restaurant crowded with Indian families enjoying authentically presented dishes while a group of Mancunian lads tuck into mounds of chips with their curry.

1 **Ambala Sweet Centre**
67 Wilmslow Road
(restaurant and sweet centre)

2 **Al Noor**
71 Wilmslow Road
(restaurant)

3 **Ittifaq Supermarket**
87 Wilmslow Road
(shop)

4 **Jewel in the Crown**
109 Wilmslow Road
(restaurant)

5 **Shezan**
119 Wilmslow Road
(restaurant and takeaway

6 **Paradise**
123 Wilmslow Road
(restaurant)

7 **Tandoori Kitchen**
131 Wilmslow Road
(restaurant and takeaway)

8 **Sanam Sweet Centre**
141 Wilmslow Road
(restaurant and sweet centre)

9 **Sanam**
145–51 Wilmslow Road
(see entry)

10 **Amee Supermarket**
195 Wilmslow Road
(shop)

11 **Tabak**
199–201 Wilmslow Road
(restaurant)

12 **Ravi Food Store**
213 Wilmslow Road
(shop)

13 **Sanam Sweet House and Restaurant**
Wilmslow Road
(restaurant and sweet centre)

14 **Wazi Food Store**
239 Wilmslow Road
(shop)

15 **Royal**
Wilmslow Road
(restaurant)

16 Shere Khan
1 Ifco Centre,
Wilmslow Road
(restaurant)

17 Shezan
64 Wilmslow Road
(restaurant)

18 Eastern Touch
76 Wilmslow Road
(restaurant)

19 Punjab
88 Wilmslow Road
(restaurant)

20 Nawab
100 Wilmslow Road
(restaurant)

**21 Manchester
Grocers**
114 Wilmslow Road
(shop)

22 Indian Cottage
Wilmslow Road
(restaurant)

23 Jilami's
124 Wilmslow Road
(grocers)

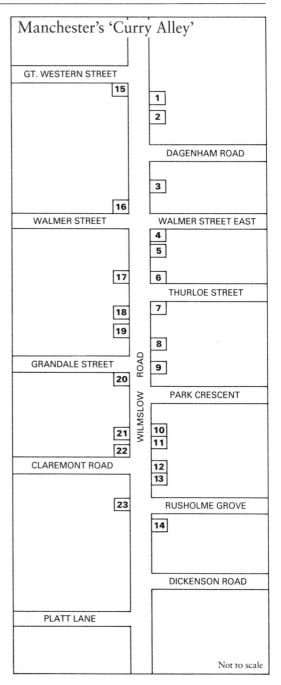

Manchester's 'Curry Alley'

GT. WESTERN STREET

DAGENHAM ROAD

WALMER STREET   WALMER STREET EAST

THURLOE STREET

GRANDALE STREET   ROAD

WILMSLOW   PARK CRESCENT

CLAREMONT ROAD

RUSHOLME GROVE

DICKENSON ROAD

PLATT LANE

Not to scale

HAMPSHIRE

Basingstoke · map 2

Pizza Express

The White House, Winchester Road
☎ BASINGSTOKE (0256) 54439

Open all week 11.30am–midnight

Part of the popular chain which is the pick of the pizza bunch. See London entry.

No-smoking area • Access, Amex, Diners, Visa

Grateley · map 2

Plough Inn

☎ GRATELEY (026 488) 221

Open all week noon–2, 7–9.30 (10 Fri and Sat)
Closed Christmas Day and Boxing Day

A well-run village pub offering a friendly welcome. Bar food is fairly standard fare but well-cooked and nicely presented. Ploughman's, chicken curry, chilli, filled jacket potatoes are constant features, backed up by a specials blackboard which is changed every couple of days. There is a tiny candle-lit dining-room for pricier evening meals.

Garden • Car-park • Wheelchair access, also WC • Access, Visa

If there are restrictions on children, these are mentioned in the details at the end of each entry.

Longstock · map 2

Peat Spade Inn

☎ ANDOVER (0264) 810612

1¹/₂m N of Stockbridge off A3057

Open all week 12.30–2.15, 7.30–10 (exc Sun and Mon D)

A recently refurbished village pub in a very rural setting and noted for friendliness and attentive service. The menu is based on fresh seasonal produce which could translate into venison or hare pie, rabbit casserole, smoked haddock and mushroom pie or chicken with chilli and garlic, accompanied by fresh vegetables. All dishes are carefully cooked to order. Good puddings.

No smoking in dining-room • No children in bar • Garden • Car-park • Wheelchair access, also WC • Access, Amex, Diners, Visa

Portsmouth · map 2

Pizza House

14 Hilsea Market, London Road
☎ PORTSMOUTH (0705) 695542

Open Mon to Sat 7–11.30 (midnight Fri and Sat)
Closed Sun, Christmas Day, Boxing Day, bank hols and Aug

Definitely not the place to go for an intimate conversation – tables are far too closely packed and the ebullient Italian owner encourages a lively atmosphere. Food is well-prepared, and there is lots of it: minestrone, pasta and pizza, made on the premises, and encompassing all the favourite combinations. Leave room for the home-made ice-cream.

Wheelchair access

Southampton   map 2

Hasty Tasty

48 High Street
☎ SOUTHAMPTON **(0703) 333038**

Open Mon to Fri 5am–2, Sat 6am–10 Closed Sun, Christmas Day and bank hols

If you find yourself in Southampton in the early morning (perhaps just off a ferry) and in need of food, then head for Hasty Tasty. It is basic but clean and will fry you up a bumper-sized breakfast for £2.40, serve you reviving tea in a mug and even make up a few sandwiches to keep you going on your journey.

Unlicensed

Kohinoor

2 The Broadway, Fortswood
☎ SOUTHAMPTON **(0703) 582770**

Open all week noon–2.30, 6–11.30 Closed Christmas Day and Boxing Day

A highly rated curry house in one of Southampton's shopping districts. The frontage is modern; inside it is decorated in shades of pink and blue with partitions and lavishly adorned taffeta. Spicy mixed kebabs, crisp onion bhajias, Kashmiri chicken with fruits and almonds, and sizzling karahi chicken have all been good. Also look for lamb pasanda and king prawn bhuna. Good pilau rice and nan bread. Drink lager.

Wheelchair access • Access, Amex, Visa

Kuti's

70 London Road
☎ SOUTHAMPTON **(0703) 221585**

Open all week noon–2.30, 6–midnight

A stylish Indian restaurant which is useful to know about if you are waiting for a cross-Channel ferry. The buffet lunch is a popular £6.50 for as much as you can eat. The menu is mainly North Indian, although dopiaza, dhansak and Madras dishes are featured. Starters include a bhel poori. Start with chaas Bombay-style – watered-down lassi with ginger, fresh coriander, cumin and fried mustard seeds.

Wheelchair access, also WC • Access, Amex, Visa

Town House

59 Oxford Street
☎ SOUTHAMPTON **(0703) 220498**

Open Mon to Sat 11.45–2 (exc Sat), 7–9.30 (exc Mon) Closed Sun

A tiny, pastel-shaded vegetarian restaurant in a smart part of Southampton. Dinner costs £12 a head, but lunch offers cheaper snacks. These range from soup, mushroom puffs with a spicy sauce and curried vegetable samosa to lentil moussaka, courgettes au gratin and mushroom Stroganoff. Crème caramel or fruit salad for dessert.

No smoking • Wheelchair access • Access, Visa

Southsea   map 2

Barnaby's Bistro

56 Osborne Road
☎ PORTSMOUTH (0705) 821089

*Open all week noon–2.30 (exc Sun),
6–11*
*Closed Christmas Day, Boxing Day and
New Year's Day*

Barnaby's is popular, offering a
reasonably priced, varied menu with
some good fish and vegetarian
choices. Moules marinière, venison
and garlic sausages, chargrilled lamb
steak teriyaki, and cashew-nut and
vegetable paella show modern globe-
trotting influences at work. Close-
packed tables could cause problems
for non-smokers.

Wheelchair access • Access, Visa

Country Kitchen

59 Marmion Road
☎ PORTSMOUTH (0705) 811425

Open Mon to Sat 9.30am–4.45
Closed Sun

A long-established and rightly
popular vegetarian café. Buying is
done with care and conscience, and
has included visiting the farm
which supplies the free-range eggs.
The café also keeps an allotment to
growing organic vegetables. The
menu changes daily and can include
stuffed seaweed rolls, lentil and nut
pâté, quiches, salads, stuffed cabbage
and a selection of cakes.

*Unlicensed, but bring your own: no
corkage • No smoking*

Pizza Express

41 Osborne Road
☎ PORTSMOUTH (0705) 293938

Open all week 11.30am–midnight

Part of the popular chain which is the
pick of the pizza bunch. See London
entry.

*No-smoking area • Access, Amex,
Diners, Visa*

Steep   map 2

Harrow Inn 🏵

☎ PETERSFIELD (0730) 62685

2m N of Petersfield

*Open Mon to Sat noon–2 (Sat 11–3),
6.30–10, Sun noon–3, 7–10.30*
Closed Christmas Day evening

Tiny, remote and idiosyncratic pub
that feels like a hostelry from another
age. Go for the special atmosphere,
the simple home-made food and the
traditional beer. Bowls of soup,
Scotch eggs, sandwiches and
enormous salads are backed up by a
hot dish such as stuffed baked
marrow. Ales are tapped from casks
behind the bar; cider is on draught
and wine is served by the glass.

No children • Garden • Car-park

You will find report forms (write a letter if
you prefer) at the back of the book so that
you can tell us about your experiences of
going *Out to Eat*. We'll put the
information to good use when we're
compiling the next edition.

Stockbridge   map 2

Mayfly

Testcombe
☎ ANDOVER (0264) 860283

Off A3051 3m N of Stockbridge

Open all week noon–2, 7–9

With such a splendid rural position by the flowing River Test, the Mayfly's popularity is obvious, it is unfortunate that this can result in poor service. Go for the huge selection of cheeses, some 30-odd to choose from, the cold cuts and the various salads, and make the most of the riverside beer garden when the weather is fine or the conservatory when dull.

Garden • Car-park • Wheelchair access, also WC • Access, Visa

Winchester   map 2

Pizza Express

1 Bridge Street
☎ WINCHESTER (0962) 841845

Open all week 11.30am–midnight

Part of the popular chain which is the pick of the pizza bunch. See London entry.

No-smoking area • Access, Amex, Diners, Visa

Pizza Piazza

Jerwy Street
☎ WINCHESTER (0962) 840037

Open all week 11am–11.30pm

A branch of one of the best pizza chains in the UK. See London entry.

Access, Visa

Wykeham Arms ★

75 Kingsgate Street
☎ WINCHESTER (0962) 53834

Open Mon to Sat noon–2, 6.30–8.30 (exc Mon D)
Closed Sun

Sandwiched neatly between Winchester College and the cathedral in the oldest part of town is this exceedingly well-run eighteenth-century inn. There is a positive no-smoking policy in several of the stylishly decorated rooms. Old oak furniture, kitchen chairs, panelling and open fires galore are shown to advantage by evening candles, fresh flowers and plants. The bar menu is based on fresh local produce and prepared in an inventive, assured way. Spinach and Stilton soup or mushrooms in fresh pesto sauce could be followed by lamb hot-pot, spicy Indonesian chicken or cottage pie. There are simple sandwiches, great desserts and good wines.

No-smoking areas • No children under 14 • Garden • Car-park • Wheelchair access, also WC

Brimfield

map 4

Roebuck ★

☎ BRIMFIELD (058 472) 230

*Open Tue to Sat noon–2, 7–10
Closed Sun, Mon, 2 weeks Feb and 1
week Oct*

This is a straightforward pub with traditional pub décor – dark, plain, wooden bar tables, beams, a pool-room – and serves excellent bar food. Seasonal produce, organic if possible, is used. Rabbit terrine with bramble chutney, plump Cornish mussels in white wine and chicken cooked in Dunkertons Cider are memorable for their fresh flavour and for Carol Evans' assured and inventive cooking style. Even a simple lunch of cheese produces home-made bread and pickles and good-condition farmhouse British cheeses. Poppies restaurant serves more expensive meals.

*No-smoking area • Garden • Car-park
• Wheelchair access • Access, Amex*

Broadway

map 4

Coach House

The Green
☎ EVESHAM (0386) 853555

*Open all week 10am–6, Thur to Sat D
6–9
Closed Oct to Feb Mon, Tue and Thur D*

Built as a barn around 1450, and once used as a studio by American artist John Singer Sargent, the Coach House now operates as a tourist attraction for today's visitors. The style is a mix of classic English tea-room – varnished tables, souvenirs and local paintings on display – and a touch of American brashness. The long menu follows suit, combining breakfast fry-ups, Sunday roasts and cream teas with pizzas, good-quality burgers and waffles with maple syrup. There are also a couple of Welsh specialities such as lamb and leek pie. Steaks are chargrilled Aberdeen Angus. There are free second helpings of most dishes, and children under 12 (accompanied by adults) eat free of charge. Wines, fruit cordials, malt whiskies and cider to drink.

*No-smoking area • Car-park •
Wheelchair access, also WC • Access,
Amex, Diner, Visa*

Goblets Wine Bar

Lygon Arms, High Street
☎ BROADWAY (0386) 852255

*Open all week noon–2, 7–9.30
Closed 2 weeks Christmas*

Goblets is separated from the Lygon Arms by a carriageway passage but maintains the old-inn style of décor: slate floor, huge inglenook, blackened beams. The food is fresh and reasonably priced. Dishes of the day supplement the short, printed menu of Worcestershire lamb and apricot crumble or Evesham plum wine and steak pie. Surprisingly few wines by the glass.

*Garden • Car-park • Wheelchair access,
also WC • Access, Amex, Diners, Visa*

Eaton Bishop   map 6

Ancient Camp Inn

Ruckhall
☎ GOLDEN VALLEY (0981) 250449

SW of Hereford, 1st right off A465,
signposted to Ruckhall and Belmont golf
course

*Open Tue to Sun noon–2, 7–9.30 (exc
Sun D)*
Closed Mon

A charming inn on a road which goes
nowhere else. It is set high above and
overlooks a beautiful stretch of the
River Wye and across the Black
Mountains into Wales. First-class bar
food includes locally made pasta,
hearty oxtail casserole, pan-fried
garlic chicken, and pork chop in cider
and apple sauce. The cooking is
assured and the surroundings are
convivial.

*No children under 10 evenings • Garden
• Car-park • Wheelchair access, also
WC • Access, Visa*

Evesham   map 4

Evesham Hotel

Coopers Lane, off Waterside
☎ EVESHAM (0386) 765566

Open all week 12.30–2, 7.30–9
Closed Christmas Day and Boxing Day

A family hotel of great charm. At
£5.80, the help-yourself lunch buffet
is such terrific value that customers
might wonder how any profit is
made. A light lunch can be chosen
from among the starters on the
printed menu – soup and a scallop

and salmon bouchée, perhaps.
Evening meals are more expensive.

*No cigars/pipes • Garden • Car-park •
Wheelchair access, also WC • Access,
Amex, Diners, Visa*

Hereford   map 4

Church Street Rendezvous

17 Church Street
☎ HEREFORD (0432) 265233

*Open Mon to Sat 10am–5, Fri and Sat
D 7–9.30, Sun L Apr to Oct noon–2.30*

Helen and Neil Clarke are a young
couple with a feeling for good food
and its preparation, and in their tiny
restaurant are making it work with
gusto. Light lunches include cheese
and spinach crêpes and grilled fresh
sardines with more substantial
offerings of lamb kebabs, fillet of
fresh cod and vegetable pasta.
Afternoon tea is served from
2.30 to 5pm.

*No smoking noon–2.30 • Wheelchair
access*

Fat Tulip

**The Old Wye Bridge,
2 St Martin's Street**
☎ HEREFORD (0432) 275808

*Open Mon to Sat 12.15–1.45 (exc Sat),
7.15–9.30*
Closed Sun and bank hol Mons

This charmingly named bistro, on
the old bridge spanning the River
Wye, offers an informal atmosphere
and decent cooking. Main courses are
pricey, but it is quite acceptable to
order just two starters. Fish

dominates the menu with fresh grilled sardines, New Zealand green mussels and Parisian fish soup, complemented by salad of goats'-milk cheese or various terrines.

Wheelchair access • Access, Amex, Visa

Gilbies

4 St Peter's Close, Commercial Street
☎ HEREFORD (0432) 277863

Open Mon to Sat 10am–11pm
Closed Sun and Christmas Day

This is a pleasant place, not far from the cathedral, for a snack or a light meal. Inside, tables look on to a large, secluded patio where there are more tables. The bar is crammed with nibbles: black and green olives, fresh chestnuts, gherkins and popcorn. An extensive blackboard menu lists everything from fondue to New Zealand mussels, by way of partridge and beef braised in ale. A good bet is pork in Dijon sauce served with baked potatoes or salad. The wine list is short but varied.

Garden • Wheelchair access • Access, Visa

Kidderminster   map 4

La Brasserie

5 Lower Mill Street
☎ KIDDERMINSTER (0562) 744976

Open Mon to Sat noon–2.15, 6.30–10
Closed Sun

A rustic sort of place, with feature arches made from reclaimed bricks, old beams and an open kitchen. Fresh fish – sardines, cod, halibut, lemon sole, salmon – features strongly on the blackboard menu together with chargrilled steaks, lamb's liver in red wine, steak and Guinness pie and a variety of salads.

No-smoking area • Wheelchair access, also WC • Access, Amex, Diners, Visa

Knightwick   map 4

Talbot Hotel

☎ KNIGHTWICK (0886) 21273

B4197 off A44 Worcester–Bromyard road

Open all week noon–2, 6.30–9.30
Closed Christmas Day evening

For an inn that has so much going for it – located in a pretty setting by a bridge over the River Teme – it is a bonus that the food is so good. A large blackboard displays an enterprising choice which could include fresh sardines, brill and tuna steaks, courgette and sweet basil gratin, an olive pâté with hunks of chargrilled bread, or pork with melted cheese. The salads that accompany main courses include sprouted beans, grated carrot and cream cheese. Don't resist the fig and yoghurt pancakes or the sticky date pudding. Generous portions and good-quality ingredients make this good value for money.

Garden • Access, Visa

Out to Eat has been compiled in the same way as *The Good Food Guide* and is based on reports from consumers and backed up by anonymous inspections.

Ledbury
map 4

Fuggles Bar, Feathers Hotel

High Street
☎ LEDBURY (0531) 5266

NW of M50 junction 2

Open all week noon–2, 7–9.30

The striking Elizabethan black-and-white building dominates even this architecturally interesting high street. Inside, modern colours and fabrics contrast well with the ancient beams and panelling. The spacious, hop-bestrewn Fuggles Bar, named after a famous hop-grower, provides satisfying food: soup, pasta, game dishes, beef casserole and dumplings, liver and bacon.

Car-park • Wheelchair access, also WC • Access, Amex, Diners, Visa

Ombersley
map 4

Kings Arms

☎ WORCESTER (0905) 620315

Off A449 Worcester–Kidderminster road

Open Mon to Sat 12.15–2.15, 6–10, Sun noon–10

A characterful, ancient, half-timbered inn (built in 1411), reputedly the first stopping point for Charles II when fleeing the battle of Worcester. The excellent bar food is an added bonus and steak and kidney pie and turkey and leek pie are firm favourites. Bouillabaisse makes a more adventurous choice and there is good bread-and-butter pudding to finish.

No children under 6 • Garden • Car-park

Ross-on-Wye
map 4

Meader's

1 Copse Cross Street
☎ ROSS-ON-WYE (0989) 62803

Open Easter to Christmas Mon to Sat 10am–2.30, 7–9.30 (exc Mon D), Jan to Easter Thur, Fri and Sat D 7–9.15 Closed Sun, Christmas Day and Boxing Day

Hungarian-born Andras Weinhardt offers hearty versions of his native cooking, both satisfying and inexpensive. Lunch includes a robust ham and bean soup, layered cabbage, both beef and pork goulash, and paprika potatoes. The evening carte is more pricey, with similar offerings, but there is a set Hungarian menu at £19 for two including a bottle of wine (not on Saturday).

No-smoking area

Stourport-on-Severn
map 4

Severn Tandoori

11 Bridge Street
☎ STOURPORT (029 93) 3090

Open all week noon–1.45, 6–11.15

A smartly decorated curry house in a Georgian building close to the river. Tandoori and masala dishes are done well, and both the house speciality of karai chicken and the lamb pasanda are worth trying, despite being pricier than the rest of the menu. Finish with patty shapta (sweet pancake) and drink lassi.

No children under 5 • Wheelchair access, also WC • Access, Amex, Diners, Visa

Weobley   map 6

Jules ★

Broad Street
☎ WEOBLEY (0544) 318206

Open all week noon–2 (exc Sun and Mon), 7.15-9.30

The Whitmarshes run a green kitchen: organically grown vegetables, free-range eggs, poultry, pork and beef. Availability and loyalty to local produce dictates much of what they cook on a daily basis. Lunch is a simple operation, keenly priced, with paprika chicken or a walnut and mushroom bake with dark orange sauce, served with baked potato. A hearty and correctly made duck cassoulet is very good value. Morning coffee and home-made cakes (from 10am) precede lunch, perhaps chocolate cake or an almond slice, and these remain available to supplement desserts. Careful, considered cooking and informal service. Evenings are more expensive.

Wheelchair access • Access, Visa

See the front of the guide for a list of each eating-place given a star for being one of the best found by the Editor during research for this book.

Whitney-on-Wye   map 6

Rhydspence Inn

☎ CLIFFORD (049 73) 262

Off A438 4m NE of Hay-on-Wye

Open all week noon–2, 7–9.30
Closed Christmas Day

A charming country pub in an out-of-the-way location. The menu here is huge, and among the 21 main courses there are four vegetable dishes including a 'three-bean casserole' and a stir-fry. Promising alternatives are roast duck, venison and trout with fennel and ginger. The wine list includes half-bottles.

Garden • Car-park • Access, Amex, Visa

Worcester   map 4

Pizza Express

1 St Nicholas Street
☎ WORCESTER (0905) 726126

Open all week 11.30am–midnight

Part of the popular chain which is the pick of the pizza bunch. See London entry.

No-smoking area • Access, Amex, Diners, Visa

Barley map 5

Fox & Hounds

nr Royston
☎ BARWAY (076 384) 459

Open all week noon–2, 6.30–10 (7-9.30 Sun)

The old, white building in the village high street dates back to the middle of the fifteenth century and has been a pub for almost 200 years. Inside, it is all old beams, inglenooks and log fires. A long menu of mostly home-made dishes ranges from spare ribs in barbecue sauce to massive fresh plaice stuffed with prawns and mushrooms; there is also plenty of choice for vegetarians. A skittle alley and children's play equipment can be found outside. Real ales and cider on draught.

No-smoking area • Garden • Car-park • Wheelchair access, also WC

Barnet map 5

Pizza Express

242 High Street
☎ 081-449 3706

Open all week 11.30am–midnight

Part of the popular chain which is the pick of the pizza bunch. See London entry.

No-smoking area • Access, Amex, Diners, Visa

Berkhamsted map 5

Boat

Gravel Path
☎ BERKHAMSTED (0442) 877152

Open Mon to Sat L noon–2.30

A convincingly revamped pub with a terrace overlooking the Grand Union Canal. Chris and Valerie Elsford run the place with good humour and a feel for neighbourhood hospitality. Lunchtime bar food is based on fresh ingredients, and moves beyond burgers and omelettes to tarragon chicken and salt-beef sandwiches with pickled cucumbers. Lamb might be served with laverbread sauce, or with apricots and nuts. There is always something for vegetarians. Free seafood nibbles for Sunday lunchtime drinkers, as well as cheese and pickles on the bar. Well-kept Fullers beers.

Car-park • Wheelchair access

Cooks Delight

360-4 High Street
☎ BERKHAMSTED (0442) 863584

Open Thur to Sat D 7–9.30 (8–late Sat), Sat and Sun L 1–3
Closed Mon, Tue, Wed and 2 weeks Christmas

Rex Tyler is a fervent 'green crusader' and his delicatessen/bookshop/tea-room-cum-restaurant is run according to strict principles. The emphasis is on macrobiotic and vegan food, and organic produce is used without compromise. Sometimes the intentions are more laudable than the results on the plate, and there have been signs that the place is resting on its laurels. Even so, it offers good-value daytime snacks – scones, salads, vegetable terrines, soups and 'clay pot' casseroles – backed up by set dinners on Thursday and Friday, and more expensive South East Asian banquets (bookings only) on Saturdays. The long list of fine teas is recommended, as is the prodigious range of organic wines, ciders and naturally brewed beers.

No smoking • Garden • Access, Visa

Chorleywood map 5

Red Lion

Chenies
☎ WATFORD (0923) 282722

Open all week noon–2, 7–10 (9.30 Sun)

No fruit machines or Muzak cloud the civilised atmosphere in this lavishly refurbished pub. Food is a big attraction and the menu is ambitious. Deep-fried Le Coucouron cheese with bramble jelly, hot mushroom, cream cheese and brandy terrine or Chinese bean salad might precede Chenies lamb pie, beef, mustard and cheese casserole or breast of chicken in ginger and grape sauce. French bread sticks and jacket potatoes come with some unusual fillings. Home-made sweets, ice-creams and sorbets to finish. Real ales and carefully chosen pub wines.

No children in bar • Family-room • Car-park • Wheelchair access, also WC • Access, Visa

Hemel Hempstead map 5

Gallery Coffee Shop ★

Old Town Hall Arts Centre, High Street
☎ HEMEL HEMPSTEAD (0442) 232416

W of M1 junction 8

Open L Mon to Sat noon–4, D theatre nights only 7–8
Closed Sun

A cheerful, well-run café/bistro set in a light, airy first-floor room with well-controlled smoking, flowers on the tables and paintings by local artists on the walls. A printed menu offers generously filled sandwiches while a blackboard gives the daily specials. Hazelnut loaf with mushrooms, pepper and dill sauce or fish boulangère both reflect the attention given to quality and flavour and come in sizeable portions. Cakes reveal imaginative flair with an Indian carrot cake with pistachio and cardamom and a tart summer pudding heavy with red berries and just sweetened by cream. Home-made lemonade or wines and beers.

No-smoking area

Hitchin map 5

Pizza Piazza

87 Bancroft
☎ HITCHIN (0462) 421101

Open all week 11am–11.30pm

A branch of one of the best pizza chains in the UK. See London entry.

Access, Visa

St Albans   map 5

Alban Tandoori

145 Victoria Street
☎ ST ALBANS (0727) 830241

Open all week noon–2.30, 6–midnight

Rated as the most creditable curry house in St Albans. The menu holds few surprises, although specialities such as hundi chicken, grilled then cooked with ground almonds, are worth pursuing. Otherwise there is the standard range of curries, tandooris and vegetables. French beans bhaji is slightly unexpected. Good-value thalis for meat-eaters and vegetarians. Usefully placed, close to the railway station.

Wheelchair access, also WC • Access, Amex, Diners, Visa

Garibaldi

61 Albert Street
☎ ST ALBANS (0727) 55046

Open all week L noon–2, Mon to Fri D 6.30–9

Local supporters reckon that this lively backstreet hostelry serves the best pub food in St Albans. The secret is good home cooking, backed up by decent salads and generous helpings of fresh vegetables. Typically the menu might range from Italian chicken and lamb masala on rice to pasta with spinach and cheese sauce. The landlord says that the pub is 'a chip-free zone'. Excellent Fullers beers, and plenty of pub games.

No smoking in conservatory • No children in main bar, or after 7pm unless eating • Garden

Kingsbury Mill Waffle House

St Michael's Street
☎ ST ALBANS (0727) 53502

Open all week 11am (noon Sun)–6 (5pm Nov to Mar)

An old watermill attractively set beside the River Ver. Waffles, plain or wholemeal, supplemented by salads and soups, dominate the menu. Eggs are free-range, flour organic and stoneground. Savoury waffles come topped with ratatouille, ham, cheese and mushrooms, tuna or cream cheese; spiced fruit and bananas and cinnamon sugar are popular sweet varieties.

Unlicensed, but bring your own: no corkage • No smoking • Garden • Car-park

Marmaris

128 London Road
☎ ST ALBANS (0727) 40382

Open all week noon–3, 6 (7 Sun)–11 Closed Christmas Day

A Turkish restaurant in a converted curry house. Inside it is cheerful and lively and the menu stays in familiar Middle Eastern territory. A full meze with dessert and coffee will just break the £10 barrier, otherwise go for starters such as taramasalata or stuffed aubergines, followed by kebabs or moussaka. Drinkable house wine. Families with children may receive a less-than-enthusiastic welcome.

No-smoking area • Access, Amex, Diners, Visa

Pizza Express

11–13 Verulam Road
☎ ST ALBANS (0727) 53020

Open all week 11.30am–midnight

Part of the popular chain which is the pick of the pizza bunch. See London entry.

No-smoking area • Access, Amex, Diners, Visa

Watton-at-Stone   map 5

George & Dragon

High Street
☎ WARE (0920) 830285

Open Mon to Sat noon–2, 7.15–10

Seafood is the main attraction in this beamed pub-cum-restaurant. The bar menu can include anything from Corsican fish soup and herring roes on toast to poached salmon with cucumber sauce. Smoked salmon comes from a curer in the village. Meat-eaters can choose coarse pâté, fillet steak in a bun, calf's liver with Madeira sauce or turkey and ham vol-au-vent. There is a limited menu on Saturday lunchtimes. More expensive meals are available in the dining-room. Greene King beers on draught; house wine by the carafe.

Licensed • No children in bars • Garden • Car-park • Access, Amex, Diners, Visa

---

Out to Eat has been compiled in the same way as *The Good Food Guide* and is based on reports from consumers and backed up by anonymous inspections.

★ after an eating-place indicates that it is one of the best found by the Editor during research for this book (see page 14 for a list).

⊚ after an eating-place indicates that it is a pub. The opening and closing times we give only relate to when food is available – the licensing hours may be different.

Ⓜ after an eating-place indicates that it is within five miles of the nearest motor-way junction. We give the relevant motorway and junction in the details. Eating-places in cities and large towns, where traffic, parking and route-finding may cause delay, do not have this symbol.

Barton-upon-Humber

map 8

Elio's

11 Market Place
☎ BARTON (0652) 635147

Open Tue to Fri L noon–2, Mon to Sat D 7–11
Closed Sun

A friendly, family trattoria serving more than the usual pizza and pasta combinations. The long menu includes lamb and beef kebabs in brandy, liver with onions and lambs' kidneys sautéed with mushrooms, red wine and cream. Cheerful and useful to know.

Wheelchair access • Access, Amex, Diners, Visa

Epworth

map 7

Epworth Tap

9–11 Market Place
☎ EPWORTH (042 787) 3333

On A161 S of M180 junction 2

Open Tue to Sat D 7.30–10
Closed Sun, Mon and Christmas Day to New Year's Day

This wine bar offers a strong wine list, reasonable prices and sturdy food. The quality is excellent – fresh, carefully handled and well presented. Parsnip and coriander soup, lasagne, beef in red wine, lamb with courgettes, steamed fillet of Scotch salmon are all praised. Sticky toffee pudding features among the desserts.

No-smoking area Sat D • Wheelchair access • Access, Amex, Visa

Grimsby

map 8

Danish Mission

2 Cleethorpes Road
☎ GRIMSBY (0472) 342257

Open all week noon–6.30
Closed Christmas Day evening

The setting is a Christian mission serving the needs of Scandinavian seamen, but the mission is also open to the public for excellent-value food. There are no pretensions, as honest sustenance is the order of the day. Lunch is a selection from the cold table, including cured herrings, Danish salamis, pâtés and salads, plus pickles and garnishes for authentic smorgasbord (open sandwiches). There are also a couple of hot dishes such as braised pork in a dark, sweet sauce. Coffee and Danish pastries throughout the day.

Unlicensed Garden

Granary

1st Floor, Haven Mill, Garth Lane
☎ GRIMSBY (0472) 346338

Open Mon to Sat noon–2.15, 7.30–9.30 (exc Mon and Tue D)
Closed Sun and 2 weeks summer

The name suggests a wholefood restaurant, but in fact this mainly seafood restaurant is so called because it takes up a floor of a converted 200-year-old grain mill. Very fresh local fish dominates the blackboard menu – lemon sole, fillet of sea trout with fresh herb hollandaise – backed up by fish soup, a daily vegetarian dish, pot roast beef and well-made desserts.

No-smoking area • Access, Visa

Scunthorpe   map 7

Giovanni's

44 Oswald Road
☎ SCUNTHORPE (0724) 281169

Open all week noon–2, 6–11 (11.30 Fri and Sat)
Closed Christmas Day, Boxing Day and New Year's Day

A popular Italian restaurant with glass-topped tables, tiled floor and cheerful service. It is strong on pastas (nearly two dozen choices, either as a starter or main course), does decent pizzas and has a few daily blackboard specials. Excellent value is offered, with generous portions and a lively atmosphere. Finish with tiramisu – Italian trifle.

Car-park • Wheelchair access, also WC • Access, Visa

South Dalton   map 8

Pipe & Glass

West End
☎ MARKET WEIGHTON (0430) 810246

Open Tue to Sun noon–2, 7–10 (exc Sun D)
Closed Mon and Christmas Day

A welcoming family pub with a charming garden and a children's play area. The soundly cooked, robust bar food includes Yorkshire pudding with onion gravy, farmhouse broth, steak and mushroom pie and a filling mixed grill. Fresh fish is often featured and ranges from grilled lemon sole to deep-fried haddock and chips.

No children after 8pm • Garden • Car-park • Wheelchair access, also WC • Access, Visa

'Wheelchair access' indicates that, according to the proprietor, entrances are at least 33 inches wide, passages 4 feet wide, and that there are a maximum of two steps. If there is access to a WC, we mention it.

ISLE OF WIGHT

Chale map 2

Wight Mouse Inn

Clarendon Hotel
☎ ISLE OF WIGHT (0983) 730431

On B3399, just off B3055 main coast road

Open Mon to Sat 11.45am–10, Sun noon–2.30, 7–9.30

One of the few pubs that genuinely caters for all the family. Children can choose between well-equipped indoor and outdoor play areas and have their own menu. Parents can sample the bar's 365 malts and other whiskies and try the fresh seafood. There are fish and chips, fisherman's platter and hot garlic prawns. Other choices include steaks, burgers and local ice-cream.

Gardens • Family-rooms • Car-parks • Wheelchair access Access

Seaview map 2

Seaview Hotel and Restaurant

High Street
☎ ISLE OF WIGHT (0983) 612711

Open all week noon–2, 7.30–9.30 (exc Sun D)

This is a pleasant family-run hotel. Bar food includes local fish – hot crab ramekin, reasonably priced lobster salad – as well as a filling and cheap workman's lunch of two eggs, sausage, baked beans and chips. There is a selection of sandwiches, and desserts include treacle sponge pudding. Breakfast, morning coffee and afternoon tea are also available.

No smoking in drawing-room • No young children in restaurant after 7.30pm • Car-park • Access, Amex, Visa

Shalfleet map 2

New Inn

☎ ISLE OF WIGHT (0983) 78314

*Open all week noon–2, 7–10
Closed Christmas Day*

An ancient inn noted for its atmospheric bars and roaring winter log-fire, and for specialising in seafood. The daily changing blackboard shows the available catch ranging from plaice, cod, Dover sole to fresh crab. Seafood curry and moules marinière are popular. Alternatives to fish take in made-to-order sandwiches and roast duck or pheasant.

Garden • Car-park • Wheelchair access

Ashford map 3

Cornerstone

25A High Street
☎ ASHFORD (0233) 642874

M20 junction 9/10

Open Tue to Sat 10am–5.30
Closed Mon, Sun and 2 weeks Christmas

Situated in one of Ashford's oldest buildings, the Cornerstone is run by Livingstones Trust, a Christian charity. A daily-changing menu of mainly vegetarian/wholefood dishes might include carrot and onion soup; bean and vegetable curry; and cashew-nut and mushroom flan, as well as chicken and apple bake. Bread, scones and cakes are baked on the premises.

Unlicensed • No smoking • Garden •
Wheelchair access

Beckenham map 3

Pizza Express

189 High Street
☎ 081-650 0593

Open all week 11.30am–midnight

Part of the popular chain which is the pick of the pizza bunch. See London entry.

No-smoking area • Access, Amex, Diners, Visa

Biddenden map 3

Claris's Tea-room

1-3 High Street
☎ BIDDENDEN (0580) 291025

Open Tue to Sun 10.30am–5.30
Closed 25 Dec to 4 Jan

Housed in one of the charming fifteenth-century half-timbered buildings that make up the high street, Claris's is old-fashioned in both looks and concept. Baked beans and well-done beef are better eschewed in favour of cheese or creamed mushrooms on toast or poached egg. For the sweet-toothed there is a wide choice of home-made cakes, and the coffee is good.

Unlicensed • No smoking • Garden •
Wheelchair access, also WC

Three Chimneys

☎ BIDDENDEN (0580) 291472

Off A262 half-way between Biddenden and Sissinghurst

Open all week noon-2, 7-10
Closed Christmas Day and Boxing Day

The atmosphere of this warren of small, nicotine-brown rooms, formerly two ancient cottages, is a strong point. This, combined with good food, means that the pub is very popular; lunch is generally a scrimmage. Inexpensive bar food includes broccoli quiche, home-baked ham or lamb casserole with rosemary. Service could be improved.

No unaccompanied children under 14 in bar • Garden and family-room • Car-park • Wheelchair access, also WC

Broadstairs map 3

Mad Chef's Bistro

35 Harbour Street
☎ THANET (0843) 69304/604609

Open all week noon–2, 6–9.30 (later at weekends)

A cosmopolitan, family-run bistro right by the harbour. Nets hang from the ceiling and the long menu centres on fish and shellfish. Starters include excellent moules marinière and squid sautéed with chillies. Main dishes range from local fish pie to baked mackerel with herbs. Paella is a speciality. There are steaks for meat-eaters, as well as a full 17-dish vegetarian menu. Set lunches and the sandwich menu are the cheapest options.

No-smoking area • Access, Amex, Diners, Visa

Bromley map 3

Pizza Express

15 Widmore Road
☎ 081-464 2708

Open all week 11.30am–midnight

Part of the popular chain which is the pick of the pizza bunch. See London entry.

No-smoking area • Access, Amex, Diners, Visa

Canterbury map 3

George's Brasserie

71-2 Castle Street
☎ CANTERBURY (0227) 765658

Open Mon to Sat 11am–10 (Fri and Sat 10.30), Sun L noon–4
Closed Christmas Day and New Year's Day

A spacious, reasonably priced brasserie serving soundly cooked food. Fashionable, eclectic influences show in the menu: bruchetta, cheese beignets, chicken noodle soup, backed up by brochette of lamb, local plaice and pasta. Ginger pudding with syllabub makes for an English finish. Service can lack direction.

No-smoking area • Garden • Wheelchair access • Access, Amex, Diners, Visa

Il Vaticano

35 St Margaret Street
☎ CANTERBURY (0227) 765333

Open all week 11.30am–10.30
Closed Christmas Day and Boxing Day

Several varieties of freshly made pasta, combined with any one of a selection of sauces, make a satisfying meal at this city centre restaurant. Carbonara, with cream and ham, or capponata, a vegetable sauce, are popular choices. There are also ravioli, cannelloni and lasagne, with baked mushrooms and Parma ham in cheese sauce to start.

No cigars or pipes • Garden • Wheelchair access • Access, Amex, Diners, Visa

All letters to this guide are acknowledged.

Chiddingstone   map 3

Castle Inn 🏅

☎ TONBRIDGE (0892) 870247

Open all week 11–2.45, 6–10.45
Closed Christmas Day evening

This ancient tile-hung pub near the castle is – like the rest of the village – owned by the National Trust. Outside is a walled garden; inside is a maze of tiny rooms on different levels. Good-value bar food takes in king prawns in garlic butter, beef and Mackeson pie, chilli and ploughman's, backed up by sweets such as Dutch apple slice with cream. Local beers on draught, as well as cider and wine by the glass. More expensive restaurant meals, including a set three-course menu for £9.50.

Garden and family-room • Wheelchair access, also WC • Access, Amex, Diners, Visa

---

Folkestone   map 3

India

1 Old High Street
☎ FOLKESTONE (0303) 59155

Open Tue to Sun noon–3, 6–11
Closed Mon

An incongruous restaurant near the town's amusement arcades, run by a cosmopolitan French/Bengali who dubs his cooking 'nouvelle indienne'. In reality, Ali Ashraf produces a familiar range of tandooris and curries, with a few unexpected items such as crab with ginger and coriander, and 'vath' (duck with cashew-nuts, raisins and cardamoms). The set-lunch menu (£5.95 including a glass of wine) lines up muglai kebab and chicken shimla alongside potage Crécy and coq au vin; other set meals begin at around £8.50 per head. Drink Kingfisher beer or Veena Indian wine.

Wheelchair access • Access, Amex, Diners, Visa

Groombridge   map 3

Crown 🏅

The Green
☎ TUNBRIDGE WELLS (0892) 864742

Open all week noon–2, 7–9.30
Closed Christmas Day and Boxing Day

Set on the sloping village green, the Crown is an attractive, characterful Elizabethan pub with small old-fashioned rooms full of beams, exposed timbers and yellowing plaster walls. Knick-knacks galore decorate the place. This is primarily a drinking pub, but the food on offer comprises decent local sausages, good soups and steak and mushroom pie.

No children under 14 • Garden and family-room • Car-park • Wheelchair access • Access, Visa

---

Harrietsham   map 3

Ringlestone Inn 🏅

nr Maidstone
☎ MAIDSTONE (0622) 859900

3m N of Harrietsham towards Wormshill

Open all week noon–2, 7–9.30

The sort of pub to take foreign visitors to – it is impressively hard to find, deep in the countryside, a former monks' hospice oozing age from the oak beams, flint walls and floors, inglenooks and ancient oak furniture. Well-kept ales, tapped from casks behind the bar, maintain the old-English image. There is a lunchtime buffet plus casseroles, curries and steaks.

Garden • Car-park • Wheelchair access, also WC • Access, Amex, Diners, Visa

Ivy Hatch   map 3

Plough ★ ⓖ

Coach Road
☎ SEVENOAKS **(0732) 810268**

Off A227 SW of M26 junction 2A

Open all week noon–2.30, 7–9.30 (exc Sun D)

A gently poached chicken breast sprinkled with fresh herbs and accompanied by a lightly dressed salad of mixed leaves is not the usual kind of food encountered in pubs. But then chefs from Alsace are not that common in them either. The assured, imaginative bar food is hard to fault. From a printed menu come light dishes, such as quiche and salad, and ratatouille with garlic bread, while a blackboard menu offers fresh haddock gratiné, saddle of venison, lamb casserole and fresh, dressed lobster. The setting is complementary: a late-eighteenth-century building with a pleasing garden, a long, narrow, pine-panelled bar which is candle-lit at night, and a more expensive conservatory restaurant.

No children under 10 evenings • Garden • Car-park • Wheelchair access, also WC • Access, Visa

Lamberhurst   map 3

Brown Trout

The Down
☎ TUNBRIDGE WELLS **(0892) 890312**

Open Mon to Sat 11.30–2, 6–10 (9.30 Sun)
Closed Christmas Day and Boxing Day evening

This is an especially charming pub specialising in fish and seafood in a pretty old cottage, much extended, surrounded by flowers. Inside, a collection of brass jugs hangs from the ceiling. Try the excellent seafood platter of half a lobster, crab, prawns and salad. Otherwise, have the grilled Dover sole; skate and trout are also good. Arrive early for a table in the bar or book for the restaurant.

Garden • Car-park • Wheelchair access, also WC • Access, Visa

Maidstone   map 3

Pizza Express

32 Earl Street
☎ MAIDSTONE **(0622) 683549**

Open all week 11.30am–midnight

Part of the popular chain which is the pick of the pizza bunch. See London entry.

No-smoking area • Access, Amex, Diners, Visa

Please let us know if you think an eating-place should be included in this guide; report forms are at the back of the book.

Marshside
map 3

Gate Inn
☎ CHISLET (022 786) 498

A28 Canterbury–Margate road, take turn-off to Chislet and pass through village

Open all week noon–2.30, 6–10.30

A thoroughly unspoilt pub, with a great atmosphere enhanced by an open fire, a garden with ducks and geese, and with chess, Ludo, dominoes and all manner of pub games available. Food fits the simple, rustic image: doorstep sandwiches of home-boiled bacon, black pudding or sausage, bean and vegetable hot-pot and ratatouille flan. Organic produce is used where possible.

No-smoking area • No children in bar • Garden and family-room • Car-park • Wheelchair access, also WC

Newnham
map 3

George Inn
44 The Street
☎ EASTLING (079 589) 237

5m SW of Faversham off A2 and W of M2 junction 6

Open Tue to Sun noon–2 (1.30 Sun), 7–10 (exc Sun)
Closed Mon and Christmas Day

A sixteenth-century, tile-hung village pub, fully beamed, with rugs on polished floorboards, high settles and fresh flowers. Bar food is imaginatively produced, with lamb-filled aubergines, a cheese-topped cottage pie, fish pie, soups and a vegetable terrine as fairly

representative choices. The carefully cooked food is served in generous portions.

Garden • Car-park • Wheelchair access, also WC

Penshurst
map 3

Spotted Dog Inn
Smarts Hill
☎ PENSHURST (0892) 870253/ 870949

Off B2188 ½m S of Penshurst

Open all week noon–2, 7–10

This is the quintessential English pub – fifteenth-century, in a lovely setting, heavily beamed, with log fires and polished-oak furniture. The bar menu offers some staunchly traditional food: home-cooked ham and beef, local Speldhurst sausages, steak and kidney pie and cottage pie. Finish with an apricot and almond suet pudding, bread-and-butter pudding or treacle tart.

Garden • Car-park • Wheelchair access, also WC • Access, Visa

Sevenoaks
map 3

Pizza Piazza
30 Dorset Road
☎ SEVENOAKS (0732) 454664

Open all week 11am–11.30pm

A branch of one of the best pizza chains in the UK. See London entry.

Access, Visa

Sissinghurst   map 3

Sissinghurst Granary

**Sissinghurst Castle Garden,
nr Cranbrook**
☎ CRANBROOK (0580) 712850

*Open all week L noon–2.30 exc Mon
Closed Mon and 22 Dec to mid-March*

A National Trust property with a
splendid country-style tea-room
housed in a restored granary. It is an
attractive, airy place, full of natural
colours of brick and pale wood, and
floor-to-ceiling glass windows
revealing extensive views. Although
the menu is limited in its scope, what
it does it does well. Salads are
interesting, savoury dishes such as
cottage pie or lamb cobbler are made
with first-class ingredients, and the
baking is good. There is always a
vegetarian dish of the day, perhaps
vegetable crumble, and jacket
potatoes provide a simple, filling
snack. Home-made cakes include
fresh, light scones and ginger cake.

*No smoking • Garden • Car-park •
Wheelchair access, also WC*

Tonbridge   map 3

Office Wine Bar

163 High Street
☎ TONBRIDGE (0732) 353660

*Open Mon to Sat noon–2, 7–9.30
Closed Sun, 3 days Christmas and bank
hols*

Antique office equipment is the
feature of the décor in this highly
rated wine bar. Inside, the walls are
white and the beams are black. A
wide-ranging, eclectic menu takes in
anything from spicy Moroccan lamb
with apricots and almonds to thick
slices of pastrami with a sweet-and-
sour sauce. Vegetables are crisp and
colourful, and sweets are served in
daunting wedges smothered in
whipped cream. Good wines from
around the world, including several
by the glass.

*Wheelchair access • Access, Amex,
Diners, Visa*

Tunbridge Wells   map 3

Pizza Piazza

76 Mount Pleasant Road
☎ TUNBRIDGE WELLS (0892)
547124

Open all week 11am–11.30pm

A branch of one of the best pizza
chains in the UK. See London entry.

Access, Visa

Sankey's

39 Mount Ephraim
☎ TUNBRIDGE WELLS (0892)
511422

Open Mon to Sat noon–2, 7–10

*Closed Sun, Christmas and bank hol
Mons*

Large, solid Victorian houses get put
to some unusual uses; this was once
an engineering works and is now a
seafood bar and restaurant. Fresh fish
dominates the menu, much of it fairly
pricey, but light bar meals of home-
made fish cakes, small Dover sole and
ocean pie are all keenly priced
enough to allow you to start with fish
soup or finish with British cheeses.

Garden • Access, Visa

Bamber Bridge   map 7

Auctioneer

ADT Car Auction Centre, Walton Summit
☎ PRESTON (0772) 324870

Behind Novotel Hotel M6 junction 29

Open Sun, Mon and Wed to Sat L 11–2.30, Fri and Sat D 7–10
Closed Tue and first 2 weeks Jan

Overlooking a car auction room in surroundings both functional and industrial, Nigel Brookes' idiosyncratic restaurant provides great-value food which, though lacking in finesse, bursts with enthusiasm. It is worth pulling off the motorway for bar snacks of steak and kidney pie, a hot roast-beef sandwich or the filling £7.95 lunch, despite the forgettable desserts.

Car-park • Access, Visa

Blackburn   map 7

Muffins Tea Shoppe

5B Town Hall Street
☎ BLACKBURN (0254) 581707

Open all week 11am–3

A down-to-earth, no-frills café opposite the central library which is very popular with lady shoppers, who must make up 90 per cent of the clientele. Traditional Lancashire dishes of hot-pot, meat pies and cheese and onion pie are complemented by home-made scones, cheesecake, trifle and cream filled eclairs. There is freshly ground coffee and a choice of teas.

Unlicensed

Pizza Margherita

New Park House, Preston New Road
☎ BLACKBURN (0254) 665333

Open all week 10.30am–10.30pm
Closed Christmas Day, Boxing Day and New Year's Day

A chain of just four, pleasant, courteously run pizza parlours. See entry for Kendal, Cumbria.

No-smoking area • Car-park • Wheelchair access, also WC • Access, Visa

Blacko   map 7

Moorcock Inn 🏅

Gisburn Road
☎ NELSON (0282) 64186

On A682 2m N of Nelson

Open all week noon–2, 7–10

A warm, welcoming Lancashire moorland inn in the heart of Pendle witch country, where visitors come from miles around for the scenery and the sound, freshly cooked bar food. Austrian dishes such as a crisply battered schweinschnitzel or goulash with noodles stand side by side with ham shank and mustard sauce, savoury pancakes and steaks.

Garden • Wheelchair access, also WC

Blackpool map 7

September Brasserie

15–17 Queen Street
☎ BLACKPOOL (0253) 23282

Open Tue to Sat noon–3, 6.30–9.30 (exc Tue D)
Closed Sun, Mon and 2 weeks New Year

A bit pricey for dinner but good value at lunchtime. Until 18 months ago, an 'organic' restaurant in Blackpool would have seemed unlikely. Now you can sip organic wine and sup on free-range chicken (with crispy bacon, cream cheese and cranberry sauce) or indulge in an old-fashioned club sandwich or a croque monsieur. A balanced, well-intentioned menu; competent, far-sighted cooking.

Access, Amex, Diners, Visa

Bolton by Bowland map 7

Copy Nook

☎ BOLTON BY BOWLAND (020 07) 205

Open all week noon–2, 7–9.30

First and foremost a pub, Copy Nook is not over-tarted-up, just clean and comfortable, and it even has a no-smoking room. Good home-made food has made this place very popular. There are soup with home-made bread rolls, creamy garlic mushrooms, steak and kidney pie,

fresh haddock and chips, and some desserts piled high with cream. Pleasant, down-to-earth service.

No-smoking area • Car-park • Wheelchair access • Access, Visa

Chorley map 7

Muffins

High Street
☎ CHORLEY (025 72) 62566

S of M61 junction 8

Open Mon, Tue and Thur to Sat 10am–4
Closed Wed, Sun and bank hols

Muffins is a friendly, town-centre tea-room. Cakes and puddings are home-made – try the scones and the coffee vanilla cake. The overall style of cooking is homely and honest and produces light meals of beef and vegetable soup, steak pie, baked mushrooms and filled baked potatoes.

No-smoking area • Wheelchair access

Turner's Smithy

Bay Horse pub, Heath Charnock
☎ ADLINGTON (025 748) 0309

Off A673 Chorley–Horwich road SE of Chorley, NW of M61 junction 6

Open Sun L noon–2, all week D 7 (6.30 Sat)–9.30 (11 Sat)
Closed Christmas Day

Something of an oddity: an English pub serving Middle Eastern food, cooked by an Armenian, in the heartlands of rural Lancashire. The cooking is somewhat toned down, no doubt to accommodate local tastes, and offers sound, but not inspired, food. Recommended are the hummus and börek, followed by moresh bademune (a tender lamb stew), with baklava to finish.

Car-park • Access, Visa

Clitheroe   map 7

Auctioneer

New Market Street
☎ CLITHEROE (0200) 27153

Open Tue to Sun noon–1.30, 7–9.30
Closed Mon, 1 week Jan and 2 weeks Sept

A sound, well-run restaurant where food is handled simply. It overlooks the open market which means that there is plenty to watch from the glassed-in veranda where an excellent, modest lunch is served. This could be a provençale fish soup followed by medallions of lamb, kidney and liver with bacon and onions, and perhaps raspberry crème brûlée to finish. Sunday lunch is £8.75. More expensive meals are available in the evening.

No children evenings • Access, Visa

Haslingden   map 7

Hazel Tree

32 Manchester Road
☎ ROSSENDALE (070 62) 11530

Open Tue to Sun 10–2 (10.30–1 Sun),
7–10 (exc Tue D)
Closed Mon and 1 week Jan

A small, simple restaurant with a strong Danish theme to the food. Lunch includes a set menu for £6.05

with choices like mushroom soup or meatballs, followed by chicken with tarragon in a wine sauce or liver and bacon. You can also snack on an open sandwich, a Danish omelette, or even smoked reindeer. Evening meals are more expensive.

Wheelchair access • Access, Visa

Lancaster   map 7

Dukes

Dukes Play House, Moor Lane
☎ LANCASTER (0524) 843215

Open Tue to Sat noon–2, 5.30–9 (9.30
Fri and Sat)
Closed Sun, Mon and bank hols

At lunchtime this theatre restaurant serves snacks and light meals for shoppers and office workers. In the evening it moves up a gear, with suppers before the show and a full à la carte menu. Tomato, orange and basil soup is the real thing, fish might include grilled salmon or coley provençale, while vegetarians are offered nut and cottage cheese loaf or tomato and onion bhajias with saffron rice. Lemon syllabub is a refreshing sweet. Wines by the glass.

Wheelchair access, also WC

Libra

19 Brock Street
☎ LANCASTER (0524) 61551

Open Mon to Sat 11am–3
Closed Sun

One of the busiest and best-value eating places in Lancaster. At lunchtime be prepared to share a table. The blackboard lists a fair range of healthy wholefood and vegetarian dishes, ranging from wholemeal quiches, filled jacket potatoes and salads to cakes and rolls. Another board lists daily specials: broccoli and cashew-nut bake is a firm favourite. Fruit salads come with yoghurt and honey.

No smoking • Garden • Wheelchair access, also WC

Pizza Margherita

2 Moor Lane
☎ LANCASTER **(0524) 36333**

Open all week 11am–10.30pm
Closed Christmas Day, Boxing Day and New Year's Day (exc evening)

A chain of just four, pleasant, courteously run pizza parlours. See entry for Kendal, Cumbria.

No-smoking area • Access, Visa

Lytham St Anne's   map 7

BBQ

Dalmeny Hotel, 19-33 South Promenade, St Anne's
☎ ST ANNE'S **(0253) 712236**

Open all week noon–2.30, 6–10

A family-run hotel with a multi-faceted food operation. The BBQ restaurant is the best bet for budget eating. As well as obvious barbecue-style dishes such as chicken with barbecue sauce, there are home-made soups, local black puddings, onion tart, steak and kidney pie with a suet crust and pasta.

Car-park • Wheelchair access, also WC • Access, Visa

Tiggis

21–3 Rear Wood Street
☎ ST ANNE'S **(0253) 711481**

Open all week noon–2, 6–11
Closed Christmas Day, Boxing Day and New Year's Day

A jolly, bustling pizza/pasta restaurant. The large, rather grand building is equally useful for snacks, family meals and parties. The best value are the pizzas and pasta dishes, but there are also blackboard specials such as kidneys in sherry sauce or chicken cordon bleu. Good vegetables, creamy sweets and excellent coffee. Italian wines by the glass or carafe. Children eat for half price at lunchtime.

Access, Visa

Whitewell   map 7

Inn at Whitewell

Forest of Bowland
☎ DUNSOP BRIDGE **(020 08) 222**

Open all week noon–2, 7.15–9.30

An old-fashioned inn – a jumble of clocks, settles, stone fireplaces, sporting prints and yapping dogs – in a splendid setting. Bar lunches include Cumberland sausage and onion gravy, local lamb pie and large Lancashire teacakes filled with ham or Coniston trout. The evening menu is less extensive. Both sticky toffee pudding and the farmhouse cheeses are first-rate.

Garden • Car-park • Wheelchair access, also WC • Access, Amex, Diners, Visa

LEICESTERSHIRE

Leicester   map 4

Bobby's

154–6 Belgrave Road
☎ LEICESTER (0533) 660106/ 662448

Open Tue to Sun and bank hol Mons 11am–10.30 (11 Fri to Sun)
Closed Mon (exc bank hols)

Leicester has one of the largest Asian communities in the country, and many of its best-value eating places are sited along Belgrave Road. Bobby's is one of the best. Mr and Mrs Lakhani offer genuine Gujerati home cooking, preparing dishes fresh each day. The menu is dominated by excellent thalis comprising snacks and starters, vegetable curries, rice, bread and sweetmeats. Otherwise, there are rice-flour dosas with coconut chutney and sambar, and unusual items such as dhokla, patis and dhebra.

Unlicensed, but bring your own: no corkage • No-smoking area • Wheelchair access • Access, Amex, Visa

Bread and Roses

70 High Street
☎ LEICESTER (0533) 532448

Open Mon to Sat 9am–4.30
Closed Sun, Christmas and New Year

Akrum Haruwash is cook and manager of this wholefood/vegetarian café in the basement of a radical bookshop. He is Palestinian and the short menu shows strong Middle Eastern tendencies, with hummus, falafel and tabouleh lining up alongside quiche, vegetable goulash and assorted salads.

Unlicensed, but bring your own •
No-smoking area

Chaat House

108 Belgrave Road
☎ LEICESTER (0533) 667599

Open Wed to Mon noon–8.30
Closed Tue and bank hols

A popular Indian vegetarian café specialising in vegetarian snacks (or 'chaat'), including onion bhajias, samosas and pani puri (hollow balls which can be filled with chickpeas and a date and tamarind sauce). Otherwise, there are dosas, vegetable curries, decent breads and a good choice of sweetmeats. Thalis from £5.75. To drink there are lassi, mango milk shake or masala milk. Take-aways are available.

Unlicensed, but bring your own: no corkage • No smoking • Wheelchair access, also WC • Access, Amex, Diners, Visa

Curry Fever

139 Belgrave Road
☎ LEICESTER (0533) 662941

Open Tue to Sun noon–2 (exc Sun), 6–11
Closed Mon (exc bank hols)

Like Friends Corner in Coventry (see entry), this restaurant offers an idiosyncratic version of Indian home cooking with some unusual touches.

Anil and Sunil Anand set up business in the late '70s, and much of their original menu has remained intact. Karahi specialities, masalas and birianis share the stage with lethally hot pili-pili chicken, egg curry and prawn vindaloo. A bowl of methi or masala chicken for six is £21.50. Vegetarians should go for the thali (£6.50). Home-made kulfi to finish.

Wheelchair access, also WC • Access, Amex, Diners, Visa

Panda

215 Fosse Road North
☎ LEICESTER (0533) 538628

Open Mon to Sat noon–10.30
Closed Sun

The setting is a red-brick Victorian house well away from the city centre. Inside, there are a few reminders that this is a Chinese restaurant; otherwise it feels almost like a dining-room in a modest seaside hotel. The menu deals in Cantonese, Pekinese and Szechuan dishes, with echoes of Chinese home cooking in the full-blooded flavours and robust handling of ingredients. Sesame prawn toasts; squid in black-bean and chilli sauce and crispy Szechuan duck show the style. Some esoteric specialities such as jellyfish with pickled cucumber, shredded pork with salted vegetables, and yin-yang rice are not always available.

Access, Amex, Diners, Visa

Rise of the Raj

6 Evington Road
☎ LEICESTER (0533) 553885

Open all week noon–2, 6–11.45

The Raj is a firm favourite. Situated on the outskirts of the prosperous

suburb of Evington, it offers, as well as an elegant décor and a cocktail list, reasonably priced North Indian cooking; £6.60 will buy a whole chicken tandoori. Karahi dishes feature and there are both vegetarian and non-vegetarian thalis.

No children under 5 • Wheelchair access • Access, Amex, Diners, Visa

Water Margin

76–8 High Street
☎ LEICESTER (0533) 516422

Open all week noon–11.30pm

This functional restaurant is probably the only venue in Leicester serving authentic Cantonese dim-sum and one-plate meals. But you must ask for the special menu, with its steamed dumplings, bowls of soup and plates of noodles with excellent fresh seafood and roast meats. Prices on the main menu have been rising steeply, but the quality of some dishes is more redolent of a local take-away.

Wheelchair access • Access, Amex, Diners, Visa

Lutterworth   map 4

Paper Tiger

27 Church Street
☎ LEICESTER (0533) 556244/ 552365

On A426 at M1 junction 20

Open Mon to Sat noon–2, 5.30–11.30
Closed Sun

Stay with the set menus for affordable eating in this highly popular Chinese restaurant. The menu brings together Cantonese,

Pekinese and Szechuan specialities – ranging from barbecued pork, steamed sea bass and aromatic crispy duck to hot-and-sour soup, crispy shredded beef with carrots and chilli, and chicken with yellow-bean sauce. Vegetarians have plenty of choice.

No-smoking area • Wheelchair access • Access, Amex, Visa

Old Dalby   map 7

Crown Inn

Debdale Hill
☎ MELTON MOWBRAY (0664) 823134

Open all week noon–1.45, 6–9.30 (exc Sun D)

Finding the Crown is a challenge: the 300-year-old inn looks more like a private house. There is no real bar, just a series of small, flower-filled rooms with open fires and antique furniture. Bar food is ambitious: beef parcels braised in rich red wine, chicken with mango, ginger and yoghurt sauce. Welsh rarebit or sirloin steak sandwiches are simpler offerings.

Garden and family-room • Car-park • Wheelchair access

Stretton   map 7

Ram Jam Inn

Great North Road
☎ STAMFORD (0780) 410776

Open all week 7am–11pm
Closed Christmas Day

Designed as an alternative to the chain restaurants lining the A1, and catering for travellers who care about food. What other roadside establishment offers espresso coffee and meaty sausages with onion marmalade? Breakfast is served from 7am to 11am, snacks are available all day, and the full menu brings barbecued ribs, crisp duck with salad and good French fries.

No-smoking area • Garden • Car-park • Wheelchair access, also WC • Access, Amex, Visa

Walcote   map 4

Black Horse

Lutterworth Road
☎ LUTTERWORTH (0455) 552684

On A427 at M1 junction 20

Open all week exc Tue noon–2, 6 (7 Sun)–9.30
Closed Tue

Thai restaurants spring up in unlikely places, although few are set amid the classic trappings of an English village pub. Landlady Saovanee Tinker hails from Thailand and she cooks a short menu of authentic specialities which can be eaten in the bar or the dining-room. Look for the Thai mixed grill, various curries, khau mu daeng (marinated pork with rice and a chilli/ginger dip) and nuer phat (strips of beef in oyster sauce). Banquets with a surprise selection of dishes can be booked in advance. English ales and bottled Thai beer.

Garden • Car-park

Out to Eat is totally independent, accepts no free hospitality and makes no charge for inclusion.

Boston   map 8

Eagle's

54–6 Main Ridge East
☎ **BOSTON (0205) 364458**

Open Tue to Sun 11-2, 6-10.30
Closed Mon

On the ground floor is the fish and chip take-away; upstairs is a fish and steak restaurant; there is also the Quarterdeck Bar on the first floor serving drinks and salads. Johnny Eagle still cooks the fish, which can be anything from haddock and skate to halibut and sole. International favourites such as prawn cocktail and chicken tikka complete the menu. Set lunches (Tuesday to Friday) will leave change from £3. To drink, there are wine by the glass, pots of tea and liqueur coffees.

No-smoking area • Car-park

Lincoln   map 8

Wig & Mitre 🏅

29 Steep Hill
☎ **LINCOLN (0522) 535190**

Open all week 8am–11pm
Closed Christmas Day

This fourteenth-century pub is set in the heart of medieval Lincoln. Run along brasserie lines, food is served all day from 8am – and that means a choice ranging from breakfast to

steak and kidney pie, home-made ravioli and crème brûlée. The restaurant is more expensive.

Access, Amex, Diners, Visa

Louth   map 8

Mr Chips

17–21 Aswell Street
☎ **LOUTH (0507) 603756**

Open Mon to Sat 9am–11.30pm
Closed Sun

A large fish and chip emporium which has been run by successive generations of the Hagan family since 1920. The bright, airy self-service cafeteria offers high chairs and a first-rate mother and baby changing-room; the no-smoking area is small. The house speciality is haddock with chips.

Unlicensed, but bring your own: no corkage • No-smoking area • Wheelchair access, also WC

Newton   map 8

Red Lion 🏅

☎ **FOLKINGHAM (052 97) 256**

On A52 10m E of Grantham

Open all week noon–2, 7–10,
Closed Mon Oct to Easter

The setting is bygone England – a village school, a fourteenth-century church and a pub nestle within the green and pleasant Lincolnshire Wolds. The pub is justly renowned for its cold meals, excellent and succulent turkey, home-pressed tongue, roast rib of beef and ham, as well as local specialities such as pork pie, stuffed chine and Lincolnshire chipolatas. The publican is also a pork butcher and his stupendous carvery shows just what can be done with a little care and a lot of skill. Beers include sensibly priced Bateman's prize-winning XXX bitter.

Garden and family-room • Car-park • Wheelchair access, also WC

★ after an eating-place indicates that it is one of the best found by the Editor during research for this book (see page 14 for a list).

⊕ after an eating-place indicates that it is a pub. The opening and closing times we give only relate to when food is available – the licensing hours may be different.

⊕ after an eating-place indicates that it is within five miles of the nearest motor-way junction. We give the relevant motorway and junction in the details. Eating-places in cities and large towns, where traffic, parking and route-finding may cause delay, do not have this symbol.

Heswall

map 7

Marco's

186 Telegraph Road, Wirral
☎ **051-342 1412**

W of M53 junction 4

Open all week D 6–10.30, plus Thur to Sat L noon–2.30
Closed Christmas Day and Boxing Day

Owned by Lynda and Renzo Garavello, this restaurant is named after their son who – according to Renzo – does not like Italy. His parents do not share this sentiment, and enjoy feeding appreciative diners with good British trattoria-style food. Bread sticks are still placed on every table for the chomping. What follows will usually be generous and good value. The pasta is fresh, as is almost everything else including complimentary salads. Don't leave without having an espresso or cappuccino.

Wheelchair access • Access, Amex, Visa

Liverpool

map 7

Armadillo

20–2 Matthew Street
☎ **051-236 4123**

Open Tue to Fri noon–3, 5–6.45 and 7.30–10.30, Sat noon–5, 7.30–10.30
Closed Sun, Mon, Christmas and bank hols

As much a part of the Liverpool scene as the Cavern and the Beatles

tourist trail, Martin and Angela Cooper's informal restaurant continues to draw the crowds. Best value is the lunch/early supper menu, which is strong on flavour and variety: falafels with tahini sauce; Arbroath fish stew; pork and sage meatballs poached in cider. Vegetarians might be offered baked marrow stuffed with nuts and vegetables, or red cabbage and chestnut lasagne. There is a more expensive dinner menu. Well-chosen, fairly priced wines.

Access, Visa

Bluecoat Café Bar

Bluecoat Chambers, School Lane
☎ **051-709 5297**

Open Mon to Sat 10am–5
Closed Sun and bank hols

Part of a complex of craft and book shops and community arts ventures housed in eighteenth-century style off Liverpool's main shopping street. Queues develop quickly for the fresh, inexpensive dishes: wholemeal pizzas, quiches, baked potatoes and some very good dressed salads. Try and hit an off-peak moment to enjoy the place at its best.

No-smoking area • Wheelchair access, also WC

All details are as accurate as possible at the time of going to press, but chefs and owners often change, and it is wise to check by telephone before making a special journey.

Casa Italia

Temple Close, 40 Stanley Street
☎ **051-227 5774**

Open Mon to Sat noon–10
Closed Sun, Christmas Day
and Boxing Day

Part of a triumvirate of Italian eating
places housed in a large building near
the site of the Cavern Club. The
Casa Italia is the cheap and cheerful
side of the business, offering a fairly
safe choice of pastas and a large
selection of very similar pizzas. But
the cooking is sound, flavours
pronounced, and there is a brisk,
bustling atmosphere.

Everyman Bistro

9–11 Hope Street
☎ **051-708 9545**

Open Mon to Sat noon–midnight
Closed Sun

A popular bistro beneath the
Everyman Theatre, a model of
providing good food on a modest
budget. Fresh ingredients, a menu
changing twice daily and an inventive
style of cooking draw an enthusiastic
crowd. Spicy lamb is an all-time
favourite, closely followed by cheese,
leek and potato gratin. Desserts are
superb, especially the orange devil's
food cake.

No-smoking area until 8pm • No
children after 9pm

Far East

27–35 Berry Street
☎ **051-709 3141**

Open all week noon–11

Rated by many of its loyal followers
as Liverpool's archetypal Cantonese

restaurant. You can eat cheaply from
the list of dim-sum snacks and one-
plate rice and noodle dishes: prawn
dumplings, Chinese mushrooms with
meat balls, chicken and glutinous rice
in lotus leaves, char siu with noodles
in soup. The full menu runs to 200
affordable dishes; vegetarians have a
separate section and there are
challenging daily specials such as
deep-fried duck with yam croquette
and oyster. Drink tea or Tiger beer.

Car-park • Wheelchair access, also WC
• Access, Amex, Diners, Visa

Jenny's

Old Ropery, Fenwick Street
☎ **051-236 0332**

Open Mon to Sat noon–2.15 (exc Sat),
7–10 (exc Mon)
Closed Sun, 24 Dec to 1 Jan, last week
Aug and 1st week Sept

A grey suit sort of seafood restaurant
– comfortable and correct with a
familiar menu and lots of creamy
sauces. It is the well-priced table
d'hôte of three courses plus coffee for
£9.95 that earns the listing here,
offering deep-fried baby squid,
prawns, fillet of brill or plaice,
provençale beef stew and rich
desserts.

Access, Amex, Visa

Refectory

The Anglican Cathedral, St James
Mount
☎ **051-709 6271 ext 142**

Open all week 10am–4.30

Liverpool's massive Anglican
cathedral is one of the city's most
spectacular architectural sights,
attracting scores of tourists, school

parties and visitors. The Refectory is to one side of the huge nave. Excellent home-baked cakes, scones and biscuits are served with tea or coffee. A short lunch menu offers soup, ploughman's and salads as well as hot dishes such as tagliatelle with mushrooms or bangers and mash.

Unlicensed • No-smoking area • Car-park • Wheelchair access, also WC

Shangri-La

37 Victoria Street
☎ **051-255 0708/227 2707**

Open all week noon (4pm Sun)–midnight

An up-market Cantonese restaurant with smart décor and helpful staff. The kitchen provides a consistent level of cooking, largely in the mainland Cantonese tradition, but with some Beijing and Szechuan dishes too. Lemon chicken and crispy duck have been praised. Go in a group for the best value.

Access, Amex, Diners, Visa

Tate Gallery Coffee Shop

Tate Gallery, Albert Dock
☎ **051-709 3223 ext 2211**

Open Apr to Sept Tue to Sun 11am–6.45, Oct to Mar 11am–4.45
Closed Mon

The Coffee Shop is stark but stylish with grey lino, steel chairs and matt-grey, Formica-covered round tables and situated on a double balcony on the mezzanine level of the gallery. It is run by Juliet Shield who, until recently, was responsible for La Grande Bouffe restaurant. Nearly everything is made on the premises, and salads are exceedingly fresh. In the summer and on Saturdays and Sundays there is a 'quick' self-service counter.

No smoking • Wheelchair access, also WC

Yuet Ben

1 Upper Duke Street
☎ **051-709 5772**

Open Mon to Sat noon–2.30 (exc Sat), 5–11.30
Closed Sun and 2 weeks in summer

Opened by Mr and Mrs Lau in 1968 and advertised as Liverpool's 'first and original Peking-style restaurant'. The 100-dish menu blends the authentic and the westernised, and it pays to look for the genuine specialities. Dishes include lamb with leeks, hot spiced chicken, cold smoked fish, pickled rainbow vegetables, crispy duck, noodles and spare ribs. Reports suggest this is a creditable alternative to some of the high-profile venues in Liverpool's Chinatown.

Wheelchair access • Access, Amex, Diners, Visa

Blickling map 8

Buckinghamshire Arms

☎ AYLSHAM (0263) 732133

Adjacent to Blickling Hall on B1354 NW of Aylsham

Open Tue to Sat D 7–9.30, Sun L noon–1.45
Closed Mon

A natural and comfortable stop after snooping around Blickling Hall or walking in the surrounding countryside. Arrive here with a big appetite and you will be well rewarded. After a drink in one of the two bars, head for the restaurant, which glories in unashamed English country cooking. If rabbit is on the menu, you will be told that the creature in question was shot by one of the barmen. Most produce is similarly slain or grown in the locale: plenty of pheasant and duck. Also recommended are the lobster, prawn and salmon and the steak and venison pies. There are beers from Adnams and Greene King and a serviceable wine list. Lunchtime bar food is also available.

Car-park • Wheelchair access, also WC • Access, Visa

Brancaster Staithe map 8

Jolly Sailors

☎ BRANCASTER (0485) 210314

Nr King's Lynn, half-way between Hunstanton and Wells, beside A149

Open all week noon–2, 7–9 (10 Fri and Sat)
Closed Christmas Day

Brancaster harbour has been declared pollution-free by the EC, and this 200-year-old pub takes full advantage of it. Locals, yachting types, birdwatchers and walkers come here for big bowls of local mussels, as well as oysters and cockles from time to time. Home-made soup is served in a mug and the bar menu also includes chunky chicken and mushroom pancakes and vegetarian moussaka. Sweets are made on the premises. Food is served all day during July and August. There are more expensive restaurant meals. Greene King beers and a better-than-average pub wine list.

No-smoking area in restaurant • Garden and family-room • Car-park • Wheelchair access • Access, Diners, Visa

Burnham Market map 8

Fishes'

Market Place
☎ FAKENHAM (0328) 738588

Open Tue to Sun noon–2, 6.45–9.30
(9 winter weekdays)
Closed Mon, Sun D Oct to June and 3
weeks Jan

A pleasant, informal restaurant overlooking the village green. As the name suggests, fish, all of it local, predominates with perhaps just one meat choice, often home-baked ham or smoked goose. The great value three-course lunch for £8.95 offers crab soup, salmon fish-cakes, whole plaice and syllabub among a selection of choices. Dinner is slightly more expensive.

No children under 5 evenings •
Wheelchair access

Downham Market map 5

Cock

43 Lynn Road
☎ DOWNHAM MARKET (0366)
385047

Open Wed to Mon noon–2 (exc Sun), 7–
9.30
Closed Tue and 1 week at Christmas

Julie Hassell's cooking draws quite a crowd to the neatly kept pub she runs with her husband Roger. Sound, honestly prepared food includes good home-made soups, beef and vegetable casserole, curries, baked avocado with chestnuts in Stilton and cottage pie. Bread-and-butter pudding and treacle tart for dessert.

No-smoking area • No children in bar •
Garden • Car-park • Wheelchair access

Great Yarmouth map 5

Mastersons

113 Regent Road
☎ YARMOUTH (0493) 842747

Open Tue to Sat 11.30am–3
Closed Sun, Mon, Christmas Day and
Boxing Day

A classic wet-fish shop with a wide range of fish for sale including home-smoked bloaters and sprats. Attached is a fish and chip restaurant and take-away. Restaurant customers can choose a piece of fresh fish from a range including haddock, cod, plaice and skate and have it fried to order.

King's Lynn map 8

Riverside

27 King Street
☎ KING'S LYNN (0553) 773134

Open Mon to Sat noon–2, 7–10
Closed Sun

The restaurant is part of a complex which includes a theatre and coffee-shop housed in a converted fourteenth-century warehouse. On fine days food can be eaten on the terrace overlooking the River Ouse. The quick-lunch menu is varied and well done, taking in omelettes, lasagne, curries, steak and kidney pie, and quiche and salad. Evenings are more expensive.

No-smoking area • Garden • Car-park
• Access, Visa

Norwich   map 5

Andersens

52 St Giles Street
☎ NORWICH (0603) 617199

*Open Mon to Wed 8am–7pm, Thur to
Sat 8am–9.30pm
Closed Sun*

A taste of Denmark comes to
Norwich in this converted
eighteenth-century town house with
a prestigiously revamped courtyard.
The menu focuses on 'smorgasbord'
– open sandwiches with toppings
ranging from smoked eel with
scrambled eggs and chives to
'frikadeller' (Danish meat balls) with
sweet-and-sour cucumber salad.
Breakfasts are served throughout the
day: look for the Bornholm omelette
(with kipper, radish and chives,
served in the pan). More substantial
evening meals are available Thursday
to Saturday. Drink iced akvavit with a
Danish beer chaser.

*No-smoking area • Wheelchair access •
Access, Visa*

Bombay

43 Timber Hill
☎ NORWICH (0603) 619908

*Open all week noon–3, 6–midnight
Closed Christmas Day*

Quality ingredients, handled with
precision, give an impression of
above-average standards at this
Indian restaurant. The food here is
familiar but rarely disappointing.
Basics like samosas and prawn poori
are carefully presented and satisfying.
King prawn rogan josh is authentic
and properly spiced.

Access, Amex, Diners, Visa

Mange Tout

22–4 White Lion Street
☎ NORWICH (0603) 617879

*Open Mon to Sat 11.30am–10.30pm
Closed Sun*

An informal, plain bistro offering the
option of a snack or a full meal.
Portions are generous and the
cooking sound. There is a wide range
of salads – niçoise, salade bleue and
chef's salad – and hot French bread
and jacket potatoes come with a
variety of fillings. Daily specials
might be a sweetcorn and broad bean
roulade or stuffed fillet of plaice
wrapped in vine leaves.

*No-smoking area • Access, Amex,
Diners, Visa*

Pizza Express

15 St Benedict Street
☎ NORWICH (0603) 622157

Open all week 11.30am–midnight

Part of the popular chain which is the
pick of the pizza bunch. See London
entry.

*No-smoking area • Access, Amex,
Diners, Visa*

Pizza Piazza

1 All Saints Street
☎ NORWICH (0603) 667809

Open all week 11am–11.30pm

A branch of one of the best pizza
chains in the UK. See London entry.

Access, Visa

All letters to this guide are acknowledged.

Scole   map 5

Crossways

☎ DISS (0379) 740638

Open all week 11.30–2.15, 6–10

Undistinguished from the outside but
worth a visit. The owner, Peter
Black, is proud of his well-priced
wine list, and the bar food, though
fairly unsophisticated, is honestly
produced and of reasonable quality.
Moussaka is made correctly with
minced lamb, and moules marinière
are carefully cooked. Otherwise,
there are steaks, curries, a vegetarian
choice and good chips.

*Garden and family-room • Car-park •
Wheelchair access • Access, Amex,
Diners, Visa*

Stow Bardolph   map 5

Hare Arms

☎ DOWNHAM MARKET (0366)
382229

Open all week noon–2, 7–10
Closed Christmas Day and Boxing Day

A pleasant and extremely popular
country pub. With bar food that
takes in seasonal crabs and lobster,
fresh lemon sole and local pheasant,
as well as standards such as steak,
Guinness and oyster pie, Stilton and
bacon soup and generously filled
sandwiches, it is advisable to arrive
early. The owners, David and Tricia
McManus, uphold high standards for
both food and service.

*No-smoking area • No children under
10 in bar • Garden • Car-park •
Wheelchair access*

Thornham   map 8

Lifeboat

Ship Lane
☎ THORNHAM (048 526) 236

Open all week noon–2, 7–10

Good walks through coastal flats help
build up an appetite for the fresh fish
served in the bar of this old and
popular pub – fillet of cod in a crisp
batter with hand-cut chips or a
simply grilled fillet of plaice. There
are also sandwiches, ploughman's and
a couple of vegetarian dishes.

*Garden and family-room • Car-park •
Wheelchair access, also WC • Access,
Amex, Diners, Visa*

Wells-next-the-Sea   map 8

Moorings ★

6 Freeman Street
☎ FAKENHAM (0328) 710949

*Open Mon and Fri to Sun L 12.30–2,
Mon and Thur to Sun D 7.30–9
Closed Tue, Wed, 24 Nov to 13 Dec, 24–
26 Dec, New Year's Day and 2–21 June*

The word 'local' peppers the menu:
local asparagus, local organic beef,
local cockles, local dabs, even locally
cured and smoked ham. Moorings is
deservedly popular (booking is
essential) for the simple cooking and
fresh flavours. Fish dominates the
menu from crab soup to cockle pie
and poached sea bass, while
imaginative meat and vegetarian
dishes are skilled and assured. Two
courses will cost £8.95 or £11.95 (still
good value) a head.

No smoking • Wheelchair access

NORTHAMPTONSHIRE

East Haddon map 4

Red Lion

☎ NORTHAMPTON (0604) 770223

*Open all week L 12.30–2, D Mon to Fri
7–9.30*
Closed Christmas and New Year

This substantial stone building is part
village hostelry and part hotel.
Home-cooked bar food is one
attraction of the place, and the best
choice is at lunchtime. The regularly
changing menu might include soup
from the stockpot, curry or lamb and
leek pie, followed by traditional
puddings. In the evenings, the menu
may be limited to sandwiches and
ploughman's. There are more
expensive restaurant meals. Charles
Wells beers on draught.

*Garden and family-room • Car-park •
Access, Diners, Visa*

Easton on the Hill map 4

Exeter Arms

Stamford Road
☎ STAMFORD (0780) 57503

*Open all week noon-3, 7-10.30
(exc Sun D)*

A few short, sharp choices are affixed
to the blackboard of this pleasant pub
every day. These might include fresh
asparagus or spinach and Gruyère
fritters or, as main courses, halibut
and braised guinea-fowl. First-class
ingredients are used in most cases.
Simple English food incorporating
just a few 'exotic' influences.

*Garden • Car-park • Wheelchair access,
also WC • Access, Visa*

Fotheringhay map 5

Falcon Inn

☎ COTTERSTOCK (083 26) 254

*Open Tue to Sun 12.30–2, 6.45–9.45
Closed Mon*

In the shadow of the church stands
the Falcon, a fine Victorian pub
whose relaxing lounge bar boasts two
open fires. Bar food is sound and
satisfying and provides a varied menu
– vegetable broth, roast local
pheasant, carbonnade of beef, fresh
Grimsby cod au gratin, roast rack
of lamb. Its popularity is well
deserved.

*Garden • Car-park • Wheelchair access,
also WC • Access, Visa*

You will find report forms (write a letter if
you prefer) at the back of the book so that
you can tell us about your experiences of
going *Out to Eat*. We'll put the
information to good use when we're
compiling the next edition.

Northampton   map 4

Edwards of Crick

The Wharf
☎ NORTHAMPTON **(0788) 822517**

Open Tue to Sun 10.30am–9.30
(4.30 Sun)
Closed Mon and 26 Dec to 4 Jan

A converted red-brick wharf by the
Grand Union Canal run with verve
by Hermione Ainley. A flexible
informality is enhanced by cooking
that tries hard and provides good
value for money. The downstairs
coffee-house brings light snacks of
cheese on toast, home-made pizzas,
Edward's dog – a sausage sandwiched
in home-made bread – and more
substantial casseroles. There is a
pricier restaurant upstairs.

Garden • Car-park • Wheelchair access,
also WC • Access, Amex, Visa

Weedon Bec   map 4

Narrow Boat Inn

Stowehill
☎ WEEDON **(0327) 40536**

E of M1 junction 16

Open all week noon–2, 7–9.30 (10 Fri
and Sat) exc Mon D
Closed Christmas, New Year

A very busy roadside pub alongside
the A5, with a big garden backing on
to the Grand Union Canal. On
Sundays, the high-raftered family-
room is packed out with visitors. In
the bar there is a straightforward
menu of pub grub – ploughman's,
chilli, steak and ale pie – backed up
by a few dishes from the more
expensive restaurant menu. Well-
kept Charles Wells beers.

Garden and family-room • Car-park •
Wheelchair access • Access, Visa

NORTHUMBERLAND

Kiln Pit Hill map 10

Manor House Inn

Carterway Heads, nr Shotley Bridge
☎ Consett **(0207) 55268**

On A68 2m S of Kiln Pit Hill

Open all week noon–2.30, 7–9.30

An old stone coaching-inn offering unusual bar meals that reflect dedication to sound ingredients. There is always a soup, then perhaps Cumberland sausage with mustard sauce, spicy lamb casserole with aubergines, or a steak sandwich. Meals can be a bargain: a generous fillet of salmon with new potatoes and salad for £4.25. Sticky toffee pudding is a must.

Garden • Wheelchair access • Access, Visa

Morpeth map 10

La Brasserie Gourmet

59 Bridge Street
☎ **Morpeth (0670) 516200**

Open Tue to Sun 11.30–2, 6.30–11 (exc Sun D)
Closed Mon

Useful in an area not well served by decent eating places. A three-course special lunch for £4.50 is exceptional value, with six main-course choices including lemon sole with parsley sauce, steak and kidney pie and lasagne. The early dinner menu (6.30–8.30pm) is equally good value at £6.50. The evening carte is more expensive.

Access, Amex, Diners, Visa

Rochester map 10

Redesdale Arms Hotel

☎ Otterburn **(0830) 20668/20530**

On A68 4m NW of Otterburn

Open all week summer noon–3, 5.30–10, winter 7–9; bar meals all day

A charming, 600-year-old, family-run coaching-inn with the atmosphere of a genial country pub. The cooking here is 'farmhouse' and available all day. Portions are big; prices are extremely modest. Considering the plethora of fox-hunting memorabilia, including a mounted fox head, it comes as a surprise to find a separate menu replete with inventive vegetarian dishes. Among these are vegetable pie with walnut or puff pastry, leek and lentil cobbler, bean and cider casserole, cheese and rice puffs and nut, corn and cheese casserole. A limited choice of beers.

Family-room • Car-park • Wheelchair access • Access, Diners, Visa

Seaton Sluice map 10

Waterford Arms

☎ 091-237 0450

On A193 between Blyth and Whitley Bay

Open all week noon–2.15, 7.30–9.30

The harbour is nearby, so fresh fish is the speciality in this large 1930s pub situated where Seaton Burn runs into the sea. Portions are gargantuan: seafood platter is spectacularly arranged on a 'foot-wide' plate, massive fillets of fried fish can measure up to 16 inches in length. There are also good specials such as swordfish, poached salmon and grilled halibut steak with cheese. Meat-eaters are offered steaks, pies and leek pudding with mince and vegetables. There are rustic soups to start, mighty banana splits to finish, with Samson Bitter on handpump, as well as refreshing white wine by the bottle.

No children after 9pm • Car-park • Wheelchair access

Warenford map 10

Warenford Lodge

nr Belford
☎ BELFORD (0668) 213453

Just off A1 4m SE of Belford

Open Tue to Sun noon–1.30, 7–9.30
Closed Mon, winter Tue to Thur L

An easy turn off the A1 makes this comfortably furnished pub an ideal journey-breaker. There is a wood-burning stove and the food is excellent. A varied menu takes in

Northumbrian fish soup, home-cooked ham with pease pudding, kofta balls, cannelloni and Syrian lamb roll, all based on first-class produce and an inventive, assured cooking style.

Children under 14 in reserved dining area, evenings only • Car-park • Wheelchair access, also WC • Access, Diners, Visa

Warkworth map 10

Jackdaw

34 Castle Street
☎ ALNWICK (0665) 711488

Open Tue to Sat 10–5 (exc Thur), 7–9.30 (exc Thur), Sun 12.30–2
Closed Mon (exc bank hols) and Thur

One of those small, inviting local café/restaurants where fresh ingredients combined with honest home-cooking ensure a loyal following. Fish, especially lemon sole, is bought daily from the nearby market while steak and kidney pie and beef olives are other stalwarts. Baking is excellent – first-class scones come with home-made jam. Sunday lunch (£6.95) is excellent value.

No-smoking area • Wheelchair access

When you book a restaurant table, you're making a contract with the restaurant and you must be given a table, within reasonable time of your arrival. If not, the restaurant is in breach of contract and you can claim a reasonable sum to cover any expenses you had as a result, e.g. travelling expenses.

Wooler

map 10

Ryecroft Hotel

Ryecroft Way
☎ WOOLER (0668) 81459

Open all week noon–2
Closed first 2 weeks Nov and 1 week
Christmas

A rather unprepossessing building
that has a redeeming feature: the
cooking is considered and assured.

The bar, the focal point of the hotel,
offers a short, inexpensive lunch
menu of soup, salmon pancake,
tagliatelle with mushrooms, baked
trout. Sunday lunch in the restaurant
is a bargain at £8 – three courses
including a roast and an excellent
sticky toffee pudding. There are
more expensive restaurant meals in
the evening.

Garden • Car-park • Wheelchair access
• Access, Diners, Visa

★ after an eating-place indicates that it is one of the best found by the Editor
during research for this book (see page 14 for a list).

🍺 after an eating-place indicates that it is a pub. The opening and closing times
we give only relate to when food is available – the licensing hours may be different.

🛉 after an eating-place indicates that it is within five miles of the nearest motorway junction. We give the relevant motorway and junction in the details. Eating-
places in cities and large towns, where traffic, parking and route-finding may cause
delay, do not have this symbol.

Nottingham map 7

Ben Bowers

128 Derby Road, Canning Circus
☎ NOTTINGHAM **(0602) 413388**

Open Mon to Sat noon–2.30, 6–10
Closed Sun, Christmas and New Year

There is something for everyone in this prettily decorated building at the top end of Derby Road. It is actually three eating-places under the same roof, and the best value is in the Victoria Bar. Snacks and simple home-cooked dishes range from soup and fresh pasta to mushroom Stroganoff, backed up by pâté, beignets and cold platters. More ambitious, more expensive meals are served in the two restaurants with their lacy curtains, pink tablecloths and potted palms.

Access, Amex, Visa

Jack Sprat's

23–5 Heathcote Street
☎ NOTTINGHAM **(0602) 410710**

Open D Mon to Sat 7–10 (10.30 Fri and Sat), L by arrangement
Closed Sun, Christmas Day, Boxing Day and bank hols

A converted Victorian corner shop on the fringes of the Lace Market. The exterior is black and white; the menu divides its loyalties between fish and vegetarian dishes. On the one hand there might be butterfly trout with peanut sauce or spicy Caribbean snapper; on the other, look for goats'-milk cheese wrapped in vine leaves, aubergine Parmesan and spinach and mushroom pancakes with tomato and sour cream. The best place in Nottingham to drink organic wines.

Wheelchair access

Loch Fyne Oyster Bar

17 King Street
☎ Nottingham **(0602) 508481**

Open Mon to Sat 9am–9pm
Closed Sun

Right in the heart of land-locked Nottingham is this splendid oyster bar and seafood shop specialising in items that are air-freighted overnight from the parent company in Cairndow (see entry). Outside is maritime blue paintwork; inside are hefty Scots pine tables and chairs. Seafood is the main business: oysters, plump mussels tossed in white wine and cream, grilled kippers, plates of smoked salmon and gravlax. Call in for a full meal, an open sandwich, a bowl of soup or a cup of tea and a cake. The style is flexible and the mood is laid back. Decent wines by the glass, and Guinness to drink.

Wheelchair access • Access, Amex, Visa

Ocean City

100–4 Derby Road
☎ NOTTINGHAM (0602) 410041

*Open Mon to Sat noon–2.30, 6–11.30,
Sun noon–10.30*

A cavernous Cantonese restaurant,
close to the university. Lunchtime
dim-sum include good-value stuffed
bean curd roll, mixed vegetable
dumpling and chicken buns.
Choosing satisfactorily from the carte
is more expensive and it is worth
asking for the cheaper one-plate rice
or noodle dishes of barbecued pork
or roast duck on the special Chinese
menu.

*Wheelchair access • Access, Amex,
Diners, Visa*

Rita's Café

15 Goosegate, Hockley
☎ NOTTINGHAM (0602) 481115

*Open Mon to Wed 9am–5pm, Thur to
Sat 9am–10pm*
*Closed Sun, Christmas, New Year and
bank hols*

You will find this café above the
Hiziki Wholefood Collective shop.
The cooking is predominantly vegan,
and dishes are listed on a blackboard.
Typically, there might be carrot and
garlic soup; tempeh (soya bean)
cutlets with tomato sauce; jacket
potato with leek and butter-bean
sauce; and cauliflower and courgette
tandoori. Meatless burgers and
spaghetti bolognese, stir-fries and
salads complete the picture. The
owners are applying for a licence;
meanwhile, bring your own alcohol.

*Unlicensed, but bring your own: no
corkage • No smoking noon–2, also no-
smoking area*

Saagar

473 Mansfield Road, Sherwood
☎ NOTTINGHAM (0602) 622014

*Open all week noon–2.30, 5.30–
midnight*
Closed Christmas Day

An elegant Regency-style restaurant
quietly situated in the suburb of
Sherwood (two miles North of the
city centre) and specialising in North
Indian cooking. A loyal following
praises the makhani chicken tikka and
the lamb korma, the creamy sauce
sharpened with mint. Portions are
more than generous, especially in the
set tandoori special meal (£20 for
two) which defies completion.

*No pipes • No children under 7 after
7pm • Car-park • Access, Amex, Visa*

Sonny's ★

3 Carlton Street, Hockley
☎ NOTTINGHAM (0602) 473041

Open Mon to Sat noon–2.30, 7–11
*Closed Sun, Christmas Day and Boxing
Day*

The bright new star of Nottingham's
eating-out scene, Sonny's is white,
inside and out: white paintwork,
white curtains and spherical white
lampshades, contrasting with bare,
black floorboards. The style and
trimmings mix the functional and the
fashionable: pieces of warm baguette
in Chinese bamboo steaming baskets,
mineral water in fluted, American-
style tumblers, dishes placed on plain
white plates. Straight out of the
global village, the menu is an eclectic
mix of up-to-the-minute café/
brasserie ideas, dominated by the
chargrill: beancakes with crème
fraîche; merguez sausages with potato
and apple purée; chicken with wild

mushrooms and grilled polenta are supplemented by daily fish and pasta dishes. Warm salads and jazzy risottos for vegetarians. Good-value set lunches at £7.95. Reasonably priced wines.

Wheelchair access • Access, Visa

Plumtree   map 7

Perkins Bistro

Old Railway Station
☎ PLUMTREE (060 77) 3659

Open Tue to Sat noon–2, 7–10
Closed Sun and Mon

An attractive bistro with a sunny conservatory and well-disposed staff.

Food is excellent, based on prime ingredients and an assured hand in the kitchen. A light, budget-conscious lunch of soup followed by lamb's liver and bacon lyonnaise or a ham omelette is possible, and snacks can be taken at the bar. The evening menu, though pricey, still represents good value.

Car-park • Wheelchair access • Access, Amex, Visa

A restaurant manager can't insist on people not smoking, unless it's specifically a no-smoking restaurant or a no-smoking area. If it is, smokers could be asked to leave if they don't stop. If in doubt, check beforehand what the smoking arrangements are.

OXFORDSHIRE

Abingdon

map 4

Prince of India

Ock Street
☎ ABINGDON (0235) 523033

Open all week noon–3, 6–11.30

Locals rate this the best Indian restaurant in Abingdon. There are no surprises on the menu – apart from lobster butterfly as a starter – but the quality is high. Chicken tikka masala, bhuna gosht and chicken biriani have all been recommended. Not as cheap as some other curry houses, but always popular. Drink lager.

Wheelchair access, also WC • Access, Amex, Diners, Visa

Banbury

map 4

Oliver's Bar

Cromwell Lodge Hotel, North Bar
☎ BANBURY (0295) 259781

M40 junction 11

Open all week noon–2, 7–9.30
Closed 25 Dec to 2 Jan

Centrally placed, just north of the famous Banbury Cross, stands Cromwell Lodge, worth noting as a place for simple, but well-cooked bar food. Minestrone soup comes thick with fresh vegetables, fish and mushroom pie packed with fish (tuna, swordfish and haddock), chilli con carne spicy and made with quality ground beef. Chips are hand-cut and crisp.

No-smoking area • Garden • Car-park • Wheelchair access • Access, Amex, Diners, Visa

Brightwell Baldwin

map 4

Lord Nelson Inn

☎ WATLINGTON (049 161) 2497

Off B480 SW of M40 junction 6

Open all week noon–2, 7–10

An attractive stone-built inn dating from the seventeenth century. Despite a well-modernised interior it still retains some charm, enhanced by a pretty back garden swept by a huge weeping willow. An interesting menu produces dishes almost daunting in size – it has been known for customers to ask for remaining food to be wrapped up to take home. A lunchtime-only dish of Welsh rarebit with crispy bacon certainly fitted the house style, embellished with potato salad, coleslaw and salad greens and representing exceptional value for money at £3.75. Otherwise, there is duck and orange pie, fettuccine al pesto (made with fresh basil) and thick spinach soup.

No children in bar • Car-park • Wheelchair access, also WC • Access, Amex, Diners, Visa

Burford map 4

Lamb

Sheep Street
☎ BURFORD (099 382) 3155

Open Mon to Sat noon–2
Closed Sun, Christmas Day and
Boxing Day

Tucked out of sight of the tourist-bound high street, this inn of mellow charm offers a relaxing atmosphere behind its 500-year-old walls. Antique furniture, open fires and fresh flowers are the setting for dependable and straightforward bar lunches of soundly made soups, beef goulash, steak sandwiches and a selection of ploughman's and salads.

No children in bar • Garden • Car-park
• Wheelchair access • Access, Visa

Chadlington map 4

Tite Inn

☎ CHADLINGTON (060 876) 475

Off A361 between Chipping Norton and Burford

Open all week noon–2, 7–9 (exc Mon D)
Closed Christmas Day and Boxing Day

On the fringes of the village, this is a classic, stone-built Oxfordshire pub. Inside, there are Windsor chairs and a modern stone fireplace. Food is served in the bar and the little restaurant, and the menus are similar. Starters such as puréed vegetable soup, pâté or mixed seafood cocotte

might be followed by home-made lasagne, braised lambs' kidneys with port, or grilled trout with almonds. Dishes come with decent fresh vegetables or salads. Cask beers, wine by the glass.

Garden • Car-park • Wheelchair access

Chinnor map 4

Sir Charles Napier Inn

Sprigg's Alley
☎ RADNAGE (0494) 483011

Open Tue to Fri noon–2 (bar food)

From Chinnor follow signs to Bledlow Ridge to the top of Beechwood Hill, then the sign to Radnage and Sprigg's Alley. Although ostensibly a pub, the emphasis is strongly on food and the inn's remote situation precludes just dropping in for a drink. A blackboard menu offers pricey but interesting bar food, available weekday lunches only. (There is a more expensive restaurant also open in the evening.) The quality is high, both in food and standard of service. First-class pasta carbonara or a warm salad of scallops and bacon, followed by saddle of lamb with caper sauce, are served with good bread, and complemented by an attractive setting and a confident hand in the kitchen. Good puddings but poor coffee.

No children under 14 • Car-park •
Wheelchair access • Access, Amex, Visa

Chipping Norton map 4

Nutters

10 New Street
☎ CHIPPING NORTON (0608)
641995

Open Tue to Sat 9am–6
Closed Sun, Mon and 3 days Christmas

On the ground floor there is a wholefood restaurant catering for vegetarians, vegans and meat-eaters, while upstairs there is a health and lifestyle centre. Meat from the Real Meat Company, locally baked bread and other local produce all ensure honest, fresh cooking with a simple approach. Soup, baked potatoes, quiches, pasta and low- or no-sugar home-made cakes are always available.

No smoking • Garden

Churchill map 4

Chequers Inn

☎ KINGHAM (0608) 658309

Open all week 11.30am–2, 7–10

A sturdy village-centre pub standing in the shadow of a grand-looking church. The cars filling the car-park are not there for the décor, which is best described as a hotch-potch. The inventive, well-cooked bar food is the big attraction. Thick country vegetable soup, rabbit casserole, fish lasagne and perfect vegetables all come in generous quantities. Desserts are piled equally high.

No children under 14 • Car-park •
Wheelchair access

Goring Heath map 2

King Charles Head

nr Pangbourne
☎ GORING-ON-THAMES (0491)
680268

Open all week noon–2, 7–9.30
Closed Christmas Day

Situated next to splendid beech woods, this pub offers imaginative cooking and a comprehensive selection of beers. Blackboard specials have included trout 'smoked to an old Norwegian recipe' and a salad containing red cabbage, peanuts, peaches and pineapple. Sometimes it works, sometimes it doesn't, but the food is usually good value. Try the parsnip soup or the grilled avocado and Stilton. Hand-pumped Brakspear, Marston, Adnams and Theakstons.

Garden • Car-park

Longworth map 4

Blue Boar

Tucks Lane
☎ OXFORD (0865) 820494

Open all week noon–2, 7–10
Closed Christmas Day

This is the sort of charming English pub that tourists dream of – thatched, low-beamed ceiling, a real fire, oak furniture and a welcoming atmosphere. A blackboard lists the reasonably priced bar food: deep-fried squid, garlic mushrooms, beef and Guinness pie, chicken pie and lasagne. Treacle tart to finish.

Garden • Car-park • Wheelchair access,
also WC

Maidensgrove   map 2

Five Horseshoes

nr Henley-on-Thames
☎ HENLEY-ON-THAMES (0491)
641282

Off B480/B481

Open all week noon–1.45, 7–10 (exc Sun D)

A remote seventeenth-century pub on a common above the Chiltern beechwoods. Above-average food draws the crowds, and the home-made puddings are renowned for miles around. Otherwise, the blackboard has something for everyone, taking in giant mussels' with garlic butter, grilled calves' livers with sage and rack of lamb, as well as Stilton soup, shepherd's pie and ploughman's. Also look for the avocado and walnut pâté, and Scotch salmon with mustard, dill and tomato sauce. Barbecues are staged in the large garden, where there are wonderful views. Brakspears beers.

No children under 14 • Garden • Car-park • Wheelchair access • Access, Visa

Marsh Baldon   map 4

Seven Stars

☎ NUNEHAM COURTENAY (086 738)
255

Just off A423 at Nuneham Courtenay

Open all week noon–2.15, 7–9.45

Fresh vegetables and proper hand-cut chips are greatly appreciated in this family-run village pub. A short menu has some imaginative pub dishes such as chicken wings in chilli and garlic, feuilleté of prawns and Stilton, cod

and spinach in a plaited pastry parcel with fresh parsley sauce and chicken en croûte. Soup, pâté, ham on the bone and liver and bacon are more traditional offerings. There is also a salad bar. Sunday lunch is a roast.

Garden • Car-park • Wheelchair access, also WC

Oxford   map 4

Al-Shami

25 Walton Crescent
☎ OXFORD (0865) 310066

Open all week noon–midnight

Persevere to find Al-Shami, tucked away in a residential street. Sticking to the hot and cold meze would provide an inexpensive meal of creamy hummus, halloum cheese pastries, fried sweetbreads and Armenian beef sausages, especially as the £1 cover charge includes an enormous salad. Shawarma is a generous main course and pastries come in threes for dessert.

Wheelchair access, also WC

Blue Coyote

36–7 St Clements Street
☎ OXFORD (0865) 241431

Open all week noon–11

This is an Arizonan dream of cacti, clay-effect walls and unpolished pine, the atmosphere punctuated by tiny spot lighting and a cool soundtrack. It attracts a stylish crowd, too, for the regional American dishes with a heavy New Mexico slant. On offer are successful grilled chicken and cheese enchiladas and good tamales, but there has been criticism for the weak spicing and some meagre portions.

No-smoking area • Wheelchair access • Access, Visa

Browns

5–11 Woodstock Road
☎ OXFORD (0865) 511995

Open all week 11am–11.30pm
Closed Christmas Eve to Boxing Day

Browns is one of a family of three informal, lively American-style restaurants (see entries for Brighton and Cambridge) with continuous service from breakfast to 11.30pm. The menu offers pasta, salads and hot sandwiches with game, chicken and fisherman's pies, roast ribs, vegetarian dishes and fresh fish. Desserts are gooey and satisfying.

No-smoking area • Wheelchair access, also WC

Café MOMA

30 Pembroke Street
☎ OXFORD (0865) 722733

Open Tue to Sun 10am (2pm Sun)–5.30 (9.30 Thur)
Closed Mon

Vegetarian dishes dominate the menu at this white, uncluttered café below the Museum of Modern Art. Soups such as tomato and red lentil or pea and lettuce, a salad of spinach and Parmesan, Mediterranean pasta, lentil and walnut burgers and courgette and mushroom loaf set the tone. Desserts include almond peachcake and chestnut cheesecake.

No smoking • Wheelchair access, also WC

Go Dutch

18 Park End Street
☎ OXFORD (0865) 240686

Open all week noon–2.30, 6–11
Closed Christmas

Go Dutch offers an impressive range of traditional pancakes from the Netherlands, served in blue-and-white-tiled surroundings opposite the railway station, freshly prepared and served with refreshing speed. Generous 12-inch-plus discs of dough are covered with any number of savoury, vegetarian, sweet or alcoholic toppings. Ham is from the bone, not a packet. All pancakes are recommended as benefiting from a dollop of 'stroop', a traditional cane sugar syrup at each table.

Heroes

8 Ship Street
☎ OXFORD (0865) 723459

Open Mon to Sat 9am–7.30
Closed Sun and bank hols

The best doorstep sandwiches in Oxford are served in this tiny place tucked away behind the Bodleian Library. Wooden stools are lined up around the walls, there are newspapers to read and rock music for entertainment. The choice of bread takes in baguettes and pitta as well as the usual sliced loaf; the range of fillings caters for all tastes. Brie with walnuts, curried chicken, avocado and prawn line up alongside cheese and pickle. Cooked breakfast, soup and cakes complete the picture. Take-aways are available.

Unlicensed • No-smoking area • Wheelchair access

Nosebag

6–8 St Michael's Street
☎ OXFORD (0865) 721033

*Open Mon to Thur 9.30am–10pm
(5.30pm Mon), Fri to Sun 9.30am–
10.30pm (9.30pm Sun)
Closed Christmas Day and Boxing Day*

An ancient building houses a card and
gift shop on the ground floor and this
pine-furnished café on the first. The
choice of food is extensive and
includes cream of vegetable soup,
leek and bacon crumble, tuna quiche,
beef lasagne and beef and vegetable
pie. There are half a dozen salads and
many cakes. The place is very
popular with students at tea-time.

No smoking

Pizza Express

The Golden Cross
☎ OXFORD (0865) 790442

Open all week 11.30am–midnight

Part of the popular chain which is the
pick of the pizza bunch. See London
entry.

*No-smoking area • Access, Amex,
Diners, Visa*

Pizza Piazza

Cantay House, 39 Park End Road
☎ OXFORD (0865) 793443

Open all week 11am–11.30pm

A branch of one of the best pizza
chains in the UK. See London entry.

Access, Visa

All letters to this guide are acknowledged.

St Aldates Coffee House

94 St Aldates
☎ OXFORD (0865) 245952

*Open Mon to Sat 10am–4.30 (5.30 Sat)
Closed Sun and bank hols*

The Coffee House is owned by St
Aldates church and run by volunteers
from the congregation. Christian
books line the oak-panelled walls and
the atmosphere is as wholesome as
the food. A short, sensible menu of
jacket potatoes, quiches and salads is
backed up by hot lunchtime specials
such as honeyed pork with rice, and
there is always something for
vegetarians. The home-made cakes
and puddings are a star attraction,
ranging from flapjacks and
shortbreads to fudge cake and fruit
sponges. There is a pleasant choice of
herbal teas, as well as coffee and
juices.

*Unlicensed exc lunchtime • No smoking
• Wheelchair access*

Wykeham Coffee Shop

15 Holywell Street
☎ OXFORD (0865) 246916

*Open all week 10.30am (noon Sun)–
5.30*

A tiny place serving very simple food
all day. Sandwiches range from the
standard cheese and pickle to the
more exotic banana and brown sugar.
Ploughman's lunch and filled jacket
potatoes come in a variety of
combinations. The place becomes
exceedingly busy at tea-time when
warm scones, hot, spiced bread
pudding and chocolate cake draw a
host of students.

No smoking

Shenington   map 4

Bell

The Village Green
☎ EDGE HILL **(0295) 87274**

Just off A422 Banbury–Stratford road

Open all week noon–3, 7–10.30 (exc Sun D)

A pub with an attractive restaurant which in winter is warmed by a log fire in a glorious stone inglenook. Shire-horse tack dominates the décor. Outside, in summer, the village green beckons. Home-style cooking is translated here to mean veal and apricot casserole, mustard rabbit, hock (bacon) and raisin on rice, and pheasant in claret. At least one vegetarian dish is promised. A sound choice for unpretentious, rustic eating.

Wheelchair access • Access, Visa

Shipton-under-Wychwood   map 4

Lamb Inn

High Street
☎ SHIPTON **(0993) 830465**

Open Tue to Sun noon–2, 7–10 Closed Mon

One of those solidly built, sturdy Cotswold-stone inns that is popular not just for its traditional good looks but also for some fine bar food. This is served in the flagstoned, beamed bar and the food reflects the inn's simplicity – mussels and hare pâté make light snacks or can be starters

to a more substantial meal of vegetable pie or lasagne.

No smoking in restaurant • No children under 14 • Garden • Car-park • Wheelchair access • Access, Amex, Visa

Sibford Gower   map 4

Wykham Arms

Colony Lane
☎ SWALCLIFFE **(029 578) 351**

Open Tue to Sun noon–2, 7–9.30 Closed Mon, Christmas Day and Sun D Nov to Feb

A well-cared-for thatched village pub with a cosy, friendly atmosphere. Bar food, with better main courses than starters, includes beef and Guinness pie, ham and eggs, vegetarian chilli and spinach and mushroom lasagne. Thick, irregular-cut chips are preferable to the microwaved jacket potatoes.

Garden and family-room • Car-park • Wheelchair access, also WC • Access, Visa

Wantage   map 2

Beetons

1st Floor, Post Office Vaults Shopping Mall
☎ WANTAGE **(023 57) 69901**

Open Mon to Sat 9am–5 Closed Christmas Day and New Year's Day

Shoppers converge on this small, friendly café on the first floor of the mall. Food is served through the day and there is always a selection of sandwiches and cakes to go with morning coffee or afternoon tea. Lunch brings hot dishes such as chicken curry, steak and kidney pie and roast pork, served with excellent fresh vegetables. Puddings consist mainly of ice-creams. Full English breakfasts start the day.

Unlicensed • No smoking

Waterperry   map 4

Waterperry
Gardens Teashop ⓣ

Waterperry Gardens, nr Wheatley
☎ ICKFORD **(0844) 339254/339226**

Off A418 N of M40 junction 8

Open all week 10am–5.30
Closed Christmas, New Year and 4 days July

Part of a centre that includes a garden shop, nursery and formal gardens. A spotlessly maintained shed-like building houses the tea-room (spreading out on to the lawn in summer) and offers properly served leaf tea, some home-baking and savouries such as chicken pie, cheese flan and various quiches.

No-smoking area • Garden • Car-park • Wheelchair access, also WC

Woodstock   map 4

Garden Bar

Feathers Hotel, Market Street
☎ WOODSTOCK **(0993) 812291**

Open all week L 12.30-2.15

The Feathers is a delightful hotel, liberally strewn with antiques and with a stone-floored bar (decorated with stuffed birds) which opens out on to a charming courtyard garden. Here, some imaginative and, for the quality, surprisingly inexpensive bar lunches are served: local game terrine, venison casserole, braised hare and lamb hot-pot. Finish with Feathers steamed pudding.

Access, Amex, Diners, Visa

Acton Scott — map 6

Working Farm Museum Café

☎ MARSHBROOK (069 46) 306/7

Off A49 3m S of Church Stretton

Open mid-Mar to Oct Tue to Sun
all day
Closed Mon and Nov to mid-Mar

A café housed in a former Victorian
school and run in connection with
the historic working farm which
shows what rural and agricultural life
were like at the turn of the century.
The café provides food in keeping
with this image: Shropshire fidget pie
(bacon, apples and onions), beef in
old ale, various ploughman's as well
as home-made cakes. Some produce
comes from the museum's garden.

Unlicensed • No smoking • Garden •
Car-park • Wheelchair access, also WC
(in museum)

Dorrington — map 6

Country Friends

☎ DORRINGTON (074 373) 707

On A49 6 miles S of Shrewsbury

Open Tue to Sat L noon–1.45
Closed Sun, Mon and 2 weeks end July

The black-and-white half-timbered
building dates from 1600. In the last
few years Charles and Pauline
Whittaker have turned it into a
relaxing, welcoming small hotel. Bar
snacks, served at lunchtime, give a

remarkably inexpensive insight into
the kitchen's innovative style.
Choose, from a short blackboard
menu, a carrot and marjoram soup
with a home-made granary roll and,
from half a dozen snacks, perhaps
sole and crab mousse on pasta, duck
quenelles with mushroom and bacon
sauce or Stilton doughnuts with
salad. Puddings come from the
restaurant dessert menu. More
expensive evening meals are available
in the restaurant.

No smoking in restaurant • Garden •
Car-park • Wheelchair access • Access,
Amex, Visa

Easthope — map 4

Wenlock Edge Inn

Hilltop
☎ BROCKTON (074 636) 403

3¹/₂m from Much Wenlock, on Church
Stretton Road

Open Tue to Sun noon–2, 7–9
Closed Mon

Originally a pair of eighteenth-
century quarrymen's cottages, this
stone-built inn is now an
unpretentious, family-run hostelry
complete with old settles and
inglenooks. No fruit machines or
Muzak disturb the peace. The
kitchen delivers home-cooked food
prepared from fresh ingredients: real
tomato soup, rich game pâté, baked
ham with home-made chutney. Hot,
savoury pies are outstanding,
vegetables are locally grown and
'nursery puddings' range from

chocolate fudge pudding to fruit tart or peach sundae. Real ales and some well-chosen wines by the glass.

No smoking in dining-room • No children under 14 in bar • Garden • Car-park • Wheelchair access, also WC

Shrewsbury   map 7

Goodlife

Barracks Passage, 73C Wyle Cop
☎ SHREWSBURY (0743) 50455

Open Mon to Sat 11.30am–3
Closed Sun and bank hols

It can get crowded and chaotic in this tiny wholefood/vegetarian restaurant tucked away in a historic part of town. The attraction is the down-to-earth home cooking and the freshly prepared food. Quiches, lots of salads and jacket potatoes are the basics; hot dishes such as vegetable paella, broccoli crumble, and mushroom and peppers in wine are more sophisticated. Baking is done with organic wholemeal flour and soya margarine. Wine by the glass or coffee to drink.

No-smoking area • Wheelchair access

Philpotts

Abbots House, Butcher Row
☎ SHREWSBURY (0743) 236654

Open Mon to Sat 8.30am–2.30
Closed Sun

Made-to-order take-away sandwiches are all Philpotts does, but it does

them well. The permutations are inventive: blackpudding, bacon and tomato, bacon and avocado, crispy bacon, smoked trout in dill sauce, pastrami and mustard with dill pickle, coronation chicken. There are five kinds of cheese, a daily breakfast and lunchtime special, soup and espresso.

Unlicensed • No smoking

Windmill Tea Room

Sutton Grange Nursery, Oteley Road
☎ SHREWSBURY (0743) 56866

Open all week 9.30am–6.30

This tea-room is currently situated in a Portakabin set in a garden surrounded by a stream and ornamental ducks. Snacks and teas are served outside, weather permitting, and there are hopes to expand the operation. Helen Atkins' forte is baking, and on a good day there could be 30 different kinds of cake. Lasagne, shepherd's pie, simple salads and sandwiches (white bread only) are savoury options.

Unlicensed • Garden

You will find report forms (write a letter if you prefer) at the back of the book so that you can tell us about your experiences of going *Out to Eat*. We'll put the information to good use when we're compiling the next edition.

SOMERSET

Ashcott
map 1

Ashcott Inn

50 Bath Road
☎ ASHCOTT **(0458) 210282**

Open all week noon–2, 6.30–9.30 (10 Fri and Sat)

A welcoming pub that has no less than two log fires and a very pretty walled garden. It is a food-oriented place with half a dozen or so fresh fish dishes available every day. Thick and tasty bacon and parsnip soup or a generous prawn and avocado salad make a good start, followed perhaps by moules marinière, fish pie, pasta or moussaka. Treacle tart to finish.

No children in bar • Garden • Car-park • Wheelchair access, also WC • Access, Visa

Brent Knoll
map 1

Goat House Café

Bristol Road
☎ BRENT KNOLL **(0278) 760995**

Just off M5 junction 22

Open all week 9am–4.30

Brent Knoll rises above the Somerset wetlands beside the busy A38, not far from junction 22 of the M5. The Goat House, not surprisingly, deals in goat products – everything from cheese and ice-cream to hand-knitted mohair sweaters and scarves. In the café, next to the goatyard, the emphasis is on home cooking: filled jacket potatoes, sandwiches and pizzas are backed up by blackboard specials such as barbecued chicken, haddock and prawn bake and vegetarian lasagne.

Unlicensed, but bring your own: no corkage • No-smoking area • Car-park • Wheelchair access

Bridgwater
map 1

Nutmeg House

8–10 Clare Street
☎ BRIDGWATER **(0278) 457823**

N of M5 junction 24

*Open Mon to Sat 9.30am–5
Closed Sun and Christmas Day*

Just off the high street is this pleasant café-cum-restaurant, with tables outside in the summer. During the week, there are decent lunches ranging from open sandwiches and filled jacket potatoes to mushroom Stroganoff, beef and Guinness casserole with horseradish dumpling, and tuna and pasta bake. A daily roast features nicely cooked meat and plenty of vegetables, and there are good sweets such as plum and almond tart. Evening meals on Fridays and Saturdays are more ambitious and more expensive. Wine by the glass.

No-smoking area • Wheelchair access • Access, Amex, Diners, Visa

Castle Cary

map 2

Old Bakehouse

High Street
☎ CASTLE CARY (0963) 50067

Open Tue to Sat 9.30am–5
Closed Sun and Mon

Carol Sealey says that she only serves
her customers what she would give
her family. Her vegetarian shop/café
is dedicated to wholesome home
cooking, using natural and organic
ingredients where possible.
Mushroom croustade, lentil rissoles
with tomato sauce, and cashew-nut
roast with red wine sauce show the
style, with Salcombe dairy ice-
creams, exotic sorbets and popular
toffee date pudding to finish. Wine
by the glass.

No smoking • Wheelchair access

Cranmore

map 2

Strode Arms

West Cranmore
☎ CRANMORE (074 988) 450

Off A361 3½m E of Shepton Mallet

Open all week noon–2, 7–9.30 (10 Fri
and Sat) exc Sun D winter
Closed Christmas Day

A collection of early fifteenth-century
cottages opposite the village duck
pond make up this atmospheric pub,
complete with the usual beams and
inglenook fireplaces. Food is
standard, but good, pub fare: soup,
steak and kidney pie, pasta with ham
and mushrooms, and the speciality
poacher's bowl of poultry, game and
meat, pastry topped. Treacle tart or
bread pudding for dessert.

No children under 14 exc in dining-room
• Garden • Car-park • Wheelchair
access, also WC • Access, Visa

Dunster

map 1

Tea Shoppe

3 High Street
☎ MINEHEAD (0643) 821304

Open all week noon–4.30 (weekends only
1 Nov to Christmas)
Closed 2 Jan to mid-Mar and weekdays
Nov to Christmas

Few touristy villages can boast such
an ideal tea-shop: an early fifteenth-
century cottage which has retained
some fine original features and serves
good food. Local produce, cooked on
the Aga, is used in lunches of ham,
pure pork sausages with home-made
mustard, and hot bread pudding with
clotted cream. Morning coffee and
afternoon tea are supplemented by a
wealth of cakes.

No smoking • Wheelchair access •
Access, Visa

Frome

map 2

Settle

Cheap Street
☎ FROME (0373) 65975

Open Mon to Sat noon–2.30
Closed Sun

Margaret Vaughan found fame with
her TV series about home-made
wine, and the fruits of her labours can
be sampled in this traditional beamed
tea-room. A few settles echo the
name of the place and there is a
Welsh dresser loaded with bottles

and home-made cakes. The cooking is in keeping, with old-fashioned and local dishes stealing the show. Typically, there might be shepherd's pie with roast parsnips, kedgeree and treacle tart, backed up by omelettes, jacket potatoes and pies with wholemeal pastry. Frome Bobbins are apricots, figs and sultanas steeped in cider and baked in pastry.

No-smoking area • Wheelchair access • Access, Visa

Leigh upon Mendip
map 2

Bell Inn

☎ MELLS (0373) 812316

5m W of Frome off A361

Open all week noon–2, 7–10.30
Closed Boxing Day

A peaceful seventeenth-century village pub with blackened beams, a log-burning stove in a massive inglenook and gleaming brasses galore. Food, when home-cooked by landlady Mrs Jackson, is a delight. Avoid the obvious bought-in dishes and go for home-made soups, game pie, rabbit casserole or steak and kidney pie. Good ham sandwiches and an excellent chocolate steamed pudding too.

No children in bar • Car-park • Access, Amex, Diners, Visa

'Wheelchair access' indicates that, according to the proprietor, entrances are at least 33 inches wide, passages 4 feet wide, and that there are a maximum of two steps. If there is access to a WC, we mention it.

Monksilver
map 1

Notley Arms

☎ STOGUMBER (0984) 56217

On B3188 5m S of Watchet

Open all week noon–2 (1.45 Sun), 7–9.30 (9 Sun)
Closed Christmas Day and first 2 weeks Feb

A popular village pub with a beamed, L-shaped bar, plain wooden tables, chairs and settles and light classical music in the background. Food is all-important and fresh ingredients are prepared with an assured hand. Good Chinese-style pork with stir-fry vegetables, vegetarian leek and mushroom croustade and home-made pasta show the range and style of cooking.

Garden and family-room • Car-park • Wheelchair access

North Perrott
map 2

Manor Arms

☎ CREWKERNE (0460) 72901

On A3066 2m E of Crewkerne

Open Tue to Sat noon–2, 7–9.45
Closed Sun and Mon

Rex and Jane Gilmore have refurbished and transformed this stone-built village pub into a lively venue with excellent value food. Simple dishes such as home-made pâté, seafood crumble and chicken curry are served in the bar. The restaurant is more ambitious, but still affordable. Mushrooms in mustard sauce is a favourite starter, escalope of veal with herbs and garlic is a

well-reported main course.
Otherwise, the menu ranges from
steak and kidney pie to salmon in puff
pastry with asparagus and prawn
sauce. Excellent French fries and
fresh vegetables. Three-course
Sunday lunch is £5.50 (children £4).
Wines by the glass, local beers.

*Garden • Car-park • Wheelchair access
• Access, Visa*

Taunton   map 1

Pizza Piazza

39 East Street
☎ TAUNTON (0823) 322087

Open all week 11am–11.30pm

A branch of one of the best pizza
chains in the UK. See London entry.

Access, Visa

Wells   map 2

Cloister

West Cloister, Wells Cathedral
☎ WELLS (0749) 76543

*Open Mon to Sat 10am–5, Sun 2–5
Closed 2 weeks Christmas*

Visitors to this charming Somerset
cathedral are generally well advised

to break bread at the Cloister. Here,
bistro-style translates as meaning
home-made soup, cassoulet or
salmon and asparagus flan. It is all
pretty basic but incredibly
wholesome. As well as lunches,
you can get morning coffee and
afternoon tea.

*Unlicensed • No smoking • Wheelchair
access, also WC*

Fountain Inn

1 St Thomas Street
☎ WELLS (0749) 72317

*Open all week 11.30 (noon Sun)–2,
6 (7 Sun)–10 (9.30 Sun)
Closed Christmas Day and Boxing Day*

Close to Wells Cathedral, the
Fountain dates from the fifteenth
century, but its look and style are
closer to the nineteenth. It is a warm,
welcoming pub whose attractions
include a choice of some 50 Spanish
wines and imaginative, honestly
cooked food. Blackboard choices
offer a spinach and cream cheese
roulade, fresh Poole mussels and
pan-fried breast of duckling.

*Family-room • Car-park • Wheelchair
access • Access, Amex, Visa*

See the back of the guide for an index of
eating-places and an index of locations.

STAFFORDSHIRE

Lichfield map 4

Eastern Eye

19B Bird Street
☎ LICHFIELD (0543) 254399

*Open L Fri and Sat noon–2.30, D all
week 5–midnight
Closed Christmas Day evening and
Boxing Day*

The popular choice for Indian food
in the Lichfield area, Mr Salam's
compact restaurant maintains a high
profile attracting celebrities as well as
loyal locals. The menu is a promising
mixture of curry house stalwarts, such
as tandoori chicken, lamb korma and
prawn patia, and more unusual
regional dishes from Kashmir,
Bengal, Bihar and Uttar Pradesh.
Look for marinated chicken with
apricots and yoghurt; mutton cooked
with spinach and green chillies; and
king prawn with bamboo shoots.
Good-value thalis.

Access, Amex, Diners, Visa

Stafford map 7

Curry Kuteer

31 Greengate Street
☎ STAFFORD (0785) 53279

M6 junctions 13/14

This well-established curry house
close to a bridge over the River Sow
has a new chef and has been given a
lavish dose of redecoration. The
décor is dominated by a goldfish
pond and a waterfall; there are plants
in the lounge and chandeliers in the
main dining-room. The menu is less
ostentatious than the décor might
suggest, concentrating on familiar
curries and tandooris. Karai dishes,
cooked in an iron skillet, are notable,
as is pati shapta (a sweet pancake).
Good-value thalis. Drink lager.

*No-smoking area • No children under 4
• Car-park • Wheelchair access • Access,
Amex, Diners, Visa*

Tutbury map 7

Ye Olde Dog & Partridge

High Street
☎ BURTON ON TRENT (0283)
813030

*Open Tue to Sat noon–2, 6.30–9.30
Closed Sun, Mon, Christmas Day and
Boxing Day*

A pub dating from the fifteenth
century with that bent-with-age half-
timbered look is always popular, but
this former coaching-inn packs them
in with an excellent carvery too.
Everything is well presented. Dishes
include smoked salmon, baked ham,
pork and beef and seafood. There are
inventive salads and hot soups.
Lighter snacks, including sandwiches,
are available in the bar at lunchtimes.

Car-park • Access, Amex, Visa

If there are restrictions on children, these
are mentioned in the details at the end of
each entry.

Uttoxeter

map 7

Tudor Fayre

Market Place
☎ UTTOXETER **(0889) 564946**

Open all week 9.45am–3
Closed Christmas Day

Tudor Fayre offers remarkable value and portions which would, indeed, placate a hungry Tudor courtier. A note on the menu warns that 'helpings are generous. If you require a smaller meal, please ask.' Here is value for money on a grand scale: roast beef, Yorkshire pudding and vegetables for £3. Sweets are 75p each. Plastic tablecloths combine with replica civil war breastplates and swords, mounted on red-flock wallpaper, creating an atmosphere of homeliness.

★ after an eating-place indicates that it is one of the best found by the Editor during research for this book (see page 14 for a list).

⊙ after an eating-place indicates that it is a pub. The opening and closing times we give only relate to when food is available – the licensing hours may be different.

⊕ after an eating-place indicates that it is within five miles of the nearest motor-way junction. We give the relevant motorway and junction in the details. Eating-places in cities and large towns, where traffic, parking and route-finding may cause delay, do not have this symbol.

Aldeburgh
map 5

Aldeburgh Fish & Chip Shop

226 High Street
☎ ALDEBURGH (0728) 452250

*Open summer all week 11.45–1.45,
5–9, winter Tue to Sat D 5–9
Closed Sun, Mon in winter, Christmas
Day and New Year's Day*

An unlikely mix: a traditional fish and
chip shop that also sells home-
smoked salmon. Excellent fresh fish –
cod, plaice or skate – is cooked in
spectacularly light, crisp batter and
accompanied by big helpings of
chips. The salmon comes as prime
slices, off-cuts or frozen pâté. For a
stately meal on the beach bring your
own lemon wedges and a bottle of
white wine, and have the salmon as a
starter. Take-away only.

Unlicensed • No smoking

Regatta Wine Bar

171–3 High Street
☎ ALDEBURGH (0728) 452011

Open all week noon–2.15, 6.30–10

Uninspiring from the outside but
bustling and lively inside, the Regatta
Wine Bar is a popular, inexpensive
alternative to the adjoining
restaurant. There is high praise for
soup, whether mushroom, parsnip,
leek and potato or cauliflower and
coconut; and steak and kidney pie
and cheese and onion quiche are also
justly popular. Great chocolate and
brandy mousse for dessert.

*Wheelchair access, also WC • Access,
Visa*

Clare
map 5

Peppermill

Market Square
☎ GLEMSFORD (0787) 278148

*Open Tue to Sun L noon–2, Thur to Sat
D 7–9
Closed Mon*

An atmospheric little restaurant (it
only seats 20) situated in part of the
former medieval Moothall. Roger
and Julene Steele offer simple,
carefully prepared snacks of
sandwiches, salads, omelettes and
jacket potatoes and the more
substantial fisherman's pie or nut
roast. Afternoon tea is available in
summer and evening meals are
available by booking only.

Unlicensed • Access, Visa

Dunwich
map 5

Flora Tea Rooms

Dunwich Beach
☎ WESTLETON (072 873) 433

*Open all week 11am–6
Closed mid-Dec to 8 Mar*

Really good fish and chips are
becoming a rarity in Britain, which

probably explains the long queues outside the Flora Tea Rooms, which now seats 106 – such is the success of this former beach hut. Fresh fish from the Dunwich boat, cooked in the lightest of crisp batter, is made even more memorable when eaten on the benches in the sand dunes. Fast, efficient service.

Unlicensed, but bring your own: no corkage • No-smoking area • Car-park • Wheelchair access, also WC

Ship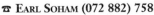

St James Street
☎ WESTLETON (072 873) 219

Open all week noon–2, 7.30–9

A nautical pub looking out across salt marshes to the sea. Locally caught fish features strongly on the blackboard menu with plaice prepared in the Ship's own batter and chips a well-liked choice. There is also fresh fish of the day, seafood salad, home-cooked ham, hearty soups and some good puddings. A very popular pub.

No children in bar • Garden and family-room • Car-park • Wheelchair access

Earl Soham   map 5

Victoria Inn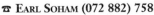

☎ EARL SOHAM (072 882) 758

3m W of Framlingham on A1120

Open all week noon–2, 6.30–10

A splendid traditional village pub that nails its colours to the mast. Beer is brewed on the premises, and the menu is honest home cooking with a

wholefood accent. Dye-free kippers, home-made beefburgers and chilli share the bill with fish pie, meatless lasagne and sweet-and-sour kidney beans. Rice is brown, and the bread is wholemeal. Ploughman's, salads and chocolate mousse make up the supporting cast.

Garden • Car-park

Ipswich   map 5

Café Marno

14 St Nicholas Street
☎ IPSWICH (0473) 253106

Open Mon to Sat 10.30am–4.30
Closed Sun and bank hols

Formerly Marno's Food Reform, this easygoing vegetarian café has been given a face-lift and a new name by current owners, Angie Allen and Hazel Sayer. A daily blackboard menu features dishes such as apple and parsnip soup, tagliatelle with mushrooms and cream, and vegetable moussaka. The nut roast is highly rated, as is the fruit Pavlova. There is a small selection of wines and beers, including Greene King Abbot Ale.

No-smoking area • Wheelchair access, also WC • Access, Amex, Diners, Visa

Orwell House

4 Orwell Place
☎ IPSWICH (0473) 230254

Open Tue to Sat noon–2.30, 7–9.30
Closed Sun and Mon

A realistically priced bistro, an alternative to the more expensive restaurant housed in the same Georgian shell. The menu changes monthly, offering good, straightforward soups, salads and terrines to start, and main courses like mousseline of seafood, skate wings meunière, lamb cutlets reformé and boeuf bourguignonne. Finish with chocolate truffle cake.

Wheelchair access • Access, Amex, Diners, Visa

Ixworth   map 5

Pickerel at Ixworth

High Street
☎ PAKENHAM (0359) 30398

Open all week noon–2, 7–10

True to its name, this sixteenth-century timber-framed pub puts the emphasis on fish. Pickerel Pie is packed with white and smoked fish, prawns and mushrooms; poached salmon is served with mayonnaise and salad and there are pints of prawns and plates of smoked halibut. Meat-eaters can settle for pea and ham soup, and steak and kidney pie; vegetarians might be offered mushroom and nut Stroganoff. The affordable restaurant has a few more ambitious offerings such as halibut and sesame steak and venison in tarragon and cream sauce. Lovely atmosphere, well-kept Greene King beers.

No children in bar • Family-room • Car-park • Wheelchair access • Access, Amex, Visa

---

All details are as accurate as possible at the time of going to press, but chefs and owners often change, and it is wise to check by telephone before making a special journey.

Laxfield   map 5

King's Head

Gorams Mill Lane
☎ UBBESTON (098 683) 395

Open all week 11–3, 6–10.30
Closed Christmas Day

Nothing has changed here in 200 years; the front room is filled by the massive horseshoe-shaped settle surrounding the fire, and both of the tiny side rooms have well-worn deal tables, chairs and pews. The back room contains the casks of beer, and there is no modern bar. Of Tudor origin, this thatched pub is worth a detour just to experience the step back in time, but the food is equally attractive. Home-made soups, sandwiches, pork and apple pie, steak and kidney pie, lamb chops, oak-smoked kippers, and roasts for Sunday lunch (for which bookings must be made) are the simple offerings.

Garden • Car-park • Wheelchair access

Newmarket   map 5

Jane's Wine Bar

29 High Street
☎ NEWMARKET (0638) 668031

Open Mon to Sat 9.30am–4.30
Closed Sun and 3 days Christmas

A pink-walled wine bar in the basement of an up-market clothes shop. Owner Jane Webb says that everything is made on the premises, from the cauliflower soup, salads and quiche to scones and flapjacks. The menu also takes in omelettes, filled jacket potatoes and specials such as chicken curry. There are teas, coffee and wine to drink. A useful venue for a snack when shopping.

No-smoking area • Access, Amex, Diners, Visa

Orford

map 5

Butley-Orford Oysterage

Market Square
☎ ORFORD (0394) 450277

Open all week noon–2.15, 6–8.30 (exc winter Sun to Thur D)
Closed Christmas Day, Boxing Day and 2 weeks Jan

In the middle of the village, with the smokery at the back, this is a simple café/restaurant on two floors with a shop. Oysters are de rigueur, and you should also sample the smoked fish – mackerel, sardines, eel, wild salmon – or the fresh dressed crab. Anything that requires sauces tends not to work and accompanying salads are dull.

Wheelchair access

King's Head

Front Street
☎ ORFORD (0394) 450271

Open all week noon–2, 6 (7 winter)–9

The Shaws' ancient village inn serves good fresh fish in the bar. Go for the grilled lemon sole, which spill over the plate and are big enough for two, and make sure to try fresh buttered samphire with it, if available. There are also well-priced local lobster, dressed crab and fish pie. Leave room for the treacle and ginger pudding.

No children in bar • Garden • Car-park • Diners

Snape

map 5

Golden Key

Priory Road
☎ SNAPE (072 888) 510

Open all week noon–2 (2.30 Sun), 6.30 (7 Sun)–9

An unpretentious, prettily situated old pub serving good, inexpensive bar snacks. Sausage, egg and onion pie remains a firm favourite, closely followed by quiches such as smoked haddock or spinach and mushroom. Steak and mushroom pie comes with potatoes and fresh vegetables for £4.95 and there is treacle and walnut tart to finish.

No children under 14 • Garden • Car-park • Wheelchair access, also WC

Southwold

map 5

Crown

90 High Street
☎ SOUTHWOLD (0502) 722275

Open all week noon–1.45, 7–9.15

A civilised eighteenth-century inn serving good wines by the glass. This is complemented by generous but pricey bar food. Take note that you can only order food if you have a table, not always an easy thing to achieve. Local smoked buckling and fresh herrings with mustard sauce are starters large enough for main courses, perhaps preceded by leek and lentil soup and followed by cheesecake. Just 100 yards down the road, the Swan (under the same ownership) offers more spacious, calm surroundings for some limited-choice bar lunches.

*No smoking in dining area • No children
under 7 Christmas or New Year • Car-
park • Wheelchair access, also WC •
Access, Amex, Visa*

Squiers

71 High Street
☎ SOUTHWOLD (0502) 723354

*Open all week exc Tue 9am–5
Closed Tue*

The outside of Squiers looks like a
sweet shop, which indeed is part of its
identity; closer observation reveals a
menu in the window which runs the
gamut from breakfast (a vegetarian
version as well as the more
traditional) to cream teas, taking in
snacks and lunch on the way. The
back tea-room is comfortable, and
the majority of dishes, such as Suffolk
ham bake and rich gingerbread, are
home-made.

*No smoking at lunchtime • Wheelchair
access*

Stoke-by-Nayland map 5

Angel 🏵

Polstead Street
☎ COLCHESTER (0206) 263245/6

*Open all week noon–2, 6.30–9
Closed Christmas Day and Boxing Day*

A comfortable restored inn with a
lounge bar furnished with wing
chairs, a deep sofa and wood-burning
stove. The main bar has a huge log
fire and a mixture of beams, timbers
and exposed brickwork. Bar food is
inventive, featuring first-class dishes
of mushrooms stuffed with snails in
garlic butter, baked stuffed green
peppers, sauté of lambs' kidneys in

mushroom and juniper sauce and
beef and venison pie. There is a dish
of three separate griddled fish,
usually hake, sole and plaice and
three different salads of pork, lamb
and gammon.

*No children • Car-park • Wheelchair
access, also WC • Access, Amex, Diners,
Visa*

Walberswick map 5

Mary's

Manor House
☎ SOUTHWOLD (0502) 723243

*Open Tue to Sun L noon–2, Fri and Sat
D 7.15–9
Closed Mon, and Tue to Thur Nov to
Easter*

A nautical theme pervades Mary's
and fish is a strong point on the
menu, delivered twice weekly from
Lowestoft; slip soles come from
Walberswick itself. Dishes are all
modestly priced. Home-made soups
are well-flavoured and hearty sausage
casserole and steak and kidney pie
come with crisp chips and a selection
of buttered vegetables. Gooey
desserts.

*No smoking in dining area • Garden •
Car-park • Wheelchair access, also WC*

Parish Lantern

Village Green
☎ SOUTHWOLD (0502) 723173

*Open Mon to Wed (exc Jan and Feb)
and Fri to Sun L noon–2.30
Closed Thur, and Mon to Wed Jan to
Feb*

Mary Allen's main business is the
craft shop, but the tiny tea-room

(extending into the small, well-sheltered garden in summer) does a roaring trade. The menu features mainly sandwiches, including pastrami, prawns and smoked salmon, or else there are smoked cod's roe, hot buttered toast and teacakes. There is a good selection of cakes and service is cheerful.

Unlicensed, but bring your own: no corkage • Garden • Wheelchair access • Access, Visa

Potter's Wheel

Village Green
☎ SOUTHWOLD (0502) 724468

Open all week L noon–2.15, Sat and Sun D 7.30–9
Closed Christmas to Easter

Leslie Scott's unassuming, single-storey clapperboard building is a must for cake-lovers. Light scones, rich, moist fruit cake, lemon sponge and coffee cake are all displayed in the entrance. For lunch, there are steak and kidney pie, fresh cod or plaice, and various vegetarian dishes, all well-cooked and served in filling portions.

Garden

Westleton   map 5

Crown

nr Saxmundham
☎ WESTLETON (072 873) 273/239

Open all week L noon–2.15
Closed Christmas Day and Boxing Day

A well-run, well-maintained village pub with a laudable attitude to segregating smokers, there is even a no-smoking dining conservatory.

Fresh fish, delivered daily, dominates the menu – cod, plaice, lemon sole or haddock either grilled or poached. Otherwise, there are steak and kidney pie, sandwiches or steak. Treacle pudding is a popular dessert. A more expensive restaurant menu is available in the evening.

No-smoking area • No children in bar • Garden • Car-park • Wheelchair access, also WC • Access, Amex, Diners, Visa

Woodbridge   map 5

Royal Bengal

4–6 Quay Street
☎ WOODBRIDGE (039 43) 7983

Open all week noon–2.30, 6–11

Decent Indian restaurants are thin on the ground in east Suffolk, but this well-established venue continues to deliver the goods. The setting is a white-painted building, just up the road from the station; inside it is pure curry house, with flock wallpaper, wall-hangings of tigers, and waiters in cavalry-style tunics. The menu includes good sheek kebab served with tamarind sauce, chicken dopiaza and devastatingly hot lamb vindaloo. Rice and breads are up to the mark. Drink lager.

No children under 6 • Car-park • Wheelchair access, also WC • Access, Amex, Diners, Visa

A restaurant manager can't insist on people not smoking, unless it's specifically a no-smoking restaurant or a no-smoking area. If it is, smokers could be asked to leave if they don't stop. If in doubt, check beforehand what the smoking arrangements are.

Wine Bar ★

17 Thoroughfare
☎ WOODBRIDGE **(039 43) 2557**

Open Tue to Sat noon–2, 7–9.45
Closed Sun, Mon, Christmas Day and
Boxing Day

The setting is a colourfully decorated room above a provisions shop. In the confined space of a domestic-sized kitchen, Sally O'Gorman works wonders, cooking to order, changing her menu every week and offering exceptional value for money. Dishes are enterprising and there is always something imaginative for vegetarians. Pan-fried monkfish is served with horseradish cream and ribbons of mooli and cucumber; stuffed saddle of lamb comes with roasted garlic and a juniper sauce. Aubergine 'two ways' is one, grilled with pesto sauce, two, marinated with capers and gherkins, deep-fried and served with grilled sweet peppers. Tarts, terrines and unusual home-made ice-creams to finish. Decent affordable wines are available by the glass.

No children under 16

Wrentham   map 5

Quiggins

2 High Street
☎ WRENTHAM **(050 275) 397**

Open Tue to Sun noon–2, 7–10 (exc
Sun D)
Closed Mon

A comfortable, attractive restaurant on the A12. The lunch menu offers a fair choice at a reasonable price; sound cooking with fresh ingredients makes a stop worthwhile. Mushroom soup, pork schnitzel and steak and kidney pie with ale, fisherman's pie and lasagne show the range. Dinner is more expensive.

Garden • Car-park • Access, Visa

Camberley · map 2

Pizza Express

53 Park Street
☎ CAMBERLEY (0276) 21846

M3 junction 4

Open all week 11.30am–midnight

Part of the popular chain which is the pick of the pizza bunch. See London entry.

No-smoking area • Access, Amex, Diners, Visa

Cheam · map 3

Superfish

64 The Broadway
☎ 081-643 6906

Open all week 11.30–2 (2.30 Sat), 5.30–11 (11.30 Fri and Sat)
Closed Christmas Day, Boxing Day, New Year's Day and L other bank hols

A small, enterprising chain of Surrey-based fish and chip shops. See Tolworth entry.

Unlicensed, but bring your own: no corkage

When you book a restaurant table, you're making a contract with the restaurant and you must be given a table, within reasonable time of your arrival. If not, the restaurant is in breach of contract and you can claim a reasonable sum to cover any expenses you had as a result, e.g. travelling expenses.

Croydon · map 3

Hockney's

98 High Street
☎ 081-688 2899

Open Mon to Sat noon–5.30, 6–10 (exc Mon D)
Closed Sun, Christmas and New Year

Simon Beckett produces vivid vegetarian food in this restaurant linked to a wholefood shop and Croydon's Buddhist Centre. Menus are international, plundering the Mediterranean and the Far East as well as more familiar wholefood territory. Samosas, quiches, soups and falafels are backed up by daily dishes ranging from lasagne and mushroom brioche to tjoan thung (a Chinese bean curd casserole with potatoes, bulgar wheat, brussels sprouts and chestnuts). Parfaits and yoghurt-based sweets to finish; lassi, elderflower cordial and juices to drink.

Unlicensed, but bring your own: corkage £1.50 • No smoking • Access, Amex, Diners, Visa

Pizza Express

3 South End
☎ 081-680 0123

Open all week 11.30am–midnight

Part of the popular chain which is the pick of the pizza bunch. See London entry.

No-smoking area • Access, Amex, Diners, Visa

Dorking   map 3

Pizza Express

235 High Street
☎ DORKING **(0306) 888236**

Open all week 11.30am–midnight

Part of the popular chain which is the pick of the pizza bunch. See London entry.

No-smoking area • Access, Amex, Diners, Visa

Pizza Piazza

77 South Street
☎ DORKING **(0306) 889790**

Open all week 11am–11.30pm

A branch of one of the best pizza chains in the UK. See London entry.

Access, Visa

Dunsfold   map 3

Sun Inn 🏵

The Common
☎ GODALMING **(0486) 49242**

Open all week noon–2, 7–10
Closed Christmas Day

From the outside this is a charming Georgian pub on the village green, inside there are the exposed timbers and high ceiling of a converted seventeenth-century barn. No less than three open fires add to the warm welcome. Leek and potato soup, garlic mussels, lamb noisettes and

pork dijonnaise are just some of the bar food choices. Walnut sponge with butterscotch sauce to finish.

No children • Garden • Wheelchair access • Access, Amex, Diners, Visa

East Moseley   map 3

Superfish

90 Walton Road
☎ **081-979 2432**

Open all week 11.30–2 (2.30 Sat),
5.30–11 (11.30 Fri and Sat)
Closed Christmas Day, Boxing Day,
New Year's Day and L other bank hols

A small, enterprising chain of Surrey-based fish and chip shops. See Tolworth entry.

Egham   map 3

Bar 163

High Street
☎ EGHAM **(0784) 432344**

Open Mon to Sat noon–2.30, 7–10.30
Closed Sun and bank hols

Just the place for a snack rather than a meal. An extensive menu changes daily but might include a plate of Stilton and Brie (£2.30), a 'bacon' club sandwich (£2.80) or a beef casserole (£4.50). Steamed puddings are a speciality. A busy rendezvous, so be patient.

Access, Amex, Visa

Epsom
map 3

Pizza Express

8 South Street
☎ EPSOM (0372) 729618

Open all week 11.30am–midnight

Part of the popular chain which is the
pick of the pizza bunch. See London
entry.

*No-smoking area • Access, Amex,
Diners, Visa*

Pizza Piazza

34 South Street
☎ EPSOM (0372) 724049

Open all week 11am–11.30pm

A branch of one of the best pizza
chains in the UK. See London entry.

Access, Visa

Ewell
map 3

Superfish

Bypass Road
☎ 081-393 3674

*Open all week 11.30–2 (2.30 Sat),
5.30–11 (11.30 Fri and Sat)
Closed Christmas Day, Boxing Day,
New Year's Day and L other bank hols*

A small, enterprising chain of Surrey-
based fish and chip shops. See
Tolworth entry.

Ewhurst
map 3

Windmill Inn

Ditch Hill
☎ CRANLEIGH (0483) 277566

On B2127 2m E of Cranleigh

*Open all week noon–2.30, 7–10 (exc
Sun and Mon D)
Closed Christmas Day evening*

The spectacular views of the South
Downs are unchanged, but new
owners have raised the tone of this
woodside pub. Eating is now the
main business in the re-vamped bar,
and a blackboard menu offers
excellent food along the lines of air-
dried beef with mustard sauce; grilled
goat's-milk cheese with salad; and
lamb and mint sausages with mash.
Beef casserole is served in a giant
Yorkshire pudding with potatoes,
beans and carrots. Up-market
sandwiches and first-rate puddings.
Real ales, wine by the glass.

*Garden • Car-park • Wheelchair access
• Access, Amex, Visa*

Farnham
map 2

Pizza Piazza

68A Castle Street
☎ FARNHAM (0252) 721383

Open all week 11am–11.30pm

A branch of one of the best pizza
chains in the UK. See London entry.

Access, Visa

Godalming   map 2

Pizza Piazza

78 High Street
☎ GODALMING (0483) 429191

Open all week 11am–11.30pm

A branch of one of the best pizza
chains in the UK. See London entry.

Access, Visa

Guildford   map 3

Rumwong

16–18 London Road
☎ GUILDFORD (0483) 36092

*Open Tue to Sun noon–3, 6–11 (10.30
Sun D)*
*Closed Mon, last 2 weeks June and 24 to
28 Dec*

Some of the most enjoyable Thai
cooking south of the river is served in
this well-established restaurant. Eat
western-style in the main dining area,
or recline on cushions in the
authentic Khan Tok Room. For a
cheap meal, stay with the list of quick
lunch or supper dishes – one-plate
meals based on rice or noodles.
Otherwise, the menu offers plenty of
treats, from creamy roast duck curry
with coconut and pineapple to deep-
fried prawns in garlic batter. Soups,
satays and salads form the back-up.
Drink tea or Singha Thai beer.

Wheelchair access • Access, Visa

See the back of the guide for an index of
eating-places and an index of locations.

Kew   map 3

Newens & Sons

288–90 Kew Road
☎ 081-940 2752

Open Tue to Sat 10am–5.30
Closed Mon and Sun

A shop and tea-room where all the
food is made on the premises and
people queue up outside to get a
table, especially for the renowned
cream teas. A roast or steak and
kidney pie are the only hot dishes at
lunch, otherwise there are Newens'
popular pies: veal and ham and
chicken. Baking is first-class and the
winter log fire welcome after a walk
in Kew Gardens.

*No smoking • Wheelchair access, also
WC*

Kingston upon Thames   map 3

Dining Hall

Griffin Passage, Market Square
☎ 081-547 1696/1656

*Open all week exc Sat noon–3 (5 Sun),
7–midnight (10.30 Sun)*

Decent fare at reasonable prices in an
outstanding setting. The food here is
not remarkable except in the context
of Kingston, a true culinary
wasteland. The outstanding setting is
a first-floor rococo hall complete
with antique mirrors opposite
windows festooned with muslin
drapes. Candlelight and some
spectacular chairs reinforce the

impression of a Venetian palazzo. Apart from Parma ham and ogen melon there are crespolini filled with spinach and ricotta to start. Main-course options revolve around chicken, kidneys, trout, wood pigeon and duck. The Café Canale downstairs is cheaper and more studenty.

Access, Amex, Visa

La La Pizza

138 London Road
☎ **081-546 4888**

Open all week 5.30pm–11.30
Closed Christmas Day, Boxing Day, New Year's Day and Easter

Luigi Abbro claims that his family-run restaurant serves the largest selection of pizzas in the UK. Twenty-eight versions are on offer, with myriad toppings and crisp – yet moist – bases. There are plenty of options for vegetarians. The menu is filled out with pastas and salads; the garlic bread is excellent. Good for boisterous parties.

Wheelchair access, also WC

Pizza Express

41 High Street
☎ **081-546 1447**

Open all week 11.30am–midnight

Part of the popular chain which is the pick of the pizza bunch. See London entry.

No-smoking area • Access, Amex, Diners, Visa

Morden   map 3

Superfish

20 London Road
☎ **081-648 6908**

Open all week 11.30–2 (2.30 Sat),
5.30–11 (11.30 Fri and Sat)
Closed Christmas Day, Boxing Day, New Year's Day and L other bank hols

A small, enterprising chain of Surrey-based fish and chip shops. See Tolworth entry.

New Malden   map 3

Pizza Piazza

69 High Street
☎ **081-942 2865**

Open all week 11am–11.30pm

A branch of one of the best pizza chains in the UK. See London entry.

Access, Visa

Redhill   map 3

Pizza Piazza

3 Linkfield Street
☎ **REDHILL (0737) 766154**

Open all week 11am–11.30pm

A branch of one of the best pizza chains in the UK. See London entry.

Access, Visa

Richmond   map 3

Kozachok

10 Red Lion Street
☎ 081-948 2366

Open Mon to Sat D 6.30–11
Closed Sun

A cosmopolitan crowd homes in on this pleasing East European restaurant, which has Russian owners and Polish waiters. The menu is an accessible mix of Russian, Ukrainian and Slavonic dishes from bortsch and marinated herrings with dill and sour cream to beef Stroganoff, schnitzels with various toppings and stuffed cabbage leaves. Meat-eaters might choose Cossack-style venison with potato dumplings, or marinated steak with red cabbage; vegetarians could try buckwheat layered with mushrooms and onions, and topped with sour cream. Excellent charlotte russe and fruit-filled blinis to finish. Drink vodka (from a choice of 30) or Bulls Blood wine.

Wheelchair access • Access, Amex, Visa

Mrs Beeton's

58 Hill Rise
☎ 081-940 9561

Open all week, all day (times vary)

Faded it might be, but Mrs Beeton's is certainly not tired. This ladies' co-operative has been running for years and offers good home cooking in a laid-back, friendly environment. Different ladies cook at different times – Greek with Ada on Mondays, Malaysian with Pili on Thursdays.

Portions are generous. On Sunday evenings, three courses are £9.95.

Unlicensed, but bring your own: corkage £1 per table • Wheelchair access

Pizza Express

20 Hill Street
☎ 081-940 8951

Open all week 11.30am–midnight

Part of the popular chain which is the pick of the pizza bunch. See London entry.

No-smoking area • Access, Amex, Diners, Visa

Refectory

6 Church Walk
☎ 081-940 6264

Open Tue to Sun 10am–5
Closed Mon, Christmas to New Year and Easter

What a service Harriet and Martin Steel are providing with their dedication to keenly priced English food. Lunch includes London Particular soup, potted meat, chicken and mushroom pie or cidered pork and apples, with a steamed chocolate pudding for afters. Morning coffee or afternoon tea come with home-baked cakes. The eighteenth-century refectory setting is charming.

No smoking L • Garden • Wheelchair access, also WC • Access, Visa

---

Out to Eat is totally independent, accepts no free hospitality and makes no charge for inclusion.

Shamley Green   map 2

Red Lion Inn

On the Green
☎ GUILDFORD (0483) 892202

On B2128 4m SE of Guildford

Open all week 10am–midnight

It is hard to eat within our budget here, but the Red Lion is a comfortable, solid, traditional pub, overlooking the cricket green, with antique furniture, lots of pictures and a real fire – well worth a visit. Good-looking, well-filled sandwiches and ham, egg and chips are the cheapest options.

No children under 5 • Garden • Car-park • Wheelchair access, also WC • Access, Amex, Diners, Visa

Staines   map 3

Pizza Express

12 Clarence Street
☎ STAINES (0784) 456522

Open all week 11.30am–midnight

Part of the popular chain which is the pick of the pizza bunch. See London entry.

No-smoking area • Access, Amex, Diners, Visa

Surbiton   map 3

Ajanta

114 Ewell Road
☎ 081-399 2567

*Open all week noon–2, 6–midnight
Closed Christmas Day and Boxing Day*

A medium-priced Indian restaurant that shows rare vibrancy and brio and outstanding use of fresh ingredients in a satisfying range of traditional dishes. Starters include chicken tikka (£2.15) and mushroom kebab (£2.20), while a good main course is king prawn masala (£6.95).

Wheelchair access • Access, Amex, Diners, Visa

Sutton   map 3

Pizza Express

4 High Street
☎ 081-643 4725

Open all week 11.30am–midnight

Part of the popular chain which is the pick of the pizza bunch. See London entry.

No-smoking area • Access, Amex, Diners, Visa

Thames Ditton map 3

Albany

Queen's Road
☎ 081-398 7031

Open all week L noon–2.30
Closed Christmas Day

A sprawling Victorian pub with a spacious Thames-side terrace overlooking Hampton Court Gardens. Bar food, in the form of a fresh, good-quality buffet, is available lunchtimes only. There are thick slices of ham, rare beef, good French bread, decent cheeses, salads and a small choice of hot dishes such as pasta, ham and cheese bake. There is also a more expensive evening menu.

No children evenings • Garden • Car-park • Access, Amex, Diners, Visa

Tolworth map 3

Superfish

59 The Broadway
☎ 081-390 2868

Open all week 11.30–2 (2.30 Sat),
5.30–11 (11.30 Fri and Sat)
Closed Christmas Day, Boxing Day,
New Year's Day and L other bank hols

A small, enterprising chain of Surrey-based fish and chip shops (see Cheam, East Molesley, Ewell, Morden and West Byfleet). All are light and bright, spotlessly clean, and offer a small selection of crisply cooked fresh fish to eat in or take away. Choose from fillets of haddock, plaice, huss or sole, or whole plaice on the bone. Chips are well cooked.

Walton-on-Thames map 3

Pizza Piazza

14 Bridge Street
☎ WALTON-ON-THAMES (0932)
220153

Open all week 11am–11.30pm

A branch of one of the best pizza chains in the UK. See London entry.

Access, Visa

West Byfleet map 3

Superfish

51 Old Woking Road
☎ BYFLEET (0932) 340366

Open all week 11.30–2 (2.30 Sat),
5.30–11 (11.30 Fri and Sat)
Closed Christmas Day, Boxing Day,
New Year's Day and L other bank hols

A small, enterprising chain of Surrey-based fish and chip shops. See Tolworth entry.

Alfriston

map 3

Drusillas Thatched Barn

Drusillas Corner
☎ ALFRISTON (0323) 870234

Open all week 10am–6
Closed Christmas Day

Drusillas – an ancient, heavily-timbered barn – is now the heart of a fully fledged family theme park, complete with a zoo, adventure playground, fudge factory and miniature railway. The main restaurant combines 'family restaurant' clichés (burgers, chilli, and fish fingers for the kids) with a few faintly regional ideas – Sussex Broth to start, Tipsy Sussex Squire to finish. Fish and chips are good and fresh; giant Sussex sausage is a real monster, but the pick of the menu is the excellent additive-free dairy ice-cream. English wine by the glass.

No-smoking area • Garden • Car-park • Wheelchair access, also WC • Access, Amex, Visa

Sussex Ox

Milton Street
☎ ALFRISTON (0323) 870840

1m NE of Alfriston

Open all week noon–2, 7–9.30 (exc Sun D winter)
Closed Christmas Day, Boxing Day evening and New Year's Day evening

Turn off the A27 to find this big country pub with stunning views of the South Downs. This is a hostelry geared to the family, with toys in the dining-room and sturdy play equipment outside. Big portions of decently prepared food range from cod and chips, garlic chicken and bangers and mash to snacks such as local goats'-milk cheese. Good treacle tart or apple crumble to finish. Harveys beers on draught; limited wines.

No-smoking area • Garden • Car-park • Wheelchair access, also WC

Brightling

map 3

Jack Fuller's

☎ BRIGHTLING (042 482) 212

On Robertsbridge–Brightling road

Open Tue to Sun noon–2.30, 7–9.30 (exc Sun D)
Closed Mon

Formerly the Fuller's Arms, the renaming underlines the strong emphasis on food; the owners describe themselves as a restaurant freehouse. English-inspired dishes produce gammon and onion pudding, beef stew and dumplings and cauliflower crumble. Vegetarians are well catered for – there is even a vegetarian spotted dick on a wonderful hot-pudding lovers' list.

Garden • Car-park • Wheelchair access • Access, Diners, Visa

Brighton   map 3

Abracadabra

29 Tidy Street
☎ Brighton (0273) 677738

Open Tue to Sat 10am–5.30, Fri and Sat D 7–10
Closed Sun, Mon and Christmas Day

A very unusual café, oddly appealing, which offers tarot readings at your table. There is also an in-house hairdresser. The menu is imaginative and the cooking is ambitious, although it does not always work: the apple strudel has too heavy a wholemeal crust and the lamb hot-pot can be too dry. But on the whole flavours are positive and dishes generally satisfying.

Access, Visa

Al Duomo

7 Pavilion Buildings
☎ Brighton (0273) 26741

Open all week noon 2.30, 6–11.30
Closed Christmas Day

Not far from the Royal Pavilion is this excellent-value, no-frills trattoria. It may look a bit like a pizza parlour, but the cooking is genuine. Apart from giant pizzas with lots of toppings, there are authentic pasta dishes such as penne matriciana and spaghetti carbonara, backed up by blackboard specials. To finish, try the profiteroles and tiramisu cake. Drinkable Italian wines.

Wheelchair access, also WC • Access, Amex, Visa

Al Forno

36 East Street
☎ BRIGHTON (0273) 24905

Open Tue to Sun noon–2.30, 6–11.30
Closed summer Mon, winter Sun/Mon and Christmas Day

Related to Al Duomo (see previous entry), with the same menu and the same lively atmosphere. The restaurant is on two floors and there is a terrace with colourful hanging baskets that has a few tables for outdoor eating. Good spaghetti bolognese. Young, attentive waiters keep the place running with good humour.

Access, Amex, Visa

Annie's

41 Middle Street
☎ BRIGHTON (0273) 202051

Open all week noon–11

This is not the smartest place in town, or the cheapest, but it is an adequate family diner. Home-spun decoration matches – mostly – home-made English food. This translates as pie: steak and kidney, steak and oyster, turkey and chestnut, lamb and apricot, chicken and asparagus and fish. It is the kind of place where an office party brings slow service to a standstill. Enjoy gooseberry fool, treacle tart, or a sponge. The 'kids' menu' is good value at £1.50.

Access, Amex, Diners, Visa

The factual details under each eating-place are based on information supplied by the restaurateur.

Black Chapati ★

**12 Circus Parade,
New England Road
☎ BRIGHTON (0273) 699011**

*Open Wed to Sun L 12.30–2, Tue to
Sat D 7–10.30
Closed Mon*

Because Steve Funnel, the chef, is not
Indian he strives very hard to make
his cooking as authentic as possible,
using an innovative style and drawing
inspiration from all over the sub-
continent, Burma and Thailand to
produce something that is far
removed from the standard curry
house offerings. The use of fresh
herbs and spices really shines through
in bhel poori, kerala chicken curry
and Goan roast duckling. The
Sunday lunch buffet is £6.95, but the
rest of the menu is just out of our
price range. We feel, however, that
this small, ultra-casual and minimalist
black and white restaurant offers
exceptional value for money.

*No children after 9pm • Wheelchair
access • Access, Visa*

Browns

**3–4 Duke Street
☎ BRIGHTON (0273) 23501**

*Open all week 11am–11.30pm
Closed Christmas Eve, Christmas Day
and Boxing Day*

Browns is one of a family of three
informal, lively American-style
restaurants (see entries for Oxford
and Cambridge) with continuous
service from breakfast to 11.30pm.
The menu offers pasta, salads and hot
sandwiches with game, chicken and
fisherman's pies, roast ribs,
vegetarian dishes and fresh fish.
Desserts are gooey and satisfying.

*No-smoking area • Wheelchair access,
also WC • Access, Amex, Visa*

La Caperon

**113 St Georges Road,
Kemp Town
☎ BRIGHTON (0273) 680317**

*Open Tue to Sun noon–2, 7–10.30 (exc
Sun D)
Closed Mon*

A tiny restaurant seating 30 in its two
rooms, one of which is non-smoking.
The three-course lunch for £3.95 is
amazing value and caters well for
vegetarians: home-made leek soup,
spinach and orange terrine, tomato
and mushroom roulade. There are
roast chicken and steak and kidney
pie for meat-eaters. Sunday lunch at
£5.95 offers more choice.

No-smoking area • Access, Visa

Clarence Wine Bar

**Meeting House Lane
☎ BRIGHTON (0273) 720597**

*Open all week 11–3, 6.30–11
Closed Christmas Day and Boxing Day*

A place crowded with young people,
and noisy with loud background
music and a live pop group on certain
evenings. It is friendly and
entertaining. Food is decent, offering
popular dishes rather than anything
imaginative: burgers, lasagne, filled
jacket potatoes and macaroni cheese
with banoffi pie for dessert.

*Garden • Wheelchair access • Access,
Amex, Diners, Visa*

Cripes

7 Victoria Road
☎ BRIGHTON (0273) 27878

Open all week noon–2.30, 6–11.30
Closed Christmas and New Year

A good-value crêperie specialising in buckwheat 'galettes'. Savoury versions range from chicken and asparagus to mozzarella and avocado with olives and tomato. All come with a crisp, dressed salad. To finish there are sweets along the same lines, including lemon and honey, or stewed apple and Calvados. Fresh filter coffee, wine by the glass.

Food for Friends ★

17–18 Prince Albert Street, The Lanes
☎ BRIGHTON (0273) 736236
12 Sydney Street, North Laines
☎ BRIGHTON (0273) 571363

Open all week 9am (9.30 Sun)–10pm

An informal, unpretentious vegetarian café which, of all the eating establishments in the Lanes, remains best for food and value. Long queues and shared tables do not deter custom. Breakfast starts the day with organic bread, pain au chocolat, croissant and Danish baked on the premises. Both lunch and dinner feature imaginative, eclectic dishes – crespolini Fiorenza, Virginia spoonbread bake, Turkish falafel – all prepared from organic produce where possible. There can be a heavy-handedness to some of the dishes but portions are generous and the food tastes fresh. The selection of salads is good, and desserts and cakes

are well made. The Sydney Street address is also a take-away.

Unlicensed, but bring your own: no corkage • No-smoking area • Wheelchair access, also WC

Häagen-Dazs

4 Prince Albert Street
☎ BRIGHTON (0273) 747448

Open all week 11am–11pm
Closed Christmas Day, Boxing Day and New Year's Day

Ice-cream at this stylish American ice-cream parlour is marvellous, made from pure ingredients and offering fresh flavours in generous portions. Some of the composite offerings on the menu are worth exploring. Chocoholic sundae speaks for itself or try raisin muffin with vanilla ice-cream.

Unlicensed • No smoking

Latin in the Lane

10 King's Road
☎ BRIGHTON (0273) 28672

Open all week noon–2.15, 6.30–11

A happy Italian trattoria, which is generally noisy and busy. It is not cheap. To keep the bill down, go for pasta and salads. But that is no hardship; the pasta is home-made and ingredients making up the wide choice of sauces are first-class – the olive oil used in dressing, and for the proper mozzarella, tomato and basil salad is thick, green and virgin.

Access, Amex, Diners, Visa

Mock Turtle

4 Poole Valley, off East Street
☎ BRIGHTON (0273) 27380

Open Tue to Sat 10am–6
Closed Sun, Mon, Christmas and 2
weeks autumn

This is essentially a cake shop serving light lunches, and very popular for an unlicensed place. The atmosphere is convivial and everyone shares tables which are adorned with flowers. The menu offers bacon and eggs and chipped potatoes, pork sausages and fillets of plaice, all of an excellent standard. Friendly and good value.

Unlicensed, but bring your own: no
corkage • No smoking on ground floor •
Wheelchair access

Pizza Express

22 Prince Albert Street, The Lanes
☎ BRIGHTON (0273) 23205
90 Western Road
☎ BRIGHTON (0273) 26333

Open all week 11.30am–midnight

Part of the popular chain which is the pick of the pizza bunch. See London entry.

No-smoking area • Access, Amex,
Diners, Visa

Slims

92 Churchill Square
☎ Brighton (0273) 24582

Open Mon to Sat 11.30am–3
Closed Sun

Against the odds, this mainly no-smoking health-food hangout may be holding its own in what could be the most unprepossessing shopping centre in the country. Grab a tray and queue at the counter for daily specials like spinach and mushroom quiche, vegetable curry and cheese and tomato flan, as well as excellent apricot sponge and pleasant honey and walnut flapjacks. This is no-nonsense cooking at reasonable prices.

No-smoking area • Wheelchair access

Chichester   map 2

Pizza Express

27 South Street
☎ CHICHESTER (0243) 786648

Open all week 11.30am–midnight

Part of the popular chain which is the pick of the pizza bunch. See London entry.

No-smoking area • Access, Amex,
Diners, Visa

St Martin's Tea Rooms

3 St Martin's Street
☎ CHICHESTER (0243) 786715

Open Tue to Sat 9am–6
Closed Sun and Mon

The Georgian façade of Keith Nelson's tea-room hides a much earlier interior and an attractive brick paved garden – the only place where smoking is allowed. The food is vegetarian, except for wild smoked salmon, and the produce used is organic where possible. Customers can check the ingredients of the dishes they order from a list at the counter. Welsh rarebit, red dragon pie or mushroom and courgette bake with salads of aduki beans, apple and potato and fruity coleslaw are all good. Only soups lack depth, based on a vegetable stock that is too light. Baking is superb – try the lightest of scones or a moist carrot cake topped with yoghurt.

No smoking, exc in garden • Garden • Wheelchair access

Salad House

14 Southgate
☎ CHICHESTER **(0243) 788822**

Open Mon to Sat 8am–5.30
Closed Sun

A counter-service café strong on cakes, vegetarian dishes and a selection of proper leaf teas. The bread is made on the premises. Nut roast and apple sauce, parsnip and tomato bake, spinach and cottage cheese crêpes and a variety of salads are backed up by home-cooked ham, generously filled sandwiches and good scones.

No-smoking area

Shepherds Tea Rooms

35 Little London
☎ CHICHESTER **(0243) 774761**

Open Mon to Sat 9.15am–5
Closed Sun

As the Tea Council's 1990 'Teaplace of the Year', Shepherds can promise a proper cup of tea. There is also a wide range of good savoury snacks: generously filled sandwiches, well-flavoured soups such as broccoli and cheese, the biggest jacket potatoes imaginable (when we visited) and the house speciality, rarebits. Barmbrake

or scones are recommendable from a gooey selection of cakes.

No-smoking area • Wheelchair access

Chilgrove   map 2

White Horse

☎ EAST MARDEN **(024 359) 219**

Open Tue to Sun L noon–2, Tue to Fri D 7–9.30
Closed Mon and Feb

An out-of-the-way location for an exceedingly convivial pub, famous for its restaurant and extensive wine list (some splendid wines, many by the glass). Straightforward bar meals of braised oxtail, boiled silverside of beef, grilled fresh fish and pigeon are all based on local produce and sound cooking skills.

No children under 14 • Garden • Car-park • Wheelchair access, also WC • Access, Diners, Visa

Cousley Wood   map 3

Old Vine

☎ Wadhurst **(089 288) 2271**

On B2100 Lamberhurst–Wadhurst road

Open all week noon–2, 6.45–9.30

Food is all-important at this old, comfortably appointed pub. The standard of cooking is sound and portions are generous. Soup or garlic mushrooms precede peppered chicken breasts in cream sauce, poached salmon and prawn en croûte, lamb curry or grilled halibut with capers and lemon juice. Mushroom Stroganoff is a good vegetarian choice.

Garden • Car-park • Wheelchair access • Access, Diners, Visa

Cuckfield   map 3

King's Head

South Street
☎ HAYWARDS HEATH (0444) 454006

Open all week 11am (noon Sun)–9
Closed Christmas Day evening

In one bar the low, nicotine-yellow ceiling is plastered with banknotes of all currencies, while pitch pine panelling covers the walls of the public bar, which offers darts and pool. In short, this is an unspoilt village pub with plain, good food to match: fish pie, cottage pie, steak and kidney pie, macaroni cheese, sandwiches and filled rolls. The restaurant is more expensive.

Garden • Wheelchair access, also WC • Access, Amex, Visa

Eastbourne   map 3

Bosworth's

8 Bottom Road
☎ EASTBOURNE (0323) 23023

Open all week 11am–11pm
Closed Christmas Day, Boxing Day and Easter Sun

Bosworth's is the sort of wine bar every town should possess, with an excellent, fairly priced wine list from

a good range of countries and with a decent selection by the glass. The short, regularly changing blackboard menu offers chargrilling, vegetarian dishes and good taramasalata and smoked salmon.

No children between 2 and 14 • Access, Amex, Diners, Visa

Brasserie Upstairs

Enterprise Centre, Station Parade
☎ EASTBOURNE (0323) 643889

Open Mon to Sat 10am–3, Fri and Sat D 7–11.30
Closed Sun and bank hols

Hard by the railway station but hardly the place for a romantic brief encounter, this is just the place for a spot of train-spotting combined with a cheering, light meal. The menu is more varied than first impressions might lead you to expect. Warm bacon and avocado salad is good, but the spinach and feta cheese pancake is too cheesy. Other options are open sandwiches, minute steaks, pasta, fillets of trout with prawns and almonds and smoked salmon omelette. Espresso coffee and swift service.

No-smoking area • Access, Amex, Visa

Pizza Piazza

4 Pevensey Road
☎ EASTBOURNE (0323) 410312

Open all week 11am–11.30pm

A branch of one of the best pizza chains in the UK. See London entry.

Access, Visa

Elsted   map 2

Three Horseshoes

☎ HARTING (0730) 825746

5m W of Midhurst

*Open all week noon–2 (2.30 Sun),
6.30–10
Closed Christmas Day*

Rough plastered walls, yellow and
bulging with age (*circa* 1500), gnarled
beams, a massive log-burning fire and
a rural setting make a splendid
location for some sound pub food.
Fresh fish is a speciality, particularly
at weekends, with whole Selsey
plaice, fried clams and dressed crab.
Thick, home-made soup,
ploughman's, steak, chilli and filled
jacket potatoes complete the picture.

*No children between 2 and 14 • Garden
• Wheelchair access, also WC*

Firle   map 3

Ram ★

nr Lewes
☎ GLYNDE (0273) 858222

Off A27 Lewes–Eastbourne road

Open all week noon–2, 7–9

A genuinely simple seventeenth-
century inn with few frills but a warm
welcome. Blackened beams, low
ceilings, dark wooden tables and
chairs, a smoky log fire in the
no-smoking room and a lovely flint-
walled garden all add to the charm.

The bar menu is imaginative and the
cooking displays an enthusiasm which
extends to the careful purchasing of
local free-range produce. Fish
chowder with scallops is thick and
full of flavour, and there is lentil and
lovage soup with herby garlic bread.
Rabbit pie, home-cooked ham, fresh
plaice fillets or lamb cutlets give an
idea of the regularly changing dishes.
Spotted dick, Sussex pond pudding
and a rich bread pudding make for a
traditional finish.

*No-smoking area • Garden • Car-park
• Wheelchair access • Access, Visa*

Fletching   map 3

Griffin Inn

☎ Newick (082 572) 2890

Off A272 at Piltdown

*Open all week noon–2.30, 7–9.30 (exc
Sun D)*

Dark beams, panelling and copper-
canopied fireplaces create the right
atmosphere at this sixteenth-century
pub opposite the village church. Bar
food is standard fare with toad-in-
the-hole, steak and kidney pie, and
chicken and leek bake representative
of the conventional menu; treacle tart
and bread-and-butter pudding to
finish.

*Garden and family-room • Car-park •
Wheelchair access, also WC • Access,
Diners, Visa*

Fulking   map 3

Shepherd and Dog

The Street
☎ BRIGHTON (0273) 857382

*Open all week noon–2, 7–9.30 (exc
Sun D)*

An attractive tile-hung pub in a
peaceful setting. Inside it is all rustic
artefacts, highly polished gateleg
tables and fresh flowers. Bar food
includes a 'farmer's lunch' of grilled
sausages, steak and kidney pie, beef
and Guinness pie and roast duck in
orange and red wine sauce. There is
locally smoked salmon in the 'squire's
lunch'. A busy, popular pub.

*No children in bar • Garden • Car-park
• Wheelchair access, also WC • Access,
Visa*

Hartfield   map 3

Anchor Inn

Church Street
☎ HARTFIELD (0892) 770761

*Open Mon to Sat noon–2, 6–10, Sun
noon–1.30, 7–10*

No fruit-machines, juke-boxes or
television to drown out the friendly
atmosphere of this traditional pub in
the village main street. The best
choice is in the bar, and fish is a
strong point, with heaped bowls of
mussels in season, poached Scotch
salmon, and prawn and crab curry on
the menu. Otherwise, there might be
beef kebabs, Mexican chilli and
various kinds of ploughman's. There

are usually half a dozen real ales to
drink. Go early – especially in
summer.

*Garden and family-room • Car-park •
Wheelchair access, also WC • Access,
Visa*

Hastings   map 3

Porters Wine Bar

56 High Street
☎ HASTINGS (0424) 427000

Open all week noon–2 (exc Sun), 7–10

Old Hastings is worth exploring and
Porters Wine Bar just the place to
end up in. It is everything a wine bar
should be – a friendly, bustling place
with lots of room for drinking at the
bar. Food is fresh and well cooked:
smoked cod and broccoli gratiné,
beef and Guinness pie, lamb and okra
curry, chilli pork sausages with potato
pancakes. A popular place – no
bookings.

*Garden • Wheelchair access • Access,
Visa*

Horsham   map 3

Pizza Piazza

3 Denne Road
☎ HORSHAM (0403) 62029

Open all week 11am–11.30pm

A branch of one of the best pizza
chains in the UK. See London entry.

Access, Visa

Lewes
map 3

Pailin

19–20 Station Street
☎ LEWES (0223) 473906

Open Mon to Sat noon–2, 6.30–11
Closed Christmas Day and Boxing Day

Formerly the home of Trumps, this sixteenth-century building now houses a quiet, comfortable Thai restaurant. The short menu may seem westernised, but the kitchen offers good-value light meals, prepared with care and served with speed. Mushroom soup with lemon grass, dry fish curry (including mussels and crab claws), and stir-fried chicken with mushrooms and ginger have all been good. Rice and vegetables are up to the mark. Try the Thai egg custard as a curiosity. Set meals from around £10 per person. The house wine from Gascony is a snip at £6 a bottle.

Access, Amex, Diners, Visa

Ronnie's Wine Bar

197 High Street
☎ LEWES (0273) 477879

Open 1 May to 30 Sept Mon to Sat noon–10, Sun noon–2.30, 7–9.30 and 1 Oct to 31 Apr Mon to Fri noon–2.30, 6–10, Sat noon–10, Sun 7–9.30

Ronnie's is a large, faded place, smoky when busy, offering decent but unambitious food. Lasagne, spaghetti bolognese, burgers and jacket potatoes are followed by light, steamed sponge puddings and good espresso. Wines are limited in scope but cheap.

No pipes • No children in bar • Wheelchair access, also WC • Access, Amex, Diners, Visa

Mayfield
map 3

Rose & Crown

Fletching Street
☎ Mayfield (0435) 872200

Open all week noon–2, 7–9.30

Five blackboards announce a huge range of foods in this pretty, white, weather-boarded pub with seats outside. Moules marinière and pâté appear alongside mixed grills and braised pork chops in a good dark mushroom and onion sauce. There are also chef's specials such as lamb in rosemary and redcurrant sauce, plus an entire board devoted to sweets: look out for the superb banoffi pie and chocolate hazelnut meringue. Abundant vegetables are served on side dishes. Real ales and decent wines by the glass.

No children under 11 in restaurant • Garden • Car-park

Midhurst
map 2

Maxine's

Red Lion Street
☎ MIDHURST (073 081) 6271

Open Wed to Sun noon–1.45, 7–9.30 (exc Sun D)
Closed Mon, Tue and Boxing Day

Skilful and consistent cooking and smooth, well-pitched service attract a loyal following. Maxine's inclusion here is for the excellent set-price menu available at lunch and dinner (except Saturday evening). £9.95 buys three courses: perhaps soup, lambs' kidneys and sweetbreads in a cream sauce, and profiteroles to finish.

Access, Amex, Diners, Visa

South Harting   map 2

White Hart

High Street
☎ HARTING (0730) 825355

Open all week 11–2, 7–10 (exc Mon D)
Closed Christmas Day and Boxing Day

An attractive village pub with exposed beams, polished wood floor covered with rugs, plain tables, a large log fire, plants and knick-knacks. Standard bar food is fresh and well made: vegetable soup, toad-in-the-hole, liver and onion casserole, steak and kidney pie. Bread-and-butter pudding is a favourite dessert.

Garden and family-room • Wheelchair access

Ticehurst   map 3

Bull

Three-legged Cross
☎ TICEHURST (0580) 200586

½m N of Ticehurst

Open all week noon–2.30, 7–10 (exc Sun D)

The low-beamed rooms with floors of brick or flagstone can only hint at

the pub's reputed 600 years. It is a friendly place made more welcoming, especially in winter, by the large central fireplace. Bar food is of solid traditional English dishes: bubble and squeak, steak and kidney pie or cottage pie. In the evening there are also more elaborate meals in the restaurant.

Garden • Car-park • Wheelchair access, also WC

Tillington   map 2

Horseguards

☎ PETWORTH (0798) 42332

Open all week noon–2, 7–10
Closed Christmas Day

Once a pub, now more of a restaurant, though the bar survives as an anteroom to the exposed beams of the dining-room. The food shows the change in gear, leaving ploughman's far behind, in favour of cajun spiced halibut with a béarnaise sauce, or seafood fricassee. Inventive cooking which often works well. It can get a bit pricey, but whatever dish is chosen will be worth it.

Garden • Wheelchair access • Access, Visa

You will find report forms (write a letter if you prefer) at the back of the book so that you can tell us about your experiences of going *Out to Eat*. We'll put the information to good use when we're compiling the next edition.

West Hoathly map 3

Cat Inn

☎ EAST GRINSTEAD (0342) 810369

Open all week 12.15–1.45, 7.15–9.30
(exc Sun D)
Closed Christmas Day, Boxing Day and
New Year's Day

An old smugglers' inn in a lovely
position close to the church and
offering an excellent choice of well-
cooked but pricey food. Fresh
ingredients give a seasonal ring to the
menu and cold weather brings
comforting dishes such as ox-tail
casserole and steamed puddings.
Otherwise, there is fresh salmon
salad, boeuf bourguignonne and tipsy
trifle.

No children in bar • Car-park

Worthing map 3

Pizza Express

Stanford Cottage, Stanford
Square, Warwick Street
☎ WORTHING (0903) 821133

Open all week 11.30am–midnight

Part of the popular chain which is the
pick of the pizza bunch. See London
entry.

No-smoking area • Access, Amex,
Diners, Visa

All details are as accurate as possible at the
time of going to press, but chefs and
owners often change, and it is wise to
check by telephone before making a
special journey.

★ after an eating-place indicates that it is one of the best found by the Editor
during research for this book (see page 14 for a list).

 after an eating-place indicates that it is a pub. The opening and closing times
we give only relate to when food is available – the licensing hours may be different.

after an eating-place indicates that it is within five miles of the nearest motorway junction. We give the relevant motorway and junction in the details. Eating-
places in cities and large towns, where traffic, parking and route-finding may cause
delay, do not have this symbol.

Gateshead   map 10

Marquis of Granby

Streetgate, Sunniside
☎ 091-488 7813

*Open all week noon–2 (2.15 Sun), 6.30–
10 (exc Sun D)*

This stone-built pub on the main
Gateshead to Consett Road (A692)
describes itself as a restaurant, and
food is the main business. High
points of the regularly changing
blackboard menu are specials such as
spicy goulash and salmon marquis –
poached and served with a lemon
sauce and prawns. To start, there are
decent garlic mushrooms and prawn
cocktail; to finish, there are nursery
puddings such as treacle tart or
spotted dick. Well-kept Theakstons
beer.

Car-park • Wheelchair access, also WC

La Piazza

596 Durham Road, Low Fell
☎ 091-487 5810

*Open Mon to Sat noon–1.45, 6–10.30
Closed Sun, Christmas Day, Boxing Day
and New Year's Day*

On busy nights up to a dozen cooks
can be seen at work in the open
kitchen of this lively Italian
restaurant. The long menu centres on
spot-on pizzas and pasta dishes,
backed up by gutsy home-made
minestrone, huge bowls of mussels,
and garlic mushrooms on toast. Fillet
steaks will bump up the bill. To
finish, there are luscious banana splits
and gâteaux. Three-course set meals
are excellent value at lunch and
dinner. The house wine is reasonable.
Turnover is fast, but booking is
advisable.

Access, Diners, Visa

Newcastle-upon-Tyne   map 10

Eastern Taste

277 Stanhope Street, Fenham
☎ 091-273 9406

Open all week noon–midnight

Some of the best-value Indian food in
Newcastle is served in this all-day
restaurant and take-away. 'No fancy
décor, No Dickie Bow Ties,' says a
note on the menu, which has a huge
choice of tandooris and curries, from
lamb tikka and keema kurma to
chicken bhuna and prawn patia.
Chicken karahi gosht is a bestseller,
and there is an enterprising range of
vegetables including tinda and karala,
as well as bhindis and chickpeas.

*Unlicensed, but bring your own: no
corkage • Wheelchair access, also WC*

Roman Way Pizzeria

Westgate Road
☎ 091-273 1991

*Open Mon to Sat noon–2.30 (exc Sat),
5.30–11*
*Closed Sun, Christmas Day, Boxing Day
and New Year's Day*

A young, energetic crowd supports
this lively pizzeria sandwiched
between the bowling alley and a
fitness gym opposite the general
hospital. The décor is the standard
mix of rough-plastered walls, neon
signs and greenery in the windows.
Excellent pizzas with interesting fresh
toppings are the mainstays, backed up
by pasta and a few Middle Eastern
ideas such as shashlik and falafel. The
house wine is reasonable, and the
atmosphere is bustling.

*Wheelchair access • Access, Amex,
Diners, Visa*

Rupali

6 Bigg Market
☎ 091-232 8629

*Open all week noon–2.30 (exc Sun),
6–11.30*

This is still Newcastle's favourite
curry house. There are bargain
lunches and early dinners (6–7pm
Monday to Wednesday, 7–8pm
Sunday) with cut-price drinks and a
Thursday Happy Night (6–11.30pm)
– four courses for £6.95 with a glass
of wine and liqueur coffee. The carte
offers a culinary tour of the Indian
sub-continent with a good tandoori
and vegetarian selection.

Access, Amex, Diners, Visa

North Shields   map 10

Kristian

Fish Quay
☎ 091-258 5155

Open Mon to Sat 11am–9
*Closed Sun, Christmas Day and Boxing
Day*

On the quay opposite the unloading
sheds, this well-known local chippie
scores with the freshness and quality
of its fish. Cod, haddock and lemon
sole are cooked to perfection and
served straight from the pan.
Greaseless chips are at their best
when supplies of good-sized 'old'
(main crop) potatoes are available.
Pots of excellent strong tea to drink.
Spotless, functional décor, fast
service, queues at peak times.

*Wheelchair access, also WC • Access,
Visa*

Alderminster map 4

Bell Inn ★

☎ STRATFORD-UPON-AVON (0789)
450414

On A34 4m SE of Stratford-upon-Avon

Open all week noon–2, 7–10
Closed Christmas Day and evenings 26
to 27 Dec, New Year's Eve and New
Year's Day

A roadside inn with a plain façade
that hides a pleasant, characterful
interior. The strength is in the food,
which is both imaginative and
attractively presented. A daily-
changing blackboard menu can
produce a well-balanced carrot and
orange soup, a light ham and
asparagus quiche, and an enjoyable
peach and almond tart. Crispy topped
lamb in cider or hazelnut roast with
spicy tomato sauce are more filling
alternatives. The quality of
ingredients used is unimpeachable
and reflected to some extent in the
price, but well worth the small extra
cost. Service is well pitched,
professional and friendly. Of the
several bars, one is no-smoking. It is
advisable to book in the evening.

No-smoking area • Garden • Car-park
• Wheelchair access, also WC • Access,
Visa

'Wheelchair access' indicates that,
according to the proprietor, entrances are
at least 33 inches wide, passages 4 feet
wide, and that there are a maximum of
two steps. If there is access to a WC, we
mention it.

Rugby map 4

Eastern Eye

10 Henry Street
☎ RUGBY (0788) 543444

Open all week noon–2.30, 6–midnight
Closed Christmas Day and Boxing Day

Peacock motifs embellish the décor
in this civilised Indian restaurant
opposite the Rugby Theatre. A
standard menu of generous dhansaks,
kormas and bhunas is backed up by
interesting specialities and tandooris.
Look for spiced chicken wings, kid
josh (meat curry with cashews and
coconut milk) and akbary masala
(chicken cooked in a cream sauce
with minced meat). Lamb dishes
show up well, as in hussaini kebab
and sultan puri pilau. Waiters are
courteous, but the use of trolleys can
slow down the service. Drink lager.

Wheelchair access • Access, Amex,
Diners, Visa

Ryton-on-Dunsmore
map 4

Ryton Gardens Café

**National Centre for Organic
Gardening**
☎ COVENTRY (0203) 303517

On A45 5m SE of Coventry

Open all week 10am–5

Ryton Gardens is a showpiece for
'green gardening' and small-scale
food production, its café an advert for

organically grown food. The gardens' own vegetables, fruits and herbs provide the basis for satisfying soups, spinach roulade and leek croustade accompanied by good salads and fresh wholemeal bread. Cakes and desserts can be heavy. Delicious, home-made apple juice.

No smoking • Garden • Car-park • Wheelchair access, also WC Access, Visa

Stratford-upon-Avon map 4

Slug and Lettuce

38 Guild Street
☎ STRATFORD-UPON-AVON (0789) 299700

Open all week noon–2.15, 5.30–9.15 (Thurs to Sat noon–9)
Closed Christmas Day, Boxing Day and New Year's Day

This jazzily re-vamped pub feels more like a rumbustious bistro/wine bar than a traditional watering hole. Inside, the long L-shaped room has panelled walls, pine tables and views of the open-plan kitchen. The food is vividly international, with dishes listed on blackboards. Sautéed chicken livers; leek, tomato and tuna bake; chicken breast with avocado and garlic show the style. Otherwise, there might be black pudding with mustard sauce or squid stuffed with rice, prawns and spinach. Sweets are in a similar vein. Ansells beers and guest ales; wines by the glass.

Garden • Wheelchair access, also WC • Access, Visa

South Warwickshire College Training Restaurant

The Willows North, Alcester Road
☎ STRATFORD-UPON-AVON (0789) 266245

Open Mon to Fri L 12.15–1.30, Mon, Tue and Thur D 7.30–9.30
Closed Sat, Sun and college hols

Under the watchful eye of their tutors, catering students run this good-value restaurant with enthusiasm. The set lunch at £4.50 offers a simple-choice, three-course menu which could include minestrone, a ragoût of beef, pineapple gâteau or a savoury Scotch woodcock. Dinner is £10.50 but still tremendous value for money.

No-smoking area • Car-park • Wheelchair access, also WC • Access, Visa

Warwick map 4

Fanshawe's

22 Market Place
☎ WARWICK (0926) 410590

M40 junction 15

Open Tue to Sat 11.30–2, 6–10
Closed Sun, Mon, Christmas Day, Boxing Day and 2 weeks Oct

David Fanshawe moved from Kenilworth to open his own restaurant in a converted shop in Warwick's market-place. The style is pleasantly informal and menus are flexible. Best lunchtime value are the brown-bread sandwiches and snacks, backed up by dishes such as venison and black cherry pie, grilled red mullet with chervil butter, and filled croissants. There are separate menus for vegetarians and young children. Dinners are more expensive. A dozen affordable wines.

Wheelchair access • Access, Amex, Visa

See the back of the guide for an index of eating-places and an index of locations.

Pizza Piazza

33 Jury Street
☎ **WARWICK (0926) 491641**

M40 junction 15

Open all week 11am–11.30pm

A branch of one of the best pizza chains in the UK. See London entry.

Access, Visa

★ after an eating-place indicates that it is one of the best found by the Editor during research for this book (see page 14 for a list).

after an eating-place indicates that it is a pub. The opening and closing times we give only relate to when food is available – the licensing hours may be different.

after an eating-place indicates that it is within five miles of the nearest motorway junction. We give the relevant motorway and junction in the details. Eating-places in cities and large towns, where traffic, parking and route-finding may cause delay, do not have this symbol.

Birmingham   map 4

Adil Tandoori

148–50 Stoney Lane, Sparkbrook
☎ **021-449 0335/9296**

Open all week 12.30–3.30, 6–12.30

Opened in 1976, Adil lays claim to being the original Birmingham balti house. Recently it has acquired cult status, amassing more newspaper column inches than any of its neighbours and drawing crowds from far beyond Sparkhill and Sparkbrook. The décor is a mixture of the garish and the spartan; the atmosphere and food are the attractions. The menu centres on baltis, cooked and served authentically in Kashmiri cast-iron dishes, and the choice stretches from mince with chickpeas to prawns with lotus roots. Vegetables are unusual, and include mustard leaf, valor (Kashmiri beans), tinda and karala (bitter melon). Superlative breads. There is an excellent off-licence next door; Adil 2 is at 130 Stoney Lane.

Unlicensed, but bring your own: no corkage • No-smoking area • Access, Amex, Diners, Visa

Chung Ying

16–18 Wrottesley Street
☎ **021-622 5669**

Open all week noon–midnight (11 Sun)
Closed Christmas Day

Chung Ying has lost none of its vigour over the years and still remains the pick of Birmingham's Chinese restaurants. The cooking is as fresh and down-to-earth as ever, with the fast-working, but not corner-cutting, kitchen and waiters delivering some superb food. The list of 40 dim-sum represents the best value for money, and is dominated by hand-made rather than ready-made specialities: excellently textured, steamed beef ball with Chinese mushrooms, paper-wrapped prawns, and a glorious stuffed green pepper. The mighty portions that make up the one-plate rice and noodle dishes are the cheapest alternatives on the full menu.

Wheelchair access • Access, Amex, Diners, Visa

Chung Ying Garden

Thorp Street
☎ **021-666 6622**

Open all week noon–midnight (11 Sun)

Like its close relative, the Chung Ying (see entry above), this is a Cantonese restaurant with a vengeance. The menu is a monster, running to more than 350 dishes, including 30 specialities and a good section for vegetarians. Eat cheaply from the list of 40 dim-sum: familiar items such as crab meat and shark's-fin dumplings, paper-wrapped king prawns and stuffed green pepper are served until 5pm; more esoteric morsels – braised ox-tripe, steamed chickens' feet and yam croquettes – are always available. Otherwise, there is a prodigious choice of one-plate soup, rice and noodle dishes. Drink tea.

Wheelchair access • Access, Amex, Diners, Visa

College of Food, Tourism and Creative Studies, Training Restaurants

Summer Row
☎ 021-235 2753

A La Carte
Ground floor

Open Tue to Fri D 6.45–8
Closed Sat, Sun, Mon and college hols

Continental
Third floor

Open Mon to Fri L 11.30–1.30
Closed Sat, Sun and college hols

Rooftop
Eighth floor

Open Mon to Fri noon–12.30,
6.45–7.15 (exc Fri D)
Closed as above

Summer Row
Ground floor

Open Mon to Fri L noon–1, Tue and
Wed D 6.45–7.15
Closed as above

These are four very different restaurants, run by catering students under strict supervision and giving a wide culinary choice. Summer Row provides a three-course, limited-choice menu for £6.50, offering perhaps cream of carrot soup and breast of chicken with garden herbs. The informal Continental provides a far-reaching culinary view of the world with Cantonese sweet-and-sour pork or an Italian tagliatelle al pesto. The Rooftop deals in short-choice specialist menus, haute cuisine in style, which is then explored more fully in the A La Carte. Some of the best-value food in Birmingham is to be had in these restaurants. Booking is advisable.

Continental unlicensed, but bring your own: no corkage • No-smoking areas in all restaurants • Wheelchair access to Continental • Access, Visa in all restaurants

Days of the Raj

51 Dale End
☎ 021-236 0445

Open all week noon–2.30 (exc Sat and Sun), 7–11.30

Sandwiched between a multi-storey car-park and a night-club, the Raj negates its faceless exterior with coolly elegant rattan and cane furniture and soft colours. The menu of mainly tandoori and Northern Punjabi dishes is considered to be among the best in Birmingham. Nan is outstanding. Best value is the £5.95 lunchtime buffet. Queue and wait to be served.

Wheelchair access, also WC • Access, Amex, Diners, Visa

Horts Wine Bar

17–18 Edgbaston Shopping Centre, Harborne Road, Edgbaston
☎ 021-454 4672

Open Mon to Fri noon–10.30 (11 Fri), Sat and Sun noon–2.30, 7–11 (exc Sun D)
Closed Christmas Day, Boxing Day, New Year's Day and bank hol Mons

Horts is situated on the fringes of Five Ways and is a popular venue at lunchtime, especially in fine weather when customers spill out of the dark interior on to the tree-lined pavement. The menu is typical of the standard wine bar repertoire – hot ham and leek pie, lasagne, pork with peppers and chilli, backed up by quiches, seafood and salads. Sweets and cheeses can be variable in quality.

Children weekends only

Maharaja

23–5 Hurst Street
☎ 021-622 2641

Open Mon to Sat noon–2.30, 6–11.30
Closed Sun, Christmas Day, Boxing Day
and last 2 weeks July

Handily situated, a few doors from the Hippodrome, and rated by many as the best Indian restaurant in central Birmingham. The dining-room is modest and slightly cramped at peak times, but the kitchen delivers consistently good North Indian and Punjabi dishes. Curries and vegetables outshine tandoori specialities. Look for chicken bhuna masala, rogan josh and thick pulpy aloo palak. Decent rice and breads. Drink lager or house wine.

Wheelchair access • Access, Amex,
Diners, Visa

Rajdoot

12–22 Albert Street
☎ 021-643 8805/8749

Open all week noon–2.15 (exc Sun),
6.30–11.15
Closed Christmas Day, Boxing Day and
L bank hols

For many years, this city-centre restaurant has been dispensing good-quality North Indian and Punjabi

cooking in an ornate setting of sculpted figurines, carving and brasswork. Dim lights add to the deliberately exotic ambience of the place. Set lunches (£7) are a popular feature, otherwise choose carefully from the main menu to keep the bill within limits. Chicken tikka, rogan josh and brinjal bhaji are typical dishes; jeera chicken with cumin seeds and quail makhari are specialities. Drink lager or house wine.

No-smoking area • Wheelchair access,
also WC • Access, Amex, Diners, Visa

Royal Al-Faisal

136–40 Stoney Lane, Sparkbrook
☎ 021-449 5695

Open all week noon–midnight
Closed Christmas Day

Like football teams, balti houses provoke strong partisan loyalties. Royal Al-Faisal is no exception. It is sandwiched between the two branches of the Adil (see entry) but its supporters rate it as highly as its much lauded neighbours. It is a big place with a big menu to match. The range of baltis takes in everything from fish with mushrooms to lotus roots and excellent tarka dhal. The cooks turn out first-rate breads including parathas, roti and chapatis.

Unlicensed, but bring your own: no
corkage • No-smoking area •
Wheelchair access • Access, Amex,
Diners, Visa

All details are as accurate as possible at the time of going to press, but chefs and owners often change, and it is wise to check by telephone before making a special journey.

Thai Paradise

31 Paradise Circus, Queensway
☎ 021-643 5523

Open all week noon–2.30 (exc Sat and Sun), 6–midnight

A small Thai restaurant in a concrete jungle close to the city library complex. Standards have slipped since it first opened, with slow service a common complaint. The food, however, is still good: fish soup with lime and the hot spicy soup have both pleased, and sweet-and-sour Thai fish and chicken with stir-fried vegetables have been very satisfying. Can be smoky.

Wheelchair access • Access, Amex, Diners, Visa

Coventry   map 4

Friends Corner

547–9 Foleshill Road
☎ COVENTRY (0203) 686688/
689962

Open Tue to Sat noon–2.30, 5.30–10.30
Closed Sun and Mon

Don't expect the predictable flavours of the high-street curry house in this idiosyncratic restaurant at the top end of Foleshill Road. Mr and Mrs Deen produce something close to genuine Indian home cooking with dishes such as fish deep-fried in gram flour, mint-flavoured lamb tikka, urd dhal and quails with spinach. The menu also has its share of old favourites, but given a new twist with very distinctive spicing. Excellent breads: try the fried batura. Drink lassi or lager.

Access, Amex, Diners, Visa

Ostlers

166 Spon Street
☎ COVENTRY (0203) 226603

Open Mon to Sat 11am–10.30
Closed Sun

The setting is an old timbered building in the historic and carefully restored suburb of Spon, a short walk from the city centre. Jean Jinks and Suzanne Davies offer a range of nourishing home-cooked dishes right through the day. 'Crock-pots' are a speciality: moussaka, chilli, cod provençale, goulash. There are also traditional pies such as meat and potato, as well as useful vegetarian options. Steaks and duck may take the bill into double figures. House wine by the glass.

Wheelchair access • Access, Visa

Stourbridge   map 4

Mister Dave's

15 High Street, Lye
☎ LYE (0384) 393698

Open Mon to Sat D 6–11.30
Closed Sun

Queues form early outside David Homer's high-street balti restaurant. Inside, there is no flock wallpaper or sitar music, but the food is strictly authentic. Kashmiri baltis are served and eaten from cast-iron pans; knives and forks are provided on request, otherwise the idea is to use your fingers and make use of the excellent nans and chapatis as accompaniments. Finish with colourful barfi or other Indian sweets.

Unlicensed, but bring your own: no corkage • Wheelchair access

Wolverhampton   map 4

Bilash Tandoori

2 Cheapside
☎ WOLVERHAMPTON (0902) 27762

Open all week noon–2.30 (exc Sun),
6–11
Closed Christmas Day and Boxing Day

The Khan family runs this curry house opposite the tiered brickwork of Wolverhampton Civic Centre. Bangladeshi dishes dominate the menu, but the names can be confusing: kolia, chorchori, laziz. Kush-kush is cooked with herbs, sultanas and almonds; the Katmandu dish sounds Nepalese, although the ingredients include 'Madras curry spice'. Otherwise, there are Kashmiri baltis served from blackened cast-iron 'woks' and good-value thalis. A note on the menu says that all vegetables are bought daily. 'Spicy flour balls' come free of charge as a starter.

Wheelchair access • Access, Amex,
Diners, Visa

★ after an eating-place indicates that it is one of the best found by the Editor during research for this book (see page 14 for a list).

🍺 after an eating-place indicates that it is a pub. The opening and closing times we give only relate to when food is available – the licensing hours may be different.

🛢 after an eating-place indicates that it is within five miles of the nearest motor-way junction. We give the relevant motorway and junction in the details. Eating-places in cities and large towns, where traffic, parking and route-finding may cause delay, do not have this symbol.

Sparkhill and Sparkbrook are cut by three sinuous arterial roads. Bleak-looking Stoney Lane is undergoing bouts of demolition and development, yet it boasts the best restaurants and sweet centres in the area. Stratford Road seems more prosperous, with its banks, jewellers and garment shops. Its restaurants, too, are generally more plush than most of their neighbours.

Ladypool Road is the bustling, cosmopolitan heart of the district, full of shops and all kinds of eating houses. Restaurants come and go, but some flashy new arrivals, including Chandni and Khan Chacha's, suggest there is still money for investment in lavish ventures. High-profile greengrocers such as Imran Enterprises and Raja Brothers rule the pavements with their sprawling fruit and vegetable stalls. Places such as Saleem's are the Asian equivalent of coffee bars with their jukeboxes and Formica-topped tables. There is also a dogged English presence in the shape of Harrington's butchers and Joseph Trippas bakers shop.

Birmingham has other Indian neighbourhoods but this area has made its name as the centre of the balti industry. The word 'balti' generally refers to a shallow metal dish in which meat, fish and vegetables are cooked and served. The style originated in Kashmir, and the first balti cafés appeared in Birmingham in the mid-1970s. At first, these places were strictly local venues for the community, but recently many of them have been 'discovered' and as a result they now attract a new, western audience.

The best balti houses produce the real thing, although others take short-cuts by *serving* so-called 'baltis' in deep two-handled dishes that have not been near the stove. Microwaves are standard for re-heating tandooris and snacks; one brilliant exception is the Milan Sweet Centre, where samosas are cooked from scratch and other items are heated in huge shallow pans. Chapatis and roti are the essential accompaniment for baltis, and the quality of these breads would put most of London's new-wave Indian restaurants to shame.

1 **Chandni**
127–9 Ladypool Road
(restaurant)

2 **Lunch Box Tandoori**
139 Ladypool Road
(restaurant)

3 **Shabab Tandoori**
163 Ladypool Road
(restaurant)

4 **Sona**
213 Ladypool Road
(sweet centre and take-away)

5 **Jilani Supermarket**
273–5 Ladypool Road
(shop)

6 **Jaaneman**
279 Ladypool Road
(vegetarian restaurant and sweet centre)

7 **Rasool Supermarket**
345–7 Ladypool Road
(shop)

8 **Bismillah Food Store**
349 Ladypool Road
(shop)

9 **Shandar**
351 Ladypool Road
(restaurant)

10 **Khyber Balti House**
365 Ladypool Road
(restaurant)

11 **Punjab Paradise**
377 Ladypool Road
(restaurant)

12 **Imran Enterprises Centre**
156–60 Ladypool Road
(shop)

13 **Raja Brothers**
160–6 Ladypool Road
(shop)

14 **Commonway Supermarket**
180–2 Ladypool Road
(shop)

15 **Khan Chacha's**
204–6 Ladypool Road
(restaurant)

16 **Ladypool Greengrocers**
210 Ladypool Road
(shop)

17 **Sheikh Brothers**
248 Ladypool Road
(halal butchers)

18 **Saleem's**
256 Ladypool Road
(café and sweet centre)

19 **Imran Tandoori**
264–6 Ladypool Road
(restaurant)

20 **Plaza Tandoori**
278 Ladypool Road
(restaurant)

21 **Shaheenshah**
328 Ladypool Road
(sweet centre and take-away)

22 **Milan Sweet Centre**
191 Stoney Lane
(take-away sweet centre)

23 **Azad Supermarket and Butchers**
156 Stoney Lane
(shop)

24 **Adil**
148–50 Stoney Lane
(restaurant – see entry)

25 **Royal Al-Faisal**
140 Stoney Lane
(restaurant – see entry)

26 **Adil 2**
130 Stoney Lane
(restaurant)

27 **Rapyal Halal Butchers**
98 Stoney Lane
(shop)

28 **Sanam**
84 Stoney Lane
(restaurant)

29 **Rasoi Indian Kitchen and Balti Room**
321 Stratford Road
(restaurant)

30 **Grand Tandoori**
343–5 Stratford Road
(restaurant)

31 **Shahi Nan Kabab**
353 Stratford Road
(take-away)

32 **Butt's Tandoori Balti House**
373 Stratford Road
(restaurant)

33 **Royal Naim Tandoori**
417 Stratford Road
(restaurant and sweet centre)

34 **Mushtaq Sweet Centre**
451–3 Stratford Road
(sweet centre)

35 **Sajed Tandoori**
511 Stratford Road
(restaurant)

36 **Pak Butchers**
515 Stratford Road
(shop)

37 **Amer Tandoori**
786 Stratford Road
(restaurant)

38 **Lunch House Tandoori**
464 Stratford Road
(restaurant)

39 **Sheikh Brothers**
4 Warwick Road
(halal butchers)

40 Baba Kebab House
362 Stratford Road
(restaurant and take-away)

41 Sher Khan
360 Stratford Road
(restaurant)

42 Minar Restaurant and Chaat House
7 Walford Road
(restaurant)

43 Kilimanjaro
9A Walford Road
(restaurant – Indian and East African)

44 Majesty Tandoori
284 Stratford Road
(restaurant)

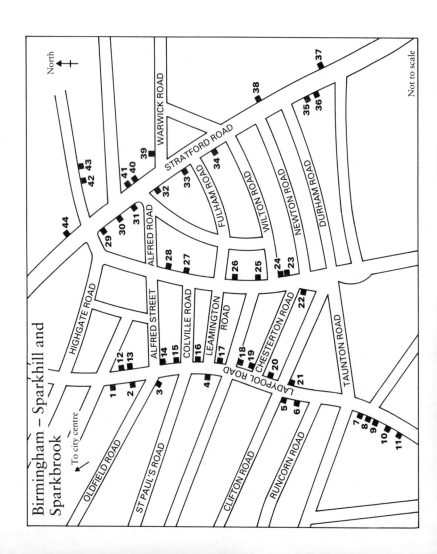

Birmingham – Sparkhill and Sparkbrook

WILTSHIRE

Avebury map 2

Stones ★

☎ AVEBURY (067 23) 514

Open all week 10am–6

In a converted stable block overlooking the great Avebury stone circle is a highly original restaurant; 'think global – cook local' is the philosophy of owners Hilary Howard and Michael Pitts. This is realised in buying as organically as possible and by supporting small growers and producers whose products are converted into dishes such as spinach polpettini with wholewheat pasta, aubergine and apricot korma, squash filled with mushroom and pine-nut with a chasseur sauce and parsnip pyramids. Although Stones is self-service and totally vegetarian, the queue for lunch may well include people who have driven from London just for the food.

No-smoking area • Garden • Wheelchair access, also WC

Bradford-on-Avon map 2

Dandy Lion ⊚

35 Market Street
☎ BRADFORD-ON-AVON (022 16) 3433

Open all week noon–2.30, 7–10

John Levis, formerly of the Red Lion at Lacock, is hoping to reproduce his successful formula at this town-centre pub. Rugs cover polished boards, there are flowers, antiques and a decent selection of bar food: omelettes, pork and apple casserole, spinach and courgette hot-pot, hot sticky toffee pudding with clotted cream. More expensive restaurant meals are available.

No children in bar • Access, Visa

Brinkworth map 2

Three Crowns ⊚

☎ BRINKWORTH (066 641) 366

Open all week noon–2, 6.30–9.30
Closed Christmas Day

A relaxed and easygoing pub in beautiful surroundings with the emphasis on straightforward, well-cooked bar food. There are no starters, but main courses are more than ample, with accompanying fresh vegetables cooked to perfection. Duck is cooked until pink, thinly sliced and not fatty and there is tender pork with Dijon mustard sauce. Home-made desserts are excellent. Very popular.

Garden • Wheelchair access, also WC • Access, Visa

Out to Eat has been compiled in the same way as *The Good Food Guide* and is based on reports from consumers and backed up by anonymous inspections.

Corton map 2

Dove Inn

☎ WARMINSTER **(0985) 50378**

Open all week noon–2.30, 7–9.30 (exc Sun and Mon D)

The Dove could not be in a more pleasant spot, deep in the countryside with doves cooing and roses climbing up the wall. The pub is more like a cottage; even the bar looks like someone's sitting-room. There is an inventive array of bar food, including garlic potatoes with anchovies and green and black olives, and gazpacho, among the game pie, fresh salmon and ploughman's.

No children in bar • Car-park • Wheelchair access, also WC • Access, Amex, Diners, Visa

Devizes map 2

Bear Hotel

Market Place
☎ DEVIZES **(0380) 722444**

Open all week noon–2, 7–10
Closed Christmas Day and Boxing Day

The Bear is a famous old coaching-inn which still exudes a strong sense of age and history from its solid, old-fashioned public rooms. Simple, well-made food (there is also a more expensive restaurant) includes fresh sandwiches, Devizes pie with Cumberland sauce, ploughman's or grilled salmon steak supported by some tempting desserts.

No-smoking area • Car-park • Wheelchair access, also WC • Access, Visa

Wiltshire Kitchen

12 St John's Street
☎ DEVIZES **(0380) 724840**

Open daily 9am–5.30
Closed 1 week Christmas/New Year

All the food is prepared on the premises in this light, airy café and the cooks draw heavily on their own recipes. The menu changes every day. Soups, such as potato and coriander, plus colourful salads are backed up by quiches, ploughman's and dishes ranging from vegetable lasagne to seafood crumble and chicken in lemon sauce. Sweet and savoury roulades are a speciality and the place is noted for its cakes, puddings and ice-creams. Evening meals for booked parties only.

No smoking • Wheelchair access

Lacock map 2

Red Lion

High Street
☎ LACOCK **(024 973) 456**

Open all week 12.15–2.30, 6.30–10 (9.30 Sun)
Closed Christmas Day

Deep-red walls set off by blackened timbers and beams, chairs and tables of genuine antiquity, a giant hearth burning enormous logs, stuffed animals everywhere – with an interior like this, no wonder this unusual village pub is filled with tourists. Bar food includes soup, turkey and apricot pie, broccoli and spinach bake, and some homely puddings.

No children in bar • Garden • Car-park • Access, Visa

Marlborough · map 2

Polly Tea Rooms ★

26-7 High Street
☎ MARLBOROUGH (0672) 512146

Open all week noon–3

One of the best traditional tea-rooms in the land, with classic old-world décor, beamed ceilings and flowery tablecloths. The strength of the place is its excellent home baking – breads, pastries, gâteaux, scones – complemented by hand-made chocolates and ice-cream specialities. Lunch features home-cooked dishes with a vegetarian bias, such as carrot and courgette roulade, or cauliflower, leek and potato bake. As well as teas and coffee there might be home-made lemonade to drink.

No-smoking area • Wheelchair access • Access, Amex, Diners, Visa

Sun Inn

High Street
☎ MARLBOROUGH (0672) 512081

Open all week noon–2, 7–9.30

A lively, pleasant sixteenth-century inn whose main bar has atmospheric appeal with its heavy beams and dark panelling. The bar food, which is cooked carefully from fresh ingredients, offers fairly standard fare: shepherd's pie, chilli, filled jacket potatoes, cod and chips, open baguettes and good salads. There is a more expensive restaurant.

Garden • Access, Visa

If there are restrictions on children, these are mentioned in the details at the end of each entry.

Pitton · map 2

Silver Plough

White Hill
☎ FARLEY (072 272) 266

Open all week noon–2, 7–10
Closed Christmas Day

This village inn boasts two signs: one depicts the Plough as constellation, the other shows the plough as farm tool. The inn also has an extremely pretty flower-filled garden. The best-value food is served in the bar, from a menu that ranges from duck breast and fennel salad and fresh linguine with bacon and basil sauce, to cottage pie. More elaborate and more expensive meals are served in the dining-room, which is housed in a modern extension down a couple of steps from the bar. Real ales and a much-better-than-average pub wine list.

Garden • Car-park • Wheelchair access, also WC • Access, Amex, Diners, Visa

Ramsbury · map 2

Bell

☎ MARLBOROUGH (0672) 20230

Open all week noon–2, 7–9.30 (exc Sun D)
Closed Christmas Day

From the outside, the Bell appears to be an unassuming village pub; inside, a pleasant atmosphere is created by fresh flowers, highly polished tables and cheerful service. Bar food ranges from very filling pies – beef and ale or fisherman's – to a Wiltshire bacon butty and Cumberland sausages with bubble and squeak.

Traditional steamed puddings, such as jam roly-poly, are available.

Garden • Car-park • Wheelchair access, also WC • Access, Diners, Visa

Rowde
map 2

George & Dragon

High Street
☎ DEVIZES (0380) 723053

Open Tue to Sun noon–1.45, 7–9 (exc Sun D)
Closed Christmas Day, Boxing Day and New Year's Day

Nestling against the vicarage walls, this is a sturdy eighteenth-century village pub, recently refurbished. Helen and Tim Withers have worked hard to put the place firmly on the food map with such offerings as a well-balanced fish soup, home-made pasta with a clear, simple seafood sauce, and decent bread-and-butter pudding.

Garden • Car-park • Access, Visa

Salisbury
map 2

Harpers

6 Ox Row, The Market Place
☎ SALISBURY (0722) 333118

Open Mon to Sat noon–2, 6.30–10 (10.30 Sat)
Closed Sun

This is an informal first-floor restaurant capably run by Adrian and Ann Harper. Best value is the 'Shoppers' Special' lunch menu with prices ranging from £4.30 for one course to £6.70 for three courses.

Light lunch and supper dishes are also available, such as casseroled beefsteak with herb dumplings, and pasta with tomato and basil sauce. Great chocolate mousse for dessert.

Access, Diners, Visa

Hob Nob Coffee Shop

65 The Close
☎ SALISBURY (0722) 332151

Open Mon to Sat 10.30–4.30, July and Aug Sun 2–5
Closed Sun (exc July and Aug) and 31 Oct to 1 Apr (or Easter, if earlier)

This coffee-shop is attached to the South Wiltshire Museum. Good home-made cakes and speciality teas are the backbone of the menu. Otherwise, there is home-made vegetarian soup, a range of sandwiches, plus a daily main dish. Special vegetarian lunches for a minimum of eight people can be booked a week in advance: mushroom bake and ratatouille crumble are typical of the menu.

Unlicensed, but bring your own: no corkage • No smoking • Garden • Wheelchair access, also WC

Just Brahms

68 Castle Street
☎ SALISBURY (0722) 28402

Open Mon to Sat noon–2, 7–10.30
Closed Sun

This is a two-part operation: in the bistro, single-course or snack meals are provided, while in the restaurant there is a more expensive à la carte menu, although both menus may be mixed in either area. Croque-monsieur, wholemeal and watercress crêpes filled with Arbroath smokies, beef chilli lasagne and open sandwiches give the span of the lighter menu.

Access, Amex, Visa

Michael Snell Tea Rooms

8 St Thomas's Square
☎ SALISBURY (0722) 336037

Open Mon to Sat 9am (8.30 Sat)–5.30
Closed Sun

Michael Snell's skill as a baker and pâtissier have earned the tea-room attached to his shop an excellent local reputation, and it is always packed. Mille-feuilles, almond bretzel, walnut butter cream gâteau are made to a high standard. Flans, such as asparagus, cheddar and mushroom, are available all day, while lunch (11.30am–2.30pm) offers salads, beef curry and lasagne.

Unlicensed • No-smoking area •
Wheelchair access

Swindon   map 2

Pizza Express

Havelock Square
☎ SWINDON (0793) 616671

Open all week 11.30am–midnight

Part of the popular chain which is the pick of the pizza bunch. See London entry.

No-smoking area • Access, Amex, Diners, Visa

Wootton Bassett   map 2

Emms ⊕

147 High Street
☎ SWINDON (0793) 854783

On A420 W of M4 junction 16

Open Mon to Sat L noon–2, Thur to Sat D 7–9
Closed Sun

Loyal customers consider Marilyn Pullen's cheerful little coffee-shop-cum-restaurant the best thing to have ever happened to Wootton Bassett. Good service and excellent home-made food are the keynotes. There are simple filled sandwiches of home-made gammon or chicken, mushroom quiche, savoury crêpes, boeuf bourguignonne and some first-class baking.

Wheelchair access

Out to Eat is totally independent, accepts no free hospitality and makes no charge for inclusion.

The factual details under each eating-place are based on information supplied by the restaurateur.

YORKSHIRE

Bolton Abbey
(N Yorks)   map 7

Devonshire Arms
☎ BOLTON ABBEY (075 671) 441

Open all week noon–2, 7–10

Fortune has smiled on this former
coaching-inn: it has been lovingly
restored and boasts some fine
antiques and paintings from
Chatsworth House, seat of the Dukes
of Devonshire. Now a comfortable
hotel, it is set in delightful
surroundings. Bar food includes soup,
open sandwiches, salads, roasts,
curries and chilli. There is a more
expensive restaurant.

*No smoking in restaurant • Garden •
Car-park • Wheelchair access, also WC
• Access, Amex, Diners, Visa*

Tea Cottage
The Green
☎ BOLTON ABBEY (075 671) 495

Open all week 9.30am–5
Closed winter

A picture-postcard cottage tea-room
with a charming garden, views on to
the ruins of Bolton Abbey, and
flagstoned floors and beams inside. It
is family-run on splendidly old-
fashioned lines, offering for lunch
simple filling food – home-made
steak pie, grilled gammon, egg and
chips, and sticky toffee pudding. It
also serves one of the best afternoon
teas in the area.

*No-smoking area • Garden • Car-park
• Wheelchair access, also WC*

Bradford (W Yorks)   map 7

Bharat
502 Great Horton Road
☎ BRADFORD (0274) 521200

*Open Tue to Sun noon–2, 6–midnight
(exc Sun D)*
*Closed Mon, Christmas Day and Boxing
Day*

Bradford's legions of Indian cafés and
sweet centres are renowned for their
rock-bottom prices, uncompromising
cooking and minimal décor. Bharat is
different. The two-storey building
stands on one of the roads climbing
the hill out of town; inside, it has
white stuccoed walls hung with
sequined pictures. The menu holds
few surprises, spanning the full range
of tandooris and curries, but there is
care in the kitchen and a healthy note
in the well-trimmed meat, ungreasy
sauces and strong showing of
vegetarian dishes. Navratan biriani,
karai lamb and chicken jalfrezi are all
above average. Good-value thalis and
cheap set lunches are available. The
restaurant has a proper wine list;
there is also Kingfisher lager.

*Car-park • Wheelchair access • Access,
Amex, Diners, Visa*

All letters to this guide are acknowledged.

Pizza Margherita

Argus Chambers, Hallings
☎ BRADFORD **(0274) 724333**

Open all week 11am–11pm

A chain of just four pleasant,
courteously run pizza parlours. See
entry for Kendal, Cumbria.

No-smoking area • Access, Visa

Sweet Centre

110–12 Lumb Lane
☎ BRADFORD **(0274) 731735**

Open all week 8am–2am

To the right is the shop and take-
away selling snacks and sweetmeats;
to the left is the restaurant, with its
own entrance. Inside, there are
functional oblong pine tables,
imitation panelling and perspex
mirrors on the walls. The menu deals
in the familiar mix of baltis, masalas,
bhunas and tikkas, backed up by
samosas, pakoras and a few oddities
such as curried brains and pigs'
trotters. Main dishes come with three
warm roti and multi-coloured rice.
Spicing is fresh; portions are
generous. Soft drinks and mango
juice to drink.

*Unlicensed, but bring your own: no
corkage • Wheelchair access, also WC*

A restaurant manager can't insist on
people not smoking, unless it's specifically
a no-smoking restaurant or a no-smoking
area. If it is, smokers could be asked to
leave if they don't stop. If in doubt, check
beforehand what the smoking
arrangements are.

Elland (W Yorks)   map 7

Berties Bistro

7–9 Town Hall Buildings
☎ ELLAND **(0422) 371724**

M62 junction 24

*Open Tue to Sat D 7 (6.30 Sat)–10.30
(11 Fri and Sat), 5–9 Sun
Closed Mon*

A popular bistro, which might be why
prices have crept up in the last year
or so – it is now hard to find a starter
under £4.95. Grilled black pudding,
scallop and bacon terrine, roast loin
of pork and suprême of chicken give
a hint of the menu. Quality can be
variable. Berties Bombe for dessert.

Wheelchair access

Fewston (N Yorks)   map 7

Swinsty Tea Garden

Fewston House
☎ BLUBBERHOUSES **(094 388) 637**

Off A59 7m W of Harrogate

*Open Sat and Sun 11am–5
Closed Mon to Fri*

They grow their own vegetables and
only use organic flour at this
enterprising tea-room quietly
situated by a lovely reservoir. Only
vegetarian dishes are available:
courgette, brazil and hazelnut crisp,
cannelloni in cheese sauce, herb nut
roast with pepper sauce, as well as
baked potatoes, salads and soups.
There is a wide choice of cakes.

*Unlicensed • No smoking • Garden •
Car-park*

Gargrave (N Yorks)   map 7

Edmondson's

3 High Street
☎ SKIPTON **(0756) 749498**

*Open Tue to Sun 11.30am–1.30 (exc
Tue), 5–10*
Closed Mon, Jan and bank hols

A family-run fish and chip shop of
over 60 years' standing, still cooking
traditionally in pure dripping and
home-made batter. Fresh haddock is
the house speciality, and the king-size
portion is daunting. A more exotic
selection takes in swordfish, shark
and tuna steaks, or else there is the
more down-to-earth home-made
steak and kidney pie.

Wheelchair access, also WC

Goathland (N Yorks)   map 10

Mallyan Spout Hotel

☎ WHITBY **(0947) 86206**

*Open all week D 7–8.30, Sun L 12.15–
1.45*

Generous portions and value for
money are not the only reasons why
the bar food at this friendly country
hotel is so popular. Good ingredients
– fresh fish from Whitby and
Scarborough, local cheeses, home-
made conserves and chutneys – make
a noticeable difference to just a
simple cod and chips or a hearty
Yorkshire pudding with roast lamb.

*No-smoking area • No children under 6
evenings in restaurant • Garden and
family-room • Wheelchair access •
Access, Amex, Diners, Visa*

Golcar (W Yorks)   map 7

Weavers Shed

Acre Mill, Knowl Road
☎ HUDDERSFIELD **(0484) 654284**

2½ miles from M62 junction 23

*Open Tue to Fri L noon–1.45, Tue to
Sat D 7–9.15*
*Closed Sun, Mon, first 2 weeks Jan and
last 2 weeks July*

An eighteenth-century cloth mill,
kept as original as possible – which,
as everything is bare stone, can result
in the dining-room feeling cold. The
sound-value three-course lunch with
coffee for £9.50 is a warming affair –
start with Yorkshire pudding and
onion gravy or a home-made soup,
followed by beef casserole or pork
chop with apple and cider. Desserts
are of mixed quality.

*Car-park • Wheelchair access • Access,
Amex, Visa*

Harome (N Yorks)   map 10

Pheasant Hotel

☎ HELMSLEY **(0439) 71241**

Open all week L noon–2
Closed mid–Dec to end Feb

A motley collection of village
buildings has created The Pheasant –
a shop, smithy and two cottages.
Character and atmosphere ooze out
of beams, stone walls and the sturdy
oak furniture. Lunchtime bar food
offers home-made soup, steak and
kidney pie, a fish pie and perhaps a
roast. Vegetarians have a reasonable
choice and desserts include a

memorable walnut and caramel
meringue.

Car-park • Wheelchair access, also WC

Harrogate (N Yorks) map 7

Bettys ★

1 Parliament Street
☎ HARROGATE (0423) 502746

Open all week 9am–9pm
Closed Christmas Day, Boxing Day and
New Year's Day

The original Bettys (see entries for
Ilkley, Northallerton and York)
opened in 1919 and is one of the last
outposts of the traditional tea-room.
Prices are by no means low but the
excellent quality of everything makes
it worthwhile. Whether you want a
cream tea, a fresh salmon sandwich, a
hot bacon muffin, an omelette or
something on toast, Bettys is always a
delight. The successful formula of
having everything home-made means
that the bakery produces over four
hundred different lines, including
cakes, chocolates, bread, scones and
muffins. Speciality teas and rare
coffees feature. The evening menu
includes a very late breakfast and rösti
with bacon or smoked salmon.

No-smoking area • Access, Visa

Garden Room

Harlow Carr Botanical Gardens,
Crag Lane
☎ HARROGATE (0423) 505604

Open all week 10.30am–5 (or dusk)

A simple restaurant at the entrance to
the popular Botanical Gardens.

Home-made cakes and scones
accompany morning coffee and
afternoon teas, and light snacks as
well as the more substantial lunch
menu provide excellent value. Good
soups, quiches and jacket potatoes are
backed up by fresh fish, steak au
poivre and chicken provençale.

No smoking • Car-park • Wheelchair
access, also WC

William & Victoria

6 Cold Bath Road
☎ HARROGATE (0423) 506883

Open Mon to Sat noon–2 (exc Sat),
6–10
Closed Sun

A stylish basement bar near the Pump
Room. A sparse version of Victorian
décor includes a mini oenology
library. Otherwise, lots of empty
bottles predominate. A no-nonsense
menu is chalked on the blackboard.
Aubergine and tomato bake is light
and spiced with cinnamon; chicken
livers in green peppercorn sauce can
be a bit clumsy; poached salmon with
cucumber sauce is as good as you will
find anywhere. Banana-and-caramel
pudding for the sweet-toothed only
and school-dinner rice pudding with
jam. Convivial, but service has been
frosty on occasion.

No children under 5 • Access, Visa

See the front of the guide for a list of each
eating-place given a star for being one of
the best found by the Editor during
research for this book.

Haworth (W Yorks)   map 7

Weavers

15 West Lane
☎ HAWORTH (0535) 43822

*Open Tue to Sat D 7–9.15, Sun L
noon–1.30
Closed Mon, 2 weeks Christmas and 2
weeks July*

A converted group of weavers'
cottages houses this informal
restaurant. A commitment to local
produce together with the use of
home-grown herbs, salads and some
vegetables are strong points. A rich
venison stew and a beef-steak hot-pot
typify the menu.

Access, Amex, Diners, Visa

Hebden Bridge
(W Yorks)   map 7

Innovation

Bridge Mill, St George's Square
☎ HEBDEN BRIDGE (0422) 844160

*Open Wed to Mon 9.45am (1pm
Sun)–5
Closed Tue, Christmas Day, Boxing Day
and New Year's Day*

A small, bright café at the back of a
gift and clothes shop. It is a friendly
place serving a varied selection of
home-made snacks and cakes.
Galettes (French-style pancakes)
come with a variety of fillings, as do
toasted sandwiches and jacket
potatoes. Otherwise, there are
quiches, turkey, ham and chestnut pie
and a selection of cakes and gâteaux.

*No-smoking area • Wheelchair access •
Access, Visa*

Watergate

9 Bridge Gate
☎ HEBDEN BRIDGE (0422) 842978

*Open Sat to Thur 10am–5
Closed Fri, Christmas Day, Boxing Day
and New Year's Day*

A cheerfully informal café with a
standard snack menu: sandwiches,
filled jacket potatoes, soup, and some
substantial casseroles, pies and pasta
dishes. Baking is of a high quality,
making morning coffee or afternoon
tea a real treat. Both 'Nutty Vera'
cake and carrot cake are highly
recommended but there are also
cheesecakes, chocolate gâteau, coffee
cake and fruit pies.

*Unlicensed • No-smoking area • Garden
• Car-park • Wheelchair access, also
WC*

Hetton (N Yorks)   map 7

Angel ★ ⊚

☎ CRACOE (075 673) 263

Off B6265 between Skipton and
Grassington

Open all week noon–2.30, 6–10

First and foremost a Dales village
pub of beams, standing timbers and
log fires that is trying hard not to be
overwhelmed by the sheer volume of
custom in the wake of praise and
awards for the bar and restaurant
food. Bar food is indeed terrific value
for money, imaginative and fresh.
Fish is a speciality, and fish soup
(£1.95), queenie scallops (12 for
£4.40) and poached Scotch salmon in
a delicate white wine, tomato and dill
sauce (£5.95) are remarkable both for
the price and quality of the cooking.
Venison, lamb cutlets and steaks

appear among less highly praised meat dishes. Sticky toffee pudding or Dales cheeses for dessert.

Car-park • Wheelchair access, also WC • Access, Visa

Hovingham
(N Yorks)   map 7

Worsley Arms

☎ HOVINGHAM (0653) 692236

Open all week noon–2, 7–9

A pleasant inn, with an attractive garden complete with stream. Excellent service is combined with some enterprising bar food: well-made soup, mushroom tart, good ploughman's, chicken roulade, lambs' kidneys and chestnut loaf. The set restaurant lunch is £9 for three courses and coffee, but dinner is more expensive.

No cigars/pipes • Garden • Car-park • Access, Visa

Huddersfield
(W Yorks)   map 7

Good Food Café

15 Upperhead Row
☎ HUDDERSFIELD (0484) 535118

*Open Mon to Sat 7.30am–5pm
Closed Sun*

Bowls of home-made stew are best-sellers in this daytime café opposite the bus station. Inside, it looks like a pizzeria, with round tables, green pointed chairs and marble-effect tiles on the floor. This is no-nonsense, affordable home-cooking for all to see as it happens behind the serving counter. The menu moves on from breakfast fry-ups to excellent sandwiches, with hot roast beef cut straight from the joint, filled jacket potatoes, Yorkshire puddings topped with meaty gravy and old-fashioned puds such as ginger sponge and custard. Pots of tea, wine by the glass.

No smoking

Memsahib Eastern Eatery

37–9 Queensgate
☎ HUDDERSFIELD (0484) 422002

Open all week noon–2.30, 6–midnight

A family-run tandoori house whose comfortable surroundings and friendly service have done as much for its popularity as the keenly priced, honestly prepared food. All the old familiar dishes (tikkas, kormas, dopiazas and masalas) appear on the extensive menu, but the more adventurous (with 24-hours' notice) can sample unusual Pakistani dishes such as lambs' brains or quails.

Wheelchair access • Access, Visa

Ramsden's Landing

Aspley Wharf, Wakefield Road
☎ HUDDERSFIELD (0484) 544250

Open all week noon–2 (exc Sat and Sun), 6–10 (10.30 Sat)

A brasserie with a crowded bar and above-average, French-inspired food. There are nibbles at the bar – handy if you are kept waiting for a table, which you shouldn't be, however, as this is a big place. Well-executed, imaginative cooking prevails. To start, there might be poached Finnan haddock with an aïoli sauce or smoked sea trout with a dill and honey sauce. To follow, you could have duck breasts with blackberry sauce, rack of lamb, chicken dhansak or calf's liver and bacon. Blackboard specials include 'stuffed pig'. Professional puddings and a reasonable vegetarian section.

No-smoking area • Car-park • Wheelchair access, also WC • Access, Visa

Ilkley (W Yorks)   map 7

Bettys ★

32–4 The Grove
☎ ILKLEY **(0943) 608029**

*Open all week 9am–7 (9 Fri to Sun)
Closed Christmas Day, Boxing Day and New Year's Day*

All small towns should possess a Bettys (see entries for Harrogate, Northallerton and York). The daytime menu covers a wide range of cakes, tea-breads, omelettes, filled rolls and muffins, and home-made ice-cream, all served by delightful waitresses. In the evening, light dishes of smoked Wensleydale croquettes, chicken provençale and some delicious cakes are available.

No-smoking area • Wheelchair access • Access, Visa

You will find report forms (write a letter if you prefer) at the back of the book so that you can tell us about your experiences of going *Out to Eat*. We'll put the information to good use when we're compiling the next edition.

Kirkburton
(W Yorks)   map 7

Wiz Tea Rooms

22a North Road
☎ HUDDERSFIELD **(0484) 607822**

*Open Mon to Sat 11.30am–4
Closed Sun and bank hols*

A green plastic, privet-edged teapot spouts puffs of steam outside this eccentric tea-room. An imitation bear stands by the door, a stuffed sheep acts as a seat for children and display cabinets are filled with curious medical memorabilia. No wonder the place bills itself as the Wiz Bizarre Studio Café. The food is less extreme: nutritious soups such as courgette and apple, sandwiches made from good bread and fresh ingredients, savoury flans and dishes such as vegetable curry. Treacle tart is wholesome, and chocolate cake comes with home-made chocolate sauce. There is a good choice of teas.

Unlicensed • Car-park • Wheelchair access, also WC

Leeds (W Yorks)   map 7

Bibis Pizzeria

16 Greek Street
☎ LEEDS **(0532) 430905**

*Open Mon to Sat noon–2.15, 6–11.15
Closed Sun and bank hols*

A cheerful, lively Italian restaurant with Roman forum-style décor and open-plan kitchen. Its informality and varied menu make it ideal for family occasions. Pasta and pizzas are backed up by well-made soups, moules marinière, salads and doughy home-made bread. No bookings are taken, so long queues may form after 8pm.

Wheelchair access • Access, Amex, Visa

Brett's Fish Restaurant

12–14 North Lane, Headingley
☎ LEEDS (0532) 755228

Open Tue to Sat L 11.30–2.15, Mon and Thur tea 4–7.30
Closed Sun and 2 weeks summer

The oak-panelled dining-room of this traditional fish and chip shop (family-owned since 1919) is well patronised by cricket fans during the season as it is close to Headingley cricket ground. Classic fish and chips and good home-made desserts include a terrific treacle sponge. There is a local rivalry between Brett's and close neighbour Bryan's (see entry below).

Unlicensed, but bring your own: no corkage • Garden

Bryan's

9 Weetwood Lane, Headingley
☎ LEEDS (0532) 785679

Open Mon to Sat 11.30am–11.30pm
Closed Sun, Christmas Day and Boxing Day

For more than 50 years, Bryan's has been serving impeccable fish and chips Yorkshire-style in typically generous North Country portions. Superb fresh haddock ('baby' or 'jumbo' size) is the first choice; the chips are fried in dripping. Refurbishment has cheered up the décor, and the menu has been expanded to include seafood platter, trout and a range of salads. Drink

strong tea. Senior citizens can buy a set lunch for under £4 (from 2.30 to 4.30pm).

Unlicensed • Car-park • Wheelchair access, also WC • Access, Diners, Visa

Darbar

16–17 Kirkgate
☎ LEEDS (0532) 460381

Open Mon to Fri L 11.30–2.30, all week D 6–11.30
Closed Christmas Day

The carefully considered décor includes a fine 300-year-old carved wooden door imported from a mansion in Pakistan. The food is equally considered, with lamb in various guises – kebabs, bhuna gosht, karahi gosht or dopiaza gosht – singled out for praise for being tender and fat-free. Good tandoor roti and nan.

No-smoking area • Access, Amex, Visa

Hansa

72–4 North Street
☎ LEEDS (0532) 444408

Open Tue to Sun noon–2, 7–10 (11.30 Fri and Sat)
Closed Mon, Christmas Day and Boxing Day

A Gujerati restaurant in a row of converted Victorian shops not far from the Grand Theatre and the Opera House. Inside, it is decorated in 'Asian bohemian' shades of green and red; the tent-like ceiling is swathed in fabric. High points from the menu are light, crisp samosas, masala dosai with sambar and coconut chutney, and vegetable curries such as spinach and potato bhaji. Unusual vegan desserts include lapsi, made from bulgar wheat cooked with sultanas, cardamom, fennel and cinnamon. Drink lassi or lager.

No-smoking area • Wheelchair access

Hon Wah

4 The Headway
☎ LEEDS (0532) 440750

Open all week noon–midnight
Closed Christmas Day and Boxing Day

An unobtrusive but pleasantly agreeable Cantonese restaurant in the city centre. The menu does not include dim-sum, but a good lunch can be built from the list of appetisers: prawn toasts, succulent capital spare ribs, deep-fried prawn balls and rainbow ground chicken. Otherwise, the menu has good noodle dishes and specialities such as sliced duck with orange sauce. Excellent toffee pineapple to finish. Drink Chinese tea or lager.

Car-park • Wheelchair access, also WC • Access, Visa

Jumbo

120 Vicar Lane
☎ LEEDS (0532) 458547/458324

Open all week noon–11.45pm

The Jumbo is a far friendlier and warmer place than it once was, and offers consistently good dim-sum, listed as snacks on the menu, huge platefuls of chow mein and well-liked full menu dishes such as saday sliced beef, baked spare ribs with salted pepper and fillet steak with OK sauce.

Access, Amex, Visa

Salvo's

115 Otley Road, Headingley
☎ LEEDS (0532) 755017

Open Mon to Sat noon–2, 5.30–11
Closed Sun

A loyal, regular following sometimes creates queues outside. The owners know how to cope: they venture outside armed with menus and complimentary garlic bread. Consideration for customers even extends to providing menus in braille. They claim to make 'the best pizzas in the North'. Look out for shark steak with a tomato, citrus and chilli sauce, calf's liver with balsamic vinegar and a red-pepper sauce and non-Italian king prawns in coconut and tamarind curry (chef Gip Dammone enjoys travelling in the Far East). Casual but with slick service.

Wheelchair access • Access, Visa

Linthwaite
(W Yorks)   map 7

Bull's Head

31 Blackmoorfoot
☎ HUDDERSFIELD (0484) 842715

Open all week 11am–10

Norman's Yorkshire Pudding Sandwich (two puddings with slabs of roast beef and gravy between them) is a major draw in this lively old stone pub off the beaten track. Other dishes change regularly and the kitchen makes plentiful use of herbs, spices and pulses: split-pea dhal; spinach, lentil and mushroom gratin; and butter-bean and parsnip carbonnade appear alongside hot beef teacakes, good steaks with real fresh chips, and specials such as chicken and apple crumble with cider sauce. But the real highlights are the home-made sweets – sticky toffee pudding with toffee sauce; spicy banana cake; brandy and apricot meringue and more besides. Real ales.

No children after 8pm • Family room • Car-park • Wheelchair access, also WC

Marsden (W Yorks) map 7

Olive Branch
Manchester Road
☎ HUDDERSFIELD (0484) 844487

Open all week L noon–2, Tue to Sun D 5 (7.30 Sun)–9.30

A sturdy, stone-built roadside pub between Huddersfield and Manchester. The owners are from Holland, and the décor is a mix of 'olde English' trappings with wooden clogs and embroidered pictures of figures in Dutch costume. A standard menu of good home-made pâté, soup (such as prawn and cucumber), steaks and burgers is bolstered by blackboard specials. Beef bourguignonne comes with rice, proper chips and salad; otherwise there might be prawn butterflies, Barnsley chops and vegetable lasagne. Home-made gâteau or apple pie to finish. Sunday roasts are very good value.

Garden • Car-park • Wheelchair access • Access, Visa

All details are as accurate as possible at the time of going to press, but chefs and owners often change, and it is wise to check by telephone before making a special journey.

Moulton (N Yorks) map 10

Black Bull
☎ DARLINGTON (0325) 377289

Open Mon to Sat noon–2, 6.45–10.15
Closed Sun and 23–31 Dec

Over the years this black-and-white village pub with its ancient bar and huge log fire has evolved into a very civilised eating place. It's well run with sound food and service, and always busy. Lunchtime bar snacks include excellent quiches, Welsh rarebit, seafood pancake, sandwiches and salads. The several restaurants are more expensive.

No children under 7 • Car-park • Wheelchair access, also WC • Access, Amex, Visa

Northallerton
(N Yorks) map 10

Bettys ★
188 High Street
☎ NORTHALLERTON (0609) 775154

Open all week 9am (10 Sun)–5.30
Closed Christmas Day, Boxing Day and New Year's Day

One of the smaller Bettys (see entries for Harrogate, Ilkley and York), so there are often queues, especially for lunch. Delightful waitresses serve Welsh rarebit, light omelettes, Yorkshire cheese lunch, some alluring cakes and tea-breads (try the 'fat rascals'), accompanied by a selection of unusual teas and rare coffees. A real treat.

No-smoking area • Wheelchair access • Access, Visa

Nunnington
(N Yorks)   map 7

Royal Oak

☎ NUNNINGTON (043 95) 271

*Open all week noon–2 (exc Mon),
6.30–9*

An inn with pleasing terrace views
and a diligent licensee, Anthony
Simpson. By way of decoration he has
amassed collections of farm tools,
copper jugs and keys. His efforts to
provide good food are popular with
locals. Apart from a daily special, a
typical menu will include chicken
liver pâté and seafood hors d'oeuvres
– smoked mackerel, rollmops, sweet
herring and prawns with apple in
marie rose sauce. Hearty steak and
kidney casserole with herb dumpling
or roast chicken are crowd-pullers.
Above-average wine list.

No children under 5 • Car-park

Otley (W Yorks)   map 7

Westbourne Fisheries

132 Bradford Road
☎ OTLEY (0943) 463203

*Open L Wed, Fri and Sat 11.30am–
1.30, D Wed to Fri 4.30pm–6.30, Sun
3.30–7 (4–6 winter)
Closed Mon, Tue and 1 week Christmas*

The atmosphere is homely and cosy;
there is a gas fire, just seven Formica-
topped tables, mock wood panelling
and cheerful service. This is a fish
and chip shop serving generous-sized
fish in crisp, light batter, good chips
and correct mushy peas well seasoned

with pepper. Pots of strong tea are
promptly refilled.

Unlicensed • Garden • Car-park

Pateley Bridge
(N Yorks)   map 7

Sportsman's Arms

Wath-in-Nidderdale
☎ HARROGATE (0423) 711306

*Open all week noon–2, 7–9.45 (exc
Sun D)*

In a lonely but lovely spot this former
coaching-inn still caters for the
traveller and its good food is well
known. Bar food features omelettes
made from the inn's own free-range
hens, locally-made cheeses,
Nidderdale lamb and trout, the latter
served in a variety of ways, and good
soups. A traditional Sunday lunch for
£9.50 is served in the restaurant,
which also serves more expensive
evening meals.

*Garden • Car-park • Wheelchair access,
also WC • Access, Amex, Diners, Visa*

Pickering (N Yorks)   map 10

Mulberries

Bridge Street
☎ PICKERING (0751) 72337

*Open all week 10am–5
Closed Sun in Jan, Feb and Nov*

Everything is home-made at this
charming, carefully restored tea-
room. Scones and cakes are the
ultimate temptation but light lunches

are good, too. Apart from soup you may find salmon mousse and salad for £2.50 or tongue and coleslaw for £3. Then it's on to bread-and-butter pudding or lemon pavlova.

No-smoking area • Garden

Pudsey (W Yorks)   map 7

Aagrah

483 Bradford Road
☎ BRADFORD (0274) 668818

Open all week noon–11.30 (midnight Fri and Sat)
Closed Christmas Day evening

Friendly, attentive service and a sure grasp of what a vegan will or will not eat mark out this pleasant North Indian restaurant. Lazat dar – chicken and lamb with onion, tomato, mushrooms and nan – is generous and satisfying, tarka dhal excellent. (See entries for Shipley and Skipton.)

No-smoking area • Car-park • Wheelchair access, also WC • Access, Amex, Diners, Visa

Cravens

32 Lowtown
☎ PUDSEY (0532) 551396

Open all week 11.30–2, 4.30–10.30 (Sun noon–10.30)

The new owners of this fish and chip restaurant have had many years' experience in the trade and use only the freshest ingredients available. The choice of fish might extend beyond haddock and plaice to hake and halibut. Salads are available.

Car-park • Wheelchair access, also WC • Access

Scarborough
(N Yorks)   map 10

Dilt's

2 Princess Square
☎ SCARBOROUGH (0723) 500146

Open all week summer noon–midnight, winter Wed to Sat noon–1.30, 8–10.30
Closed winter Sun to Tue

A remarkable little fish and chip shop/restaurant tucked away in the old part of town not far from the harbour. Inside it is pure old Yorkshire, with dark wood panelling, fishing nets and storm lamps on the walls. Ian Smith cooks and runs the place with real North Country ebullience. Excellent fresh fish, ranging from cod, haddock and wooff (cat fish) to Dover sole and occasionally brill, is perfectly fried in crisp batter and served with good chips. Slices of brown bread are spread with proper butter. The wine list is impressive for a chippie; otherwise bring your own. Take-aways are available.

Hanover Fisheries

14 Hanover Street
☎ SCARBOROUGH (0723) 362062

Open all week 11.30–1.30 (exc Mon), 8 (4.30 Thur and Fri)–11.45
Closed Christmas and New Year

A long-established chippie handily placed opposite the railway station. Peter Haire maintains high standards, uses fresh fish, and keeps his prices low. Pizzas supplement the standard output of the friers. Take-aways only.

Unlicensed • No smoking

Small Fry

52 North Street
☎ SCARBOROUGH (0723) 367448

Open Tue to Sat 11.30–2, 4.15–7.15 (10.15 Thur and Fri) exc Sat D
Closed Sun, Mon and Christmas Day

Run by the Holmes family, Small Fry is a tiny take-away fish and chip shop in a row of Victorian cottages at the bottom end of Westborough shopping precinct. Fish comes from local boats where possible and all frying is done in vegetable oil.

No smoking • Wheelchair access

Settle (N Yorks)   map 7

Liverpool House

8 Chapel Square
☎ SETTLE (072 92) 2247

Open Mon, Tue, Fri and Sat L noon–2, all week D 7 (1 sitting)
Closed Christmas and Jan

Liverpool House was built in the mid-eighteenth century as a gatehouse for a proposed waterway. It is now a comfortable, homely guest house open to non-residents for snacks and evening meals. Simple, home-cooked food is the trademark here, with baking a strong point. Well worth a stop during the day for cakes, tea, and snacks of soup, sandwiches and omelettes. There is

only one sitting for dinner, at 7pm sharp, which must be booked in advance.

No-smoking area • Car-park • Access, Visa

Sheffield (S Yorks)   map 7

Bay Tree

119 Devonshire Street
☎ SHEFFIELD (0742) 759254

Open Mon to Sat L noon–2.30, Thur and Fri D 6.30–9
Closed Sun

A splendid place for a quick, inexpensive vegetarian lunch, the Bay Tree is run by Brenda Tyssen and Linda Crabtree, who also prepare the fresh, attractive-looking food. The daily changing menu could feature green peppercorn roulade, vegetables in satay sauce, a fish dish, and black-eye beans with spinach and juniper berries. Figs in frangipane stand out among good desserts.

Unlicensed, but bring your own: corkage 50p • No smoking • Wheelchair access

Crucible Coffee Shop

Crucible Theatre, Norfolk Street
☎ SHEFFIELD (0742) 760621

Open Mon to Sat 10am–9
Closed Sun

Open to the general public and theatre-goers alike, the theatre coffee-shop is a popular meeting place for shoppers. The food has a wholefood/vegetarian emphasis – vegetable soup, baked potato with

vegetable chilli, and various salads –
although meat-eaters are catered for.
There is a selection of cakes and
pastries and a generally lively
atmosphere.

*No-smoking area • Wheelchair access,
also WC*

Fat Cat

24 Alma Road
☎ SHEFFIELD (0742) 728195

Open all week L noon–2.30
Closed Christmas Day

A health-conscious pub with a no-
smoking room, real ales and
wholesome food served with North
Country generosity. The tiled
fireplaces, old mirrors and posters
reflect the past, while the loyalty of
the place is to community arts and
alternative entertainments. A menu
of substantial dishes might take in
lightly salted hefty tomato and
vegetable soup; sausage and pasta
casserole; and prawn and potato
curry. Bread is granary; sunflower
margarine is used instead of butter
and there are fruit crumbles with
proper custard to finish. Draught
beers, ciders and some drinkable
wines.

*No-smoking area • Garden •
Wheelchair access*

Just Cooking

16–18 Carver Street
☎ SHEFFIELD (0742) 727869

*Open Mon to Sat 11.45–3.30,
7.30–9.45*
Closed Sun

Just Cooking, situated alongside the
town hall, is a popular lunchtime
eatery frequently attracting long

queues. Food on display at the
counter looks good and freshness is a
mark of the ingredients. Crisp,
imaginative salads and cold dishes are
particularly noteworthy (including
excellent honey-roast ham) and
desserts are irresistible, especially the
chocolate roulade.

No-smoking area • Wheelchair access

Nirmal's

189–93 Glossop Road
☎ SHEFFIELD (0742) 724054

*Open Mon to Sat L noon–2.30, all week
D 6–midnight (1am Fri and Sat)*

Nirmal Gupta is still one of the few
Asian female chefs in the country and
her cooking has acquired an enviable
local reputation. Apart from skilful
tandooris and subtly spiced curries,
she offers daily specialities such as
chicken jalfrezi. Also look for her
special soup served with cream and
almonds, potato 'chops' filled with
lentils and onions, and nan bread
stuffed with paneer (Indian curd
cheese). There are stuffed bhindis
among the vegetables and a different
dhal each day. Drink Kingfisher or
Tiger beer.

*Wheelchair access, also WC • Access,
Amex, Visa*

Shelley (W Yorks)   map 7

Three Acres Inn

Roydhouse
☎ HUDDERSFIELD (0484) 602606

From Shelley take Flockton road for 1m

Open all week noon–1.45, 7–9.45

Situated within 100 yards of the
Cemley TV mast, the Three Acres

Inn creates the feeling of being on top of the world, with views stretching for miles. Bar food is available at lunchtime only, with an extensive choice of sandwiches – the fashion among regular groups is to order a large and attractively presented selection and a bowl of chips – grilled gammon and pineapple, a meaty steak and kidney pie and sausage and mash with onion gravy. There is a good-value two-course set lunch in the restaurant for £6.95; evening meals are more expensive. The inn is exceptionally well run, spacious and comfortable, with cheerful and friendly service.

Car-park • Wheelchair access • Access, Amex, Visa

Shipley (W Yorks)   map 7

Aagrah

27 Westgate
☎ BRADFORD (0274) 594660

Open all week noon–midnight
Closed Christmas Day evening

Part of a small chain of North Indian curry houses (see entries for Pudsey and Skipton). Aagrah has a local reputation for serving good-quality Asian food, and consistent standards keep the place busy. Vegetarians are well catered for and there is a welcome no-smoking area. Try the Kashmiri dishes and the house speciality lamb Hyderabad.

No-smoking area • Access, Amex, Diners, Visa

Skipton (N Yorks)   map 7

Aagrah

Unicorn House, Devonshire Place
☎ SKIPTON (0756) 790807

Open all week D 6–midnight (11 Sun)

Another of this small, popular chain of curry houses (see entries for Pudsey and Shipley), family-run in a caring manner. There is a no-smoking area and a good vegetarian selection of food. Dishes come from all over the Indian sub-continent with balti chicken, Hyderabad dishes and chicken zafrani representative of a long list of specialitities.

No-smoking area • Car-park • Wheelchair access, also WC • Access, Amex, Diners, Visa

Herbs

10 High Street
☎ SKIPTON (0756) 790619

Open Mon to Sat (exc Tue) 9.30am–4.45
Closed Tue, Sun, Christmas Day, Boxing Day and New Year's Day

Part of the Healthy Life Natural Food Centre, the vegetarian Herbs offers simple food – soups, sandwiches, salads, filled pancakes and vegetable casseroles – made from fresh local produce and unadulterated wholefoods. There is a fair range of desserts and cakes to accompany the dozen or so herbal teas on offer.

Unlicensed • No smoking

Staithes (N Yorks)   map 10

Endeavour

1 High Street
☎ WHITBY (0947) 840825

Open Mon to Sat noon–2, 7–10
Closed Sun, 23 to 26 Dec and 6 Jan to
12 Mar

Lisa Chapman offers carefully
cooked, well-presented food. Prices
are not low, but such is the quality
offered here that it is well worth any
extra cost. Local fish includes brill,
served with parsley hollandaise or
there is succulent calf's liver and
onions.

No children under 8

Sutton Howgrave
(N Yorks)   map 7

White Dog 🏵

☎ MELMERBY (076 584) 404

¹/₄m off A1 on Masham–Thirsk road

Open Tue to Sun L noon–2
Closed Mon, Christmas and New Year

A quiet village setting for a peaceful
pub, its two rooms looking more like
the front rooms in the adjoining
cottages than conventional bars. Bar
food is available lunchtimes only
from a regularly changing menu
which might include lamb casserole,
steak and kidney pudding and a thick-
crusted venison pie, with lighter
choices of sandwiches, salads and
omelettes.

No-smoking area • No children, exc in
garden • Garden • Car-park •
Wheelchair access

Threshfield
(N Yorks)   map 7

Old Hall 🏵

☎ GRASSINGTON (075 675) 2441

Open all week 11.30–2, 6.30–9.30
Closed Mon Jan to May

The Old Hall is a thriving, bustling
pub and a complete internal
refurbishment and new extension
mirrors this success. Food is
competent and certainly varied, with
sag gosht and chicken satay in among
the fresh fish dishes and the
carbonnade of beef. Desserts are a
weak point and could be improved.
Service is friendly and efficient.

Car-park • Wheelchair access, also WC

Whitby (N Yorks)   map 10

Elizabeth Botham & Sons

35–9 Skinner Street
☎ Whitby (0947) 602823

Open Mon to Sat 9am–5
Closed Sun

Founded in 1865, and still a family-
run establishment, this is a local
institution famous for quality baking.
The sparse upstairs café serves
legendary strawberry tarts in summer
and equally good gingerbread at
Christmas. Potted meats, sausages
and meat pies are distinctive. There is
also a set menu which invariably
features roast beef and Yorkshire
pudding. The local girls who serve
are friendly. Just the place for an
enormous cream tea.

No-smoking area • Wheelchair access •
Access, Visa

Magpie Café

14 Pier Road
☎ WHITBY (0947) 602058

Open all week 11.30am–6.30
Closed late Nov to Mar

Go early, for the Magpie handles only freshly landed fish and the queues quickly build up. With half a lobster and salad for £8.95 you can see why. Fish comes grilled, poached or fried, but the café's fame lies with its fish and chips of Whitby cod or haddock which feature in the great-value special lunches. Bread and butter comes automatically as does the tea, unless specifically declined in favour of the wine list. Salmon is fresh from the River Esk. Meat-eaters are simply catered for with steak and kidney pie, gammon and steaks. The 30 desserts are all made on the premises and include a memorable sticky toffee pudding. Restricted diets and children are well catered for.

No-smoking area

Shepherd's Purse

Sanders Yard, 95 Church Street
☎ WHITBY (0947) 604725

Open all week noon–2, 6–9 (exc winter D)
Closed Christmas Day and Boxing Day

Making a change from the fish and chip shops that dominate the eating scene in Whitby is this wholefood vegetarian café. Dishes include a lentil and fennel bake, cashew-nut pâté and aubergine and red-bean casserole. Salads are crisp, and cakes, especially the sticky variety like pecan pie, are good. Re-heating is by microwave, which can make pastry unappetisingly soggy.

No smoking • Access, Visa

Silver Street Fish and Chip Shop

22 Silver Street
☎ WHITBY (0947) 603087

Open Tue to Sat 11.30–1.30, 8–11.30 (exc Wed D)
Closed Sun and Mon

Just a take-away fish and chip shop but undoubtedly one of the best in Whitby. Derek and Mary Webb put all the emphasis on fresh fish and locally grown potatoes, with the food then cooked to order as the customer waits. Only those in a hurry are served the fish cooked in advance and held warming in the top – an admirable practice.

Unlicensed • Wheelchair access

Trenchers

New Quay Road
☎ WHITBY (0947) 603212

Open all week 11am–9
Closed Dec to Mar

The nearest rival to the remarkable Magpie Café (see entry). Inside, it is purpose-built, with fixed seating, plastic menu cards and loud pop music. But the quality of the food is well above that of the average family restaurant. Fish is landed fresh from the quay and deftly fried in excellent batter. Chips are crisp and ungreasy; salads may contain unexpected exotic ingredients such as star fruit, and sweets include sumptuous ice-creams. House wine, keg beer and pots of tea.

Wheelchair access

Please let us know if you think an eating-place should be included in this guide; report forms are at the back of the book.

York (N Yorks)   map 7

Bettys ★

6–8 St Helen's Square
☎ YORK **(0904) 659142**

Open all week 9am–9pm
Closed Christmas Day, Boxing Day and
New Year's Day

Frederick Belmont used the interior designers who worked on the liner *Queen Mary* to create this, the most stylish of the Bettys chain of tea-rooms (see entries for Harrogate, Ilkley and Northallerton). Some 60 years later the huge plate-glass window is still polished daily and a pianist plays in the evenings. The excellent quality of the food and traditional service justify the higher-than-normal tea-room prices. During the day speciality teas and rare coffees complement tea-breads and scones, smoked salmon muffin, and Yorkshire rarebit with ham. In the evening chicken provençale, scrambled eggs and smoked salmon, and very late breakfasts draw the crowds.

No-smoking area • Wheelchair access •
Access, Visa

Miller's Yard Café

Miller's Yard, Gillygate
☎ YORK **(0904) 610676**

Open Mon to Sat L noon–2.30

Run as a workers' co-operative with the Gillygate Wholefood Bakery. The self-service café is part of a collection of converted buildings near the City Art Gallery, and there are tables in the courtyard. Breads and pastries come from the bakery, salads can contain some unexpected fresh herbs, and much of the produce is organic. Solid, robust, hot and cold dishes range from aubergine and potato curry to layered terrine; the tofu cheesecake is highly rated.

Unlicensed • No smoking inside café •
Garden

St William's

3 College Street
☎ YORK **(0904) 634830**

Open all week noon–2.30

A lovely old building close to York Minster, founded in the fifteenth century. Today, St William's College is partly a museum, partly an all-day self-service restaurant. Popular at lunchtime (be prepared to queue), the restaurant offers raised cold pies, terrines, a range of salads, Lancashire hot-pot and good, old-fashioned bread-and-butter pudding.

No-smoking area

Taylors Tea Rooms

46 Stonegate
☎ YORK **(0904) 622865**

Open all week 9am–5.30

Owned by the estimable Bettys Tea Rooms but well established in its own right as a purveyor of fine teas and coffees. The tea-room is above the shop in a handsome sixteenth-century building. Half the menu lists speciality teas and coffees, the other half superb cakes, sandwiches, omelettes and things on toast. The higher-than-expected prices reflect York's tourist industry.

No-smoking area • Access, Visa

ISLE OF MAN

Castletown map 9

Chablis Cellar

21 Bank Street, Castletown
☎ (062 482) 3527

Open Tue to Sun L noon–3, Fri and Sat
D 7–9
Closed Mon

An informal harbourside restaurant
filled with fresh flowers and the smell
of freshly baked bread. Large
windows give waterside views. Food
is well cooked in an unfussy manner
and keenly priced. Expect savoury
mince pie, lasagne, seafood pancake
and chicken Mexican served with
vegetables or salad. Finish with
treacle tart.

Car-park • Wheelchair access, also WC

Douglas map 9

Bowery

4 Athol Terrace, Queen's
Promenade
☎ Douglas (0624) 6280

Open Mon to Sat 12.30–2, 7.30–10
Closed Sun and winter bank hols

An American-style restaurant serving
standard American and Tex-Mex
dishes. It is unlike anything else on
the island, not just for the food it
serves but for the outstanding, well-
motivated level of service given.
There is a wide range of burgers,
steaks and good salads. Burritos,
tacos, nachos and potato skins back
up the menu.

No-smoking area • Wheelchair access,
also WC (men only)

SCOTLAND

Aberdeen
(Grampian)   map 11

Craighaar Hotel

Waterton Road, Bucksburn
☎ ABERDEEN **(0224) 712275**

Open all week D 6.30–10 (8 Sun)
Closed Christmas Day, Boxing Day and
New Year's Day

Tacked on to the edge of a housing
estate, this unprepossessing modern
building nevertheless provides some
good bar food. Fish is an attraction,
whether a plate of oysters, a herring
platter, haddock, sole or plaice, while
lamb cutlets or curries are substantial
meat courses. There is a more
expensive restaurant strong on 16-
ounce steaks.

Car-park • Access, Amex, Diners, Visa

Megna Tandoori

11 Dee Street
☎ ABERDEEN **(0224) 572065**

Open all week noon–2, 5–midnight
Closed Christmas Day

A superior curry house forging a
reputation for good-value, high-
quality Indian food. Onion bhajias
are nice and crisp; vegetable rogan is
mainly peas and potatoes but topped
with lightly cooked tomatoes and
slivers of green pepper. House
specialities include bataire masala
(quails) and chicken makhani (cooked
with coconut and almond).
Otherwise, lamb chop masala is a
good bet. Finish with the fruit salad.

Access, Amex, Diners, Visa

Arbroath (Tayside)   map 11

But 'n' Ben

Auchmithie
☎ ARBROATH **(0241) 77223**

3m NE of Arbroath

Open Wed to Mon noon–2.30, 4–5.30,
7.30–10
Closed Tue

A 'but 'n' ben' is a two-roomed
cottage, and the atmosphere of
Scottish village life still pervades this
splendid restaurant run by Margaret
Horn and her family. Lunches, high
teas and evening meals show off the
quality of the local produce and the
special skills of home baking. Platters
of impeccably fresh seafood share the
bill with pan-grilled Aberdeen Angus
steaks. Otherwise, there are Arbroath
smokies, home-made soups, quiches,
and mince with tatties and skirlie.
Baskets of wholemeal bread are
reliable fixtures. Wine by the glass.

No smoking in restaurant • Wheelchair
access, also WC • Access, Amex, Visa

Arisaig (Highland)   map 11

Arisaig Hotel

☎ ARISAIG **(068 75) 210**

On A830 Fort William–Mallaig road

Open all week 12.30–2

The Arisaig Hotel is an unremarkable
Jacobean building, but a scenic drive,
fine views and an inexpensive bar
lunch strong on local seafood make it
an attractive proposition. There are
locally smoked salmon, Arisaig king

prawns, fried lemon sole, Mallaig herring in oatmeal or steaks, venison pâté and gammon for meat-eaters. Over 100 malt whiskies are on offer.

Family-room • Car-park • Access, Visa

Aviemore (Highland) map 11

Winking Owl

Grampian Road
☎ Aviemore (0479) 810646

Open Mon to Sat noon–2.30, 5–9.30, Sun 12.30–2.15, 6.30–9.30

A varied menu, strong on Scottish produce and low prices, is the attraction at this open-all-year pub. Much is home-made: the chicken and game pâté, devilled parsnip soup, venison pie. Roast rib of prime Scotch beef with vegetables and potatoes is great value at £3.80. Fillet of fresh haddock is popular. Finish with home-made whisky mousse. Morning coffee from 11am.

No children after 8.30pm • Garden • Car-park • Access, Amex, Diners, Visa

Ayr (Strathclyde) map 9

Stables

Queen's Court, 41 Sandgate
☎ Ayr (0292) 283704

Open Mon to Sat 10am–10pm (5 Mon) Closed Sun and Nov evenings

The Stables, in a pleasant, renovated eighteenth-century courtyard, caters well for tourists and locals alike with a coffee-house-style daytime menu and a more expensive evening restaurant. Scotch broth with a hunk

of locally made bread, open sandwiches, haggis, chicken stovies, ham and haddie pie (bacon and haddock), fresh baked cakes, scones and oatcakes feature on the keenly priced day menu.

No smoking in main dining-room • Garden • Wheelchair access • Access, Amex, Diners, Visa

Cairndow

(Strathclyde) map 11

Loch Fyne Oyster Bar ★

Clachan Farm
☎ CAIRNDOW (049 96) 276/236

At the head of Loch Fyne

Open all week 9am–9pm

Food with a view and oysters for everyman. This good-value oyster bar, right at the head of spectacular Loch Fyne, is part and parcel of an enterprise including a smokehouse, produce shop and home-delivery service. Oysters from local beds are the stars of the show – served au naturel or baked – but the menu covers all kinds of provisions from home-cured gravlax, dressed crab, Loch Fyne kippers and fried herrings in oatmeal to platters of smoked venison, or Scottish cheeses with oatcakes. To drink there are well-chosen, appropriate wines (several by the glass), imported bottled beers and pots of tea – not to mention champagne and Guinness. Eat in the pine-furnished café or sit outside. A branch has opened in Nottingham (see entry).

Garden • Car-park • Wheelchair access, also WC • Access, Amex, Visa

Canonbie

(Dumfries & Galloway)   map 9

Riverside Inn

☎ CANONBIE (038 73) 71512

Open Mon to Sat L noon–2, Sun D 7–9
Closed 2 weeks Feb

Canonbie is no longer on the main
road into Scotland but this bar still
fills up at lunchtime, such is the pull
of the food. A laudable effort is made
to buy organic produce, also free-
range chickens and wild salmon.
Soups are excellent, the salad
dressing, made with walnut oil, is
good and haddock and chips comes
with home-made tartare sauce.
Evenings are more expensive.

Garden • Car-park • Wheelchair access,
also WC • Access, Visa

Colonsay

(Strathclyde)   map 11

Isle of Colonsay Hotel

☎ COLONSAY (095 12) 316

Open bar all week 12.30–1.30, 7–8.30,
Virago's restaurant Wed to Sat noon–8
Closed Virago's Sun to Tue, Virago's
and bar Nov to Feb

The ferry from Oban takes two and a
half hours (and it does not run every
day), lending credence to the claim
that this eighteenth-century hotel on
a beautiful Hebridean island is the
most isolated in Great Britain. Kevin
and Christa Byrne make all their own
bread and preserves and grow
vegetables in the hotel garden.
Locally caught seafood plays an
important role, appearing as the
mainstay of the Virago's evening
restaurant menu (Wednesday to
Saturday). Creel-caught prawns,
crabs, mussels and oysters are backed
up by Tobermory smoked trout,
smoked eel, mackerel and salmon. In
the bar, simple lunches of home-
made soup, filled rolls and cheese are
extended in the evening to include
boeuf bourguignonne and venison in
red wine. A more expensive menu is
available in the hotel's other
restaurant.

No smoking in restaurants • Garden •
Car-park • Wheelchair access, also WC
• Access, Amex, Diners, Visa

Drybridge

(Grampian)   map 11

Old Monastery

☎ BUCKIE (0542) 32660

Off A98 at Buckie Junction on to
Drybridge Road, follow for 2m – don't
turn right into Drybridge village

Open Tue to Sat noon–1.45, 7–9.30
Closed Sun, Mon, 3 weeks Jan and 2
weeks Nov

A remote Gothic retreat erected by
the Dominicans at the turn of the
century. The views are stunning. The
restaurant is sited in the chapel, the
bar in the cloisters. Lunch is well-
priced with choices from the mini à la
carte ranging from game terrine,
cheese and chive omelette and
Aberdeen Angus steak to Moray fish
feast. Finish with Drambuie parfait.
Evenings are more expensive.

No smoking in restaurant • No children
under 8 • Garden • Car-park • Access,
Amex, Visa

Dulnain Bridge
(Highland)   map 11

Muckrach Lodge Hotel
☎ DULNAIN BRIDGE (047 985) 257

Open all week noon–2

A simple, unpretentious hotel serving
some sound lunchtime bar snacks.
The sandwiches (listed as substantial
on the menu) take pride of place and
include wild Spey salmon, poached or
smoked, home-cooked gammon and
ox tongue. Omelettes, soups, North
Sea sole and lamb's liver and bacon
provide for most appetites and there
is steamed syrup sponge to finish.

*Garden • Car-park • Wheelchair access,
also WC • Access, Amex, Diners, Visa*

Dundee (Tayside)   map 11

Raffles
18 Perth Road
☎ DUNDEE (0382) 26344

*Open Tue to Fri noon–2, 6–9 (10.30
Fri), Sat 10am–10.30pm
Closed Sun, Mon, Christmas Day,
Boxing Day, 2 weeks early Jan and 2
weeks July/Aug*

Overlooking the River Tay and
charmingly decorated, Raffles offers
well-judged, carefully prepared, if
slightly fussy, food at reasonable
prices. Spiced barbecue lamb comes
with nut butter and rhubarb sauce,
breast of chicken is stuffed with
chicken mousse, mushrooms and
cream. Vegetarians fare well with
vegetable pie or lasagne.

Wheelchair access

Dunfermline (Fife)   map 11

New Victoria ⊕
2 Bruce Street
☎ DUNFERMLINE (0383) 724175

W of M90 junction 3

*Open Mon to Sat 9am–9.30pm
Closed Sun, Boxing Day and 1 to 3 Jan*

Eating here is like stepping back in
time. Scotch broth, Irish stew with
dumplings and steamed jam sponge
sum up the food and the style of this
restaurant with views of the ancient
abbey. A long menu, including 18
main courses, ranges from roast beef
and fried haddock to grilled pork
chops. There are also a few meatless
dishes and salads. Wine by the glass.

No-smoking area • Access, Visa

Dunkeld (Tayside)   map 11

Tappit Hen
7 Atholl Street
☎ DUNKELD (035 02) 472

*Open all week 10.30am–5 (exc Sun Oct
to Easter)
Closed Sun Oct to Easter*

Martin and Louise Dibbs run a
charming coffee-shop with the
emphasis firmly on sound home
baking. This produces light scones
and sponges, rich fruit cake, date and
walnut loaf and good coffee cake.
There is a simple choice of filled rolls
and sandwiches made to order: roast
beef, ham, and the popular egg and
cress. Home-made soups and
ploughman's complete the picture.

Unlicensed • No-smoking area • Visa

Dunvegan
(Highland)   map 11

Three Chimneys
Colbost, Isle of Skye
☎ GLENDALE (047 081) 258

Off B884 3m W of Dunvegan

Open Mon to Sat 12.30–2, 7–9
Closed Sun and mid-Oct to March

A restaurant located along a single-track road in the north-west tip of Skye can only be described as remote. It is also enjoying some success, so much so that a £10 budget can only withstand lunch here. This provides a Scottish-inspired menu of home-made bread, oysters, soups, local mussels, partan pie (crab) and fresh salad.

No smoking • Car-park • Access, Visa

Eddleston (Borders)   map 9

Horse Shoe Inn 🏅
☎ EDDLESTON (072 13) 225

On A703 4m N of Peebles

Open all week noon–2.30, 6–10

Basically a steak and burger place backed up by home-made minestrone soup, garlic prawns, beef bourguignonne and home-made apple pie. The range is not particularly imaginative, but portions are large and prices, even for steaks, reasonable. Service can be indifferent.

Garden and family-room • Car-park •
Wheelchair access, also WC • Access,
Amex, Diners, Visa

Edinburgh
(Lothian)   map 11

Baked Potato Shop
56 Cockburn Street
☎ 031-225 7572

Open all week 9am–7pm in winter,
9am–11pm in summer

A tiny take-away, just off the Royal Mile, with a couple of stools and barely room for four people inside. The theme is baked potatoes with fillings, but the range goes far beyond cheese and coleslaw. On the cold side there might be mushroom and soured-cream salad; hot fillings range from vegetable curry to vegetarian haggis (nuts, lentils and oatmeal served with turnips). All fillings can be served with pitta bread as an alternative to potatoes. To drink there are freshly squeezed juices and home-made yoghurt drinks.

No smoking • Wheelchair access

Bamboo Garden
57A Frederick Street
☎ 031-225 2382

Open all week noon–midnight
Closed 3–4 days Jan

Locals reckon that this basement Chinese restaurant avoids most of the Edinburgh clichés. The menu features a good range of dim-sum and there are some reasonably priced set menus. Recommended dishes have included prawn and shark's-fin dumplings; honey-fried chicken and phoenix-tail prawns in chilli sauce. Crispy roast duck and barbecued pork are excellent. A plate of fried noodles with beansprouts makes a filling alternative to rice. Drink tea or white wine.

Wheelchair access, also WC • Access, Amex, Visa

Cellar No. 1

1A Chambers Street
☎ **031-220 4298**

Open Mon to Sat noon–2.30, 6–9.30
Closed Sun, 2 days Christmas and 3 days New Year

A long, narrow cellar bar, comfortably appointed and situated below a wine shop. Wine is taken seriously here with a list of some 30 available by the glass. A daily blackboard supplements the printed menu of keenly priced dishes. Gnocchi, squid in a piquant tomato sauce, wild Scottish smoked salmon and the big sandwich, a filled poppy-seed bun, are popular.

No children under 14 • Access, Visa

Chan's

1 Forth Street
☎ **031-556 7118**

Open Wed to Mon 5.30–11.30, Fri noon–2
Closed Tue, Christmas Day, Boxing Day and 4 days Chinese New Year

Cantonese, Pekingese and Szechuan dishes share the bill in this light, airy restaurant, but the unexpected bonus is a fully-fledged list of vegetarian specialities. Bean curd, mushrooms and cashew-nuts dominate, but the kitchen can deliver some excellent results: crispy wun-tun filled with sweetcorn, deep-fried bean curd with black-bean sauce, a hot-pot of braised

mixed vegetables and deep-fried cucumber with satay sauce have all been enjoyed. Otherwise, the menu takes in everything from steamed lemon sole with ginger and spring onion to roast duck with fried noodles. Excellent value.

Access, Amex, Diners, Visa

Chinese Home Cooking

21 Argyle Place
☎ **031-229 4404**

Open all week D 5.30–11
Closed Christmas Day

A no-frills, no-nonsense Chinese restaurant serving big portions of good food to the inhabitants of Edinburgh's bed-sit land. Décor is a functional mix of stucco, imitation panelling and tables lined up along the walls. The menu may read like that of a take-away, but dishes have the flavour and quality of genuine home cooking. Barbecued spare ribs, sweet-and-sour king prawns and char siu pork with mushrooms have been recommended.

Unlicensed, but bring your own: no corkage

Doric Tavern

15 Market Street
☎ **031-225 1084**

Open Mon to Sat noon–10.30
Closed Sun, Christmas Day and Boxing Day

While some claim that the Doric's best days are past, the cooking here still has its moments. The red walls can seem oppressive in the daylight and the menu can't be accused of inventiveness. But there are enough occasions when its solid, unpretentious style wins through. Look out for couscous merguez, braised lamb with lemon and almonds or monkfish with peppercorns. Some good, cheap wines but, in general, the list is too short. The set-price, three-course lunch is a bargain at £8.50.

No children under 14 in bar • Access, Amex, Diners, Visa

Engine Shed Café

19 St Leonard's Lane
☎ **031-662 0040**

Open Mon to Fri 10.30am–4
Closed Sat, Sun, 1 week Christmas and 1 week Easter

Run by Garvald Community Enterprises, a charity dedicated to supplying employment training to people with special needs, the Engine Shed Café occupies an airy upstairs room off a charming old courtyard. Aggressively vegetarian, it offers a soup, two hot dishes and a selection of salads each weekday. Tofu – plain, marinated and smoked – is a regular crowd-puller. An excellent choice of herbal teas, fruit juices and baked goods.

Unlicensed • No smoking • Garden • Car-park • Wheelchair access, also WC

Fruitmarket Gallery Café Bistro

29 Market Street
☎ **031-225 2383**

Open Tue to Sun 10am–5.30
Closed Mon and Christmas Day

An attractive café/bistro on the second floor of the art gallery. A wide-ranging blackboard menu might take in guacamole with pitta bread or

cream of lettuce soup, followed by beef and mushroom pie or courgette parmigiano. Crisp, fresh salads come with decent vinaigrette dressing, and there are ice-creams and luscious fruity sweets to finish. Friendly, helpful staff.

No-smoking area

Gallery Café

Scottish National Gallery of Modern Art, Belford Road
☎ **031-332 8600**

Open all week noon–4.30
Closed Christmas and New Year

In the basement of the National Gallery of Modern Art is this well-designed, aesthetically pleasing café. Crowds flock in for good-value lunches of carrot and coriander soup, chicken and pepper pie with salad, lamb curry and garlic sausage pizzas. Jacket potatoes, savoury croissants and salads, home-baked cakes and Scottish cheeses served with oatcakes complete the picture. There is wine by the glass, as well as teas, coffees and bottled beers. A beautiful terrace and garden are available for fine-weather eating.

No-smoking area • Garden • Car-park • Wheelchair access, also WC

Helios Fountain

7 Grassmarket
☎ **031-229 7884**

Open Mon to Sat 10am–6 (8 during Aug), also Aug Sun 11am–5
Closed Sun (exc Aug)

Occupying an imposing former Bank of Scotland building, this simple, self-service vegetarian café is at the back of a book, toy and craft shop. Only organic or bio-dynamically grown ingredients are used. The daily-changing menu is imaginatively thought out, including, perhaps, spinach and coconut soup and butter-bean goulash; cakes such as carrot and prune are available all day.

Unlicensed • No smoking • Wheelchair access • Access, Visa

Henderson's

94 Hanover Street
☎ 031-225 2131

Open Mon to Sat 8am–11pm
Closed Sun, 2 days Christmas, 2 days New Year and bank hols

Henderson's is a victim of its own popularity: the relentless queues at popular meal times and trawling for a table with a laden tray can take the enjoyment out of the inventive and mainly organic vegetarian food. The buffet operates all day with vegetable curry and mushroom flan among the hot dishes, a wide range of salads and some imaginative cakes and desserts.

No-smoking area • Visa

Howie's

75 St Leonard's Street
☎ 031-668 2917

Open all week 12.30–2 (exc Mon and Sat), 6.30–10
Closed 1 week Christmas

The restaurant occupies the converted front room of a house in a tenement building. Inside, there is an assortment of stripped-wood tables decorated with tiny vases of dried flowers. Three-course fixed-price menus (£4.90 lunch; £9.90 dinner) offer excellent value for dishes such as game terrine with Cumberland

sauce; butterfly lamb chop with crab-apple sauce; and freshly made sherry trifle. There is always something for vegetarians. Good ingredients, generous portions.

Unlicensed, but bring your own: no corkage • Access, Amex, Visa

---

Kalpna ★

2–3 St Patrick's Square
☎ 031-667 9890

Open Mon to Sat noon–2 (exc Sat), 5.30–10.30
Closed Sun, Christmas and New Year's Day

Undoubtedly one of the best Gujerati restaurants in Britain. Everything has an air of simplicity and delicacy: the plain décor, the courteous service and the wonderful vegetarian food. Start with bhel poori, a dish frequently abused, and experience a real balance of textures and flavours. Gobi badami (cauliflower cooked in yoghurt, tomatoes, peas and nuts with herbs and spices) or shahi sabzi (mixed vegetables laced with spinach in cream and fresh coriander) give some indication of the inventiveness at work. Thalis (set meals) are excellent value and a good introduction if the food is unfamiliar. Even the desserts are made on the premises.

No smoking • Wheelchair access • Access, Visa

Lazio

95 Lothian Road
☎ 031-229 7788

Open all week noon-2.30am (3 Fri and Sat)

The décor is simple and the turnover of customers fast. Stick to the pasta and pizza choices (nothing unfamiliar) to stay within a reasonable budget. Otherwise, meat dishes have been praised and could be chosen for a one-course meal. Chicken noodle soup is well done. Desserts demonstrate 20 different things to do with ice-cream. Good-humoured service with a flourish.

Wheelchair access • Access, Amex, Diners, Visa

Loon Fung

32 Grindlay Street
☎ **031-229 5757**

Open all week noon (2 Sat and Sun)–midnight

A bright, cheerful Cantonese restaurant not far from the Usher Hall and the Lyceum. Excellent dim-sum (termed 'high tea' on the menu) are served throughout the day and there is a comprehensive list of noodle or rice one-plate dishes. Go in a group to make the most of the carte; judicious ordering should keep the bill down.

Access, Amex, Visa

New Edinburgh Rendezvous

10A Queensferry Street
☎ **031-225 2023**

Open Mon to Sat noon–2, 5.30–11.15, Sun 1–11.30
Closed 3 days Chinese New Year

Edinburgh's original Pekingese restaurant is up a flight of stairs in the west end of the city. Useful snacks and one-plate meals, such as grilled dumplings or soft noodles with minced pork and yellow-bean sauce, back up a menu of dishes ranging from crispy seaweed with dried

scallops to braised mixed vegetables and deep-fried bean curd with pork. Portions are enormous. Cheap lunches and good-value set meals.

No children under 5 evenings • Access, Amex, Diners, Visa

Philippine Islands

36 Broughton Street
☎ **031-556 8240**

Open Mon to Sat D 6.30–11
Closed Sun

Reputedly the only Filipino restaurant in Scotland. The décor is colourful and so is the food. Food is served in pottery bowls and comes adorned with sculpted vegetables and orange peel. The menu has some excellent choices for vegetarians, such as deep-fried tofu with soya and chilli dip, crisp vegetables in coconut milk, and beansprouts and tomato in black-bean sauce. Good rice and salads. Live music.

Wheelchair access • Access, Amex, Visa

Pierre Victoire

10 Victoria Street
☎ **031-225 1721**
8 Union Street
☎ **031-557 8451**
38 Grassmarket
☎ **031-226 2442**

Open Mon to Sat noon–3, 6–11
Closed Sun

Having perfected a winning formula of extraordinary value for money, fresh ingredients and informality, Pierre Levicky has moved on to open two more branches of his highly popular restaurant. The Victoria Street original – a converted coffee bar near the Grassmarket – sets the style, but all follow a similar pattern. The three-course set lunch (around £5) might feature leek and potato soup, grilled fillet of sole with ginger and spring onion, plus a sweet. The short evening carte is reasonably priced for two courses such as mussels steamed with coriander, then roast rib of beef with Stilton and red wine. Good-value, drinkable house wine.

Wheelchair access, also WC • Access

Raj

91 Henderson Street
☎ 031-553 3980

Open all week noon–2.30, 5.30–11.30

The setting is a corner overlooking the newly renovated shore of Leith. Inside, the wooden walls and extraordinary, elaborate ceiling complete with fans give the place a faded colonial air. Bangladesh is the inspiration for the cooking, with a few detours into Bengal for fish, the North West frontier for tandooris and 'The British Indian Army Mess'. The quality of vegetable dishes such as brinjal bhaji, aloo jeera and tarka dhal shows the capabilities of the kitchen. Chura mutter (peas with orange juice) is a speciality. There are good-value thalis for meat-eaters and vegetarians. Drink lassi, juices or lager.

Wheelchair access, also WC • Access, Amex, Visa

'Wheelchair access' indicates that, according to the proprietor, entrances are at least 33 inches wide, passages 4 feet wide, and that there are a maximum of two steps. It there is access to a WC, we mention it.

Royal Meadow

22 Valleyfield Street
☎ 031-229 1978

Open Tue to Sun 5pm–midnight (1am Fri and Sat)
Closed Mon

One of a cluster of new Malaysian restaurants springing up around Edinburgh. The real bargains here are the set lunches and pre-theatre dinners (£5 for three courses plus coffee), but the full menu is also reasonably priced. Prawns in batter with a spicy dip, curry puffs, and king prawns in a spicy sauce made with coconut milk are good introductions to the cuisine. Mixed vegetables and fried rice are up to the mark.

Wheelchair access • Access, Visa

Seeds

53 West Nicholson Street
☎ 031-667 8673

Open Mon to Sat 10am–8, 3 weeks Aug (festival) all week 11am–11pm
Closed Sun, Easter, 2 weeks Christmas and 1 week early Sept

Expect to share a table in this well-established co-operative café close to the university. The team of cooks rings the changes and new dishes appear all the time. Milk, butter and yoghurt are on offer, but the cooking is purely vegan; organic produce is used where possible. Interesting salads and satisfying soups are backed up by substantial dishes such as black-eyed beans and tomatoes with rice, or pumpkin and lentil bake. Desserts are usually sugar-free.

Unlicensed, but bring your own: no corkage • No smoking • Wheelchair access

Shrimps

107 St Leonard's Street
☎ 031-667 9160

Open Mon to Sat 11.30am–3.30
Closed Sun, Christmas and New Year's
Day

Shrimps' basic, junkshop décor fits in
neatly with print wallpaper and
matching curtains, aspiring to the
Victorian parlour look. Choose
between 14 open-face sandwiches
(£2.75–£3.50) and six large salad
plates. The smoked salmon is good;
the prawns are frozen.

Wheelchair access, also WC

Singapore Sling

503 Lawnmarket, The Royal Mile
☎ 031-226 2826

Open all week D 6 (5.30 Sat and Sun)–
11 (midnight Fri and Sat), Mon to Sat
L noon–2 (2.30 Sat)

Claims to be the only Malaysian/
Singaporean restaurant in Edinburgh,
which means that the cooking is
multi-cultural, with influences from
China and India as well as South East
Asia. Satays, coconut-based curries
and dishes such as beef rendang and
sambal goreng line up alongside hot-
and-sour Assam seafood, beef in
oyster sauce and sweet-and-sour king
prawns. Laksa soup and noodle dishes
such as mee goreng make good-value
snacks or single-dish meals.
Rambutans, mangoes and sago
pudding with palm sugar to finish.
Drink Tiger beer or try an exotic
cocktail.

Wheelchair access • Access, Amex,
Diners, Visa

Terrace Café

Royal Botanic Gardens
☎ 031-552 0616

Open all week 10am–3
Closed 3 days Christmas

The Botanic Gardens are a delight,
and the Terrace Café has the added
attraction of panoramic views over
the city skyline. Food is self-service
and a limited menu might feature
ratatouille, bean casserole and fillets
of lemon sole florentine. There are
also good-looking salads and a choice
of home-made cakes and sweets, such
as carrot cake with cream cheese
icing. Reporters have recommended
the place as a speedy venue for
a baked potato and a bottle of
Becks beer.

No smoking • Car-park • Wheelchair
access, also WC

Waterfront Wine Bar

1C Dock Place, Leith
☎ 031-554 7427

Open Mon to Sat noon–2.30 (3 Fri and
Sat), 6–9.30 (10 Fri and Sat), Sun
12.30–3
Closed Christmas Day, Boxing Day,
1 and 2 Jan

On fine days the waterside terrace
relieves the pressure at this popular
wine bar that has many charms,
including spacious conservatory and
pleasant, cosy bars. A list of some 100
wines complements the selection of
food: mussels, West Coast oysters,
hot game terrine, chargrilled lemon
sole, pigeon breasts in cherry sauce.
Sound, assured cooking; good
service.

No-smoking area • No children under 5
• Wheelchair access • Access, Visa

Whighams Wine Cellars

13 Hope Street
☎ 031-225 8674

Open Mon to Sat noon–2.30
Closed Sun

Whighams, in the centre of
Edinburgh's financial area, serves
lunch only. The besuited banking
clientele who crowd the many nooks
and crannies (best to book) enjoy a
short and keenly priced menu strong
on fresh ingredients. Seafood is a
feature – oysters, gravlax, asparagus
and langoustine tartlet –
accompanied by inventive soups,
pasta and rare roast beef.

Visa

Falkland (Fife)   map 11

Kind Kyttock's Kitchen

Cross Wynd
☎ FALKLAND (0337) 57477

Open Tue to Sun noon-5.30
Closed Mon and Christmas Eve to 3 Jan

Falkland Palace attracts the visitors,
the Dalrymples' simple restaurant
feeds them. Pleasant, efficient service,
good, plain food and low prices are
the keynotes here. Home-made
wholemeal bread accompanies
omelettes and Scotch broth and there
are baked jacket potatoes, salads and
sandwiches. An afternoon tea of
Scotch pancakes is a must.

No-smoking room • Wheelchair access •
Access, Visa

Please let us know if you think an eating
place should be included in this guide;
report forms are at the back of the book.

Fordyce (Grampian)   map 11

Hawthorne

nr Portsoy
☎ PORTSOY (0261) 43003/43911

Open Easter to summer Tue to Sun
noon–2.30, 7.30–9.30; reduced opening
in winter
Closed Mon, Christmas Day and Boxing
Day

Fordyce is a detour worth making;
the village is idyllic and Hawthorne
provides first-class quality food at low
prices. Cooking is inventive, assured
and well-balanced. Summer light
lunches include a delicious
mushroom soup, venison stew-pot,
salmon, and a selection of Scottish
cheeses. Come the evening it is still
possible to have three courses
for £10.

No smoking • Wheelchair access, also
WC • Access, Visa

Fort William
(Highland)   map 11

Crannog Seafood Restaurant ★

Town Pier
☎ FORT WILLIAM (039770) 5589/
3919

Open all week noon–2.30, 6–10

The setting is spectacular,
overhanging Loch Linnhe with
superb sea views. Opened as an outlet
for the plentiful supplies of seafood
landed by Scottish Crannog
Seafoods, the uncomplicated menu
allows the outstanding quality of the
fish to shine through. Lunch offers
the best value. A rich, fresh-tasting

bouillabaisse, smoked mussels with aïoli or moules marinière, then baked mackerel in cider sauce or mixed seafood pasta will just about do it. Fleshy, sweet langoustine in a pungent garlic butter with potatoes and a great mixed salad would make a satisfying one-course meal.

No-smoking area • Car-park • Wheelchair access, also WC • Access, Visa

---

Glasgow
(Strathclyde)   map 11

Babbity Bowster

16–18 Blackfriars Street
☎ **041-552 5055**

Open restaurant Mon to Sat noon–3 (exc Sat), 5–11.30, Sun 12.30–3.30, café-bar all week 8am–midnight (11 Sun)

The original building was designed in the eighteenth century, although there are few echoes of the past in its new incarnation as café-bar/restaurant. The splendid décor is a major attraction, with pine woodwork, beams, black blinds and red paintwork; a period fireplace is one reminder of the history of the building. Food is served in the downstairs bar and the slightly more expensive upstairs restaurant. The kitchen can be inconsistent, but there have been good reports of haggis with neeps, hot goats'-milk cheese on toast, and pan-fried pork chop with herbs. Ingredients are fresh, and simple dishes work best. Lively, raucous atmosphere.

No children under 14 in café-bar during licensing hours • Car-park • Wheelchair access • Access, Amex, Visa

Balbir's Vegetarian Ashoka

141 Elderslie Street
☎ **041-248 4407**

Open all week noon–2 (exc Sun), 5–11.30
Closed Christmas Day, New Year's Eve and New Year's Day

Balbir Sing Sumal has conquered Elderslie Street with a series of lively, popular curry houses. The vegetarian food served here is soundly cooked, served in lavish helpings and is thoroughly enjoyable, with vegetable masala, stuffed parathas and channa strongly recommended. Meat-eaters should try Balbir's Ashoka Tandoori, the original restaurant (at 108 Elderslie Street, 041-221 1761/1762).

No-smoking area • Wheelchair access • Access, Amex, Diners, Visa

---

La Bavarde

19 New Kirk Road, Bearsden
☎ **041-942 2202**

Open Tue to Sat noon–1.30, 6.30–9.30
Closed Sun, Mon, last 3 weeks July and 2 weeks Christmas

Bread is made on the premises daily and pasta and chutneys are also home-made. There is a solid dedication to realistic prices and the £6 three-course lunch menu is great value. Pigeon and date pie, tripe Italian-style, tagliatelle al pomodoro, grilled herrings with oatmeal and roast ham spare ribs leap over established culinary frontiers. Dinner is more expensive.

Wheelchair access • Access, Amex, Diners, Visa

See the back of the guide for an index of eating-places and an index of locations.

Café Gandolfi

64 Albion Street
☎ 041-552 6813

Open Mon to Sat 9am–11.30pm
Closed Sun

In a converted, wood-panelled Victorian pub in the newly revived Merchant City, this attractive, bistro-type café serves some enjoyable dishes. Prepare for mixed-bean salad with tofu dressing, mixed-bean salad with blue cheese dressing and choux pastry stuffed with Stilton. If none of this appeals, the menu also offers New York pastrami on rye, cold baked Cumbrian ham with pease pudding, smoked venison with gratin dauphinois, marinated herring and potato salad, and Finnan haddock and potatoes. For dessert try papaya or mango fruit salad. An excellent 'good morning menu' features cheese or ham on an Italian roll.

Wheelchair access

Café Qui

Cochrane Street
☎ 041-552 6099

Open all week 10am–10.30pm
Closed Christmas Day and New Year's Day

Glasgow's new Italian Centre encompasses a superbly decorated, spacious restaurant producing a wide range of popular Italian dishes for lunch and dinner. Quality ingredients go into minestrone, tagliatelle, spaghetti bolognese and pizza, all offered at affordable prices. The upstairs café – open all day – is more informal with a shorter menu of Italian breads, pizza and pasta.

Access, Amex, Diners, Visa

Café Rogano

11 Exchange Place
☎ 041-248 4055/4913

Open Mon to Sat noon–11 (midnight Fri and Sat)
Closed Sun and bank hols

A fine art deco building is the splendid setting for the Rogano restaurant and its inexpensive café offshoot. The latter is open all day for food such as poached mussels, Cullen skink, casserole of lambs' kidneys, mushrooms and sausages, cod, salmon and oyster pie or spinach and peanut lasagne.

Access, Amex, Diners, Visa

Loon Fung

417 Sauchiehall Street
☎ 041-332 1240

Open all week noon–11.30

Excellent dim-sum are the highlights for affordable eating in this spacious restaurant at the top end of Sauchiehall Street. A good choice might include steamed beef dumplings with ginger and spring onion, stuffed duck's web and chicken meat with whole baby corn wrapped in a skin of dried bean curd. Sweet lotus buns and slabs of jelly-like water-chestnut cake make an unusual finish. The full menu has esoteric Cantonese specialities as well as more familiar items such as fried squid with green pepper and black-bean sauce. Portions are impressively generous. Drink tea or Chinese beer.

Access, Amex, Visa

Out to Eat has been compiled in the same way as *The Good Food Guide* and is based on reports from consumers and backed up by annonymous inspections.

Mother India's

1138 Argyle Street
☎ 041-337 1157

Open Mon to Sat noon–10
Closed Sun

The owners pride themselves on
serving traditional Indian food at
affordable prices. Four different
curries are the mainstay of the short
menu; karahi dishes are prepared
from scratch and there is a good-
value thali for £3.95. The 'Indian
breakfast' – served all day – is halva,
dhal and home-made yoghurt served
with puris (£3.50). Minestrone soup
and chicken Maryland are reminders
that this is a café for all-comers.

Unlicensed, but bring your own: no
corkage • Wheelchair access

Ubiquitous Chip

12 Ashton Lane
☎ 041-334 5007

Open all week noon–11
Closed Christmas Day and 31 Dec

Omnipresent the chip is not! While
avoiding the use of the fried potato,
the Chip manages to be all things to a
great swathe of Glasgow life. This
huge, plant-filled converted
warehouse is home to both a
restaurant and the Upstairs bar. The
latter offers keenly priced, soundly
cooked dishes of vegetarian haggis
with neeps and tatties, rare roast
Scotch beef, Perthshire pheasant
casserole, herring in oatmeal and
spicy sausage Creole. The use of
prime ingredients shows in just the
simplest things – satisfying home-
made soups and mild Mull of Kintyre
truckle cheddar.

Access, Amex, Diners, Visa

Willow Tea Room

217 Sauchiehall Street
☎ 041-332 0521

Open Mon to Sat 9.30am–4.30
Closed Sun

The Willow Tea Room of 1904–28
was lovingly restored to the original
design of Charles Rennie Mackintosh
in the early '80s. The present tea-
room, a triumph of art nouveau
design, is filled with reproduction
Mackintosh furniture. Open for
breakfast, light lunches of baked
potato, toasted sandwiches and
lasagne as well as delicious, old-
fashioned afternoon tea.

Unlicensed

Helmsdale
(Highland)   map 11

La Mirage

7–9 Dunrobin Street
☎ HELMSDALE (043 12) 615

Open all week noon–8.45

A warm, if eccentric, oasis in this
frozen fishing port. Barbara Cartland
takes a local cottage in the summer
and owner Nancy Sinclair is a devout
acolyte. White garden furniture
surrounds a papier-mâché tree and
further fake-vegetation is provided by
baskets of silk flowers under a slowly
revolving fan. Not quite as much
attention has been lavished on the
food, which is standard and, on the
whole, adequate. Many dishes come
deep-fried. To finish, succumb to the
home-baked scones and shortbread
rather than the standard desserts.

No-smoking room • Wheelchair access,
also WC

Invermoriston
(Highland)   map 11

Glenmoriston Arms

☎ GLENMORISTON (0320) 51206

On A82 5m N of Fort Augustus

Open all week noon–2, 6.30–8.30

Disillusioned Loch Ness monster-spotters should repair to the Glenmoriston Arms, where a spot of malt whisky sampling should prove more rewarding. Bar snacks include the inevitable haggis as well as poached wild salmon, venison in red wine, and gammon and steak pie served with chips or baked potato. Food is tasty and exceptionally cheap.

Garden • Car-park • Wheelchair access, also WC • Access, Visa

Inverness (Highland) map 11

Nico's Bistro

Glen Mhor Hotel, 9–12 Ness Road
☎ INVERNESS (0463) 234308

Open all week noon–2.15, 5–9.30

A cosmopolitan bistro in a traditionally run hotel situated on the riverbank below the castle. The menu mixes Scottish specialities with Continental and American favourites. Haggis, mussel soup, Arbroath smokies and venison casserole co-exist with hamburgers, shepherd's pie and pasta. Short wine list. Useful for the area.

No-smoking area • Wheelchair access • Access, Amex, Diners, Visa

All letters to this guide are acknowledged.

Kilberry
(Strathclyde)   map 11

Kilberry Inn ★ ⊛

☎ ORMSARY (088 03) 223

16m from Tarbert along B8024

Open all week 12.15–1.45, 8–8.45 (exc Sun D)
Closed mid-Oct to Good Fri (exc New Year)

A converted croft which is now probably a contender for the most out-of-the-way pub in Scotland – reached after 16 miles of single-track road! Lovely scenery, especially the views on to the island of Gigha, relieves the drive, and the food at journey's end is well worth the trip. John Leadbeater provides a warm welcome, aided on cold days by a peat fire at one end of the bar, a log-burning stove at the other. His wife Kathy cooks. The menu changes constantly and only the very best ingredients are used, but the Leadbeaters' most famous dishes are country sausage pie made with apples cooked in cider, and hot chocolate fudge cake. Bread, jams and chutneys are all home-made.

Family-room • Car-park • Wheelchair access, also WC • Access, Visa

Kilfinan (Strathclyde) map 11

Kilfinan Hotel

nr Tighnabruaich
☎ KILFINAN (0700 82) 201

Open all week noon–2, 7.30–9

This remote coaching-inn on a single-track country lane next to the church is strong on old-fashioned hospitality, with log fires, home comforts and a very personable welcome from the proprietor. Lunchtime bar meals might feature home-made soup, herrings in oatmeal, vegetable curry and steak and kidney pie, with ice-cream or Pavlova to finish. Full meals in the restaurant will take the bill well beyond our £10 limit. Decent house wine and draught beer in the bar.

Garden • Car-park • Wheelchair access, also WC • Access, Amex, Visa

Killiecrankie
(Tayside)   map 11

Killiecrankie Hotel

Pass of Killiecrankie, by Pitlochry
☎ PITLOCHRY (0796) 3220

Open all week 12.30–2, 6.30–9.30
Closed mid-Nov to late Feb

Refurbishment of the bar area has made it an even more comfortable spot in which to enjoy some excellent bar food. Lunch is strong on light choices, of home-cooked Ayrshire ham salad, fresh salmon salad, or an Angus beef open sandwich. Highland game casserole, Scottish lamb chops or local trout in oatmeal feature for supper. Finish with tipsy laird trifle.

Garden • Car-park • Wheelchair access, also WC • Access, Visa

A restaurant manager can't insist on people not smoking, unless it's specifically a no-smoking restaurant or a no-smoking area. If it is, smokers could be asked to leave if they don't stop. If in doubt, check beforehand what the smoking arrangements are.

Lanark (Strathclyde)   map 9

East India Company

32 Wellgate
☎ LANARK (0555) 3827

Open all week noon–2, 5.30–11.30

A simple but tastefully decorated Indian restaurant, specialising mainly in North Indian cooking. Meat and fish are of sound quality and, combined with freshly ground spices and fresh green herbs, produce satisfying tandoori lamb kebab, chicken korma and a spicy prawn jalfrezi. There are nans of all varieties and Kingfisher beer.

No-smoking area • Wheelchair access, also WC • Access, Amex, Visa

Largs (Strathclyde)   map 11

Nardini's

Esplanade
☎ LARGS (0475) 674555

Open all week noon–8.30 (10 Thur to Sun)
Closed Christmas Day

Nardini's has been in Largs for 55 years and visiting this restaurant/ cafeteria is like stepping back in time. Nothing has really changed, and the solid, old-fashioned concept of Scottish high teas of haddock or liver, bacon and tomato, both at £5.25, are as popular as the fresh pasta, home-made cakes, gâteaux and the outstanding Nardini ice-cream.

No-smoking area • Car-park • Wheelchair access, also WC • Access, Visa

Linlithgow
(Lothian)   map 11

Champany Inn Chop and Ale House
Champany Corner
☎ PHILPSTOUN **(0506) 834532**

2 miles NE of Linlithgow just off M9
junction 3, corner of A803/A904

*Open all week noon (12.30 Sun)–2
(2.30 Sun), 6.30 (6 Sat)–10
Closed 2 weeks from Christmas Eve*

Housed in the same sixteenth-
century building as the renowned
Champany restaurant, the inn offers
simpler food in plainer surroundings.
Great attention to detail means that
specially reared grain-fed chicken is
spit-roasted to maximise flavour,
Scottish lamb is cooked on the bone,
and hamburgers and sausages are
home-made. Prime Angus steaks are
pricey but exceptional.

*Car-park • Wheelchair access • Access,
Amex, Diners, Visa*

Newcastleton
(Borders)   map 9

Copshaw Kitchen
4 North Hermitage Street
☎ LIDDESDALE **(038 73) 75250**

Off A7 on B6357 17m S of Hawick

*Open Mar to Dec Wed to Mon 9.30am–
6, 7.30–9.15 (exc D Sun and Mon)
Closed Tue, Jan and Feb*

Simple, homely food is on offer at
this unpretentious, informal tea-
room. Fresh, filling soup comes with
barley fadge (Scottish wholemeal
bread), and there are home-made

beefburgers, lasagne, omelettes and
sausage rolls. Excellent baking
produces scones, rock buns,
shortbread and cream cakes. Booking
is essential for dinner in the
restaurant.

*Car-park • Wheelchair access, also WC
• Access, Visa*

Peebles (Borders)   map 9

Sunflower
4 Bridgegate
☎ PEEBLES **(0721) 22420**

*Open Mon to Sat 9.15am–5.30, 7.30–9
(exc Mon D)
Closed Sun, Christmas Day and New
Year's Day, D Tue to Thur Oct to
Easter*

Having shed the constraint of
vegetarianism, the food here has
become more interesting and
ambitious. Seating is a wee bit
cramped. There are about half a
dozen choices at each stage of the
three-course menu: you may find
pumpkin rarebit soup, mushrooms
and peppers in warm sherry vinegar
or spiced pork with lime pickle to
start. To follow, try the cassoulet
containing baby black puddings or
the beef stew with orange, rather
than the lemon sole with apple and
cider. Prices are keen and the wine
list is fair. Snacks are served all day.

*No-smoking area • Wheelchair access,
also WC*

All details are as accurate as possible at the
time of going to press, but chefs and
owners often change, and it is wise to
check by telephone before making a
special journey.

Perth (Tayside)   map 11

Brown's Coffee Parlour

67 George Street
☎ PERTH (0738) 32693

Open all week 10am–6

The word 'homely' springs to mind
the minute you walk through the
door. Popular with shoppers for
coffee, cake and light snacks, Brown's
ambitions rise no further than that.
Sandwiches, lasagne, chicken pie,
quiche and various salad
combinations are generous and well-
priced. This is the place to go in
Perth for enormous cups of strong
espresso.

Unlicensed

Timothy's

St John Street
☎ PERTH (0738) 26641

Open Tue to Sun noon–2.30, 7–10.15
Closed Mon and 3 weeks summer

For more than two decades, the
Laings' town-centre restaurant has
maintained its own distinctive style.
The menu is built around Danish-
inspired 'snitters' (starters) and
'smorrebrod' (open sandwiches), but
it looks far beyond Scandinavia for
inspiration. Snitters might feature
asparagus roll-ups, or curried eggs
with prawns. The list of 'smorrebrod'
takes in prawns and chicken with
sesame seeds and Oriental sauce;
Russian Rubies (ham with beetroot
and sour cream); and roast beef with
horseradish and mushroom salad.
Mixed platters, salads and ice-cream
sweets complete the picture.

Wheelchair access • Access, Visa

Port Appin
(Strathclyde)   map 11

Airds Hotel

☎ APPIN (063 173) 236

Off A828 N of Oban on E shore of Loch
Linnhe

Open all week L 12.30–1.30

The thought of a splendid scenic
drive followed by a simple lunch of
soup and sandwiches in one of the
most perfect settings in Scotland is
hard to resist. This welcoming early
eighteenth-century hotel, formerly a
ferry inn, offers just that, nothing
more. Soup could be pea and mint,
sandwiches are freshly prepared to
order and there is ice-cream to finish.
Lunch and dinner (8pm–8.30pm, one
sitting) in the restaurant are more
expensive.

Rhiconich
(Highland)   map 11

Old School Restaurant

Inshegra
☎ KINLOCHBERVIE (097 182) 383

On B801 midway between Rhiconich and
Kinlochbervie

Open all week noon–2, 6–8

There is an acute shortage of
restaurants in this far corner of the
British mainland, but this former
Victorian schoolhouse helps to fill a
gap. Roasts, casseroles and locally
caught fish prepared in a homely
manner epitomise the style. There is
a vegetarian menu of savoury
pancakes and lentil crumble.

Delicious bread-and-butter pudding to finish.

Unlicensed • Garden • Car-park • Wheelchair access, also WC • Access, Visa

---

Selkirk (Borders) map 9

Philipburn House Hotel

☎ SELKIRK (0750) 20747

Open all week L noon–2.30

A pleasantly converted, eighteenth-century, baronial-style country house, with fine grounds and an attractive poolside restaurant. Lunch offers some excellent and keenly priced dishes: well-made cream of asparagus soup, home-made bread, haggis and whisky pancake, lamb and apricot pie, delicious fish-cakes. Spotted dick or giant cream meringues to finish. Breakfast, morning coffee and afternoon teas are also available.

No-smoking area • No children under 5 after 7.30pm • Garden • Car-park • Wheelchair access, also WC • Access, Amex, Diners, Visa

---

Stromness (Orkney) map 11

Ferry Inn

John Street
☎ STROMNESS (0856) 850280

Open all week noon–2, 6–9.30

The mahogany-clad lounge bar resembles the inside of a schooner, complementing the fine harbour views. Generous bar food includes Stromness marinated herring, Orkney pâté, a daily roast and minute steak. There is a selection of Orkney cheeses and clootie dumpling and cream for dessert. Espresso coffee is a welcome sight.

Wheelchair access, also WC • Access, Visa

Ullapool (Highland) map 11

Ceilidh Place

14 West Argyle Street
☎ ULLAPOOL (0854) 2103

Open all week noon–6.30, 7–9

Possibly all things to all men – a hotel, restaurant, coffee-shop, bookshop, arts centre – the name means 'meeting place'. The coffee-shop is popular, the service stressed when too busy, but it is a lively, informal, laid-back sort of place offering home-made soup, stovies (lamb, potatoes and onions), local crab, fish pie, sandwiches or filled rolls and home-baked cakes. Dinners are more expensive.

Garden • Car-park • Wheelchair access • Access, Amex, Diners, Visa

---

See the front of the guide for a list of each eating-place given a star for being one of the best found by the Editor during research for this book.

WALES

Aberaeron (Dyfed)   map 6

Hive on the Quay ★

Cadwgan Place
☎ ABERAERON (0545) 570445

Open all week noon–2, 6–9 (D July and Aug only)
Closed end Sept to spring bank hol

Aptly named because this seasonal eating place in a converted coal-wharf by the quay is owned and run by the Holgate family – of honey fame. Their loyalty to local and organic produce is impressive. Lunch is a buffet featuring soup, salads, wholemeal bread with farmhouse cheeses (including organic Pencarreg), pickled mackerel, ham and pâté, followed by fruit pies and speciality honey ice-creams. During July and August there are dinners, with dishes such as vegetable hot-pot, grilled Welsh lamb with laverbread sauce, and fresh crab tartlets. Children, quite rightly, get a mini-menu of real home-cooked food. Beers, cider and wines (including some organics) to drink.

Wheelchair access

Aberdovey
(Gwynedd)   map 6

Old Coffee Shop

13 New Street
☎ ABERDOVEY (065 472) 652

Open Tue to Sun 9.30am–6 (10–5 winter)
Closed Mon (exc high summer)

Susan Griffiths' friendly daytime coffee-shop near the sea prides itself on good home-cooking and fresh ingredients. Through the day there are snacks, sandwiches and all manner of home-baked cakes and pastries to go with tea or coffee. Lunch brings salads and quiches in summer, replaced in winter by substantial hot dishes such as beef bourguignonne, braised pheasant, cottage pie and vegetarian chilli pancakes. Excellent home-made meringues with strawberries or cheesecake to finish. Sunday lunch is a splendid roast.

Unlicensed, but bring your own: corkage £2.50 • No smoking

Penhelig Arms Hotel

☎ ABERDOVEY (065 472) 215

Open all week noon– 2, 7–9.30
Closed Christmas Day

A much-loved harbourside inn which offers some excellent-value dishes for lunch. Sunday lunch of various roasts and lashings of vegetables is a bargain you must book for. For the rest of the week there are well-made soup, a light spinach and prawn roulade, home-baked ham, chicken in a cumin-flavoured cream sauce, and plaice in cheese sauce. Make room for desserts.

Car-park • Wheelchair access, also WC (ladies only) • Access, Visa

When you book a restaurant table, you're making a contract with the restaurant and you must be given a table, within reasonable time of your arrival. If not, the restaurant is in breach of contract and you can claim a reasonable sum to cover any expenses you had as a result, e.g. travelling expenses.

Aberystwyth (Dyfed) map 6

Corners

21 Chalybeate Street
☎ ABERYSTWYTH (0970) 611024

Open Tue to Sat 10–5, 7–9.30
Closed Sun and Mon

The Reynolds combine wholesome, all-day eating with substantial lunch and dinner menus. Inside this centrally located, former corner shop, the staff are friendly and the service is efficient. In the kitchen they will be preparing pork with a leek and Stilton sauce or even nut and vegetable roast with a peanut sauce. Cardigan Bay crab salad makes an occasional appearance while vegetarian dishes feature regularly. Soups are good.

Wheelchair access • Access, Visa

Bangor (Gwynedd) map 6

La Bella Vita

166 High Street
☎ BANGOR (0248) 362920

Open all week noon–2.15 (exc Sun),
6–9.15 (5–9.45 Fri and Sat)
Closed Mon winter

A small, modest Italian-style restaurant. Both pizza dough and pasta are made on the premises and you should stick to these choices if you are aiming to keep the bill below £10. The menu holds no surprises, offering well-known pasta combinations and pizza toppings, but portions are generous. Italian ice-cream and espresso coffee to finish.

No-smoking area

Betws-y-Coed
(Gwynedd) map 6

Ty Gwyn Hotel ◉

☎ BETWS-Y-COED (0690) 710383

100 yds S of Waterloo Bridge on A5

Open all week noon–2, 7–9.30

Happily placed on the outskirts of the tourist-swamped village, this charming seventeenth-century inn has a further barrier against the madding crowd – the terms of its licence state that drinkers either eat here or stay overnight. Each small room is antique-strewn, boasting a hoard of knick-knacks, prints, rugs, cushions, and a display of chairs and tables. Customers in the know head for the freshly made, well-prepared bar food rather than the more expensive restaurant. It is standard bar fare of generous portions using good prime ingredients: gammon is thickly sliced, venison sausages are meaty; there are a good selection of fish, a rich lasagne and home-made soups. Children are made welcome with smaller portions and kindly attention.

Car-park • Wheelchair access, also WC
• Access, Visa

Borth-y-Gest
(Gwynedd) map 6

Blossoms

4 Ivy Terrace
☎ Porthmadog (0766) 513500

Open Mon to Sat noon–2, 7–10
Closed Sun and winter Mon and Tue

An informal 'take us as you find us' harbour-front bistro where most tastes are catered for, including vegetarian. The lunch menu offers a range of affordable snacks from soup and garlic bread to filled baked potatoes, pasta, garlic mushrooms and spaghetti bolognese. There are salads and wholemeal sandwiches too. The evening menu is more pricey.

No-smoking area • Access, Visa

Broad Haven
(Dyfed)   map 6

Druidstone Hotel
☎ BROAD HAVEN (0437) 781221

Open all week 12.30–2.30, 7.30–10

'We like natural food, ale, people, gardens and animals,' say Rod and Jane Bell, who run this much-liked hotel overlooking the sea. Light lunches in the cellar bar are especially popular with families. Home-made terrine, 'old-fashioned' hot-pot, vegetable chilli and leek and mushroom pancakes are typical of the menu. To finish, there are ice-creams and fruit tarts. More expensive meals with exotic overtones are served in the restaurant. Reasonably priced wines.

Garden • Car-park • Wheelchair access, also WC • Amex, Visa

Out to Eat has been compiled in the same way as *The Good Food Guide* and is based on reports from consumers and backed up by anonymous inspections.

Cardiff (S Glamorgan)   map 6

Bo Zan
78 Albany Road
☎ CARDIFF (0222) 493617

Open all week noon–1.45 (exc Sun and Mon), 6–11.30
Closed Christmas Day and Boxing Day

Bo Zan specialises in Szechuan cooking but includes the most popular Peking and Cantonese dishes among its 80-plus choices. Hot and spicy dishes are asterisked. Prices have increased with the doubling in size of the dining-room and it is best to go in a group to ensure a decent selection within a reasonable budget.

Wheelchair access • Access, Amex, Diners, Visa

La Brasserie
60 St Mary Street
☎ CARDIFF (0222) 372164

Open Mon to Sat noon–2.30, 7–12.15am
Closed Sun

Out of the same mould and in the same street as Champers and Le Monde (see entries). For eating out in Cardiff this trio of wine bars offers the liveliest atmosphere and best value. Chargrilled meats and fish are backed up by dressed crab, suckling pig and baked mussels. The extensive list of well-priced wines covers the major French growing regions.

Access, Amex, Diners, Visa

Champers

61 St Mary Street
☎ CARDIFF (0222) 373363

Open all week noon–2.30 (exc Sun),
7–12.15am

There are two good reasons for
visiting Champers: to indulge in the
marvellous Riojas, many by the glass,
and to experience the first-class
chargrilled steaks. The bodega-style
wine bar runs on the sound Spanish
principle of serving great chunks of
meat. Salads, garlic bread and cheeses
back up the menu and the fresh fish is
highly recommended. No desserts.

Access, Amex, Diners, Visa

Crumbs

33 Morgan Arcade
☎ CARDIFF (0222) 395007

Open Mon to Sat 9.30am–3
Closed Sun

Judi and Dave Ashley recently
celebrated 20 years of trading in their
tiny vegetarian café. Salads are the
speciality: there is usually a selection
of six, served in wooden bowls along
with dressings and mayonnaise.
Home-made vegetable soup is served
in winter. There is a selection of
juices to drink.

Unlicensed • No-smoking area •
Wheelchair access

Chapter Kitchen

Market Street
☎ CARDIFF (0222) 372756

Open all week 10am (11.30 Sun)–9

The Chapter Arts Centre houses two
cinemas, a theatre and an art gallery
as well as two lively bars. The
Kitchen café, with its solid pine
tables, occupies most of the foyer.
Lunches centre on healthy wholefood
dishes with a vegetarian bias: soups,
jacket potatoes, stuffed aubergines,
vegetable lasagne and pizzas typify
the range. Carrot cake, flapjacks and
chocolate brownies are available all
day to go with coffee or herbal tea.
There is also a choice of wines and
juices.

Wheelchair access, also WC

Everest

43–5 Salisbury Road, Cathays
☎ CARDIFF (0222) 374881

Open all week noon–2.30 (exc Sun),
6–midnight

Highly regarded as one of the most
civilised Indian restaurants in Cardiff
– despite its austere exterior of blue
engineering bricks. Inside, it is plush
and modern, with carved wooden
screens, Indian photographs and
linen cloths on the tables. The menu
does not change, but dishes are
always distinctive and freshly spiced.
Look for the tandoori shashlik kebab
and the memorable lamb pasanda.
Details such as vegetables and breads
are well up to the mark. Best value
for vegetarians and meat-eaters are
the thalis. Drink lager.

Wheelchair access • Access, Amex,
Diners

Indian Ocean

290 North Road
☎ CARDIFF (0222) 621152/621349

Open all week noon–2.30 (exc Sun),
6–11.30

A tandoori restaurant whose pleasant, smart décor is not reflected in steep prices. Ingredients used are of a high quality and the subsequent careful spicing is such that a well-constructed lamb pasanda or tandoori chicken maintains the subtle balance between the meat flavour and the spices. Service is excellent.

Wheelchair access, also WC • Access,
Amex, Diners, Visa

Le Monde

60 St Mary Street
☎ CARDIFF (0222) 387376

Open Mon to Sat noon–3, 7–12.15am
Closed Sun, Christmas Day and New
Year's Day

Above La Brasserie and next door to Champers, a sister restaurant to both (see entries). By 8.30pm on most evenings there is a long wait for tables. This is primarily a fish restaurant: squid, scallops, mussels and oysters precede fresh grilled fish (sold by the pound). Chargrilled meats are also available. Chips from chip shop-like ranges – the kitchen is on full view.

No children under 10 • Access, Amex,
Diners, Visa

All letters to this guide are acknowledged.

Pepper Mill Diner

173 Kings Road, Canton
☎ CARDIFF (0222) 382476

Open Mon to Sat noon–2 (exc Sat),
6–9.30 (10.30 Fri and Sat)
Closed Sun, Christmas Eve to Boxing
Day and New Year's Day

The only Mexican cantina in Cardiff. Popular with vegetarians for the many unusual meatless dishes and popular with all for the comfortable surroundings and fresh, enterprising cooking. There are spinach and cheese enchiladas, chimichangas in meat or vegetarian versions, re-fried beans and corn chips. Desserts include a rich, dark and powerfully flavoured chocolate cake.

Garden • Wheelchair access, also WC •
Access, Visa

Tandoor Ghar

134 Whitchurch Road
☎ CARDIFF (0222) 615746

Open Sun L noon–2.30, Mon to Sat D
6–midnight (1am Fri and Sat)
Closed Christmas Day and Boxing Day

No artificial colours or preservatives, readily used in many other curry houses, are used here, so that a chicken tikka masala takes you by surprise with its unfamiliar brown colour. Dishes are carefully cooked to order from a short, well-explained menu, with spicing handled with great subtlety. Try the undyed pilau rice (other tandooris please note).

No-smoking area • Wheelchair access,
also WC • Access, Amex, Diners, Visa

Topoli

218 City Road
☎ CARDIFF **(0222) 494922**

Open all week noon–2 (2.30 Sun),
6–11.30 (12.30am Fri and Sat)
Closed Christmas Day, Boxing Day and
New Year's Day

As in Greece, you have the opportunity of inspecting the kitchen before you eat – by virtue of the fact that the entrance to the dining-room is through the kitchen. The chef is likely to welcome you personally. The menu here is wide-ranging, inexpensive and reasonably appealing to vegetarians. The meze, available as a starter or a main course, contains the usual. An unusual first course is maigo: king prawns wrapped in whole-grain mustard and bacon. Avoid the vegetable kebab, but indulge in the 'tropical kebab' – this is pork off the bone with onions and cooked in a light tomato, coconut and pineapple sauce (£5.75). Otherwise, the chicken garlic kebabs (marinated chicken grilled with garlic, white wine and yoghurt) should do the trick. There is a choice of four house wines.

Access, Amex, Diners, Visa

Welsh National Opera Restaurant

Princess of Wales Building, John Street
☎ CARDIFF **(0222) 464666**

Open Mon to Fri L 12.30–2.15

At lunchtimes, the WNO canteen, on the first floor of the company's head office, provides some of the best-value healthy food in Cardiff. The serve-yourself counter tempts an eccentric mix of regulars – local businessmen, shoppers, opera stars –

with salads, soups and two hot dishes per day. An excellent vegetarian venue.

No-smoking area

Carmarthen (Dyfed)   map 6

Waverley

23 Lammas Street
☎ CARMARTHEN **(0267) 236430**

Open Mon to Sat 11am–3
Closed Sun

This is a wholefood vegetarian restaurant behind a health-food shop and health-care centre. Queues form at the serving counter at peak times, but service is friendly. The choice of up to a dozen freshly made dishes includes vegetarian soup, casseroles, curries and quiches, backed up by salads. There is also a decent selection of sweets. Ingredients are organic where possible. Evening bookings for parties only.

No smoking • Wheelchair access •
Access, Visa

Clydach (Gwent)   map 6

Rock and Fountain Inn

☎ GILWERN **(087 383) 0393**

Open all week noon–2, 7 (4 summer)–
1am (summer all day Sat)
Closed Christmas Day evening

Peter Adams has transformed this aptly named out-of-the-way pub into a relaxed and imaginative hostelry offering an extensive, enterprising menu. The food is well worth a detour. Both a bar and a restaurant menu are available and you can mix and match *and* choose to eat in either room. The restaurant is pretty, with stripped-stone walls, flowers, candles and even a natural waterfall. Bar food prices are low, with lasagne, steak pie and Highland gammon steak in whisky sauce, enlivened perhaps by some unusual restaurant starters – monkfish in a beer batter, deep-fried local goats'-milk cheese. However, the more ambitious, fanciful dishes do not always work.

No-smoking area • Family-room • Car-park • Wheelchair access, also WC (men) • Access, Visa

Criccieth (Gwynedd) map 6

Blue China Tearooms

Lon Felin
☎ CRICCIETH (0766) 523239

Open all week 10am–6
Closed Jan

Spectacularly situated right on the seafront, just below the ruins of Criccieth Castle. There are views across Cardigan Bay from the sheltered garden outside. Home baking is the star attraction; scones come with home-made jam, otherwise there might be all kinds of cakes and tea breads. Salads appear in summer; soup and nourishing hot dishes in winter. Seasonal dishes are advertised to take away around Christmas-time. Unlicensed, but the tea is loose-leafed.

Unlicensed • Garden

Please let us know if you think an eating-place should be included in this guide; report forms are at the back of the book.

Crickhowell (Powys) map 6

Bear Hotel

Brecon Road
☎ CRICKHOWELL (0873) 810408

Open all week noon–2, 6.30–10

An inviting-looking town-centre coaching-inn that rewards curiosity with its good bar food. Shepherd's pie, chicken pie, cheese and asparagus pancake or steaks are fairly typical choices from a largely conservative menu, but by using fresh, prime ingredients, honest cooking skills and attractive presentation the level of these standard bar dishes is raised high. A simple lasagne is made memorable by the use of prime ground beef, a well-made sauce and the accompanying crisp, mixed leaf salad and good dressing. Spiced chickpea, parsnip and cashew-nut bake represents a small choice of vegetarian dishes. Puddings are a must.

Garden and family-room • Car-park • Wheelchair access, also WC • Access, Amex, Diners, Visa

Cynwyd (Clwyd) map 6

Fron Goch Farmhouse Kitchen

☎ LLANDRILLO (049 084) 418

On B4401 Corwen–Bala road 1¹/₂m S of Cynwyd

Open all week noon–2.30 (Oct to May weekdays bookings only), D 7.30 (bookings only) exc Tue

Sarah Stille runs an excellent, if remote, farmhouse kitchen well worth a detour for the view of the Upper Dee Valley and the food. A white Aga dominates the room, a dresser is loaded with her own marmalade and local honey, while bread and scones straight out of the oven are piled on a table. The hens roaming in the field outside provide eggs for baking and making omelettes. Some herbs and vegetables are grown in the garden. The menu is deliberately simple to keep the standard high, and freshness is highlighted by the seasonal emphasis on some of her cooking. Stop any time during the day for scones, sponge cake, or more substantial soup, home-baked ham and salad or a light quiche.

Garden • Car-park

Dinas Mawddwy
(Gwynedd)   map 6

Old Station Coffee Shop
☎ DINAS MAWDDWY (065 04) 338

On A470 1m N of junction with A458 at Mallwyd

Open all week 9.30am–5
Closed mid-Nov to mid-Mar

Eileen Minter's highly rated coffee-shop is in a converted station at the entrance to Meirion Woollen Mill – a local tourist attraction. The building is of solid greystone and slate, with tiny window lights, pine furniture and baskets of dried flowers decorating the walls. Nourishing home cooking is the order of the day, with bowls of hot soup, jacket potatoes, slabs of wholemeal pizzas and excellent fruity bara brith (Welsh fruit loaf). The place is noted for its cheese scones. There is a good range

of speciality and herb teas; wine and beer with meals only.

No smoking • Garden • Car-park • Wheelchair access, also WC

East Aberthaw
(S Glamorgan)   map 6

Blue Anchor
☎ ST ATHAN (044 675) 0329

Open all week noon–2.15

A convivial thatch- and creeper-covered pub whose interior offers a maze of thick-walled, low–beamed rooms. A brisk estuary walk is necessary to do justice to the well-cooked lunches served in the bar. It is simple and satisfying food, based on pub stalwarts such as steak and kidney pie, cauliflower cheese with bacon, a roast of the day and salads of crab, salmon or beef.

Garden • Car-park • Wheelchair access, also WC • Access, Visa

Glanwydden
(Gwynedd)   map 6

Queen's Head ★
nr Llandudno Junction
☎ ABERCONWY (0492) 546570

Open all week noon–2, 7–9

This village inn serves outstanding, home-made food with the in-built advantage of home-grown produce enhanced by well-chosen local supplies. A confident and exceedingly long menu often includes delights like green lip mussels served with a warm anchovy butter, smoked fillets of trout and crab salad with new potatoes. Apart from fish and seafood, a regular triumph is Welsh lamb. While the wine list is sufficient, a pint from the bar is an appropriate accompaniment.

No children under 7 • Car-park • Wheelchair access, also WC • Access, Visa

Goodwick (Dyfed)   map 6

Farmhouse Kitchen

Glendower Square
☎ FISHGUARD (0348) 873282

Open Tue to Sat 10.30–3.30, Sun noon–2, all week D 7–9.30 (exc winter Mon)
Closed 2 days after Christmas, 2 days at New Year

The Harveys deliver uncomplicated, honest home cooking in their deliberately rustic restaurant decked out with pottery, plants and coarse-weave carpeting. Lunches are exceptional value: around £6 will pay for three full courses such as farmhouse pâté, Welsh lamb hot-pot or chicken pie, with cheese or Upton Farm ice-cream to finish. The full menu, which caters well for vegetarians, is still affordable: lamb steak with gooseberry sauce and cod in celery cream sauce show the style. Sandwiches, snacks and afternoon teas are also available. Good-value wines.

Garden • Wheelchair access

See the front of the guide for a list of each eating-place given a star for being one of the best found by the Editor during research for this book.

Tate's Brasserie

Bay View House, Main Street
☎ FISHGUARD (0348) 874190

Open all week Easter to Nov noon–2, 7–9.30, Dec to Easter Mon to Wed and Sun D 7–9.30
Closed Nov to Easter (exc bookings)

Convenient for the Fishguard–Rosslare ferry, and justifiably popular. This is an inventive restaurant, specialising in seafood. The set menu has also offered the likes of 'African beef stew' (casseroled with peanuts and spices) and caramelised rabbit (wild rabbit cooked with orange). Thursday is Bistro Night: three courses of French food with wine for under £10. There is a casual, friendly, rustic atmosphere and an open fire in winter. A comprehensive children's menu is usually available.

Wheelchair access

Harlech (Gwynedd)   map 6

Llew Glas

Plas-y-goits, High Street
☎ HARLECH (0766) 780700

Open all week 11.30am–5
Closed Boxing Day and New Year's Day

An old stone bakery that is still just that, and more – a delicatessen, tea-room and restaurant. The latter is more expensive, though it has an imaginative £8.75 three-course Sunday lunch. The tea-room provides soup with flavour, unusual pies served with salads and fresh bread and some sound baking, as well as good speciality ice-creams.

Access, Visa

Yr Ogof

High Street
☎ HARLECH **(0766) 780888**

*Open all week Easter to Oct and Wed to
Sat Nov to Easter D 7 (5 school hols)–10
Closed Nov to Easter Sun to Tue*

Yr Ogof means 'the cave' and this
cheerful, stone-walled bistro is set
under some shops close to Harlech
Castle. The long blackboard menu of
soups, crêpes, steaks and salads is
backed up by an enterprising list of
daily specials with an international
flavour: Brazilian cod in coconut-
milk, tagliatelle verdi, chicken tikka
masala, spare ribs with sweet-and-
sour sauce. Vegetarians do well with
spinach crêpes and Stilton sauce,
bulgar wheat and walnut casserole
and bean goulash. Two courses are
usually sufficient for most appetites.
A children's menu is available until
6.30pm in the summer holidays.

Access, Visa

Haverfordwest

(Dyfed) map 6

Jemima's

Freystrop
☎ HAVERFORDWEST **(0437) 891109**

*Open all week (exc Sat) noon–2
Closed Sat and Christmas Day*

The food is fresh, simple and lovingly
prepared, and as down-to-earth as the
practical farmhouse that is now
Jemima's. Local produce brings fish
from Milford Haven and prime meat
backed up by home-made bread,
home-grown vegetables, herbs, even
watercress. Lunch is a bargain at £8
for three courses. Evening meals are
more expensive.

*No-smoking area • Car-park • Access,
Visa*

Hay-on-Wye
(Powys) map 6

Oscars

High Town
☎ HAY-ON-WYE **(0497) 821193**

*Open all week 12.15pm–5 (11am–3
Nov to Mar)
Closed Sun Nov to Mar*

Second-hand bookshops pepper Hay
with engrossed bookworms who then
repair to Oscars for the congenial
atmosphere, amiable waitresses and
honest food. Plumply filled toasted
sandwiches are made to order while
perhaps a meaty chicken curry, a
pasta Neapolitan, salads, a triple-
decker sponge cake, scones and
gâteaux will all be on display.

Wheelchair access • Access, Visa

Lamphey **(Dyfed)** map 6

Dial Inn 🏅

☎ LAMPHEY **(064 667) 2426**

*Open all week noon–2, 6.30–9.30 (10
Fri and Sat) exc Sun D winter
Closed Christmas Day*

A pleasant village pub serving fresh
local fish from Milford docks (down
the road) at budget prices: plaice on
the bone, positively spilling over the
plate, and served with chips and peas
is £3.95. There are also well-made
falafel – deep-fried chickpea balls

served with salad and French bread – and Welsh cheeses.

Garden and family-room • Car-park • Wheelchair access, also WC • Access, Visa

---

Letterston (Dyfed)   map 6

Something's Cooking
The Square
☎ LETTERSTON (0348) 840621

Open Mon to Sat L 11–2, all week D 5.30–10.30 (exc Sun D winter)

The 'something' is fish and chips – reputed to be among the best anywhere. Membership of the National Federation of Fish Friers is testimony to the seriousness of their endeavour. Chef-patron Trevor Rands is adamant that success is derived from prime-quality fish, skilfully boned, covered in light batter and cooked in pure vegetable oil. Chips will only have 'that fresh crisp taste' if the potatoes are stored at a sufficiently low temperature to prevent sugar build-up. Children are welcome and receive a free lolly if they finish everything on their plate.

No smoking • Car-park

Llangattock (Powys)   map 6

Vine Tree Inn ◉
The Legar
☎ CRICKHOWELL (0873) 810514

Open all week noon–2.30, 6.30–10

The Vine Tree, in lovely surroundings on the bank of the River Usk, is much loved for its atmosphere, low-priced food and large helpings. Excellent local bread accompanies honest, well-flavoured dishes such as eggs provençale and ham and asparagus Mornay. Both the rabbit casserole and the chicken wrapped in bacon are highly recommended.

Car-park • Wheelchair access

Llangollen (Clwyd)   map 6

Gales
18 Bridge St
☎ LLANGOLLEN (0978) 860089

Open Mon to Sat noon–2, 6–10.15
Closed Sun and Christmas to New Year

A wine bar with carefully selected wines at affordable prices and unpretentious, well-cooked food. Soup, a fair selection of salads, quiches and filled jacket potatoes are rounded off by coffee and walnut fudge pudding or home-made ice-creams. Hot dishes include spicy vegetable casserole, Hawaiian pork and creamy lemon chicken.

Garden • Wheelchair access • Access, Visa

Llanrwst (Gwynedd)   map 6

Tu Hwnt I'r Bont ★
☎ LLANRWST (0492) 640138

Open Tue to Sun and bank hol Mons 10.30am–5.30
Closed first Sun Oct to Tue before Easter

Tucked beside the bridge spanning the River Conway stands a tiny, ivy-clad cottage of immense charm. Inside, low beams, a genuine Welsh dresser and patterned china create a traditional tea-room look. The genial Holt family have the sense to keep it simple, given the size and popularity of the place; featherlight scones, served hot from the oven with mounds of butter, cream and jam, are the main attraction, but home-made bara brith, light sponges and buttery biscuits are just as good. Lunchtimes bring filled baps, pâté, ploughman's and salads; and there is always correctly served leaf tea.

Unlicensed • No smoking • Garden • Car-park • Wheelchair access

Llanynys (Clwyd)   map 6

Cerrigllwydion Arms

☎ LLANYNYS (074 578) 247

Open Tue to Sun noon–2, 7–9.30 (10 Fri and Sat)
Closed Mon

Deep in the heart of the countryside but worth a detour for the fine views down the Vale of Clwyd, this pub offers genuine friendliness and simple, honest food. It is everything you would want a pub to be – family-run and 600 years old, with its characterful small rooms intact (every one beamed and rough-walled where not panelled). Home cooking brings thick slices of home-baked ham, bacon chop, half a roast duckling or chicken, ham and mushroom pie, all proudly served with some very good chips. Vegetarians are catered for with a well-made hazelnut loaf and spicy tomato and basil sauce. Finish with cream-filled meringue or treacle and walnut tart.

Garden • Car-park • Wheelchair access, also WC • Access, Amex, Visa

Llyswen (Powys)   map 6

Griffin Inn ★

☎ LLYSWEN (0874) 754241

Open all week noon–2, 7–9 (exc Sun D)

A solidly comfortable, old-fashioned fishing and sporting inn. Walls in the Fisherman's bar are decorated accordingly and fresh river fish and game make strong appearances on the menu when in season. The food is excellent, with the same thought, care and quality put into the bar menu as into that of the more expensive restaurant. Organic produce is used when available. An excellent choice from a daily-changing menu could bring a seasonal mushroom and asparagus pancake bursting with fresh asparagus and lightly sauced, a homely ragoût of wild rabbit, ratatouille, pasta au gratin, and kidneys Turbigo. A crisp, well-dressed mixed leaf salad and well-made desserts balance the meal.

Car-park • Wheelchair access • Access, Amex, Diners, Visa

Machynlleth (Powys) map 6

Quarry Shop

13 Maengwyn Street
☎ MACHYNLLETH (0654) 702624

Open Mon to Sat 9am–5 (4.30 winter)
Closed Sun exc high summer

A relaxed, self-service, vegetarian café attached to the Centre for Alternative Technology. Organic produce (where possible) is used. Breakfast with home-baked bread, gives way to lunch of carrot soup flavoured with coriander, chickpea and sweetcorn chowder, thick wholemeal pizza and potato and spinach curry. Wholemeal, low-sugar cakes for tea. Take-away service available.

Unlicensed • No smoking • Wheelchair access

Mold (Clwyd)   map 6

Chez Colette

☎ MOLD (0352) 59225

Open Mon to Sat 11.30–2, 6.30–10 (exc Tue D)
Closed Sun and bank hols

An informal, French family-run bistro, easily found opposite the church. Food includes a lunchtime plat du jour for £3.75 and a three-course menu rapide for £8.50. Moules marinière are plump and gently cooked, chicken with orange, and beef cooked in red wine are tender and full of flavour and come with crisp roast potatoes and a well-dressed salad.

Wheelchair access • Access, Visa

Narberth (Dyfed)   map 6

Gregory's of Narberth

Market Square
☎ NARBERTH (0864) 861511

Open all week noon–5.30 (3.30 winter), Thur (exc winter), Fri and Sat D 7–9

Part of the restoration of Narberth's old and often huge buildings is a former brewery now stylishly converted into Gregory's. Light snacks include ploughman's, omelettes, salads and sandwiches, while a more substantial meal of

Glamorgan cheese sausages or Welsh lamb chops with vegetables is terrific value. Afternoon teas are available with Gregory's own bread and scones.

Wheelchair access • Access

Newchapel (Dyfed)   map 6

Ffynone Arms ⊚

☎ BONCATH (0239) 841235

On B4332 between Boncath and Cenarth

Open all week noon–2.30, 6–10

An unspoilt village pub making a laudable effort to serve Welsh dishes in among the prawn cocktail and the plaice and chips. The games-room has been turned into a bistro and here, using fresh produce, is some good plain cooking: selsig morgannwg made from cheese, leeks, herbs and breadcrumbs, lamb cooked in a fruity sauce, Glamorgan (cheese) sausages.

Garden • Car-park • Wheelchair access

Newport (Dyfed)   map 6

Cnapan

East Street
☎ NEWPORT (0239) 820575

Open Mar to Oct all week 12.15–2.30 (exc Tue), 7–8.45 (exc Sun), Nov to Jan Sun L, Fri and Sat D only
Closed Tue, winter Mon to Thur and Feb

An attractive listed Georgian building with five letting rooms and a homely restaurant specialising in Welsh dishes. Lunch offers cawl (soup), a good, rough home-made pâté, Welsh chicken and ham pie, a Welsh onion tart and an oat-based flan. There are old-fashioned trifles, crumbles and fruit pies for dessert. Cnapan also provides morning coffee, afternoon teas, and more expensive dinners.

No smoking • Car-park • Wheelchair access, also WC • Access, Visa

---

Penmaenpool
(Gwynedd)   map 6

George III Hotel

☎ DOLGELLAU (0341) 422525

Open all week 12.30–2, 7.30–8.45 (exc Sun D)
Closed 2 weeks Christmas

The food served in this cosy, stone dining-room overlooking the Mawddach Estuary is variable in quality, but hits more than it misses. The best bet appears to be Sunday lunch, and you can rely on the notable home-made pâtés and steak and kidney pie.

Garden • Car-park • Wheelchair access • Access, Amex, Visa

Penuwch (Dyfed)   map 6

Brimstone Bistro

Brimstone Wildlife Centre, Brynamlwg, nr Tregaron
☎ LLANGEITHO (097 423) 439

On B4577 between Aberarth and Aberystwyth

Open Sun L noon–2.30, all week D 7.30–9.30
Closed (tea-shop) Nov to Easter

Brimstone Wildlife Centre is a 27-acre conservation site complete with

a pets' paddock, stables and an adventure playground. The tea-shop provides refreshment for visitors during the day and becomes a bistro in the evening. During the summer, aperitifs are sipped in the tropical house among the exotic butterflies and birds. This touch of exoticism extends, also, to the wide-ranging menu: pan-fried marinated lamb is served with spinach and lemon sauce; vegetable curry is accompanied by spiced banana salad; and black cherries are flamed in white rum with home-made coconut ice-cream. Bookings only for Sunday lunch and Sunday and Monday dinner.

Garden • Car-park • Wheelchair access, also WC

Pontfaen (Dyfed)   map 6

Gelli Fawr Country House
☎ NEWPORT (0239) 820343

Off B4313 Pontfaen–Fishguard road

Open all week noon–2.30, 5–6.15
Closed some days winter (phone to check)

A handsome Victorian farmhouse with splendid views of the Gwaun Valley. As a winner of a 'Taste of Wales' award it is to be expected that Welsh dishes appear on the menu, but they do not dominate. Bar food, available for lunch and from 5pm to 6.15pm, provides a good-value sample of Frances Roughley's cooking. Soup comes with a whole loaf of delicious home-baked bread, followed perhaps by Miser's feast (a Welsh dish of potato, cheese, garlic and cream), lentil rissoles or maybe a medley of deep-fried prawns. Desserts include an excellent locally made ice-cream as well as lemon soufflé, chocolate pots, fruit pies and crumbles. Restaurant meals are more expensive.

Garden • Car-park • Wheelchair access • Access, Visa

Rhosneigr (Gwynedd) map 6

Runnelstones

☎ RHOSNEIGR (0407) 810904

Open Apr to Sept Sun L noon–1.30, all week D 7–10, Oct to Mar Sun L and Wed to Sat D only (Wed to Fri bookings only)
Closed winter Mon and Tue

This was once the village post office, which is why there is a post box in one of the restaurant walls. The cooking here is straightforward and uses fresh local produce. The table d'hôte at £10.25 offers three courses – soup, beef burgundy, pork scrumpy or fresh fish, dessert and coffee – and is good value. A traditional Sunday lunch is £7.95. À la carte is pricier.

Wheelchair access • Access, Visa

Swansea
(W Glamorgan)   map 6

Barrows

42 Newton Road, Mumbles
☎ SWANSEA (0792) 361443

Open Tue to Sat noon–3, 6–9.30 (10 Sat)
Closed Sun, Mon and Christmas Day

Described enthusiastically as very cheap, very good and with a great atmosphere. Well-flavoured soup and bacon cockles and laverbread make inventive starters, while trout wrapped in bacon and stuffed with cockles and laverbread makes an interesting main course. Otherwise, there are venison in all sorts of guises, plenty of fish choices, lamb cutlets and gammon and egg.

No-smoking area • Access, Visa

La Braseria

28 Wind Street
☎ SWANSEA (0792) 469683

Open Mon to Sat noon–2.30, 7–midnight
Closed Sun and Christmas Day

Out of the same stable as La Brasserie, Champers and Le Monde in Cardiff (see entries), the style is 'Spanish bodega', with a fish bar upstairs. Grills and salads are the key elements; steaks and kebabs share the bill with sardines, scallops and monkfish.

Wheelchair access, also WC • Access, Amex, Diners, Visa

PA's

95 Newton Road, Mumbles
☎ SWANSEA (0792) 367723

Open all week 12.30–2.30, 6–9.30
Closed 3 days Christmas and 3 weeks Oct

The initials refer to owners Paul Davies and Andrew Hetherington. They have converted a shop with a view of Oystermouth Castle into a bistro serving decent food and good wine. The former is rarely cheap but might involve veal ('dusted' with mixed herbs in lemon and white wine) or trout (stuffed with cockles and laverbread). A useful choice of wine supplied by Lay & Wheeler.

No children under 14 • Garden • Wheelchair access • Access, Visa

Roots

2 Woodville Road, Mumbles
☎ SWANSEA (0792) 366006

Open Mon and Tue noon–5, Wed to Sat 11am–9 (exc Mon winter)
Closed Sun, winter Mon and Christmas Day

A promising vegetarian restaurant on the corner of an unpromising street. Inside, there are colourful wall-hangings, ethnic decorations and fresh flowers. Drinks are listed on a hymn board. Almost everything is made on the premises, and the owners are faithful to organic produce. Lunch menus range far and wide for watercress soup, almond roast with onion and red wine sauce, stir-fried vegetable crêpes with cashews and black-bean sauce, and lasagne. Evening menus roam further afield for couscous and tempura vegetables with gado-gado sauce, as well as returning home for Glamorgan sausages with laverbread.

Unlicensed, but bring your own: corkage £1 • No-smoking area • Wheelchair access, also WC

Schooner

4 Prospect Place
☎ SWANSEA (0792) 649321

Open all week 11.45–2.15, 6.30–9 (exc Sun D)
Closed 26 to 28 Dec

A popular pub serving decently prepared, filling food at honest prices. Braised steak, steak and kidney pie, Swiss veal and plaice fillet with crab sauce are all priced at under £4 and come with plenty of vegetables. In the evening there is a carvery menu of three courses for £7.95.

Wheelchair access, also WC

Trecastle (Powys)   map 6

Castle Hotel

Main Street
☎ SENNYBRIDGE (087 482) 354

Open all week noon–2, 7–9 (exc Sun D)

A former coaching-inn, now completely refurbished and exuding a pleasant, relaxed atmosphere. Bar food is handled with care. Home-made soup, filled pancakes, tandoori chicken and grilled pork chops show the range from a fairly extensive choice. There is a more expensive evening restaurant.

Car-park • Wheelchair access • Access, Visa

Tywyn (Gwynedd)   map 6

Proper Gander

Cambrian House, High Street
☎ TYWYN (0654) 711270

Open all week 10am–5.30
Closed 3 weeks end Jan/beginning Feb

This pretty pink tea-room is a breath of fresh air in the seaside town of Tywyn. Home cooking is the order of the day; only the breads, croissants and teacakes come from the bakery next door. Cream teas feature splendid cakes, fresh sandwiches and scones with clotted cream. Lunches concentrate on special daily dishes such as liver and bacon casserole, breast of chicken in white wine and apricot sauce, and vegetable lasagne. Sunday lunch is a roast. Wines and lagers with meals.

No smoking • Access, Visa

Welshpool (Powys) map 6

Powis Castle Tea Rooms

☎ WELSHPOOL (0938) 555499

Open Easter to first week Nov Tue (July and Aug only) to Sun 11am–5.30
Closed Mon and Tue (exc July and Aug) and second week Nov to Easter

The main draw is the castle, set in magnificent grounds, in which case a visit to the National Trust-run café in the converted stables is fine for light refreshments. Short cuts are taken with some of the food, but by sticking to filled baps and choosing carefully from the cakes on display you can't go wrong.

No-smoking area • Garden •
Wheelchair access, also WC

Whitebrook (Gwent) map 6

Crown at Whitebrook

☎ MONMOUTH (0600) 860254

Between A466 and B4292 4m S of Monmouth, Whitebrook turning at Bigsweir Bridge, 2m down narrow country lane

Open all week noon–2 (exc Mon),
7–9.30 (exc Sun)

There are a number of reasons for making a detour to the Bates' pleasantly informal inn – the beautiful, remote setting in the Whitebrook valley and the consistently good bar food being two of the best. Gruyère, ham and onion tartlet, crab, prawn and pineapple pancakes, well-flavoured soups and pâté, home-made ice-creams and some sound Welsh cheeses set the tone.

No-smoking area • Garden • Car-park • Wheelchair access • Access, Amex, Diners, Visa

Wrexham (Clwyd) map 6

Coffee Shop

Library Arts Centre, Rhosddu Road
☎ WREXHAM (0978) 352334

Open Mon to Fri 9.30am–9pm (6 Sat)
Closed Sun

Mrs Gilliatt's unpretentious all-day café within the library building probably offers the best-value food in Wrexham. There are no frills – just straightforward, honest home cooking. Home-made cakes and puddings are the highlights, the omelettes are locally famous, and the menu has its full share of quiches, salads and grills, backed up by specials such as liver and bacon and cauliflower cheese.

Unlicensed • No-smoking area • Garden • Wheelchair access, also WC

LONDON BY CUISINE

AFGHAN
Buzkash (see under Caravan Serai),
  SW15
Caravan Serai, W1

AFRO/CARIBBEAN
African Pot, NW10
Bambaya, N8
Calabash, WC2
Portobello Gold, W11
Smokey Joe's Diner, SW18

AFTERNOON TEA
Athenaeum Hotel, W1
Basil Street Hotel, SW3
Coffee House, Inter-Continental
  Hotel, W1
The Dorchester, Promenade, W1
Ritz Hotel, Palm Court, W1
Savoy Hotel, Thames Foyer, WC2
Tea Time, SW4

BISTROS
Bon Ton Roulet, SE24
La Bouffe, SW11
Brahms, SW1
Bridge, SW11
Café Anjou, N3
Le Casino, SW1
La Cloche, NW6
Emile's, SW6, SW15
Gardners, W4
Jigsaw, W12
Lantern, NW6
Le Mercury, N1
Mustoe Bistro, NW1
Oliver's, W14
Pigeon, SW6
Sonny's, SW13
Surinder's, W2
Village Bistro, N6

BRASSERIES
Café Delancey, NW1, WC1
Café Pelican, WC2
Café Pelican du Sud, SE1
Café Rouge, NW3
Café Sud Ouest, SW3
Camden Brasserie, NW1
Canal Brasserie, W10
Le Poulbot, EC2
Rouxl Brittania Café, EC2

BREAKFAST
Adams Café, W12
Bistrot 190, SW7
Café Delancey, NW1, WC1
Café Kensington, W8
Coffee House, Inter-Continental
  Hotel, W1
Diana's Dining Room, EC1
Fox and Anchor, EC1
Place Below, EC2
The Place to Eat, W1
Le Poulbot, EC2
Quality Chop House, EC1
Ritz Hotel, Palm Court, W1
Rive Gauche, NW1
Rouxl Brittania Café, EC2
Tea Time, SW4
Le Tire Bouchon, W1

BURMESE
Mandalay, SE10

CAFES
Brewer Street Buttery, W1
Brompton Brasserie, SW10
Burgh House Buttery, NW3
Café de Columbia, W1
Café Delancey, NW1, WC1
Coffee House, Inter-Continental
  Hotel, W1

Diana's Dining Room, EC1
General Trading Company, SW1
Hungrys, W1
ICA Café, SW1
Lauderdale House, N19
Mildred's, W1
National Gallery, WC2
New Restaurant, SW7
New Serpentine, W2
Ooblies, N19
The Place to Eat, W1
Rive Gauche, NW1
Rouxl Brittania Café, EC2
St John's Café, NW8
Star Café, W1
Tea Time, SW4
Terrace Café Restaurant,
    Museum of London, EC2
Le Tire Bouchon, W1
Titchfield Café, W1
Waterside Café, EC1

CHINESE
China China, W1
Chinatown, E14
Cho Won, W1
Chuen Cheng Ku, W1
Dragon Inn, W2
Four Seasons, W2
Honeymoon, N8
Jade Garden, W1
Ley-On's, W1
Mr Kong, WC2
New Shu Shan, WC2
New World, W1
Poons, Leicester Street, WC2
Poons, Lisle Street, WC2
Poons at Whiteleys, W2

EAST EUROPEAN
Brewer Street Buttery, W1
Czech Club, NW6
Daquise, SW7
Navigator, SW5
Ognisko Polskie, SW7
Zamoyski, NW3

ETHIOPIAN
Ethiopia in the Year 2002, W9

FISH
La Gaulette, W1
Grahame's Seafare, W1
Lou Pescadou, SW5
Zazou Brasserie, W1

FISH AND CHIPS
Faulkners, E8
Geales, W8
Masters Super Fish, SE1
Redfords, NW11, Edgware
Seafresh Fish Restaurant, SW1
Seashell, NW1
Upper Street Fish Shop, N1

GREEK
Costas Fish Restaurant, W8
Daphne, NW1
Jason's, SW11
Microkalamaras, W2
Nontas, NW1
Vrisaki, N22
Yerakina, NW1

ICE-CREAM PARLOURS
Häagen-Dazs, NW3, WC2
Marine Ices, NW3

INDIAN/PAKISTANI/
BANGLADESHI
Anwar's, W1
Aziz, W6
Camden Tandoori, NW1
Chutneys, NW1
Curry Paradise, NW3
Diwana Bhel Poori House, NW1,
    W2
Fleet Tandoori, NW3
Gandhi's, WC1
Ganpath, WC1
Gopal's of Soho, W1
Great Nepalese, NW1
Gurkhas Tandoori, W1

Haandi, NW1
Indian Veg Bhel-Poori House, N1
Malabar, W8
Mandeer, W1
Moti Mahal, SW7
Papadams, W1
Ragam, W1
Raj Bhel Poori House, NW1
Rajput, W12
Rani, N3
Sabras, NW10
Saheli Brasserie, WC2
Spices, N16
Sree Krishna, SW17
Suruchi, N1
Surya, NW6
Taj Oriental, W2
Woodlands, SW1, W1,
    Wembley

INDONESIAN/MALAYSIAN/
   SINGAPOREAN
Makan, W11
Melati, W1 (x2)
Rasa Sayang,NW3, W1, W2, W13,
    WC2
Singapore, W4
Singapore Garden Restaurant, NW6

ITALIAN
Accademia Italiana, SW7
Bizzarro, W2
Casale Franco, N1
Como Lario, SW1
Enoteca, SW15
Formula Veneta, SW10
Frascati, NW3
Italian Graffiti, W1
Lorenzo, SE19
Marine Ices, NW3
Osteria Antica Bologna, SW11
Spago, SW7
Underground Café, NW1
Valentino's, N13
Villa Estense, SW6

JAPANESE
Ajimura, WC2
Ikkyu, W1
Men's Bar Hamine, W1
Ninjin, W1
Yoshino, W1

JEWISH
Blooms, E1, NW11
Grahame's Seafare, W1
Redfords, NW11, Edgware
Reuben's, W1

KOREAN
Bu San, N7
Jin, W1

MIDDLE EASTERN/NORTH
   AFRICAN
Adams Café, W12
Ali Baba, NW1
Efes Kebab House, W1
Falafel House, NW3
Hodja Nasreddin, N1
Laurent, NW2
Le Petit Prince, NW5
Samsun, N16
Topkapi, W1

MODERN ECLECTIC
Bistrot 190, SW7
Blueprint Café, SE1
Café Kensington, W8
First Floor, W11
Museum Street Café, WC1
Quality Chop House, EC1

MONGOLIAN
Mongolian Barbecue, W5

NORTH AMERICAN
Boardwalk, W1
Kenny's, NW3

PATISSERIES
Louis, Finchley, NW3
Louis, Hampstead, NW3
Maison Bertaux, W1
Maison Sagne, W1
Patisserie Bliss, EC1
Patisserie Valerie, W1

PIZZAS
Kettners, W1
Pizza Express N1, N12, NW3,
    NW11, SE1, SE3, SE19, SW1
    (x2), SW6, SW7, SW10, SW11
    (x2), SW14, SW15, SW16, SW19,
    W1 (x2), W2, W4, W5, W8, W11,
    WC1, Harrow, Wembley
Pizza Piazza, SW6
Pizza Place, W9
Pizzeria Castello, SE1
Pizzeria Condotti, W1

PUBS
Albion, N1
Cutty Sark, SE10
Fox and Anchor, EC1
Grapes, E14
Latymers, W6
Maple Leaf, WC2
Portobello Gold, W11
Sporting Page, SW10
White Horse on Parsons Green,
    SW6

SANDWICHES
Balls Brothers,EC2 (x5), EC3, EC4
    (x2), SE1 (x2)
See *London – Sandwich bars*

TAPAS
Don Pepe, NW8
Los Remos, W2
Meson Don Felipe, SE1

THAI
Bangkok, SW7

Bedlington Café, W4
Chiang Mai, W1
Latymers, W6
Sala Thai, W5
Sri Siam, W1
Supan, W9
Thai Garden, E2
Topsy Tasty, W4
Tui, SW7
Tuk Tuk, N1

TRADITIONAL ENGLISH
Chimes, SW1, SW19
F. Cooke, E8
Simpsons of Cornhill, EC3

VEGETARIAN
Cherry Orchard, E2
Chutneys, NW1
Country Life, W1
Cranks, EC1 (x2), EC2, EC3, W1
    (x3), WC2 (x3)
Diwana Bhel Poori House, NW1,
    W2
East West, EC1
Escape Coffee House, SE10
Food For Thought, WC2
Govinda's, W1
Greenhouse, WC1
Indian Veg Bhel-Poori House, N1
Mandeer, W1
Manna, NW3
Neal's Yard Bakery, WC2
Place Below, EC2
Raj Bhel Poori House, NW1
Rani, N3
Raw Deal, W1
Sabras, NW10
Seasons, W1
Spices, N16
Sree Krishna, SW17
Suruchi, N1
Surya, NW6
Wilkins, SW1
Woodlands, SW1, W1, Wembley

VIETNAMESE
Dalat, NW6

WINE BARS
Almeida Theatre Wine Bar, N1
Balls Brothers, EC2 (x5), EC3, EC4
    (x2), SE1 (x2)
Bibendum Oyster Bar, SW3
Carriages, SW1

Cork and Bottle, WC2
Ebury Wine Bar, SW1
Hubble & Co, EC1
Julie's, W11
Just William Wine Bar, SW11
Odette's, NW1
7 Pond Street, NW3
Shampers, W1
Wine Gallery, SW10

INDEXES

INDEX OF EATING-PLACES

INDEX OF LOCATIONS

MAPS

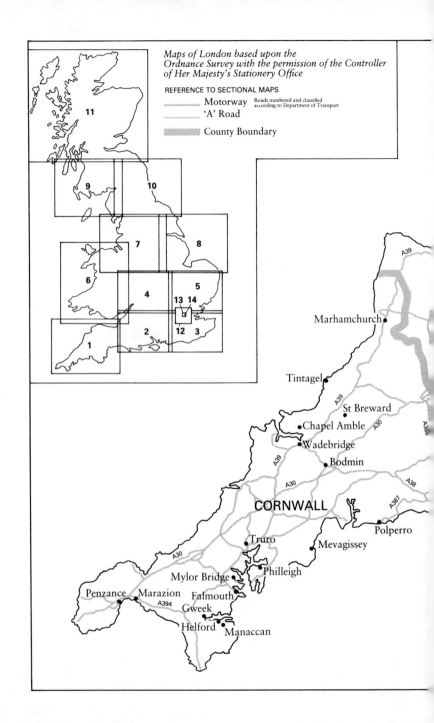

Maps of London based upon the
Ordnance Survey with the permission of the Controller
of Her Majesty's Stationery Office

REFERENCE TO SECTIONAL MAPS

Motorway — Roads numbered and classified according to Department of Transport

'A' Road

County Boundary

CORNWALL

MAP 1

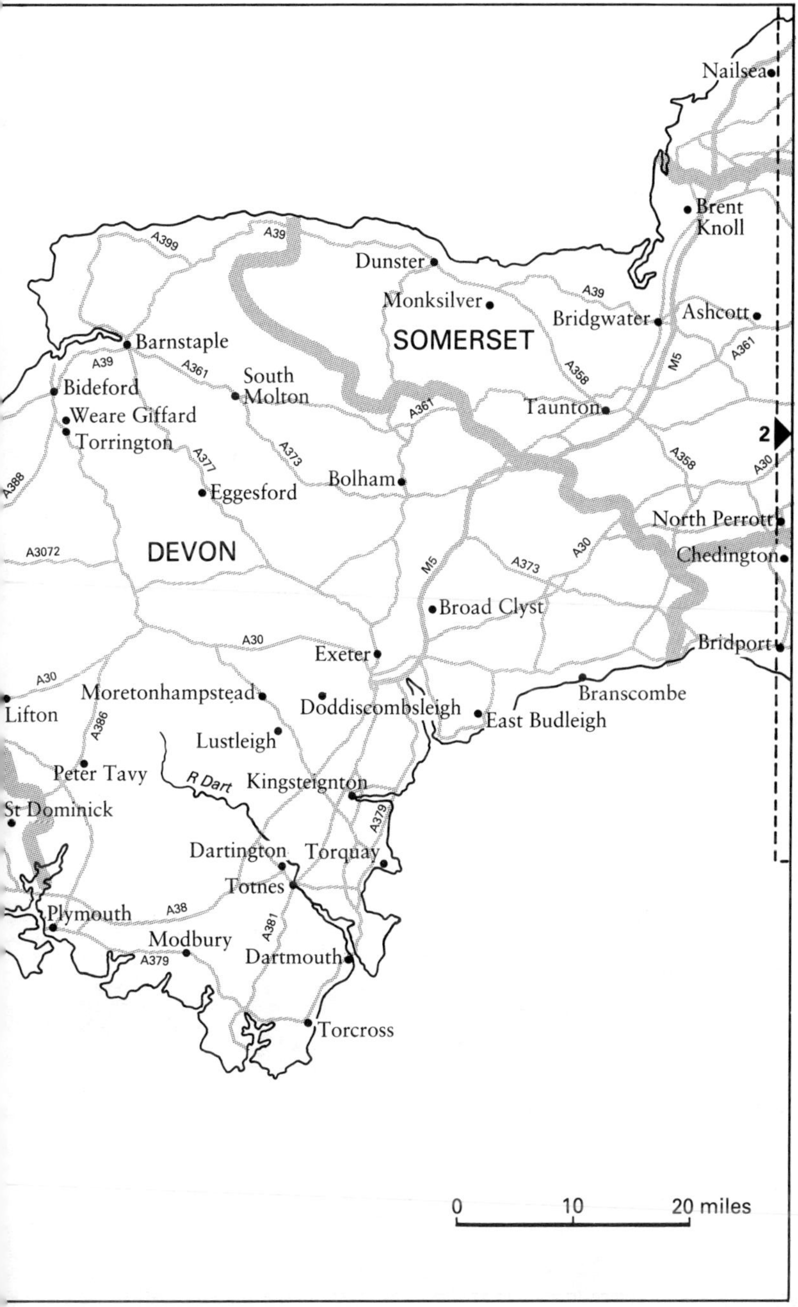

Nailsea

Brent Knoll

Dunster

Monksilver

SOMERSET

Bridgwater

Ashcott

A39

A399

A39

Barnstaple

South Molton

Taunton

Bideford

A39

A361

Weare Giffard

Torrington

A361

A358

M5

A361

Eggesford

A377

A373

Bolham

A388

DEVON

North Perrott

A358

A30

2

Chedington

A3072

M5

A373

A30

Broad Clyst

A30

Exeter

Bridport

Lifton

A30

Moretonhampstead

A386

Doddiscombsleigh

Branscombe

East Budleigh

Lustleigh

Peter Tavy

R Dart

Kingsteignton

A379

St Dominick

Dartington

Torquay

Totnes

Plymouth

A38

Modbury

A381

Dartmouth

A379

Torcross

0   10   20 miles

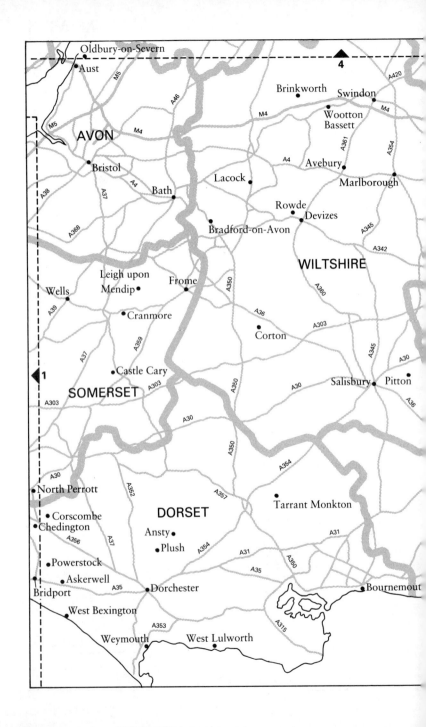

MAP 2

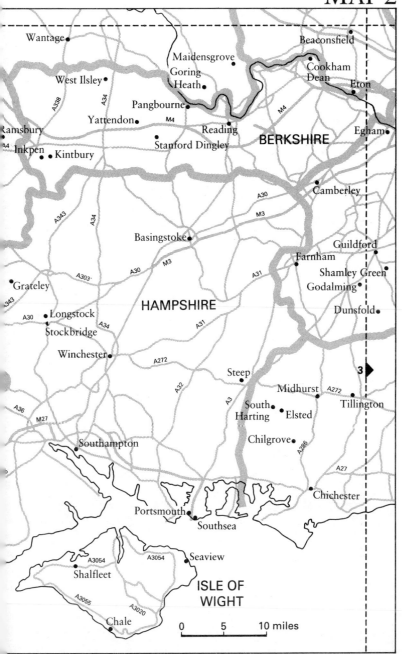

Wantage
Beaconsfield
Maidensgrove
Cookham
Dean
Goring
Heath
West Ilsley
Eton
Pangbourne
Yattendon
M4
Ramsbury
Reading
BERKSHIRE
Egham
Inkpen
Kintbury
Stanford Dingley
A338
A34
A4

Camberley
A30
M3
A343
A34
Basingstoke
Guildford
A303
A30
M3
Farnham
Shamley Green
A31
Godalming
Grateley
HAMPSHIRE
Dunsfold
343
A30
Longstock
A34
Stockbridge
A31
Winchester
3
A272
A32
Steep
A36
A3
Midhurst
A272
M27
South
Tillington
Harting
Elsted
Southampton
Chilgrove
A286
A27
Chichester
Portsmouth
Southsea
A3054
Seaview
A3054
Shalfleet
ISLE OF
WIGHT
A3055
A3020
Chale

0   5   10 miles

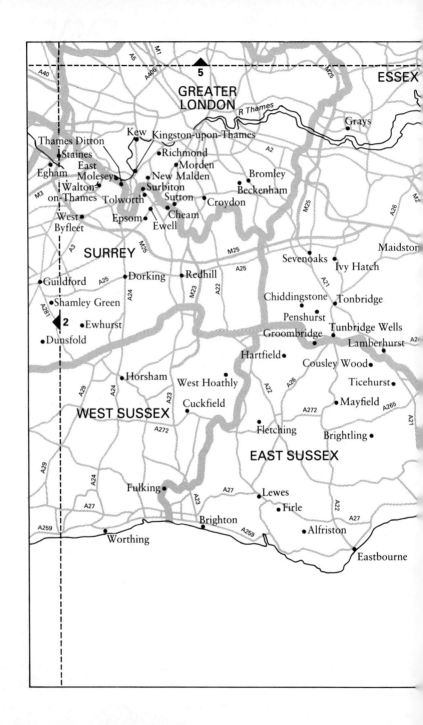

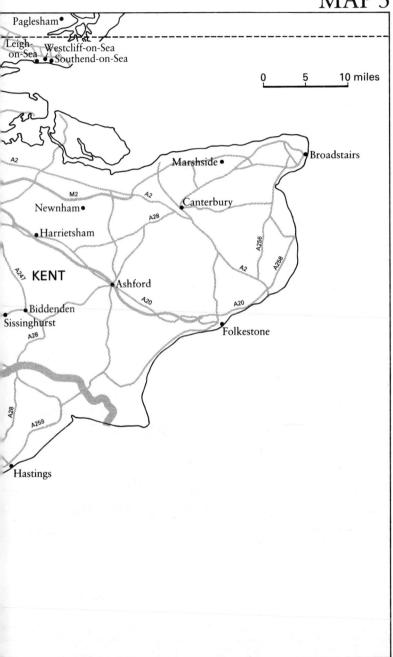

MAP 3

Paglesham •

Leigh-
on-Sea Westcliff-on-Sea
• •Southend-on-Sea

0   5   10 miles

A2

Marshside •   •Broadstairs

M2   A2
Newnham•   •Canterbury

•Harrietsham   A256

                                        A2   A258
A247 KENT

        •Ashford
                    A20
                                A20
•Biddenden   •Folkestone
Sissinghurst
        A28

A28
    A259

•Hastings

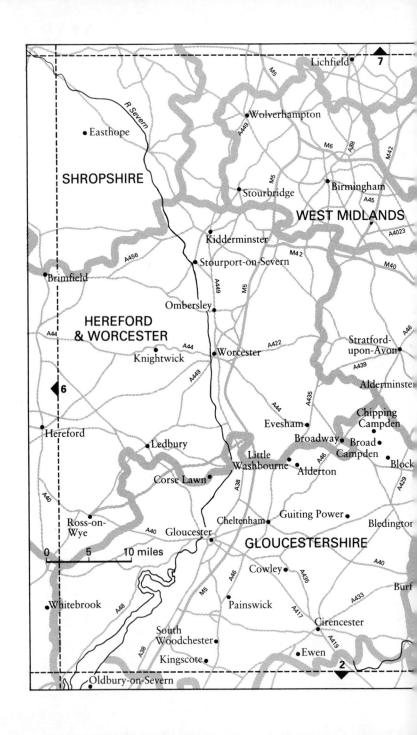

MAP 4

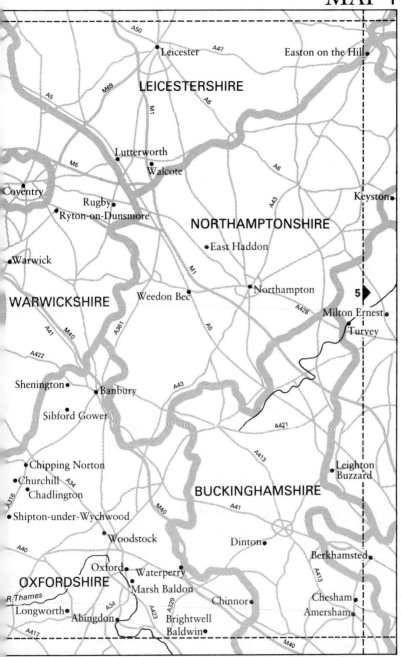

A50

Leicester   A47   Easton on the Hill

LEICESTERSHIRE

A5   M69   M1   A6

Lutterworth

M6   Walcote

Coventry   A43   Keyston

Rugby
Ryton-on-Dunsmore   **NORTHAMPTONSHIRE**

East Haddon

Warwick

Northampton   **5**

WARWICKSHIRE   Weedon Bec   A428   Milton Ernest

M1   Turvey

A41   M40   A361   A5

A422

Shenington   Banbury   A43

Sibford Gower   A421

A413

Chipping Norton   Leighton
Churchill   A34   Buzzard
Chadlington   **BUCKINGHAMSHIRE**

A316   Shipton-under-Wychwood   M40   A41

Woodstock   Dinton

Oxford   Waterperry   Berkhamsted

A40   **OXFORDSHIRE**   Marsh Baldon   A413

R Thames   A34   A329   Chinnor   Chesham
Longworth   Abingdon   A223   Amersham
Brightwell
A417   Baldwin   M40

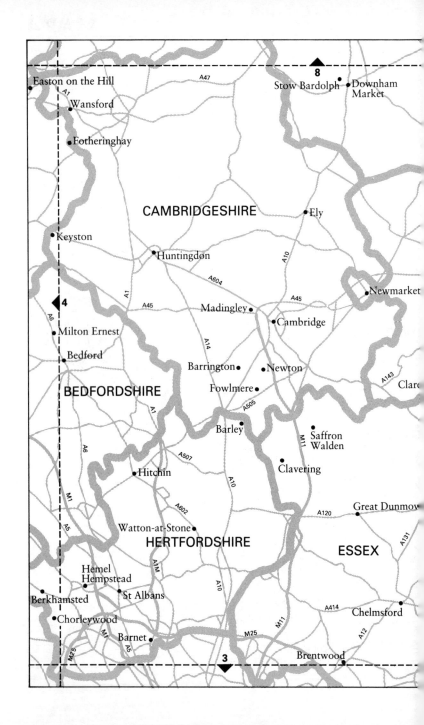

MAP 5

Norwich

Great Yarmouth

NORFOLK

A11

A140

A134

A143

A140

Scole

Wrentham

Southwold
Walberswick

Laxfield

Dunwich
Westleton

A1120

Ixworth

A45

Earl Soham

Snape

Aldeburgh

A12

SUFFOLK

Woodbridge

Orford

A134

Ipswich

A45

A12

Gestingthorpe

Stoke-by-Nayland

osfield

Dedham

A604

Harwich

A120

Colchester

A12

Witham

Maldon

Burnham-
on-Crouch

0   5   10 miles

Paglesham

MAP 6

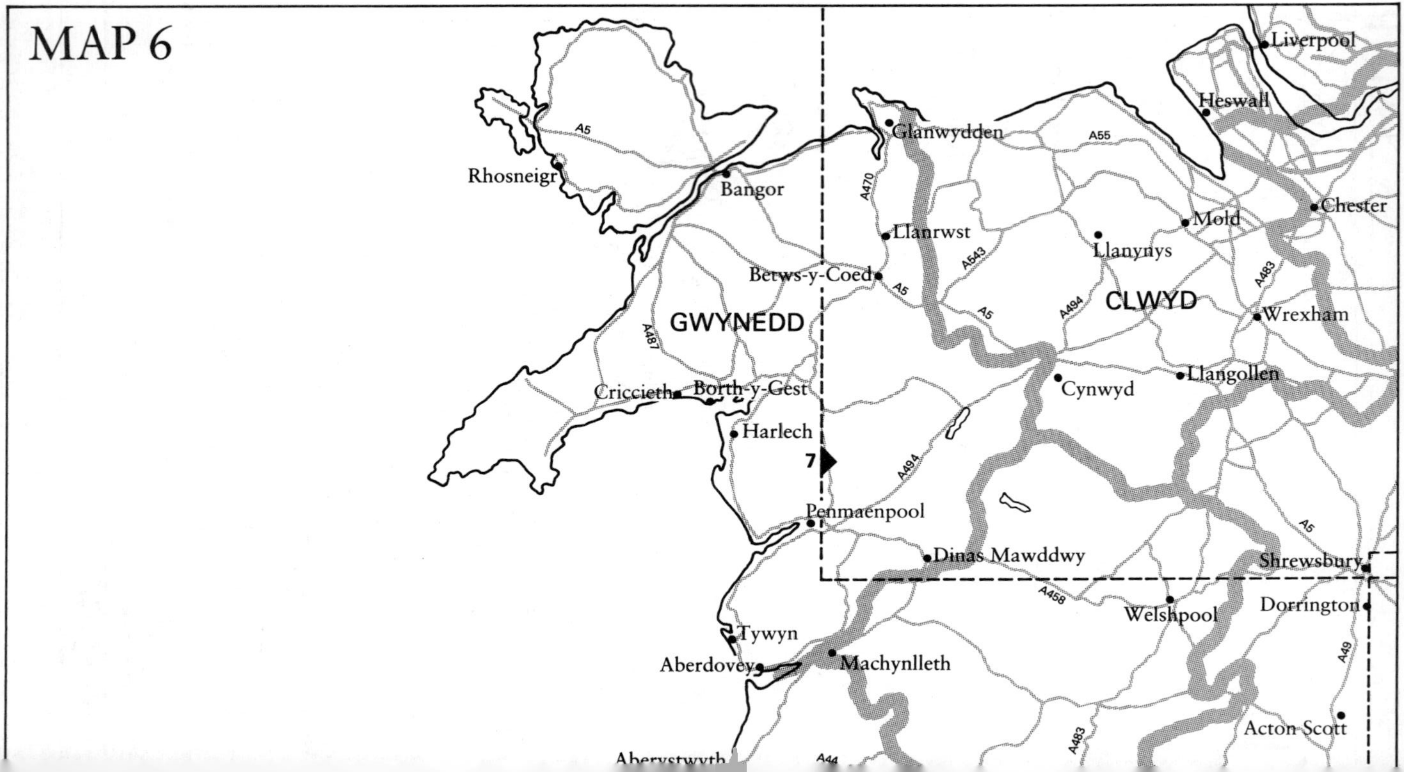

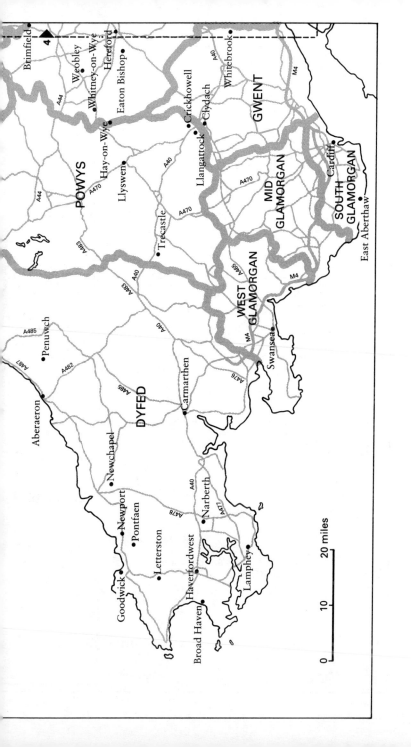

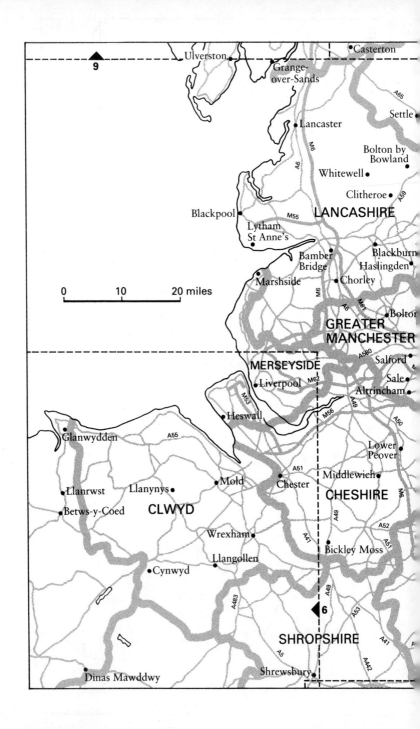

MAP 7

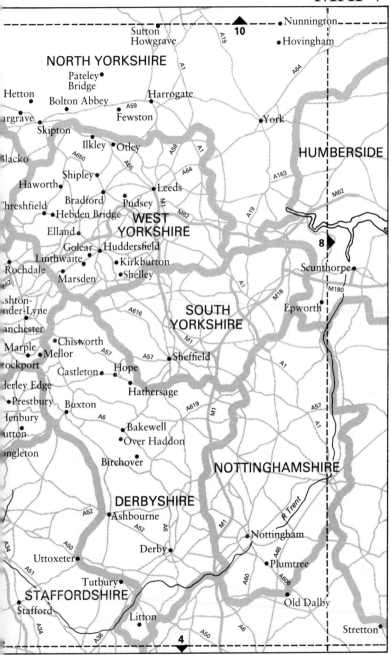

10

Nunnington •
Sutton
Howgrave
• Hovingham

NORTH YORKSHIRE
Pateley •
Bridge
Hetton
• Harrogate
Bolton Abbey •
A59
argrave • Fewston
Skipton • • York
HUMBERSIDE
Blacko • Ilkley • Otley
A650
Haworth • Shipley •
hreshfield • Bradford • Leeds
• Hebden Bridge Pudsey •
Elland • WEST
YORKSHIRE
Golcar • Huddersfield
Linthwaite • Kirkburton
Rochdale • Marsden • Shelley
8
shton-
nder-Lyne • Scunthorpe •
anchester A616
SOUTH Epworth •
Marple • Chisworth YORKSHIRE
Mellor •
tockport A57 A57 • Sheffield
Castleton • Hope
lerley Edge • Hathersage
• Prestbury Buxton •
lenbury A6
utton • Bakewell
ngleton • Over Haddon
• Birchover
NOTTINGHAMSHIRE

DERBYSHIRE
Ashbourne •
A52
A52
Derby • Nottingham •
Uttoxeter • Plumtree •
Tutbury •
STAFFORDSHIRE
Stafford • Old Dalby •
Litton
Stretton •
4

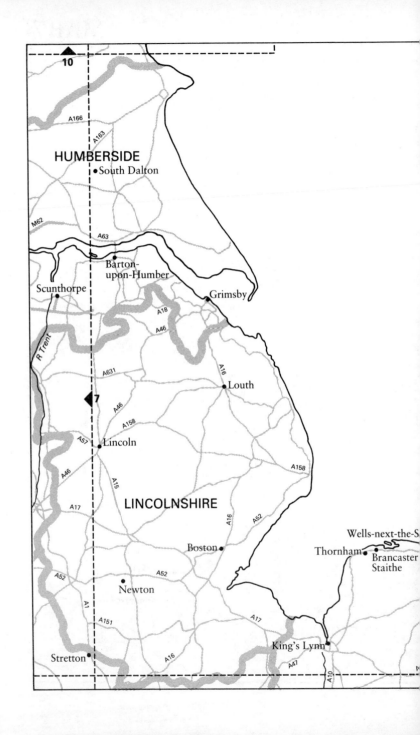

MAP 8

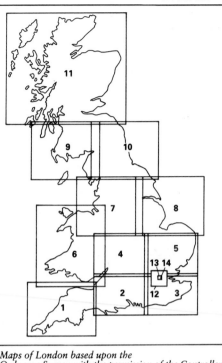

11

9 **10**

7 **8**

6 **4** **5**

13 14

2 **12** **3**

1

*Maps of London based upon the
Ordnance Survey with the permission of the Controller
of Her Majesty's Stationery Office*

REFERENCE TO SECTIONAL MAPS

Motorway Roads numbered and classified
according to Department of Transport

'A' Road

County Boundary

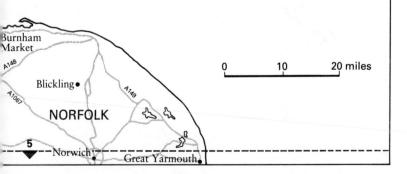

Burnham
Market

A148

Blickling●

A149

NORFOLK

A1067

0   10   20 miles

5

▼ Norwich●

Great Yarmouth●

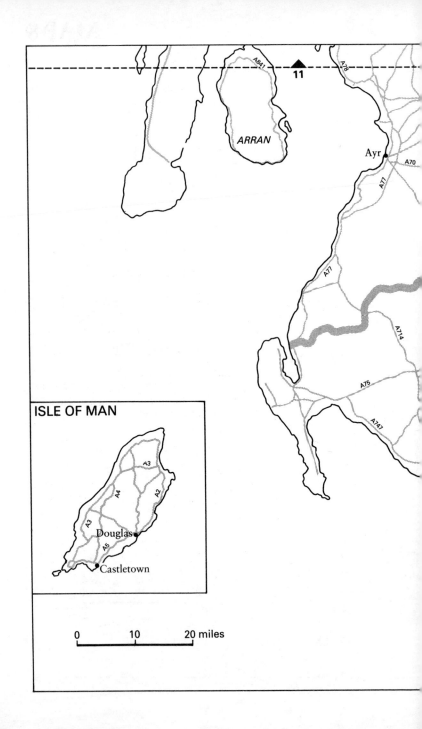

ARRAN

11

Ayr

A841

A78

A70

A77

A77

A714

A75

A747

ISLE OF MAN

A3

A4

A2

A3

Douglas

A5

Castletown

0   10   20 miles

MAP 9

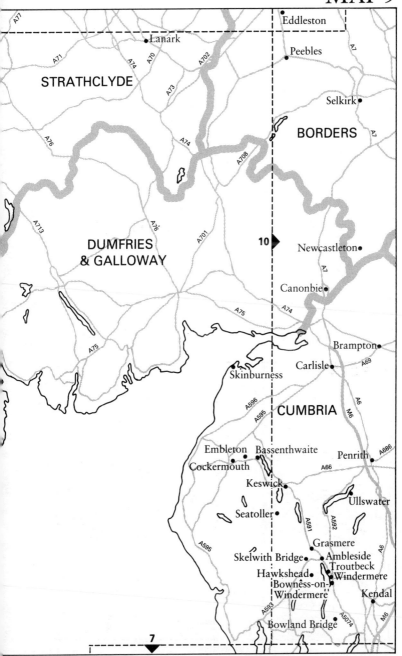

A77

Lanark

A71

A70

A73

A74

A702

A71

STRATHCLYDE

A76

A74

A708

Eddleston

Peebles

A7

Selkirk

BORDERS

A7

A713

A76

A701

**DUMFRIES
& GALLOWAY**

10 ▶

Newcastleton

A7

Canonbie

A75

A74

A75

Brampton

Carlisle

A69

Skinburness

A696

A595

CUMBRIA

A6

M6

Embleton

Bassenthwaite

Penrith

A686

Cockermouth

A66

Keswick

A591

Ullswater

Seatoller

A592

A6

A595

Grasmere

Skelwith Bridge

Ambleside

Troutbeck

Hawkshead

Windermere

Bowness-on-
Windermere

Kendal

A593

Bowland Bridge

A5074

M6

7 ▼

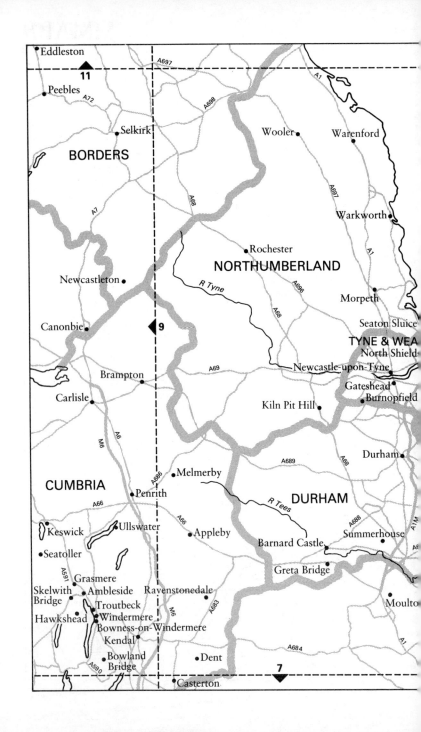

MAP 10

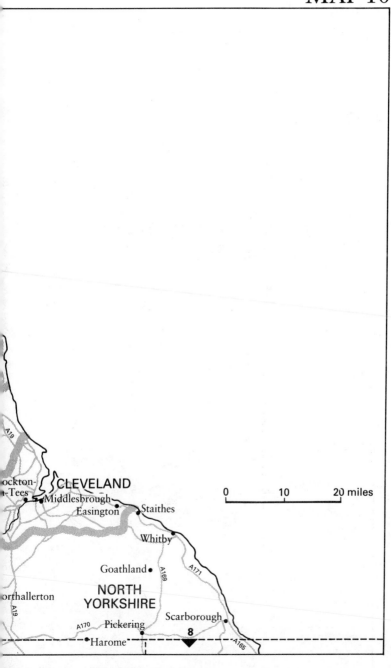

0   10   20 miles

ockton-
-Tees   CLEVELAND
•5•Middlesbrough
Easington•   •Staithes

Whitby•

Goathland •

NORTH
YORKSHIRE

orthallerton

Pickering

•Harome   8

Scarborough

MAP 11

Rhiconich

A858

LEWIS

A859

WESTERN

ISLES

Ullapool

HIGHLAND

A832

A835

A832

Dunvegan

A855

A890

UIST

A856

SKYE

A87

Invermoriston

A82

RUM

Arisaig

A830

A82

Fort William

COLL

A861

TIREE

Port Appin

A82

A828

MULL

A85

A816

Cairndow

COLONSAY

Colonsay

A83

A815

STRATHCLYDE

JURA

Kilfinan

BUTE

Kilberry

Largs

ISLAY

9

0   10   20 miles

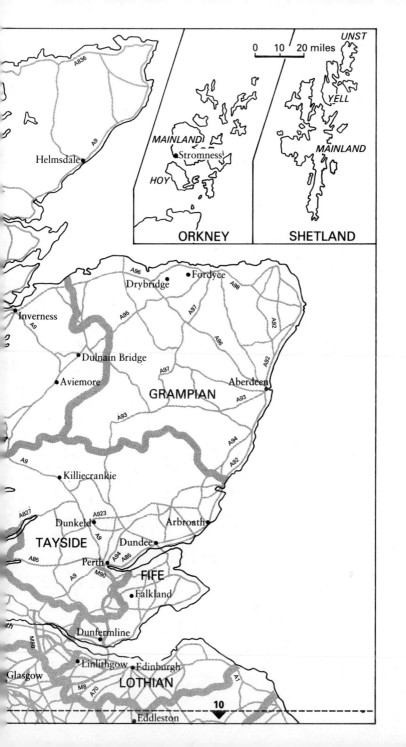

0 10 20 miles

UNST

YELL

MAINLAND

MAINLAND
• Stromness

HOY

ORKNEY **SHETLAND**

Helmsdale •

A836

A9

• Fordyce
Drybridge •

A96

A95

A97

A96

A92

• Inverness

A9

• Dulnain Bridge

A97

Aberdeen •

A93

GRAMPIAN

• Aviemore

A93

A94

A92

A9

• Killiecrankie

A827

A923

Dunkeld •

Arbroath •

TAYSIDE

A9

A85

Dundee •

Perth •

A94 A85

M90

FIFE

A9

• Falkland

Dunfermline •

M80

• Linlithgow • Edinburgh

A1

Glasgow

M8 A70

LOTHIAN

10 ▼

• Eddleston

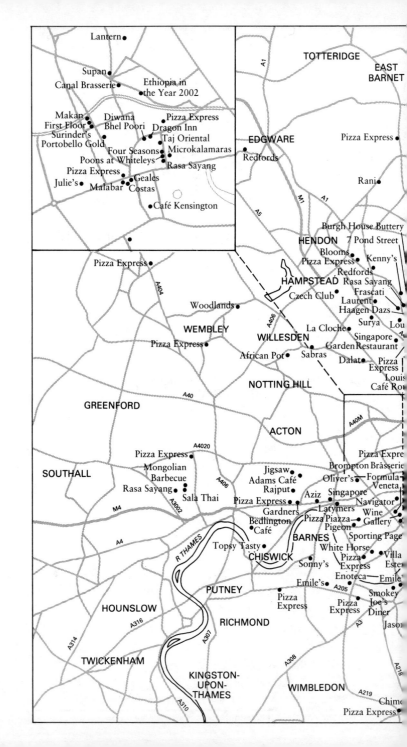

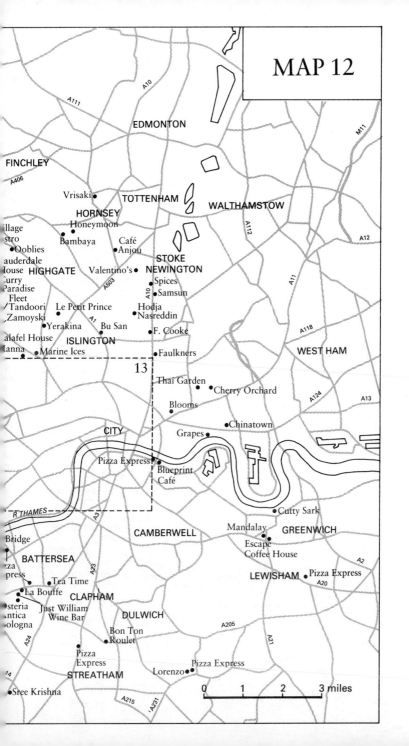

MAP 12

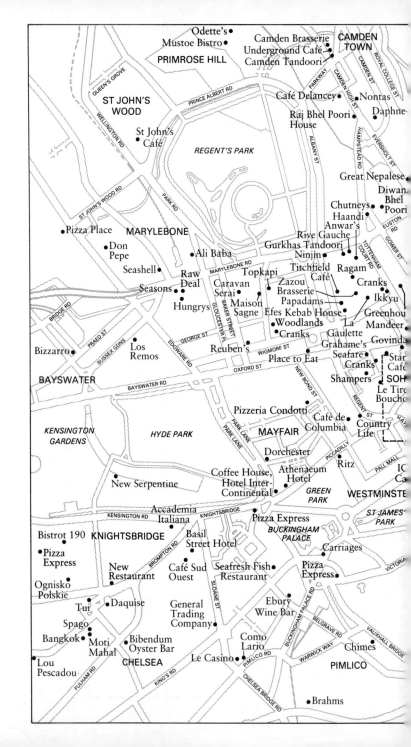

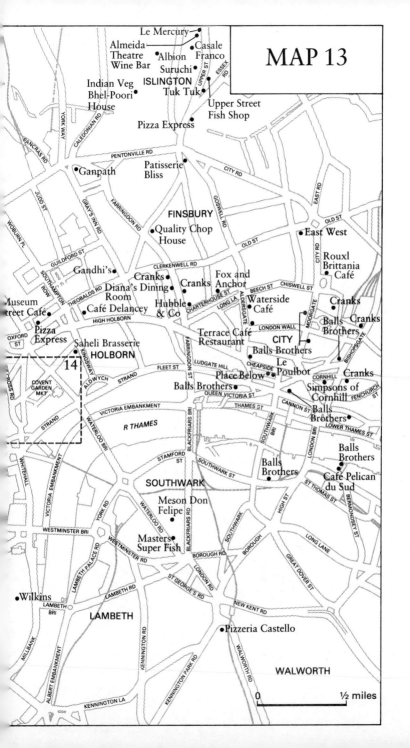

MAP 13

Le Mercury
Almeida
Theatre
Wine Bar
Albion
Casale
Franco
Suruchi
Indian Veg
Bhel-Poori
House
ISLINGTON
Tuk Tuk
Upper Street
Fish Shop
Pizza Express

Ganpath
Patisserie
Bliss

FINSBURY
Quality Chop
House
East West
Rouxl
Brittania
Café

Gandhi's
Cranks
Cranks
Fox and
Anchor
Cranks
Diana's Dining
Room
Café Delancey
Hubble
& Co
Waterside
Café
Cranks
Museum
Street Café
Balls
Brothers
Pizza
Express
Terrace Café
Restaurant
CITY
Saheli Brasserie
Balls Brothers
HOLBORN
Le
Poulbot
Cranks
Place Below
Simpsons of
Cornhill
Balls Brothers
Balls
Brothers
Balls
Brothers
Balls
Brothers
Café Pelican
du Sud
SOUTHWARK
Balls
Brothers
Meson Don
Felipe
Masters
Super Fish
Wilkins
LAMBETH
Pizzeria Castello
WALWORTH

0   ½ miles

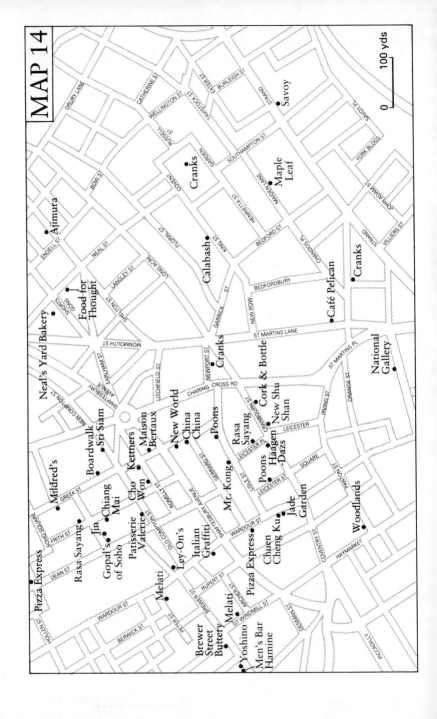

MAP 14

0   100 yds

Savoy

Maple Leaf

Cranks

Cranks

Café Pelican

Calabash

Ajimura

National Gallery

Food for Thought

Neal's Yard Bakery

Cranks

Cork & Bottle

New World

China China

New Shu Shan

Poons

Maison Bertaux

Rasa Sayang

Häagen-Dazs

Boardwalk

Sri Siam

Poons

Mildred's

Cho Won

Kettners

Mr. Kong

Chiang Mai

Jin

Ley-On's

Rasa Sayang

Gopal's of Soho

Woodlands

Patisserie Valerie

Italian Graffiti

Jade Garden

Pizza Express

Chuen Cheng Ku

Melati

Pizza Express

Brewer Street Buttery

Melati

Yoshino

Men's Bar Hamine

Report Form

To the Editor, *Out to Eat*,
FREEPOST, 2 Marylebone Road, London NW1 1YN

From my personal experience the following establishment should/should not be included in *Out to Eat*:

_____

_____

Telephone _____

I had breakfast/lunch/dinner/snack there on _____19 _____

In the space below please describe what you ate and drank, and give any other details, e.g. of service, location or atmosphere, that you wish to add.

please continue overleaf

My meal for _____ people cost £ _____ *attach bill where possible*

I am not connected in any way with the management or proprietors.
Name and address (BLOCK CAPITALS)

_____

_____

Signed_____

Report Form   OTE

To the Editor, *Out to Eat*,
FREEPOST, 2 Marylebone Road, London NW1 1YN

From my personal experience the following establishment should/should not be
included in *Out to Eat*:

_____

_____

Telephone _____

I had breakfast/lunch/dinner/snack there on _____19 _____

In the space below please describe what you ate and drank, and give any other
details, e.g. of service, location or atmosphere, that you wish to add.

please continue overleaf

My meal for _____ people cost £ _____ *attach bill where possible*

I am not connected in any way with the management or proprietors.
Name and address (BLOCK CAPITALS)

_____

_____

Signed_____

Report Form   OTE

To the Editor, *Out to Eat*,
FREEPOST, 2 Marylebone Road, London NW1 1YN

From my personal experience the following establishment should/should not be
included in *Out to Eat*:

_____

_____

                              Telephone _____

 I had breakfast/lunch/dinner/snack there on _____19 _____

In the space below please describe what you ate and drank, and give any other
details, e.g. of service, location or atmosphere, that you wish to add.

please continue overleaf

My meal for _____ people cost £ _____ *attach bill where possible*

I am not connected in any way with the management or proprietors.
Name and address (BLOCK CAPITALS)

_____

_____

Signed_____